INDIA'S SECURITY ENVIRONMENT

PROCEEDINGS OF SELECT SEMINARS HELD

BY

ASIA CENTRE BANGALORE

INDIA'S SECURITY ENVIRONMENT

Proceedings of Select Seminars held by Asia Centre Bangalore

2007–12

Asia Centre Bangalore

in association with

KONARK

Konark Publishers Pvt Ltd
New Delhi • Seattle

Konark Publishers Pvt Ltd
206, First Floor,
Peacock Lane, Shahpur Jat,
New Delhi-110 049
Phone: +91-11-41055065, 65254972
e-mail: india@konarkpublishers.com
website: www.konarkpublishers.com

Konark Publishers International
1507 Western Avenue, #605,
Seattle, WA 98101
Phone: (415) 409-9988
e-mail: us@konarkpublishers.com

Cataloging in Publication Data--DK
Courtesy: D.K. Agencies (P) Ltd. <docinfo@dkagencies.com>

India's security environment: proceedings of select seminars held by Asia Centre Bangalore, 2007-12.
p. cm.
Includes index.
ISBN 9789322008260

1. National security--India--Congresses. 2. India--Foreign relations--Asia--Congresses. 3. Asia--Foreign relations--India--Congresses. I. Asia Centre Bangalore.

DDC 355.033054 23

Editor: Satyaki Roy

Typeset by Saanvi Graphics, Noida and printed and bound at Thomson Press (India) Ltd.

Contents

Foreword

Indians, as a people, are generally considered of above average intelligence when compared with most other nationalities. However this inherent intelligence seems to be conspicuously absent when they are judged in terms of their responses to emergent situations. This built-in contradiction, perhaps, arises due to our reluctance to act decisively in crisis situations. No wonder, therefore, that in his well-known book, *The Asian Drama*, written many decades ago, the Swedish economist Gunnar Myrdal felt constrained to describe India as a 'soft state'. Her adversaries, he said, have reasons to be confident that even where India's own vital interests are involved, its leadership can be depended upon to choose the softest response available to it!

It is said that 'God helps those who help themselves'. But in India, alas, we have been reduced to merely complaining about our plight to those very countries that have befriended and armed countries that sponsor terrorism on our soil. With new challenges arising, formulation of fresh policies and firm action upon them to protect our national interest has become an urgent concern.

The Rand Corporation, the well-known US think tank, had, some 20 years ago, sent one of its senior vice-presidents to India to study the strategic policy followed by it. He had come to the rather strange conclusion that there was little evidence to show that India had evolved any strategic doctrine, until his attention was drawn to the writings of Kautilya in the 4th century BCE and the *Panchatantra* authored by Vishnu Sharma in the 6th century CE, to teach young princes the arts of strategy and tactics—a long time before Machiavelli was even born!

The application of these well-known principles of Indian diplomacy can, even today, play a crucial role, since they provide us low-cost options to safeguard national interest, as compared to the crippling cost of depending solely on military means. That would obviously require fresh initiative with newly emerging centres of power like the European Union (and its main members such as Germany and France), as well as with Japan and the Russian Federation, and even with China. The basic principles of Non-Alignment still remain valid today:If anything, these principles are more relevant than when they were first formulated by us in the 1950s.

Nevertheless, it is important to bear in mind that nothing has changed the world's perception of India more positively than our nuclear tests of May 1998. After years of pleading for Universal Nuclear Disarmament, a billion people had at long last come into their own. Respect, rather than affection, certainly matters more in relations between states. As far as we are concerned, our nuclear weapon capability is not for intimidating others, but for ensuring our security from nuclear threats or blackmail by outside powers. India has, therefore, repeatedly reiterated its readiness to work with like-minded countries towards the total elimination of all weapons of mass destruction on an equal and non-discriminatory basis. Total security for a few can only result in total insecurity for the rest.

India's geographic location astride the Indian Ocean sea-lanes gives it a strategic advantage that cannot be ignored by any power. At present, India is suffering mostly from self-inflicted handicaps and is perceived as disunited, with a weak, vacillating leadership that has no sense of direction or clearly identifiable policy. However, this situation need not continue for long. The very size of the country and its talented population will ensure that India will emerge sooner, rather than later, from its self-induced paralysis and claim her rightful place in the comity of nations.

Finally, a word about how the Asia Centre was born in the late 1990s. When it was being set up, some of the founding members argued that since the discussions would cover myriad global issues, it would be more appropriate to give the organization global nomenclature. Finally, however, it was agreed upon that the think-tank will be named 'Asia Centre', since everyone conceded that we should focus on issues as they affect us here in India, which is an integral part of Asia. As a wag put it, one has to become a father first, before aspiring to become a grandfather!

Our members, who are 50 persons in all, comprise mainly of senior retired diplomats, veterans of the three wings of our own Defence Forces, Academics, as well as veteran journalists. We have worked closely with the Ministry of External Affairs as well as the Indian Council for World Affairs in a symbiotic manner over the years, to study and contribute towards a better understanding of global issues that have an impact on India, and their long-term consequences—not viewing other countries as adversaries but bearing in mind the exhortation of our forebears who declared millennia ago: 'The whole world is our Motherland; we are all the children of this Earth!'

These summaries of the various seminars held by the Asia Centre over the past decade or so can be useful pointers to the unfolding of future events in the global scenario. It is our earnest hope that this compilation will help scholars and practitioners of international relations glimpse the future, and prepare ourselves to the maximum extent possible, against unpleasant surprises.

A.P. Venkateswaran
Chairman

Asia Centre
Bangalore
14 April 2013

'What Might be Happening in West Asia'

ASIA CENTRE BANGALORE ANNUAL LECTURE

M. Hamid Ansari
Vice President of India

15 February 2013

WELCOME ADDRESS

A.P. Venkateswaran,
Chairman, Asia Centre, Bangalore

Dear Members of Asia Centre and Distinguished guests,

It is indeed a great pleasure and privilege for all of us today to welcome in our midst the Honourable Vice President of India, Shri Hamid Ansari. We are also glad to have with us the Honourable Governor of Karnataka, Shri Hans Raj Bhardwaj, and the Honourable Minister for Technology and Fisheries Shri Asnotikar, besides senior representatives of the State and Central Governments. Shri Ansari had graciously agreed, some time ago, to deliver the annual address of the Asia Centre. It is, indeed, a happy coincidence that during his present visit to Bangalore, the Vice President has released the ten scholarly volumes written by the former Vice President B.D. Jatti on the vachanas of the great Karnataka Saint Basava, who is revered by the people of Karnataka.

You all know that apart from his presently being the second citizen of India, Shri Ansari has also had a long and distinguished service as a diplomat and represented India with distinction in many parts of the world, besides serving as India's Permanent Representative at the United Nations. That gives him a uniquely holistic view of the world and I, along with all who are present here, greatly look forward to his address to the Asia Centre.

Thank you,
Mr. Vice President,
on behalf of all at the Asia Centre.

INTRODUCTION

C.V. Ranganathan,
Vice Chairman, Asia Centre

Your Excellency Shri Hamid Ansari, Vice President of India, Your Excellency Shri Hans Raj Bhardwaj, Governor of Karnataka State, Honourable Minister Shri Asnotikar, Chief Secretary Shri S.V. Ranganath, other distinguished members of the Karnataka Government, distinguished invitees, members of the Asia Centre, ladies, and gentlemen. It is a privilege to be asked to introduce the Vice President, but his bio-data is so long that I seek your indulgence if I am very subjective in choosing what I think would interest the Asia Centre and, in fact, the entire audience.

Born in 1937, he has an MA in political science and joined the Indian Foreign Service in 1961, and he has served in a various capacities right from junior to senior-most, in a wide geographical arc extending from West Asia to Australia and many countries in between. He has been Ambassador to the United Arab Emirates, Afghanistan, Iran, Saudi Arabia, and Australia, and as our Chairman mentioned, he was also Permanent Representative of India to the United Nations in New York.

He has enormous experience in bilateral relations and ultimately in what one might call the multilateral apex center of world politics and economics.

Post-retirement, he has had several government appointments; he has been the Chairman of the 5th National Commission for Minorities, a member of the National Security Advisory Board, and Co-Chairman of the India–UK Round Table, which is a mechanism for eminent persons from India and the UK to dialogue. That apart, he has been in the educational field; he has been the Vice Chancellor of the Aligarh Muslim University, a Visiting Professor in the Jawaharlal Nehru University in Delhi, and in the Third World Academy in the Jamia Millia, also in Delhi. He was first elected Vice President of India in 2007, which also involves being Chairman of the Rajya Sabha and he has been re-elected both as Vice President and as Chairman of the Rajya Sabha in 2012. Across parties, rising above our confrontational sort of party politics he has been unanimously welcomed to once again lead the Rajya Sabha; obviously he is impartial and fair. The Vice President has written many books and numerous articles. Along with the Chairman let me express the most warm welcome to him; we in the Asia Centre and apart from the Centre those of us who have had the privilege of being his erstwhile colleagues feel proud that he is here with us. The subject of the Honourable Vice President's lecture today—a subject of contemporary importance—is 'What Might be Happening in West Asia'.

ASIA CENTRE BANGALORE ANNUAL LECTURE 'WHAT MIGHT BE HAPPENING IN WEST ASIA'

M. Hamid Ansari
Vice President of India

Some in this audience, members of a tribe adept at eulogizing or lamenting its golden past, are also familiar with the tradition and practices of command structures. It is this tradition that brings me here today, dutifully responding to the injunction of a tribal chief in the person of Ambassador A.P. Venkateswaran.

I have no hesitation in confessing that in this case compliance is a matter of pleasure.

Personal preferences apart, an opportunity to exchange views and hear alternative perspectives is always of relevance. At the same time, I am conscious of the hazards of articulating thoughts before a knowledgeable audience; I, therefore, beg indulgence if not forgiveness from those who know better.

I have chosen for today's talk a subject of considerable interest to us despite the inadequacy of attention given to it most of the time by the national media.

A word about nomenclature is relevant. In a continent called Asia, its various geographical segments have to be named logically rather than in terms of historical accidents. West Asia is therefore as logical as East Asia, South Asia, or Central Asia. Most in this audience would know that the terminology of the colonial period, naming regions as Near East, Middle East, or Far East, made sense only from the perspective of London.

Despite this, the propensity of the West Asians to call the region Middle East is, to say the least, baffling. Is it a case of 'reinforcement of the stereotype' or, to use Antonio Gramci's phrase, 'a dilution of the consciousness of what one really is'?

The Arab Spring

Allow me to begin with a proposition that might sound startling. The so-called 'Arab Spring' did not happen suddenly. What is happening in some West Asian lands today by way of political turbulence has had a long gestation, was waiting to happen, and is in the nature of serial volcanic eruptions whose intensity and duration is difficult to predict.

Some questions readily come to mind. What is the nature of the turmoil and the forces propelling it? What is its impact on different segments of society and on social relationships? What is its immediate or medium term impact on the economy? Has it influenced security perceptions of the individual states and their views on regional security? What are its implications for India and Indian interests in the country and the region?

Some facts can be recalled to understand the context. In the first place, all the lands in North Africa and West Asia (with the exception of Iran) are Arabic-speaking societies, many with tribal structures still intact, overwhelmingly Muslim, who experienced colonial or neo-colonial trauma in the first half of the 20th century. The experience of each, however, was distinct. Secondly, the structures of dominance put in place after World War I, and continued with some modifications in the second half of the century, were essentially neo-patriarchal, characterized by one Arab scholar as 'the marriage of imperialism and patriarchy.' The net result of this was historical retardation or, as the Moroccan historian Abdullah Laroui put it, 'infra-historical rhythm.'

The implications of the latter were far reaching. As early as 1928, a Lebanese lady by the name of Nazira Zain al-Din wrote about the scourge of Four

Veils—of cloth, ignorance, hypocrisy, and stagnation. This could not but impact on the nationalist upsurge that surfaced in different places from time to time. The clash of secular and Islamist nationalist traditions also became pervasive. Writing in 1996, Bassam Tibi of Syria, calling himself a post-1967 generation man, admitted the failure of the effort 'to replace the myths of Arab nationalism by an Arab enlightenment' and by 'the erosion of the legitimacy of the secular nation-state.' Similar judgments emanated from other, non-Islamist, intellectuals.

Other developments, relating to the advent of authoritarian governance combining one party and military rule, aggravated the process. It suited the regimes and also the patterns of Western dominance and strategies of the Cold War. The one exception was Palestine. It wounded the psyche of every individual in every Arab land. The grievance had merit; it was depicted poignantly by Nasser to Kennedy in 1962: 'One who did not possess gave a promise to another who did not deserve, and these two managed by power and deceit to deprive those who both owned and deserved.'

Lamentation alone, however, has never been known to correct the wrongs of history, and has not done so in the case of Palestine.

In 2002, the Arab Human Development Report identified freedom, empowerment of women, and knowledge as the three deficits that hampered human development in Arab countries. The public mood of pessimism was summed up in the remark that 'we, Arabs, do not have the power to do anything and there are certain alien forces that control our destiny'.

The despondency of two lost generations, in which modernity was imported as a product rather than as a process, also propelled a quest for alternatives: of an imagined past, an ideal of authenticity, an instrument of mobilization well rooted in the consciousness of the masses. This brought forth Islamism in different manifestations. It was psychologically reassuring. As an instrument of protest, it sought democratic governance to deny the legitimacy of the authoritarian state. Rashid al-Ghannushi, leader of an Islamist party in Tunisia, summed it up in an essay written in exile at the end of the 20th century: 'A democratic system of government', he wrote, 'is less evil than a despotic system of government that claims to be Islamic.'

The end of the Cold War and Iraq's invasion of Kuwait altered power equations. Saddam Hussain's misadventure in Kuwait left him crippled but without loosening his hold on Iraq. An external catalyst was injected on spurious ground in the shape of the Iraq War. It progressed from 'known unknowns' to 'unknown unknowns.' Its cost in human and material terms to both the victor and the vanquished is still being assessed; on the side of the former, a first estimate in 2008 by Joseph Stiglitz and Linda Bilmes put it at three trillion dollars.

The war and the prolonged period of occupation and resistance to it in all its manifestations impacted on the Arab status quo but on a delayed-action fuse. The regimes that have tumbled, and those that are challenged, failed to gauge the urge for change in the majority segments of their youthful populations. The wars in Iraq and Afghanistan also demonstrated the limits of the military capacity of the United States in a non-conventional conflict.

In August 2010, through Presidential Study Directive 11, President Obama asked his government agencies to prepare for change. According to an article by David Ignatius in *The Washington Post* of March 11, 2011, the document cited 'evidence of growing citizen discontent with the region's regimes', said the region is entering a critical period of transition, and asked his advisors to 'manage these risks by demonstrating to the people of the Middle East and North Africa the gradual but real prospect of greater political openness and improved governance.'

The military and political conflicts in the first decade of the present century brought to the fore other fault lines that have left their mark on the balance of socio-political power in individual countries of the region. These have taken the shape of:

- Ethnic assertions as with the Kurds in Iraq and Syria;
- Sectarian empowerment of Shias in Iraq and demands for rights by the Shias majority in Bahrain and Shia minority in Saudi Arabia;
- Democratic upsurges in Tunisia, Egypt, and Libya and muted rumblings in some of the GCC states; and
- The power struggle for Syria and its regional and global implications.

The impact of each set of challenges has been different. In Iraq, the Kurdish demand for greater role in governance in a highly centralized Arab state has been long standing. The US-led war against Saddam Hussain has resulted in a *de facto* autonomous Kurdish region in Iraq where the authority of Baghdad is minimal and frequently contested on matters of daily governance. In Syria domestic political discontent against one-party rule, encouraged and assisted materially by some regional and other powers, has assumed the form of a full fledged civil war with no end in sight. This has given Syrian Kurds a little elbow room though without external recognition; it is likely to be complicated by neighbouring Turkey's stern policy towards its Kurdish population. The new situation in both countries has prompted apprehensions about efforts to give shape to various projects of cartographic engineering in the region, or as Hassanein Heikal put it recently, 'a New Sykes-Picot.'

The democratization of the political process in Iraq, in the wake of the war of 2003, projected for the first time the demographic reality of the state and resulted in the emergence of Shias as the majority politico–sectarian faction. The loss of political power by the Arab Sunnis of the country was deeply resented and continues to be contested. It also has wider geopolitical ramifications. In 2004, the King of Jordan contributed, allegedly at the prompting of his chief of intelligence, the term 'Shia Crescent' to the political vocabulary of the region. Unconsciously, perhaps, it helped highlight the geopolitical gains that accrued to Iran in the wake of the Iraq War. Iran has sustained its assistance to the Hezbollah in Lebanon; there is, however, no evidence as yet of a material Iranian impulse in the simmering of discontent in the Shia segments of the Bahraini and Saudi population since this emanates from domestic factors and pre-date the Iraq War.

The immediate details of the political eruptions in the past two years in Tunisia and Egypt are known to most people; the backdrop is not. Since independence in 1956, the Tunisian public or people (sha'b) mostly subscribed to the ideal to a homogenous, united, modern, Francophile, and secular body-politic and a paternalistic relationship in a 'pact of obedience' to the Leader (Zaim.) Economic grievances did surface from time to time but did not transform themselves into movements for rights. It is this which changed when Mohamed Bouazizi set himself on fire on December 17 2010. Thenceforth, 'the people' became the point of reference. This did not mean homogeneity; gaps of perception on matters regional, generational and cultural have emerged and are aggravated by the demographic reality and high unemployment of around 18 per cent according to a World Bank study. There is an ongoing debate between Islamism and secularism but the focus even of the Islamist Al-Nahda leaders is to establish institutions that safeguard public debate and electoral choice. And yet, as the happening of February 6 was to show, derailment is always on the cards.

Egypt is the very reverse of the relative tranquillity of Tunisia though the Tunisian protests served as an inspiration. A perceptive observer has recently noted that two years after the initial turmoil 'Egyptians don't really know the balance of forces in their own homeland.' This reaffirms Leon Trotsky's observation that 'the masses go into a revolution not with a prepared plan of social reconstruction, but with a sharp feeling that they cannot endure the old regime.' The leaderless protestors in Tahrir Square and elsewhere in Egypt, fully assisted by modern communications technology and ad hoc mechanisms of defence against police tactics, focussed on toppling the Mubarak regime.

The first stage of the Egyptian revolution was essentially leaderless and reflected the aspirations of all segments of society. Its limitations became evident with the progress of events. The electoral process and the constitution-making brought to the fore the Muslim Brotherhood as the most organised socio-political force on the scene. It is strong but not unchallenged; on the other hand, while both the Salafists and the liberal-secularists have mobilised against it, they do not find convergence on critical values and tactics. The most recent events thus tend to highlight nature of the challenge: how to forge a democratic system while integrating the Brotherhood and other Islamists into the political game.

Violence, until recently, was generally avoided. Ominous signs of a reversal are now emerging. A new organisation, the Black Bloc, made its appearance in the last week of January, claiming to be 'formed in reaction to the Muslim Brotherhood's military wing.' In a first reaction, the Ministry of Interior has called them terrorists and ordered their arrest. A challenge is being mounted by the liberal-secularists, but not the Salafists, to the legitimacy of the President himself. The Brotherhood's uncompromising position on the making of the constitution and the electoral law has hardened the political divide which can only be addressed by the proposed National Dialogue.

Events in Libya, beginning in February 2011, took a somewhat different course. The discontent against Gaddafi was used as a pretext for external interference in the shape of UN Security Council action, the declaration of no-fly zone, followed by extensive bombing of Tripoli by the French and British air forces. The mysterious refuge in Britain of intelligence chief Moussa Koussa and the cooption of other figures of the Gaddafi regime in the new set up does suggest a measure of external involvement of a clandestine nature in the progress of events. Nor were miscalculations avoided; the murder of the US Ambassador in Benghazi was to show that the nature of some of Gaddafi's opponents was not fully understood.

The Challenge for Contemporary Muslim Societies

Two dimensions of the developments discussed above require closer scrutiny. The first relates economic grievances. High unemployment among the youth, and declining household incomes, has been a common factor of social unrest in all the affected countries. A World Bank report in September 2012 assessed that 'recent political changes will be meaningful if they lead to concrete social and economic development.' The Bank has emphasised the need for transparency, good governance, job creation and competitive private sector. There is also an insistence, on the part of prospective Western donors, on 'real democratic transition' taking place. A satisfying factor, from the view point of the donors, is the acceptance by the new regimes of the neo-liberal economic reforms undertaken by the previous administrations.

Less explicit, but nevertheless constraining, are the requirements of rich regional donors. There is no evidence, as yet, of these matters having been addressed comprehensively by the new administrations; tactical commitments, however, have been made. Unease about the activities of the Muslim Brotherhood in GCC states, particularly UAE's concern about Al-Islah, has acquired a higher profile in recent months. The sole exception to this is Qatar which maintains a multi-pronged relationship with the Brotherhood.

A critical question discussed in different fora and on different planes, directly as well as elliptically, is the place of Islam in society and in State policies. In a book published in 2000, the American journalist Geneive Abdo wrote that 'the religious transformation of Egyptian society appeared obvious to me shortly after I stepped out in the Cairo breeze one Sunday evening in 1993', adding that 'the Islamic revival was broad-based, touching Egyptians in every social class and all walks of life.' The only outstanding question, she concluded, 'is to what degree the religious revival will take over Egyptian society.'

The Brotherhood, with deep roots in society and in professional groupings, subscribes to the amorphous dictum 'Islam is the solution.' Some in this audience would know that in terms of the political theory of Islam, governance is to be by consultation, allegiance is conditional, and dissent admissible. This, in modern terminology, would tantamount to democratic governance. The political history of Muslim societies, however, is characterised by the opposite. The choice often is between form and content. The paradox is summed up succinctly by the French-Algerian scholar Mohammed Arkoun: 'Islam is theologically Protestant and politically Catholic.'

The challenge for contemporary Muslim societies, in the wake of the upsurge against autocratic governance, is to seek legitimacy both in the light of their own cultural authenticity and the norms of the contemporary world. Local situations, even national characteristics, would shape the contours of the debate and outcomes in individual societies. Generalised perceptions of approval or otherwise would be unhelpful.

One last aspect pertains to external impulses. Since the advent of the 21st century, the region and its countries have been witness to initiatives based on innovative doctrines emanating from Western powers. Evidence of a design is compelling. Should conclusions be drawn from it?

Constraints of time prevent me from dwelling on the situation in Yemen and Jordan. Both require watching since many similar forces are at work there. The GCC states—authoritarian and undemocratic but India and Indian friendly—are in a different time zone of political evolution and the combination of enormous wealth and small populations would in all likelihood sustain the status quo for some more time. Bahrain would be an exception to this. If and when turbulence does reach the GCC, it would impact our strategic and commercial interests significantly.

Impact on India's Bilateral Relations

How do these developments affect us in India? Needless to say, political turbulence and economic disruption on our western flank, as in other neighbouring regions, would be an unwelcome development. Formally, a change of regime would not impact on our perceptions since Indian state practice does not admit of regime recognition. Nor is India generally given to pronouncement of value judgements on the domestic set up of other countries unless such a step is motivated by more compelling considerations of statecraft. Barring a serious divergence of views on questions of our national interest, therefore, the new regimes in these countries would not have an adverse impact on our bilateral relations. On the contrary, hard economic and geopolitical interests would ensure harmonious relationships.

In the final analysis therefore the changes, voluntary and expressive of popular will, are to be welcomed. We know only too well that democratic institution-building requires commitment as well as patience and a temper of tolerance. To the extent our assistance is sought, it should be made available without being prescriptive. The transition to a democratic system would be genuine and durable as long as it is autonomous. Suggestions of imposition would be a negation of both.

There is, of course, another scenario to be reckoned with. What would happen if the democratisation process falters, if disagreements take the shape of violent dissent, if the principle of majority rule within the framework of equal rights is not adhered to, if newly installed democratic governments fail to meet public expectations on better governance, social justice, employment and growth? Would renewed turbulence induce external intervention—regional or extra regional? Would it make the region resemble Pandemonium, depicted by the poet Milton as the capital of Hell where the great Satan would be the ruling deity?

VOTE OF THANKS

Director, Asia Centre
Vice Admiral (Retd) R.N. Ganesh

It is with some hesitation that I speak to break the spell.

It is my pleasant duty to thank the Honourable Vice President for literally carving out one hour from the extremely busy schedule of his visit to Karnataka for our benefit and to give us some of his insights on a subject that is not very well studied or analysed.

It would be presumptuous of me to make any comments about what he has said; I will content myself with saying that it was a masterly survey of West Asia and from now when we read about it we will do so with that much more understanding.

It is also our pleasure to have had the Honourable Governor of Karnataka Shri Hans Raj Bhardwaj, who has also set aside the time to come and be present this evening. Shri Asnotikar, Minister for Technology and Fisheries, thank you for coming and finding the time for us.

I have a number of people whom I need to mention, but obviously we cannot go through an entire list. I would be failing in my duty if I did not mention the State administration and the tremendous support that we have got from them in organising this event, starting with the Chief Secretary who took personal interest and particularly the Department of Protocol directly under Mr Kulkarni the Additional Secretary. Their guidance was timely and extremely welcome.

The Bangalore Police have worked hard and have made things seemingly easy, and that is a sign of good organisation. We thank them.

And finally, to this magnificent hotel, the Leela Palace Hotel, their generosity and spontaneity—everything has worked here with clockwork precision; we are grateful to them for their very prompt responses to our requests which often were at short notice.

Introduction

The Asia Centre, Bangalore, was founded in 1996, with the objectives of promoting political, economic, and academic exchanges and exploring fresh Indian initiatives to meet the emerging challenges of the new global order. Since 2001, with A.P. Venkateswaran as its Chairman and Lt General (Retd) Ravi Eipe as its Director, Asia Centre has held regular seminars on various topics, reviewing regional developments from an Indian foreign policy and security perspective. From about 30 lectures and seminars conducted during this period, an editorial team has selected 14, and compiled these in the current volume. Most of them were conducted in the past three years, and the oldest selected, is a seminar conducted in 2007. Together, they cover an eventful period and make for an interesting overview of the prevailing political, economic, and strategic challenges that have faced India and which continue to confront us in the contemporary era.

Attitudes to National Security

With a large number of erstwhile diplomats and military and civil service officers amongst its members, it was natural that the seminars conducted by the Asia Centre should be imbued with concerns about foreign policy and national security. Over time, this perspective has become a feature of the Centre's seminars, and this is reflected in the proceedings of the seminars in this compendium.

Indian leaders displayed surprising indifference to national security in the first few decades after independence, with the posts of the Indian Naval and Air Force Chiefs being occupied by British officers for more than a decade after independence. Despite having faced an armed invasion by its recently excised neighbor within 68 days of its independence, the Indian State failed to internalize the vital importance of a firm foreign policy backed by military strength, for safeguarding the interests of the nation. Only a few years later,

India was again attacked, this time by China, whom India had exerted itself to befriend and whose acceptance in the UN she had advocated.

The early years did see India occupy an influential position in world affairs as the leader of the Non-Aligned Movement, largely due to Nehru's towering personality and personal rapport with world leaders.

Seminal Events

Four seminal events resulted in the gradual evolution of a more pragmatic foreign policy and a more sophisticated understanding of national power.

The first was the attack by China on our North-East and Northern borders. This was a rude awakening for India, and more specifically, for Nehru and his visions of an enduring partnership with China in a resurgent Asia.

The second was the Bangladesh War, which clearly showed that major powers like the US were guided by their own strategic objectives in times of crisis. The dispatch of the US carrier group to the Bay of Bengal to intimidate India generated great hostility towards the US in this country. Yet, it was a useful lesson to India on the dynamics of major power interactions: the US, Russia, and China all stayed clear of direct involvement in the war.

The third major event was the collapse of the USSR, on which India's decades-old dependence had led to a kind of strategic complacency. When the Soviet Union collapsed, India had to make a hard re-appraisal of its policies; ironically, it resulted in Russia doing the same. Both countries were now in need of Western capital and technology to re-boot their economies and their mutual relationship was de-emphasized in their preoccupation with the developing global situation. The government was forced to liberalize its economic policies and the resultant expansion of opportunities fundamentally changed the West's outlook on India.

The fourth event of import was India's decision to come out of the nuclear 'closet' in 1998. With the West piling on the pressure on the CTBT and MTCR, it became imperative to carry out the Pokhran-2 tests then; evidently it was felt that any further delays would have virtually shut down India's nuclear programme and closed its options for the future. India weathered the anticipated storm of protests and sanctions; with the passage of time, the US President made a policy U-turn and steered an agreement for nuclear cooperation with India despite opposition from his own Congress and the Nuclear Suppliers' Group.

It can be said that Indian foreign policy has become more seasoned in the course of these four defining events; with deeper awareness among our elected representatives of the intricacies of statecraft and the guarding of national interests. India, thus, made some progress on the road to becoming a mature power.

Brief Overview of this Book

The 14 seminars and one lecture in this compendium look critically at the developments in the region against this background. The seminars have sought to derive conclusions and policy options for India in her objective of maintaining peace and stability and moving forward, together with other countries of the region, along the road to development.

The first chapter of this book is on Afghanistan, and describes the geopolitical contest there, that impacts India's interests. The conflicting objectives of the various parties, and the implications for India, especially after the US withdrawal, are examined by the panelists. In an earlier seminar on Afghanistan, not included in this volume, Bhadrakumar, a retired diplomat had propounded the view that US interest in Afghanistan would remain irrespective of the Al-Qaeda issue. He attributed this to the US's New Silk Route grand strategy, and to the need for a Southern outlet for Central Asian oil. The centrality of the Afghan imbroglio also comes out in the chapter on India and the Shanghai Cooperation Organization.

The chapter on Iran points out India's dependence on Iranian crude, and simultaneously, India's interest in seeing that Iran does not become a nuclear power. There is an apprehension that Iran will be subjected to an attack with support by the US, over the Western allegations that it is engaged in the production of nuclear weapons. Bangladesh, Nepal, and Myanmar are the subjects of separate chapters. India has been in regular contact with Nepal and Bangladesh; there is an undercurrent of antipathy to India in both countries, created by fears of Indian hegemony and stoked by the factious polity in these countries. Myanmar, in contrast, was isolated diplomatically for several years, until a welcome change in India's policy caused a resumption of contacts. Recent events have justified this change, brought about mainly by India's Look East Policy.

It is frequently commented that India's preoccupation with the Pakistan problem comes in the way of its natural larger regional role. This may be so, but Pakistan is a clear and present danger that cannot be ignored. The three seminars that the Asia Centre has conducted on the crisis-ridden situation in Pakistan have been depressingly similar; the oft-cited elements of the syndrome: the usurpation of the State by the military, the fear that India seeks to destroy Pakistan, and the Pakistani identity crisis all are now subsumed in its Faustian pact with the Taliban to attack India. The chapter brings out the absence of options for India we must continue to engage Pakistan and seek to prevent a conflagration, while being alert and prepared.

The tepidity of India's relations with Russia has already been mentioned above. The core of the Indo–Russian relationship has been, historically, strategic cooperation in defence. Whereas the relationship with the US has also been termed as strategic, there are misgivings that the strategic agenda set by the US is not congruent with India's vision of the global order. A lecture on US–India relations by Shyam Saran, the former Indian Foreign Secretary and India's chief negotiator for the US–India nuclear agreement is also included in this chapter. The chapter on China examines the implications of its military modernization for India. While it brings out the large gap in technological and military capability, the chapter also emphasizes that the way ahead lies in a confident and balanced approach to handling the admittedly asymmetrical relationship.

One country that has not featured in this collection is Sri Lanka, which is an important piece in the regional mosaic. Asia Centre has not held a seminar on Sri Lanka, but instead organized two interactions at the 'Track Two' level in this period, that resulted in a valuable exchange of views. The meetings were conducted not by the Asia Centre alone, but jointly with the Institute of Defence Studies and Analysis, and with participation by analysts from Chennai.

The speakers at the seminar on 'India and the Indian Ocean' dealt with the subject of the Indian Ocean in both its connotations of the Indian Ocean littoral as well as the Indian Ocean as a maritime highway. The expansion of China, economically, strategically, and potentially in a military capacity in the Ocean formed a major thread of the presentations. The second-last chapter in the book deals with the crucial problem of India's energy security. The rising price of oil, its serious impact on India's balance of payments capabilities, and its use as a political tool have all been discussed. The various energy resources have been studied and analysed for their economic viability and potential in the Indian context, and the need for early steps to meet this challenge is clearly brought out. The presentations made at this seminar contain the clear warning that the current energy situation is untenable; unless India acts vigorously, its development plans will fail.

A recurring theme in this collection of seminars is the inadequate importance that has been accorded to the smaller countries in our region.

India has always had a benign influence on many of them; but with aggressive Chinese economic thrust, India is rapidly losing ground in the Indian Ocean and in the South Asian region. It behoves the government to examine this aspect and institute early corrective measures.

This volume covers a wide canvas and deals with diverse aspects of the regional scenario. Its Indian perspective on foreign policy and regional security serves as the unifying strand that binds the separate parts into a coherent whole.

R.N. Ganesh
Director
Asia Centre Bangalore

Chapter 1

India and Afghanistan

ASIA CENTRE BANGALORE
AND
THE INDIAN COUNCIL OF WORLD AFFAIRS

'The Geopolitical Contest in Afghanistan and its Impact on India's Interests'
Proceedings of the Joint Seminar on

July 25, 2009

Introduction

This seminar was the first joint endeavour by the Indian Council of World Affairs, New Delhi and the Asia Centre, Bangalore after the conclusion of an agreement between them in early 2009. The seminar was presided over jointly by A.P. Venkateswaran, former Foreign Secretary and Chairman, Asia Centre, Bangalore and S.T. Devare, Director General, Indian Council of World Affairs, New Delhi. The following were the speakers:

Brigadier (Retd) Rahul Bhonsle	Research Scholar affiliated to USI, New Delhi
Shantie M. D'Souza	Research Fellow at IDSA, New Delhi
Hormis Tharakan	Former Chief of RAW, Visiting Professor, Department of Geopolitics, Manipal University
S.K. Lambah	Former Special Envoy for Afghanistan, Currently Special Envoy in Prime Minister's Office

Nearly 45 Asia Centre members comprising of former Foreign, Defence, and Administrative Service Officers and academics attended the seminar. The presentations were followed by a discussion session. A summary of the proceedings and conclusions, recorded by A. Madhavan, former ambassador of India, is presented in the succeeding pages.

The Director, Asia Centre, Lt General (Retd) Ravi Eipe, welcomed the participants. He extended a special welcome to Sudhir T. Devare, Director General, ICWA, and S.J.S. Chhatwal, Member of the Governing Board of the ICWA. He thanked the ICWA for agreeing to sponsor joint seminars with the Asia Centre, Bangalore, this being the first of the series.

Introducing the topic of the day, he observed that Afghanistan had never been conquered by an outside power. It was also historically known as the graveyard of empires, as typified by the British and Soviet experiences of the 19th and 20th centuries respectively, and has now become a testing ground for US ambitions. Afghanistan has always been a sharply divided tribal society, with spill-overs of affiliation into North-West Pakistan, Baluchistan, and other neighbouring countries. These linkages allow interference and instability in the frontier areas of all these countries. The adage that 'the neighbour's neighbour is a friend' holds true for Indo–Afghan relations. Pakistan, which is the country in the middle, wants to negate or minimize Indian influence in Afghanistan and spread its own influence there instead. This makes for Indo–Pak conflict in Afghanistan. The Afghan scene is further complicated by the different agendas of major powers, the US along with its NATO allies, Russia, and China, apart from the Central Asian Republics.

Presentation 1: Strategic Options

Brigadier (Retd) Rahul K. Bhonsle

The presidential election on August 20 will mark another cusp in Afghanistan's turbulent history. The election had to be postponed from May 20 due to instability, especially in the south and east. The Talibanization of the vast Pashtun tribal lands and the duplicity of Islamabad have led to growing concerns over stability in the country along the Durand Line between Afghanistan and Pakistan. Two opposite views of the future can be discussed. One stressing matters that are deteriorating, and the other stressing developments that are moving reasonably well. On the plus side, we can cite the international commitment and India's stake in Afghan stabilization. That the presidential candidates could debate their programmes on TV (except that

President Karzai did not take part in the debate) is a positive signal favouring open democratic leanings. Human development indicators like health checks for children show improvement in Afghan standards. Several million refugees have returned to Afghanistan from other countries they had earlier fled to.

Since India is a major stakeholder in Afghanistan, the latter's future course is important for our security. Afghan history has seen the contest among various powers in the 19th and 20th centuries. First between Britain and Tsarist Russia, next between the US and the Soviet Union, and since the end of the cold war, between the Taliban Islamists and the non-Islamists. With the current international involvement in stabilizing Afghanistan, there are hopeful signs. Since 2006, there is a focus on security and development.

The US Secretary of State, Hillary Clinton recently said at the Council for Foreign Relations that 'in Afghanistan and Pakistan, our goal is to disrupt, dismantle, and ultimately defeat Al-Qaeda and its extremist allies, and to prevent their return to either country'. However, US commitment is not likely to be long standing, as the Secretary of Defence Robert Gates indicated almost at the same time. The American people were tired of wars in Iraq and Afghanistan.

Alternative perspectives for the next few years should be explored to identify the drivers of stabilization. The Afghan government is making some progress in tackling corruption and extending the reach of central authority to the provinces. The US 'surge' and the revised rules of engagement, which stress better contact with the people, are eliciting public response. NATO forces are also resorting less to air power. A civilian surge is delayed, due to lack of trained personnel. The coalition is intact, though its commitment is now reduced.

The Taliban is largely intact, but split into groups, such as the Quetta Shura, the Southern and Northern Commands, the Haqqani network, and Hizb-e-Islami. The last-named is linked with drug and criminal gangs supported by the Tehrik-e-Taliban Pakistan (TTP) and the Pakistani establishment. There are divisions between the local and central leadership, apart from internal divisions among the militant leaders. The improvised explosive device (IED) is the Taliban's main tactical weapon and an effective one. The Taliban employs the strategy of suicide bombers combined with fire assault in Kabul and other towns. It controls an area which could range between 30 and 70 per cent of the territory.

Pakistan has undertaken counter-militancy operations in the Malakand Agency, including Swat, Buner, and Dur, defeating the Taliban. The second phase is likely to be in South Waziristan. The US considers the operations effective, but with caveats. Attacks on the allied forces continue. The strategy is complex: targeting the leaders and the tribal militias, combined with peace deals and local agreements. Pakistan's commitment is suspect.

Russia has increased its engagement with Afghanistan. President Medvedev held a summit with the Afghan and Pakistan presidents in Moscow recently. The possibility of opening the Northern Route with Russian cooperation, for supplies to the coalition, is being considered. Iran remains in political flux. China, after the eruption of ethnic unrest and conflict in Xinjiang, lacks a clear security policy and may restrict its engagement. India's aid programme is substantial, despite Pakistan's objections, and is a success story. The AfPak region has become the base for global and regional terrorism from the Al-Qaeda, the Taliban, Lashkar-e-Toiba (LeT), Jaish-e-Mohammad (JM), and Jamaat-ud-Dawa (JUD). India, therefore, has to press on with its engagement with this region.

Among the various outcomes, we could consider three scenarios. 1) Growing stability, which is the most favoured outcome; 2) Status quo; 3) A failed state moving towards anarchy, which is the worst case scenario.

The Green Option Full-scale stability in Afghanistan is unlikely, but growing stability is possible by 2015. It would include functioning central and regional governments, the dilution of Taliban control, and increased capacity of the Afghan National Army and Police in exercising control without foreign support. Concomitantly, the bases of the other terrorist groups should be neutralized, and their militants should be drawn into the mainstream. Progress should be marked by greater consensus and cooperation among nations on stabilizing the country. A marginal reduction of external dependence for development aid and security could also be expected. The US-led commitment should be sustained by key actors: Russia, India, China, Iran, the Central Asian Republics, and Pakistan, which is most important. Pakistan should fulfil the commitment to dismantle the terrorist bases in its territory and move away from the objective of gaining 'strategic depth' within Afghanistan.

The main factors would be the resolve of the Afghan leadership and the commitment of the Afghan people. Without it, there will be no progress. The synergy of the various factors working towards stability may be reflected in a stronger resolve by the Afghans. Indian aid is also a component of the scenario.

If, on the other hand, the international consensus weakens due to lack of domestic support, and if Pakistan continues pursuing 'strategic depth' by relying on Afghanistan's Talibanization, insecurity will prevail. So the risks in this optimal scenario are manifest.

The Amber Option The status quo scenario of continued instability is likely if the US 'surge' in troops on the ground fails to improve the situation in a year or so. In such a scenario, the Afghan government will be hard pressed to firm up its authority in the provinces. Governance would remain Kabul-limited, with the Taliban holding sway in about half the country and the international commitment uncertain. Pakistan's erratic attitude to tackling the Taliban insurgency, responding only under international pressure and doles from the US, would aggravate the problem. The Afghan security forces would be weaker and dependent on international deployment of forces. It would also sap the government's resolve. If Pakistan remains ambivalent and the leadership of the Taliban/Al-Qaeda is not much affected by the allied AfPak strategy, the disruption will go on. The Afghan government and people would begin to lose heart. Corruption and parochialism will contribute to the disenchantment of the people. Other nations would then be less willing to offer aid. This scenario would lead to the worst outcome.

The Red Option The worst scenario, an unstable Afghanistan descending into anarchy, is also possible. If the institutions needed are not built up and if the terrorist groups remain active in the AfPak region, anarchy is predictable. This region will remain the matrix of regional and global terrorism. The key consequences would be the forced exit of the US troops, the further weakening of the Afghan security forces, lack of consensus among the regional powers, intra-regional conflict, Pakistan's overt support to the Taliban/Al-Qaeda, and the waning resolve of the Afghans to stabilize the country. The global recession may also reduce the ability of countries to keep up assistance to an unstable Afghanistan.

We may consider if India has viable military options to counter the Afghan insurgency with other countries. No such option can be suggested unless the following criteria are met:

1) The issue is of vital national interest;
2) We have a national consensus for the long haul;
3) International commitment and consensus are certain;
4) There is a trained and operationally ready force;
5) Logistics and sustainability are certain;
6) We have a 100 per cent chance of success.

These criteria are clearly not met, which rules out Indian intervention in Afghanistan. However, India could assist by training Afghan security forces and by expanding its present engagement through consultations. The Pakistan factor dictates gradualism and muted commitments. Training Afghan forces is a viable option.

India can also provide management expertise in organizing, for example, a security force constituted by demobilized troops. Equipment like heavy weapons and *Dhruv* and *Cheetal* helicopters, which are effective in high altitudes, could be provided at subsidized prices. Other countries concerned should, of course, concur with this type of Indian engagement.

Afghanistan needs continued international backing for a long period. Stabilization must be an international and regional priority that no single country should be expected to shoulder by itself. Pakistan should distance itself from the aim of seeking 'strategic depth' in Afghanistan.

Presentation 2: The Regional Contest

Shanthie D'Souza

Key Factors for Instability This important subject may be analysed by examining the key factors for instability in Afghanistan in its national, regional, and international aspects. After the ouster of the Taliban regime, the Bush administration failed to address the problem of Pakistan affording sanctuary to the Taliban insurgents. Its forces were too meagre, with a small security footprint in Afghanistan. This, combined with the porous border along Pakistan, enabled the Taliban to regroup and effect a comeback. Obama took office intending to stabilize Afghanistan, moving away from the Bush 'War on Terror' to the goal of stabilizing the Afghan government gradually. But herein lay a contradiction, since the immediate goal of US policy was not stability but the dismantling of terrorist outfits, mainly the Al-Qaeda. Afghanistan is not 'ungovernable', but the present scenario is adverse to the Afghan government gaining firm control, since both the regional states (mainly Pakistan and Iran) and big power contentiousness (among the US, Russia, and China) contribute to instability. The US has directed drone attacks on suspected hideouts inside Pakistan, but so far only some low-level commanders—not the leaders (some living in Quetta)—have been eliminated. Meanwhile, the Kerry–Lugar bill has sanctioned an annual grant-in-aid to Pakistan amounting to \$1.5 billion, which will go largely unaccounted for. Huge funds have been poured into Afghanistan and Pakistan, but there is little stabilization to show for it. Security and development have been on the back-burner. The success stories are not translated into stable institutions. Aid programmes have been channelled through the aid agencies of the donors rather than through the Afghan government. As a result, the aid has sapped the government, which is seen as weak, inept, and corrupt. The parallel state structure that has emerged has further reduced the effectiveness of the Afghan government and people's faith in it. The Afghan state is a *rentier* state, as it is continually dependent on outside support. It has not been able to build and run its own structure, based on its own resources.

International Military Intervention International military intervention involves two forces—NATO's International Security Assistance Force (ISAF) and the US 'Operation Enduring Freedom' force, the latter being the greater in size. They have, however, added to the exposure of the Afghan government's inadequacies. The foreign forces have not heeded the cultural sensitivities of the people; this has worsened the backlash against them. Afghans do not favour the Taliban, but the people have no choice but to comply with their dominance. The Taliban know that the US and foreign troops will not stay forever. The Pashtun saying, 'You have the watch, but we have the time' is applicable to the Americans. The US is working on its exit strategy and may withdraw or scale down its presence in the area if Obama does not gain his objectives. He has not defined his AfPak strategy time-wise, but will wish to avoid seeing it labelled his 'Vietnam.' The contradiction between the need to stay on and the need to leave will be problematic. In the latter course, regional powers will resume destabilizing Afghanistan. The AfPak policy is good, but does not deal with the backlash against American intervention in Pakistan. Attacking a few terrorist leaders will not be enough to defeat the insurgency, as the counter-strikes will involve civilian casualties. The Pakistan civilian government would be weakened, and the military could once again take over the government. The other danger is the huge Islamist threat. Meanwhile, the LeT, which has strong connections with the Taliban, is active in training posts in the Kunar province on the Afghan side of the border. India cannot rest on the assumption that the Taliban insurgency does not affect our security, particularly as the Taliban has included Kashmir in its agenda of goals and India in the list of its enemies.

'Civilian' Surge Needed The US 'surge' may lessen civilian casualties, but how it can stabilize the country is not clear. A long-term strategy is missing. Iraq and Afghanistan are different in the sense that in Iraq the insurgency was mostly urban, while it is mostly rural in the latter. Iraq had functioning state institutions in towns, but even the traditional village institutions in

Afghanistan have broken down or been radicalized. Much of the aid received from abroad has gone into salaries and administration, so that the problem of poverty and unemployment remain, feeding the Taliban movement. A civilian surge to match the military is required for provincial reconstruction. Further, while foreign attention is now focused on reclaiming the South and the East, little aid has gone to the North, where reform and rebuilding need attention.

Ineffective Reconstruction Assistance The Provincial Reconstruction Teams (PRTs), intended to aid and strengthen local authorities, are not very effective because they do not let the Afghans decide the kind of small project they should take up first. If a village requires a drinking water supply project, the PRT building a school is not much appreciated. The people have no great expectations of the PRTs; when militants attack a settlement, PRTs are of little consequence. We must remember this if India is to send out its own PRTs to Afghan areas.

Security Situation The security situation remains grim. The Taliban is constituted of diverse elements, not only Islamists but out-of-work young men, those with grievances against the state, and even thieves. US forces need to secure the supply lines for logistics, which have been disrupted on the Pakistani side by the Taliban. Alternative routes via Russia, such as the Northern route, are less feasible if Russia is reluctant to oblige due to NATO's expansion in Eastern Europe and American diplomatic penetration of Central Asia. Iran is another possibility, with the road from Zaranj to Delaram in the South–West of Afghanistan, which India has built, extendable to the port of Chahbahar; but continuing US–Iran tension rules out an early agreement. The upshot is that the US will continue to depend on Pakistan, come what may.

A Role for China China is an important regional power which can play a helpful role in the stabilization of the Afghan situation due to its influence with Pakistan, which could be utilized. The Shanghai Cooperation Organization (SCO) could be asked to engage more constructively towards normalizing Afghanistan.

Obama's Vietnam? Obama's AfPak strategy, which he would like to succeed to bolster his re-election campaign, has not been very effective. But as the Americans do not have the stomach for a long war, the outlook is that the US will leave Afghanistan after, perhaps, two more fighting seasons. Their problem is to achieve a measure of stability in Afghanistan, with the help of its allies, which are also tiring of the responsibility. The US wants India to be an active player. If the US cannot overcome the insurgency, its entire strategy would be labelled as 'Obama's Vietnam', which he would like to, somehow, avoid.

If the Pakistani civilian government is weakened through the backlash against US intervention, it is possible that the military would take over the reins again, or that the Islamist threat would loom larger still. India would be under threat too, since the Taliban has strong links with the LeT and rebel Islamists from Central Asia. A long belt of interlinked disruptions could result, stretching from Chechnya to Afghanistan, Pakistan, and India.

India's Role India is being pressed into a major role; it is already the sixth largest donor of foreign aid to Afghanistan, and Pakistan would immediately object to any increase in its aid or profile, and prevail on the US to arrange a scaling down of its Afghan presence. Pakistan is also urging the US to mediate in the Kashmir issue, an intervention India will not accept. While Richard Holbrooke, the US special envoy, has been careful to avoid discussing Kashmir, there are some in Washington who are inclined to appease Pakistan further.

India wants long-term stability to be built up in Afghanistan. Indian aid and training programmes are well appreciated by the Afghans and more could be channelled through local agencies, focusing on the neglected northern areas. But sending Indian troops to Afghanistan is not recommended; sustaining a military presence would be a big problem, and would be a red rag for Pakistan. Instead, India can use its capacity to train Afghan security personnel in high-altitude warfare, counter-insurgency, and several other operations; and to build and strengthen Afghanistan's state institutions, especially those of local government. Indian Muslims could join in the campaign to expose the un-Islamic tenets of the terrorists using the Islamic label. India could participate in combating the menace of narcotics trade; if a successful model area can be established, efforts to replicate it would be beneficial.

Inclusion of Afghanistan in South Asian Development Lastly, the aim of integrating Afghanistan into the South Asian development region should be addressed in earnest. In the longer term, energy pipelines through Afghanistan and Pakistan to India can be envisaged. Indo–Afghan trade would gain immensely from the opening of transit routes through Pakistan, if the latter can be pressed to do so. These projects, though not feasible at the present stage, should be considered for the eventual development of Afghanistan as an independent state. It can generate more employment through its integration into the larger region of free trade.

UN as Main Agency for Aid Coordination The international community has a big role, and another conference like the Bonn conference of 2001 is called for. Afghan elements that were earlier excluded but are now ready to give up armed struggle could be brought into the government set-up. Such a conference should give the lead role to the Afghans, who should be encouraged to plan their future. A non-interference pact could be negotiated and Afghanistan could be recognized as a neutral and independent state. The UN, rather than the US, should be the main agency to coordinate aid and reconstruction.

Presentation 3: The Afghan Riddle

Hormis Tharakan

Afghan and Pakistan—Solutions Interlinked The counter-insurgency drive in Afghanistan has reached a decisive stage with President Obama outlining his AfPak policy. The interconnection between Afghanistan and Pakistan in tackling the Al-Qaeda–Taliban offensive implies that the problems of one country cannot be solved without solving those of the other. This approach was mooted by Bruce Riedel, former CIA official (whom Obama has consulted), in an article in 'Foreign Affairs' in June 2007. He said, 'A critical first step towards decapitating the Al-Qaeda is for Washington to enhance its commitment in Afghanistan.' He further urged that defeating the Taliban would require significantly more NATO troops and equipment, which itself requires US leadership. To induce the shift, more US troops should be diverted from Iraq to Afghanistan. Riedel suggested a contact group of Afghanistan's neighbours could be formed, to secure Afghan borders. Iran had been helpful previously and should again be engaged in securing Afghanistan. India has been the target of terrorism by Islamist militants for long. India has given more than half of billion dollars in aid to Afghanistan and should play a bigger role there. Pakistan should not be rewarded for its selective targeting of terrorists. The new US Congress, Riedel said, should take 'a sharp look' at Pakistan's record of cooperation with the US in its regional objectives. The US should use the enhanced relationship with India after the nuclear deal and encourage improved Indo–Pak understanding and a lessening of hostility between them. Riedel acknowledged that the terrorist network in Kashmir maintained links with the Al-Qaeda.

Inclusion of Kashmir Issue in US Strategy Though Kashmir has been downplayed by Ambassador Holbrooke, it does seem to be part of the US strategy for the region. Recently, there has been an enhancement of allied military action in Afghanistan, but the UK's support is also weakening with increasing British casualties. There is friction between the US and Pakistan over strategy. In July, the *International Herald Tribune* and the *New York Times* reported that Pakistan was against the expanded anti-Taliban allied military operations in Afghanistan since this would require it to move troops from its Indian borders to its East to its Western borders. For Pakistan, the main problem was to guard against Indian offensives.

Perceptual Differences between US and Pakistan There is a growing gap in perception between the US and Pakistan despite the latter's military offensive against the Taliban in Swat, which has won plaudits in the West. The US military is convinced that Pakistan is taking on the Pakistani Taliban militants and ignoring the Afghan Taliban, which is known to have links with the Al-Qaeda. Secretary of State, Hillary Clinton, recently said in New Delhi that the planners of 9/11 had taken shelter in Pakistan, though the Pakistan foreign ministry vigorously denied the charge. The US believes that Mohammed Omar is in Quetta but Pakistan denies this and says that only two of the leaders named by the US, who pose no threat, are in Quetta. The US Army is not happy with Pakistan for its refusal to attack the Afghan Taliban. Pakistan backs Sirajuddin Haqqani, who is in North Waziristan training militants to fight the NATO.

Karzai not US Favourite The presidential election in Afghanistan (on August 20, 2009) may result in Hamid Karzai getting a second term as president. This, according to reports, would not please the West, which is backing the unpopular former World Bank official and former finance minister Ashraf Ghani. A violent reaction may follow Karzai's victory.

Dialogue with the Taliban Pakistani intelligence is pressing the West into a dialogue with the Taliban. The Pakistani record of cooperation with the Taliban features several instances of intrigues against some of its leaders. The ISI penchant for the 'good Taliban', despite burnt fingers, has been minimized by the Americans, because they still need Pakistan to carry out the campaign against the Afghan insurgency.

If Pakistan can convince the West to start a dialogue with the Taliban, the West may opt for a regime change in Afghanistan. There are some who hold the view that the troop surge is a limited mission that needs to be developed into a full nation-building project that would take a long time to succeed. The US has stopped counting the number of enemies killed in action as an index of progress.

The Afghans prefer the Taliban to government agencies, which are perceived as corrupt. The prospects of the AfPak strategy must be viewed with reservation. The US may decide to leave, since its primary target is to debilitate the Al-Qaeda and neutralize it, so that the US homeland continues to be secure from terror strikes, like those of 9/11.

Planning for the End Game In the end it should be the regional players that should cooperate to ensure Afghanistan's security. India needs to plan for the time when the US leaves and the Taliban regains ascendancy in Afghanistan, which is the Pakistani objective. India's diplomatic strategy should reach out to Iran, Russia, China, and the Central Asian Republics, all of which have a common interest in stabilizing Afghanistan, without a dominant Taliban.

Presentation 4: The Way Forward

Satinder Lambah

Introduction

Afghanistan has emerged, in our time, from being a client state in 1979 to the status of a fledgling democracy. The security situation has been deteriorating since 2006, with the civilian population, the militants, and the US–NATO troops, all sustaining more casualties. The figures for violent incidents are up in the south and east of the country. NATO is a divided house: its members are reluctant to put more troops on the ground and there are not enough troops to combat the insurgency. The US is sending 17,000 more troops, with some civilian support. The Afghan National Army is not capable of pursuing an effective campaign without NATO support.

Taliban and the Spread of Terrorism The Taliban has the advantage of sanctuaries, shelter, and recruitment potential in Pakistan. The Tariq-e-Taliban Pakistan (TTP) and the Afghan Taliban are close. The Pakistan state's loss of control over FATA is a fillip to the Taliban fighting in Afghanistan. The distinction between the Taliban, the Al-Qaeda, and groups like the LeT is becoming meaningless, since they are all fused, both operationally and ideologically. The terrorist spread is menacing. The LeT and its offshoot the JUD (active in Jammu and Kashmir), have been designated as terrorist groups by the UNSC under the Resolution 1267, which is a positive step. But the terrorist footprint extends to the whole region, including India. The present impasse is that the Taliban cannot capture power in Afghanistan, while the NATO cannot defeat the Taliban.

Narcotics Problem Two problems have complicated the situation. The first is the narcotics problem. Afghanistan is a narcotics-based state, with drugs producing 50 per cent of its GDP; 93 per cent of the world's supply of heroin comes from Afghanistan. In the southern and eastern parts of the country, there is an increase in poppy cultivation. The reasons include the higher returns for the farmer for growing poppy, poor border controls, and official collusion. The nexus between narcotics and terrorists is well known.

Problem of Refugees The refugee problem persists long after 2001, when 7 million Afghans fled to neighbouring countries. Though the UNHCR says 5 million refugees have returned, there are still about 3 million in Pakistan, Iran, and the neighbouring countries in the north. Even in India, there are about 9,200 Hindus and Sikh refugees who claim Afghanistan as their homeland but cannot yet go back because of insecurity and lack of employment prospects.

Presidential Elections The presidential election will be held on August 20 under an independent Afghan commission, aided by the UNDP. President Hamid Karzai is the front-runner, and other prominent candidates are the former Foreign Minister Abdullah Abdullah and the former Finance Minister Ghani. Karzai's vice-presidential team includes Fahim as deputy, which is not congenial to the West, but he is likely to swing the Tajik and other minority votes for Karzai. The results are to be announced in September or October.

Impact of Central Asian Neighbours Afghanistan occupies a strategic location close to Central Asia, which is rich in minerals, oil, and gas, and has been a zone of contention among the major powers for centuries. Its neighbours (Tajikistan, Turkmenistan, Uzbekistan, Kyrgyzstan, and Kazakhstan) have an important bearing and impact on the present crisis. Two new elements have to be noted: Islamic fundamentalism and terrorism, both of which have caused much of the disruption in the region. The Russian shadow also falls on it. Organized crime, drug traffic, and authoritarian regimes are unfortunate features here. After 9/11, the Central Asian Republics became frontline states in the Afghan war.

Russian Reservations At first Russia welcomed US intervention in Afghanistan, but has changed its attitude in recent years, with the advance of NATO eastward towards the Russian border and US influence gaining ground in Central Asia. Russia has the most extensive and complex economic and other interests in the Central Asian Republics.

China's Growing Role Next, we should note the growing role of China in this region. China borders some of them. With the tribes freely crossing the borders, China has its own concerns to secure. Hitherto the small republics north of Afghanistan have had a low profile there.

Iran's Interests Iran has long had an important interest in Afghan stability. It supports the Afghan Shia minority. In 2001, Iran supported the US-led war against the Taliban and Al-Qaeda and the Bonn Conference that year would not have reached a favourable agreement on Afghanistan's governance without Iran's backing. It was Iran that proposed the inclusion of the word 'democracy' for the projected Afghan government, to the pleasant surprise of the US. Iran is crucial for ensuring a stable Afghanistan. It is a member of two trilateral commissions—Pakistan–Afghanistan–Iran and Turkey–Iran–Afghanistan. Russia is also taking part in such a group—Russia–Afghanistan–Pakistan–Tajikistan. These interactions deserve India's attention.

Pakistan's Interests in Afghanistan Pakistan is a critically important neighbour. Pakistan's objectives in Afghanistan are:

1) To gain 'strategic depth';
2) Increasing Afghanistan's dependence on Pakistan;
3) Settling the Pakhtunistan issue;
4) Facilitate trade and transit to Central Asia;
5) To create a source of recruits for jihad in Kashmir;
6) Negating India's influence in Afghanistan.

Rafat Hussain, a scholar in the Institute of Strategic Studies, Islamabad, has recently written that Afghanistan and Pakistan never enjoyed smooth relations except during the four years of the Taliban regime. The factors making for friction are the Durand Line, the British drawn border in the Pashtun region, which Afghanistan never accepted, and divergence in the strategic outlook of the two neighbours as well as their different ideas of their shared faith, Islam. Afghanistan has long shunned foreign influence and interference, while Pakistan has long been an American ally, receiving protection, especially at present. Pakistan is pro-Taliban because the Taliban is anti-India and anti-secular.

Pakistan's 'Strategic Depth' Concept The concept of 'strategic depth', which Pakistan seeks in Afghanistan, is intended to give the former certain advantages in a conflict with India: Pakistan will have time to transfer key military equipment to a place of its choosing. Logistical support would be available. Places west of the Durand Line would be safe from attack. Large safe havens would be ensured. These are unlikely scenarios conjured by the Pakistani army.

The Swat Offensive Terrorism and Talibanization have spread through Pakistan and major cities like Karachi and Lahore have hidden terrorist networks; even Islamabad is not immune. The conflict in Swat is a development of the Afghan situation. In recent military operations, the Pakistani army has used air power and artillery tanks against the Taliban insurgents, a paradigm shift in strategy following a late realization that the Taliban poses a threat to the Pakistan state. The Swat offensive was also due to international concern and Pakistan's desperate need for financial support, which is tied to the effectiveness of its drive against the Taliban. But the drive has produced various problems for Pakistan, threatening regional stability and communal relations. The Pashtun refugees from Swat and other areas, numbering 2.3 million at the peak, are unwelcome in Sind and Punjab, which has embittered them as fellow-citizens and ignited a regional divide.

Further, the tactical cooperation among the jihadi groups in Pakistan has become closer. Pakistan is still reluctant to take action against the India-centric jihadi groups. The Swat operation obliged Pakistan to move some troops from its eastern border with India to the western border with Afghanistan. It indicates a measure of trust in India's peaceful intentions. For the first time since 1971, there are signs of growing fatigue among the Pakistan troops who are now called upon to fight their own people.

Conflicting Objectives

International Opinion From our point of view, international opinion inclining towards Pakistan's wish of initiating talks with the Taliban is of some concern. It is a sign of drift in the campaign against Afghan insurgency and it also makes the Afghan government appear weak. India has asked how we can distinguish the 'good Taliban' from the 'bad Taliban'. The ultimate aim of the pragmatists is to reach some kind of compromise, though the West is not willing to spell it out now. In fact, the US and Pakistani priorities are different. One is right to say that 'the watch is with the US, but time is on the side of the Taliban'.

US Objectives The main US objective is to eliminate the Al-Qaeda structure. The Americans may revive their idea of sponsoring a gas pipeline from Turkmenistan to Afghanistan and Pakistan in the longer term. The US considers Pakistan too important to ignore its concerns, and it will continue to receive US military and economic assistance despite Admiral Mullen's candour on its double dealing. One positive aspect for India is that the crisis has exposed Pakistan's policy of assistance to terrorists, which is now under greater international scrutiny.

China's Objectives China's objectives are to prevent the export of terrorism to Xinjiang and, in the long run, to sponsor a gas pipeline reaching its cities from Central Asia. Its minority communities bordering these states have ethnic links, which have to be rightly channelled. China has been sensitive to its ally Pakistan's difficulty in curbing Islamic activity in other countries, but it may play a more active role in helping Afghan stability in future.

Russian Objectives Russia's objectives are to prevent the export of terrorism to Chechnya, and to guard against the spread of drug addiction, which is already very high among Russians. Russia enjoyed the discomfiture of the US in Afghanistan, but it now wants to see the country brought to order, since the unrest of the Taliban insurgency can infect 'the soft underbelly' of Russia.

India's Interests India, for its part, wants to ensure that there is no export of terrorism and extremism from the region and no outside interference in Afghanistan. The Afghan government should exclude the Taliban, and should rely on an integrated army and police. Human rights should be protected. The UN could assist in the reconstruction, which should be given the main emphasis. India has had a long-term and strategic interest in Afghanistan. Afghan leaders up to Karzai, though from diverse regimes, had personal or familial connections with India, including education in India. We have good relations with the different strata of society. For these very reasons, the Taliban and ISI oppose Indian presence.

India's Aid Programme India has an open and visible aid programme for reconstruction, spanning all the provinces of Afghanistan, amounting to $1.3 billion so far. The projects are targeted by the Taliban militants. The main assistance programmes, which have benefited the Afghan government and are welcomed by the people, are:

1) The 218 km highway from Zaranj to Delaram in the southwest of Afghanistan that will provide a gateway to the Indian Ocean via Iran and its port of Chahbahar, greatly improving the country's trade prospects. It has already begun to boost the movement of cargo.

2) The Salma dam power project (42 MW) under construction in Herat province, which will provide irrigation to large tracts.
3) A power transmission line built over difficult mountainous areas from Pul-e-Khumri to Kabul and a substation at Chimtala for additional power from the Northern grid to Kabul.
4) The Afghan parliament house in Kabul, a symbol of our democratic linkage.
5) Restoration of the telecom infrastructure in 11 provinces.
6) Expansion of the national TV network for Kabul and the provincial capitals.

There are also many smaller projects which contribute to the health, education, and social needs of the Afghans, especially children and women. Wheat consignments, food aid to schools, the Indian Medical Missions in the capital and other cities, the Indira Gandhi Institute for Child Health, solar panels, a cold storage centre, a computer training centre, vocational training for youths, and ITEC placements in India are some of the different areas where India is helping the reconstruction and capacity building of Afghanistan. We are renewing contacts with our traditional friends, the Pashtuns.

Despite the prospect of an eventual Afghan government which includes some Taliban members, the aid programme is the way forward for India to secure its interests in the Afghan state and win the trust of its people.

Discussion

The ensuing discussions brought out several points which are summarized in the following paragraphs.

Iran's Benign Influence in the Region Ambassador Khaleeli described Iran's benign influence over several epochs on Afghanistan. The only period of stability which Afghanistan had enjoyed was when the Hindu and Iranian civilizations cooperated there.

Pakistan's Influence The Afghans are a tribal people with their own virtues and codes of behaviour and Pakistan cannot make a lasting mark on it or dominate it; Iran would have a continuing influence.

Freedom from Intruders India should favour the exit of all foreign intruders, whether the Soviet Union as in the past, the Americans today, or the Russians or Chinese in the future, as it does not serve our interests. We should keep in touch with the Taliban, good or bad, as it is good diplomacy to maintain such contacts. The Americans would leave Afghanistan eventually, and India should work to impress on the Pashtuns and the Taliban that Pakistan cannot manipulate a stable Afghanistan, and thus undo the mischief of the British-drawn Durand Line.

Arab Influence on Afghanistan There is considerable Saudi Arabian influence on the Islamic insurgents through funded 'charities.' But Turkey and India were in favour of an Afghanistan which would not exploit religious extremism as its ideology. Other Muslim countries could also help the moderating trend. The Arabs, particularly the Saudis, have spread the Deoband type of Wahabi Islam among the Afghan Sunnis, appealing to tribalism. But the Afghan Muslims, Sunnis included, have long enjoyed cultural links with the Iranian civilization and Persian is spoken widely in the country.

Russia's Rising Profile Russia was reasserting its interests in the region and the SCO could play a positive role. China's presence is also more evident in Central Asia. The US is aware of these developments and attended the Moscow Summit of the SCO at a junior level. The US clearly wants more international cooperation in Afghanistan.

NATO Supply Routes As an alternative to the Pakistan route, which has become dangerous, the Northern route too is difficult to rely on. The Iran route via the Indian-built highway in Afghanistan is potentially usable, being shorter and less costly. But the West's relations with Iran over Iran's controversial nuclear programme rules out that option at present. India has a neutral stand and will make its own decisions on bilateral relations with Iran, as with other countries. Much depends on how the Iran crisis evolves.

Scale of Assistance Projects There was a view expressed that India should not go in for big infrastructure projects in Afghanistan which draw Pakistan's opposition, but replicate the kind of projects like the hospital for children (IGCHA) in the provinces, along with small vocational training centres. It was pointed out that most of the Indian projects were small ones which women's groups were being enabled by India to oversee and execute. High visibility projects like the Salma dam were located in the relatively more stable parts of the North.

Indian Consulates in Afghanistan Pakistan viewed the Indian consulates with suspicion and alleged that they were used for fomenting trouble and for espionage. Lambah corrected a questioner and emphasised that the US had not made any call for dismantling the consulates. Clarifying the facts, he said that of the four Indian consulates, only those in Jalalabad and Kandahar, which have existed since the 1950's, are near Pakistan. They are thinly staffed and were necessary as India has a zero tariff arrangement with Afghanistan for its dry fruit export and every consignment needs to be certified by the consulate. The Pakistani criticism should not be taken seriously.

Indian Diplomatic Initiative Ranganathan suggested that India and others could initiate a regional solution, after due consultations, to stabilize Afghanistan. India should avoid the trap of insisting that the new Afghan government should be totally free of the Taliban representatives. Like Khaleeli, he would like India to establish its own contact with the Taliban.

American interest in the region was limited; the US wants India to be a more active player. It would be a positive diplomatic initiative if India could put together a group including Russia, Iran, and possibly China (whose interests intersect with India's in several areas). That way, we would be exercising autonomy and independent judgement in foreign policy. The US could perhaps persuade Pakistan to join such an initiative.

Vacation of Afghanistan by the US The US would not continue to stay in Afghanistan for the sake of oil and gas in view of Turkmenistan's long term agreement on gas with Russia. If they did stay, oil and gas would be subsidiary to their main interest which was to see that the 9/11 kind of threat was, in their judgment, eliminated successfully.

Projects in Afghanistan S.J.S. Chhatwal, Member, Governing Body and Chairman, Programme Committee, ICWA, shared the following views with the audience about the present Afghan situation:

1) Afghan scholars now go to Pakistan for study and research, and do not expect much from India in the academic field. They speak chaste Urdu, not Hindustani any more.
2) Pakistan has used the lure of money to make the Afghans (Pathans) Islamist in outlook.
3) China is investing more funds and technology in Afghanistan since the space is vacant and there is little Indian private investment coming in. It will establish growing influence in the country.
4) India, it is true, has done a lot, and generated popular goodwill. The power transmission line we have built was notable; it was turned down by Western companies for collaboration at the project stage.

5) The Indian built highway to Iran will not be open to the NATO powers and the US, since Iran has specifically refused to allow the road to be used as the allied transit route for their Afghan operations.
6) India has done well in giving 2.5 million tonnes of wheat as food aid to Afghanistan, a highly appreciated gesture.

Summary and Conclusion

The seminar produced informative and clear-cut presentations by all the four speakers. The subsequent discussion brought out some differences of opinion and emphasis, but also clarified the issues of national concern for us, mainly Pakistan's political disarray and double-dealing on fighting terrorism. India's interests as a stakeholder in the Afghan–Pakistan region were uppermost in all the presentations. They took due note of India's interest extending to the adjacent region of Central Asia and Iran.

Afghanistan is moving into a phase of painful stabilization, challenged by serious security threats from the largely Pashtun insurgents of the Taliban and the remnants of the Al-Qaeda. The Taliban has re-entered the fray as a foe of both the Karzai government and its external backers, the multi-national combine led by the US. The US itself has begun to doubt the rationale of the Afghan war, which has claimed a high price in its prestige, leadership, money, and trained personnel. The Janus-faced role of Pakistan as the frontline ally of the US and simultaneously the clandestine mainstay of the Taliban is the core problem in the present Afghan crisis. The AfPak strategy was acutely analysed by the speakers: none could forecast success for it despite the 'surge' of mostly American troops.

Since this seminar at the end of July 2009, Pakistan's army has conducted purposeful and heavily armed operations against the Taliban. The Pakistan Taliban has turned against its mentor, the Pakistan army, as well as the civilian government. The American drone attacks killed countless civilians and drove out refugees by the thousand, making the Americans objects of hate in the eyes of the Pakistani public. The reported death of Baitullah Mehsud in a drone strike on August 5 has led to a violent succession dispute among the tribal factions. The leaders of the Afghan Taliban and Al-Qaeda still remain in hiding, somewhere in the Afghan–Pakistan tribal belt.

The chief gain this summer for the countries and forces ranged against the insurgency is that the Pakistan state is now determined to eliminate at least the Pakistan Taliban. But this consolation is flawed as the militants whose targets are Indian rather than Afghan or American are still dear to the ISI as 'assets.' Pakistan is yet to be convinced of the futility of reliance on the sponsored 'jihad' against secular, democratic India.

At the root of India's Afghan problem is the fact that the US feels beholden to Pakistan, despite the latter's known perfidy, and feels obliged to pamper it with arms and other help. India sides with the US and its NATO allies in wanting to restore stability in Afghanistan and contributing to Afghan reconstruction and development; but it is hampered by the hostility of Pakistan to the Indian presence in Afghanistan, a perversity which the US is covertly supporting.

The inescapable conclusion is that India cannot tag along with the US in its AfPak policy in the key aspect of indulgence towards Pakistan's remote control terrorism. This contradiction in the policies of both the US and Pakistan has inveigled India into a tacit acquiescence of the idea that the Afghan state can be stabilized only by a broad-based government which includes the 'good Taliban', as opposed to the 'bad Taliban' who are dead against a compromise with the West and US-dependent Pakistan. The fact that one cannot distinguish the good from the bad Taliban will not deter either Pakistan or the US in seeking such a compromise. For Pakistan, this is a gateway to the revival of a Taliban-ruled Afghanistan and the concept of 'strategic depth' in case of a confrontation with India. For the US, the compromise offers a wedge of light at the end of the dark Afghan war tunnel, an exit strategy that saves face.

In this background, India's Afghan policy has to be at a remove from the US policy, but run parallel with it in cooperating to stabilize Afghanistan. India too, as some speakers at the seminar suggested, should have its own contacts among the Taliban or Taliban-sympathizing Afghans, many of whom are understandably opposed to foreign military presence and patronage. The suggestion that India should initiate groundwork for a new Afghan conference among regional powers is worth exploring.

Since India has a long-term vision of closer economic interaction with Afghanistan, we could seriously take up laying the informational foundation and contact building for potential projects. This would help the Afghans lessen their dependence on other countries. Our aim should be to enter the economic space vacated by Western investors, not with the view to buying up and exploiting precious mineral resources, as China has done, but to collaborate with Afghan partners. If a project is framed with providing employment and training for local youth, as the Indian aim, it would be better received by the people. The rich experience that Indian engineers and technicians have already gained in projects in diverse fields like electric power, highways, airline maintenance, transport, and medicine and health care should be tapped methodically by a group of select experts to advance this objective, unfazed by the current unrest and turmoil in Afghanistan.

The presidential election on August 20 may not result in a decisive victory for Karzai or the other two credible candidates in the face of Taliban-led disruption and violence. The plurality of tribal affiliations and their networks in the adjacent countries, especially in Pakistan across the Durand Line, poses a problem of Afghan national identity which can be tackled only by compromise among the tribes and understanding among the neighbours. Afghanistan can create its role as a neutral and peaceful state if it is a long-term project of international cooperation through the UN rather than any single power. India can use every means in its widening diplomatic scope, such as the SCO, the firmer bilateral relations with the US and Russia, and the commonality with China. This implies that India should encourage Pakistan to be more trustful of our policy and intentions as a benign regional power that allows it latitude but no quarter for sponsoring subversion and terrorism against us.

Chapter 2

India and Iran

ASIA CENTRE BANGALORE

'Complexity of the Situation in Iran: India's Strategic Interests and Options'
Proceedings of the Seminar on

March 22, 2008

Preface

A.P. Venkateswaran, former Foreign Secretary and Chairman of Asia Centre presided. The following speakers addressed the seminar:

Akbar M. Khaleeli	Former Ambassador to Iran
Vice-Admiral (Retd) P. J. Jacob	Former Vice-Chief of Naval Staff and former Naval Attaché in Tehran
Kesava Menon	Associate Editor, *The Hindu*, and its West Asia Correspondent from 1994 to 2002.

This report summarizes the presentations and the discussions that followed. It has been compiled by A. Madhavan, former Ambassador of India and a current member of Asia Centre.

Introduction

A.P. Venkateswaran, Chairman of Asia Centre, welcomed the participants and the speakers. He said that Iran is the centre point of world turmoil. If the US attacks or invades Iran, India's foreign policy moves would be keenly scrutinized for signs that it has succumbed to American pressure. He invited the three speakers to share their perceptions with the audience, drawing on their long experience in examining the political and strategic developments of Iran since the 1979 Revolution.

Lt General (Retd) Ravi Eipe, Director of Asia Centre, welcomed the speakers and the participants. Introducing the subject, he gave an overview of the Indo–Iranian connection, with its long history and cultural links. He stated that, for strategic reasons, a friendly Iran is invaluable to India.

India is in an evolving strategic partnership with the US. The US sees Iran as a state bent on acquiring weapons of mass destruction, and a supporter of anti-Israeli terrorism. For India, Iran is a long standing and strategically important friend. India has important economic projects in its Iran agenda, one such being the proposed gas pipeline from Iran to India via Pakistan. The US is pressing India to give up the idea of participation in it, and warns that it would entail sanctions by the US against several Indian entities.

How this dilemma will play out is a major concern.

Presentation 1: A Historical Perspective

Akbar M. Khaleeli

Iran's History Khaleeli presented a broad historical survey of Iran and the Indo–Iranian interaction since ancient times to the present. Iran, China, and India are the three enduring Asian cultures. Iran was the nodal area of the Silk Route. The speaker dwelt on the psychology of the Iranian people, the terrible sufferings they had overcome during the period of Arab ascendancy, followed by the even more terrible Mongol invasions. He extolled their pride, sense of humour, and love of independence. He expounded the beliefs and values of the Shia faith, after pointing out that Iran was Sunni-dominant for four centuries until the Safavid era. The Shias, he said, constituted, in a sense, the most continuous political party in the world. He cautioned against Indian diplomats taking a facile view that Sunni Islam as a majoritarian group is more Islamic than the Shias.

Imposition of a Pro-Western Monarchy He then spoke of Iran's humiliation in the 19th Century as a hyper-colony and contrasted it with India's condition under the British Raj. Iran had to yield control of its minerals, oil, and forestry to the European powers. It was caught up in the rivalry among Russia, France, Britain, and Germany. The Iranians of the time were not anti-American and wanted a balance between the big powers, mainly Britain and Russia, to avoid complete dominance by either. After Prime Minister Mossadeq nationalized the oil industry, the US, supported by the UK, authorized a CIA coup in 1953 to topple his government. The US brought in the Shah from Rome to head a pro-Western government in Iran.

Post-Revolution Rise of Hard-line Clerics The rise of the exiled Ayatollah Khomeini after the Iranian revolution of 1979 was a partly-nationalistic backlash by a proud people chafing under out-dated restraints. In the post-revolution phase, the moderating influence of the provisional government appointed by Khomeini was overwhelmed by the clerical hardliners. After this, the latter became more powerful and emphasized the Islamic dimensions of the Republic of Iran. Thus, a moderate course in Iranian foreign policy was hampered, if not precluded, from the start in the post-revolution period.

Khaleeli gave a brief exposition of the centrality of Khomeini's personality and political vision in shaping the constitution of Iran. One can sense that Khomeini, while asserting political control over Iran, did not want vested interests to become too comfortable and hence, in many ways, his influence in preventing back-sliding is still felt. The decimation of the Iraqi religious leadership over the past two decades has also given Iran an edge in international Shia politics. Nevertheless, Shia-ism is too intellectually vigorous and naturally dissident to become monolithic with or without Iranian influence.

Anti-American Bias The anti-American backlash of the Shah Pahlavi era is still effective. Iran's policy towards Israel and the other states of Western Asia is inevitably coloured by this bias, which the Bush administration has done nothing to offset by conciliation or understanding. The commitment of the Hezbollah in Lebanon and the Islamization of the Palestinian cause are seen as results of Iran's influence. These have caused concern in many Arab regimes while at the same time accelerating American efforts towards Israeli–Palestinian (read PLO) rapprochement, albeit on a road filled with tragic accidents.

The present Iranian government, with President Ahmedinejad at the head, is defiant in not budging in the face of American hostility to its nuclear programme. His statements questioning the legitimacy of Israel as a state and the holocaust are an oblique response, if not a challenge.

US Aided Iran to Acquire Nuclear Capability US relations with Iran should not be reduced to the single dimension of terrorism. Iran has always been more sensitive about safeguarding its sovereign rights over nuclear energy, no less than its rights over oil and gas. Iran had shown other countries the way to national control of oil resources in 1951. Iran and the US had friendly relations in the past; the earlier Shah Reza Khan made the American Millspaugh Administrator-General in Iran. Millspaugh helped to stabilize the economy and initiate modernization. The present crisis in US–Iran relations must be seen in context. It is natural for Iran to lessen dependence on oil and gas and seek other energy alternatives. The first nuclear research reactor was supplied by the US, after an agreement in 1967, under the Atoms for Peace programme. The Franco–German reactor planned for Bushehr conformed to these plans; at that time, there was no Western objection to the Shah's policy. The current confrontation over Iran's nuclear aspirations is the old Western attitude of denying energy security and diversification to developing countries. It is ironic that India, a victim of such discrimination, should now strive to align itself with such an attitude in hopes of gaining nuclear materials and equipment.

Negative Impact of India's pro-US Policy Shift This shift in foreign policy may marginalize India in its friendly relations with countries like Iran. Its indifference to the American occupation of friendly Iraq and the conversion of Iraq into a breeding-ground for Islamic terrorism and networks, when none existed earlier, could have consequences in India. For India to get involved in Iraq on USA's behalf as also its present indifference can harm our interests in Iran. If India has asserted its predominance as a regional power in the sub-continent and the Indian Ocean, it should not be surprised by Iran's dominance in the Persian Gulf.

Differentiated American Policies The US has followed different tacks in dealing with the nuclear threat from the policies of North Korea, Libya, and Iran. With the other two being more or less tackled, the US is bent on pressurizing Iran via crises in Lebanon (Hezbollah), Syria, and Central Asia. Some Arab countries may be compelled to plan for an Arab bomb to counter a feared Persian nuclear capability by going nuclear themselves: a risk which would vastly complicate American policy in the region.

Risk of Destroying Friendly Relations with Iran Does India really wish for a wider role as a consequence of the US–Iran confrontation and as a beneficiary of access to sensitive US technology? If the Indo–US deal comes to fruition, will it not make for long-term hostility in Indo–Iranian relations? It is not easy to balance our relations when two partner countries are having sharply conflicting interests. But it would be unfortunate if our government, while legitimately seeking to enlarge areas of strategic cooperation with USA, over-steps itself and gives the impression that by being in the good books of a super power, it can carelessly undo the painstaking diplomatic goodwill and friendly relations we have built up, especially since 1979 with Iran, which like China is bound to be around for a long time.

Iran's Shared Interests with India Iran wants Pakistan to be stable and prosperous, but is not in favour of changes in the status quo in Kashmir. It understands that Al-Qaeda and the Taliban are more antipathetic to Iran than even to the US. Iran has absorbed Islamic values on its own, not from Arab clerics. These factors make for Indo–Iranian rapport on the basis of shared interests and values.

Iran has diplomatic room, in that it can nimbly alter its equations with the US, Europe, and Russia. It was Iran that helped the US to oust the Taliban in Afghanistan. The West may need Iran's offices to bring about peace and order in Iraq, where sectarian conflicts are raging under American auspices.

Indian Policy Challenges If Iran is attacked by USA, would India remain unconcerned? We would not be able to parley with Iran to direct its gas eastwards instead of westwards. Will the nuclear deal with the US, which is intended to strengthen our energy security, paradoxically become a factor in sacrificing our autonomy to choose partners who could be more important for energy security and regional cooperation?

Presentation 2: A Strategic Perspective

Vice-Admiral (Retd) P.J. Jacob

Complexity of Indo–Iranian Relationship India and Iran have a very complex relationship, fraught with sub-equations. The perspectives to be considered are historical, religious, and regional, apart from the further complications of the US factor and terrorism. Bilateral relations have traditionally been positive. In January 2003, Prime Minister A.B. Vajpayee and the President of Iran, Mohammad Khatami, signed the New Delhi Declaration announcing a 'strategic partnership' between the two countries. It addressed cooperation in economic matters, hydrocarbons, science and technology, education and training, apart from collaborative work on Afghanistan's reconstruction and on global issues.

Stages of the Relationship Indo–Iranian relations can be considered in the following stages.

1) By the early 1970s, both countries had emerged as important regional powers. Iran was powerful in global oil politics and had a military presence in the Persian Gulf. India was the strategically pre-eminent

power in South Asia. Though Iran's support for Pakistan during the 1971 war had again adversely affected the warming trend in bilateral relations, Foreign Minister Swaran Singh's visit to Iran in July 1973 dispelled some mutual apprehensions. When Pakistan successfully cultivated the Arab Gulf states, Iran sought friendlier ties with India. For India, it was a welcome balance, and a new period of mutual engagement began.

2) Between 1970 and 1990, both Iran and India had common concerns, such as security threats from US hegemony, the collapse of the Soviet Union, and the stability of Central Asia. The rise of the Taliban and commercial interchanges were shared interests between India and Iran. There was convergence on the Afghan developments. Both countries backed the Northern Alliance for several years. Iran–Pakistan relations worsened, mainly because of differences over Afghanistan and sectarian terrorism in Pakistan.
3) In the decade, 1990–2001, India was a low-cost option for Iran in developing infrastructure and industry.
4) Since 9/11, both countries share concerns in containing terrorism and safeguarding energy supplies. When the US consolidated its military presence in Afghanistan and accused Iran of being part of the 'Axis of Evil', Iran wished for closer bonds with India. But Iran's nuclear programme and ambitions began to cause misgivings to the Indian government. Meanwhile, the Indo–US nuclear deal for civil nuclear energy cooperation created a dilemma for India in its relations with Iran.

Strategic Perspectives

There are various strategic perspectives to consider:

Energy Security As stated in the New Delhi Declaration, there is a complementarity of interests in this sector which needs to be developed. Iran has surplus energy resources, while India needs more energy for its rapid development. Besides, India is seeking to diversify its sources of petroleum and its products. Iran, with 5 per cent of the world's crude oil resources and 14 per cent of its natural gas reserves, is keen on the Indian market. Energy cooperation between the two is, therefore, highly desirable and logical.

India and Iran have been involved in the stalled project of a gas pipeline via Pakistan for more than 15 years. India was initially averse to dependence on a pipeline through Pakistan territory, though Pakistan was ready to give assurances for its security. The Indo–US nuclear deal has caused rethinking in India. The US probably insisted on India abandoning the pipeline project, being suspicious of Iran. It warned us of the sanctions it would be obliged to impose on our entities entering deals with Iran. India is still keen on keeping its options open. Iran said that it is ready to sign the trilateral deal, but technical issues between India and Pakistan (now under a new elected government) are hampering the process.

Defence Cooperation There is an increasing trend in defence cooperation between the two countries. They have begun to institutionalize contacts between the armed forces. A dialogue on mutual security issues and arms sales to Iran is on the cards. The 2003 Declaration included exploring cooperation in defence, so that our strategic relations have gained a subtle but significant military dimension.

Iran has a fair amount of defence equipment of Soviet manufacture. India's known capacity to manufacture such arms under licence promises complementary interests. This would boost India's military exports to West Asia, a region of geopolitical importance for us. The Defence Cooperation Agreement of 2003 was another milestone. It envisages Indian support for building a warship repair facility in the new Iranian port of Chabahar, stationing Indian aeronautical engineers at Iranian military bases to help upgrade MiG-29 fighters, engineers to refit and maintain T-72 tanks. The two countries had held joint naval exercises. Iran has sought India's assistance to service its naval and air force equipment and to develop batteries for its Kilo class submarines, these being more suitable in Gulf waters than those supplied by Russia.

Anti-Terrorism As regards terrorism, India and Iran have mainly cooperated to secure their interests in Afghanistan. Iran feared Sunni extremism by the Taliban regime. India saw the situation as a manifestation of the Islamic extremism that it was contending with in Kashmir. Both countries supported the Northern Alliance against the Taliban, in contrast to Pakistan. Both also supported the US military action to oust the Taliban regime and both seek to prevent a return of a revived Taliban regime. Both have given economic aid to Hamid Karzai's government. Other than this, Iran's anti-terrorism credentials are suspect. The assassination of Hezbollah's external operative, Imad Mughniyeh, is a sign that Iran continues to be a key player in global terrorism. It has close links with Hezbollah, Hamas, and the Palestinian

Islamic Jihad. Iran may still have a hand in aiding Al-Qaeda agents. Iran has been called the world's 'central banker of terrorism'. The US 9/11 Commission found that Iran allowed Al-Qaeda agents to use its territory as a transit into Afghanistan, though there was no evidence of Iran's involvement in the 9/11 attacks. This warrants great circumspection on India's part in joining hands with Iran in anti-terrorist actions.

Iran's Relations with Pakistan Iran–Pakistan relations are of importance to India. They have not always been smooth. Iran supported Pakistan in crisis situations, giving the latter moral, political, diplomatic, and even financial support. But after 9/11, when the US tightened its alliance with Pakistan, things have changed. Iran is, in effect, caught between two wars, in Iraq and in Afghanistan. The rise of the Taliban has made for acrimony between Iran and Pakistan, yet their relations remain close. Pakistan's nuclear cooperation with Iran indicates a certain strategic congruence. Pakistan would like normal relations with Iran, since it would otherwise have problematic neighbours on both sides. Pakistan's future course will affect its relations with Iran. If Pakistan experiences Shia–Sunni clashes, Iran would feel the impact.

India–Iran Relations For India, better relations with Iran would be an advantage vis-à-vis Pakistan. If, for instance, military cooperation moves to an Indian presence in Iran, it would add strength to our watch on Pakistani affairs. But Iran could use greater access to India to urge both India and Pakistan to moderate their policies towards each other. Iran was the first country to try for a détente and dialogue between India and Pakistan when tensions ran high in 2001.

Iran's Nuclear Policy—the Complicating Factor Iran's nuclear policy poses a serious dilemma for India. India has to go along with the world community in preventing Iran from becoming a nuclear power, since such a development would have adverse security implications for us. But to do this without impairing good relations with Iran is difficult. We would be liable to charges from Islamic countries that India, which previously opposed the double standards of the West, was now adopting them. But it is undoubtedly correct that India cannot accept a new nuclear power in the region and that it must side with the world community to ensure that Iran's programme strictly conforms to the IAEA provisions on non-proliferation. The government faces the internal problem of keeping the Opposition parties and the Left from spreading the perception that India has become the 'junior partner' of the US. These parties have also opposed any dilution of Indo–Iranian relations.

In 2005, contrary to some speculation, India voted at the IAEA for the resolution finding Iran in breach of its international obligations. This was a notable shift. It was criticised as submission to US pressure. In January 2006, the US ambassador to India linked the progress on the nuclear deal with this issue, hinting that if India did not vote with the US, the US Congress would thwart the nuclear deal. This was attacked by India's opposition parties as an affront to our sovereignty. Yet on February 4, India again voted with the majority at the IAEA in referring Iran to the UN Security Council, while also stating that it would not detract from India's close relations with Iran. However, it is in India's interest to see that Iran does not acquire nuclear weapons. Though Iran was disappointed by India's vote, our relations do not seem to have suffered too much. Pragmatism and mutual needs should govern our relations with Iran.

Indian–Israeli Ties An Irritant Another issue which can affect smooth relations with Iran is the closeness of Indo–Israeli ties. Iran being one of the staunchest opponents of Israel, the increasing exchanges between India and Israel, including our purchases of Israeli arms, could well cause misgivings and friction. Iran seems to have maintained a tolerant view of it so far. But Israel is apprehensive of close ties between India and Iran, particularly of Israeli defence technology reaching Iran through India. Israel's Prime Minister, Ariel Sharon, on a visit to India in 2003, asked for guarantees from India that it would not transfer any acquired technology to third countries, especially Iran. On the other hand, Iran was unhappy that an Indian rocket launched an Israeli spy satellite into space in 2008. Managing these counter-currents would determine the future of Indo–Iran relations.

India's Strategic Imperatives

Energy Security India must keep up its energy cooperation with Iran, including the tri-nation gas pipeline project, regardless of the Indo–US nuclear deal. India must actively pursue defence cooperation with Iran and extend it to training Iranian personnel. Naval cooperation and joint exercise to provide inter-operability will be desirable.

Anti-Terrorism Cooperate on anti-terrorism to the extent possible, keeping in mind our reservations on Iran's policies.

Nuclear Weapon Proliferation Cooperate with international efforts to make Iran follow non-proliferation norms and to ensure that Iran does not go in for nuclear weapons capability. India could impress on Iran the wisdom of complying with the IAEA requirements on inspection and safeguards to avoid sanctions and other dangers.

The enhanced engagement with Iran since the mid-1990s has deepened bilateral relations. However, India's improved relations with the US and Israel, which Iran views with suspicion, could test the leadership of both India and Iran. India has to weigh its strategic options if Iran begins to edge away from us on account of our relations with the US and Israel. India is in a sound position economically and militarily to balance its national interests and should be able to pursue its strategic imperatives without greatly ruffling one party or the other.

Presentation 3: A Media Perspective

Kesava Menon

Four Issues Kesava Menon conceded that journalists sometimes oversimplify issues. He said he would try to set out the points of view commonly taken by the media on this subject, and raise questions to delve deeper into the matter and present a clearer perspective. There are four interlinked issues which need to be examined: Iran's strategic orientation, how the US is trying to manage global affairs, how India is coping with the US, and India's position on the Iran issue and India's strategic orientation. Media coverage of inadequate depth may be responsible for the biased and superficial discussions of these issues one has seen.

Alignment with the US A current trend of opinion in our media is that in a uni-polar world, where the US is the superpower with global reach, India should align itself with the US to become one of the major powers; this, in spite of all the development that India has achieved in recent years. A contrary view (outdated to some) is that India should stick to the established principles of foreign policy and abide by certain ideals. Though we have occasionally erred by becoming over-idealistic, we have modified our stand to suit necessity. For example, by moderating our concerns for human rights and democracy where our security interests are endangered. But the one principle we cannot afford to give up is independence. This is not an expression of anti-Americanism. But, it is reasonable to be sceptical of American motives in foreign policy. The US will always give priority to its interests and will not offer free lunches. In dealing with a much bigger power, it is right and realistic for us to be cautious in our responses to their moves.

Thus, our independence should not be regarded as too idealistic. Independent judgement means that we must first ascertain the facts of a situation and understand the reality. What are the facts regarding the confrontation between the US and Iran? Why have a group of countries sided with the superpower in this?

The Facts behind Iran–US Confrontation It is asked whether Iran needs its nuclear programme in view of its abundant petroleum resources. Iran's answer is that these resources are finite and that Iranian demand for energy is growing and that other sources must be tapped. Iran signed the NPT; as such has undertaken not to develop or possess nuclear weapons, but it retains the right to obtain the know-how for a nuclear fuel cycle.

From 1980 to around 1995, Iran sought help from three countries to set up a uranium enrichment programme. In all three cases, US pressure blocked any deal. Iran then felt justified in going clandestine and obtaining plans and materials from A.Q. Khan, the discredited Pakistani scientist. There are credible reports that the US knew at the time about the actions by Khan and the complicity of the Pakistan leadership. But this information was buried in the lower echelons of the US administration.

Iran claims that from 1996, when it obtained help from Khan, till 2002 it did not undertake any action for uranium enrichment. Iran's installation of a facility to produce uranium hexafluoride and a separate facility for the centrifuge array could be regarded as controversial if not suspect. But all the technical questions concerned were sorted out to the satisfaction of the IAEA after many rounds of discussion since 2003.

In this period the Western media relayed scare stories to depict Iran as pursuing a secret nuclear weapons programme. In one instance, a document purportedly detailing the process of machining uranium into hemispherical shapes deliberately ignored the fact that it made no reference to the size or dimensions, without which no bomb or warhead could be made. Nor did the media mention that the document itself had actually been handed over by the Iranians to the IAEA, and was therefore not something concealed from it.

Iran has at every stage acceded to the requests of the IAEA for clarification. The IAEA itself has accepted that Iran's disclosures confirm to the information it has gathered through its investigations. The reports pertain to the declared sites of the Iranian programme, including the facility for uranium conversion and the centrifuge workshop. What the IAEA is unable to certify is that Iran does not have any undeclared sites, facilities, assets, and materials of nuclear technology.

Iran and the Additional Protocol That the IAEA will not certify the absence of clandestine assets is not Iran's fault. It had accepted the Additional Protocol of the NPT, empowering the IAEA to carry out surprise inspections. The latter did carry out tests impartially, including environment sampling. The bulk of its findings seemed to confirm the Iranian contention of having no clandestine programme. But Iran, being known to be fiercely independent in its foreign policy, is a victim of suspicion by other states that its territory may be hiding underground enrichment facilities.

If Iran is persuaded to accept the Additional Protocol again and if the IAEA can inspect the sites, the matter could be settled. But it is doubtful if Iran will now comply with the demands.

On the negative side, Iran's withdrawal from the Additional Protocol is cited. Further, it has resumed its enrichment of uranium after two years. Its centrifuge array has been augmented. But at every stage, Iran was reacting to provocation. Based on the IAEA Board of Governors' negative report to the UNSC, even before the inspectors had finished investigations, the UNSC imposed sanctions against Iran. This preceded the conclusion of the discussions between Iran and the EU interlocutors. Iran was bidden to suspend its enrichment programme as a pre-condition for further talks. Iran is conscious that its previous suspensions produced no benefits.

Can a War be Averted? Some analysts believe that the US has pressured the world community into a policy of shifting the goal-posts in order to provoke Iran into an indiscretion like withdrawal from the NPT, which would give its opponents a *casus belli*. This may be unrealistic since the Bush administration lacks the political capital to launch a new major military operation. It is surely aware that the costs would outweigh any advantage to be gained from such a thrust. A massive air strike would provoke Iran to counter-attack and plunge the whole region in ruinous conflict.

Can this danger be averted? The latest US National Intelligence Estimate conveys the consensus of all their intelligence services that Iran gave up efforts to develop nuclear weapons in 2003. This has prompted American strategists to advocate a cautious line rather than a belligerent one.

This gives India an opportunity. Would all the experts present agree that India could go beyond the official channels and work actively with those sections of the American strategic community that are looking for a wider range of options? The most desirable option is one where India stands to benefit from its relationship with the US, as well as Iran.

The speaker hoped that the discussion would result in a better understanding of India's Iran problem.

Discussion

The Chairman invited questions from the audience. The main points that came up during this session are summarized in the following paragraphs.

Nuclear-armed Iran is against India's Interests In reply to a question on a nuclear-armed Iran, Admiral Jacob said that it is not in India's interest to have another nuclear power in the neighbourhood. But the irony is that India can, at best, only delay such a development.

Iran and other Countries Khaleeli answered a question about the ethnic composition of the Iranians. There are minorities like Azeris and those of Turkmen stock, Ispahanis, Kurds, and Baluchis too. These minorities have lived in peace with the main population. The speaker went on to add observations on Iran and nearby countries. Turkey has benefited from the Iranian revolution. Pakistan has helped Iran to cultivate relations with China. Iran wants safe borders with Pakistan, free of ethnic contention. The impression that Iran is isolated is not correct. It has quite good relations with the Gulf countries. The Shia–Sunni problem should not be exaggerated, since both communities have lived together for long periods in Iran as well as Iraq. As for the nuclear programme, it was the Shah who first began it in Bushehr. Iran is keen on preserving its sovereignty and conserving its oil or gas as long as possible. If Iran goes nuclear, the US may even give nuclear weapons to other Gulf states. The strategic importance of a gas pipeline from Iran running eastward instead of westward should not be forgotten.

On Democracy In reply to a question on what India could do to make Iran a secular democracy, Khaleeli said that India could be a good example of such a polity. Iranian society is more integrated than the Indian. Women are given greater respect there. A democracy cannot come about by decree. It has to be a process. The Chairman concurred that a democratic country cannot tell others how to be democracies. The US has made such a mistake in Iraq.

On Iran's Role in Arabian Sea Security Admiral Jacob explained India's involvement in the construction of new port facilities for Iran in the Gulf, at Bandar Abbas and Chabahar. Iran is highly conscious of its role in the security perimeter of the Arabian Sea and the Indian Ocean.

Women in Iran Khaleeli explained that women in Iran were capable of being achievers, as was evident from example of the Nobel laureate, Shirin Ebadi.

Kesava Menon added that Iranian women are progressive. It is not rare to find women taxi drivers.

Oil Politics To a question on Central Asia's oil reserves and the politics of oil, Khaleeli said that Iran's nationalization of the oil refining company had jolted the West, which intended to keep the price of oil at one dollar per barrel. Oil diplomacy in the so-called 'New Great Game' in Central Asia had become very significant.

No Role for India in Moderating Islamic Fervour To another question by an Indian–American scientist, he said that harsh words had been exchanged between the US ('axis of evil') and Iran ('America as the great Satan'). India has no role in moderating Islamic fervour. Islam should reform itself. If Indian Muslims, numbering 150 million, can live well, that would be a great contribution to Islamic opinion. Bush acts as a Christian leader but passes off as secular, he said.

Indian Reaction if Iran is Attacked The Chairman observed that though India is now much more powerful than it was at Independence, it commands less respect. There is a high probability that the US would bomb sites in Iran, even with tactical nuclear weapons. This could happen before Bush leaves the White House, directly by the US forces or through Israel as its surrogate. What would be the Indian reaction? India should prepare its response to this eventuality if it should happen.

On Iran's pro-Shia Role in Iraq On Iran's possible aid to the Shias in Iraq in the internal conflict, Khaleeli said that formerly there was no Shia–Sunni problem in Iraq, or blatant discrimination against Shias. He did not believe Iran was promoting dissension within Iraq. After all, in the Afghan drive against the Taliban, Iran had been helpful to the US. Under American occupation, crime has increased; rape which was uncommon is now happening more often. He believes that the country could break up under the present dispensation.

Conclusion

The seminar clearly brought out the perception that the potential for mutually beneficial Indo–Iranian relationship is too important to be subordinated to the confrontation between the US and Iran, over the latter's nuclear programme. Some remained sceptical about Iran's protestation that its programme is a genuine, legitimate quest for nuclear energy and not a ruse to make nuclear bombs through uranium enrichment or plutonium extraction. But there was the conviction that the IAEA and the UNSC are under pressure from the US and the EU to apply more stringent sanctions on Iran and impose more onerous preconditions to enable any possible diplomatic resolution of the problem.

A consensus was also forming that it would be contrary to India's interests if Iran became a nuclear power, although the irony of India having become such a power in defiance of the West was also noted. In brief, there is more sympathy for Iran than has been apparent in the conspicuous foreign policy shift of the UPA government, in voting at the IAEA with the US on Iran matters. This was attributed to the desire to clinch the Indo–US nuclear deal.

India cannot ignore the fact that US policy is blind to the wanton armed attacks by Israel against Lebanon's Hezbollah. More recently, Israel carried out a lightning air strike with impunity on an alleged nuclear facility under construction in Syria. India has to distance itself from one-sided American criticism of Iran which overlooks Israeli provocations and bellicosity.

What was missing from the seminar was a parallel view of Iran's relations with Russia and with China. Both these major powers have pursued their own policies and interests towards Iran, which they rightly regard as an energy rich country with tempting lines for productive economic cooperation. They have gone along with the West in the UNSC by agreeing to impose sanctions on Iran for its non-compliance with the IAEA procedures to establish its civil nuclear credentials, but they have also retained their right to trade with Iran and to give it sophisticated technical aid for approved plans, including a nuclear reactor in Bushehr (Russian design). Iran is counting on their support to become a member of the Shanghai Cooperation Organization, unlike India. That is a strategic move worth watching. India on the other hand has been over-cautious and over-solicitous in its Iran policy to avoid American disapproval. Even Pakistan has been more forthcoming on the proposed Iran gas pipeline. Such a pipeline could be stretched to India only if the implacable confrontation between Iran and the US (and Israel) could be bypassed through diplomatic efforts.

In the month since the seminar was held, there have been developments which could augur a course correction by India. President Ahmadinejad visited New Delhi on his way back from Sri Lanka and Pakistan on April 29. India's Minister for Petroleum recently went to Pakistan to discuss the revival of the aborted plan for the Iran gas pipeline (Foreign Minister Pranab Mukherjee had visited Tehran and held talks with Iranian leaders in February 2007, keeping a line open for eventual restoration of bilateral trust and cordiality.) Even if these moves come to nought, the very fact that India and Iran are increasingly overtly seeking a more positive relationship is all to the good. National Security Adviser M.K. Narayanan has spoken of the civilizational ties between India and Iran, while Foreign Secretary S.S. Menon has stated that sanctions or military action would not provide a lasting solution, but only exacerbate the situation. 'We need to evolve something that involves Iran', he said, since non-proliferation worldwide can only succeed in a reformed system in which Iran is also a party. Such sentiments are overdue in our foreign policy.

The US, for its part, seems to be moving away from its over-rigid stance of root-and-branch hostility towards Iran, which is establishing its due place in West Asia in spite of it. The Iranian president has recently visited Baghdad and held talks with Iraqi leaders. The US must have acquiesced in it or even quietly encouraged it. The American animus against Iran has long been at work in the active instigation of dissident Iranians to overthrow the government in Tehran in 'a regime change' reminiscent of 1953. For several years now, both Israel and the US have readied detailed plans for a devastating strike at Iran's nuclear facilities and even for inflicting damage amounting to national erasure. That is, if Iran should make a false step by a sneak attack on Israeli or American strategic assets. The US can find a *casus belli* in Iran's influence with Iraqi Shias and Hamas in Palestine, Hezbollah in Lebanon, and also in Syria. The only deterrents now are the economic mess in the US, the Iraqi quagmire, and the desperation in Afghanistan.

The US has asked India to persuade Iran to cooperate with the world community by halting its drive to enrich uranium through arrays of centrifuges. This unsolicited and openly given advice has ruffled the Indian government, keen as it is to avoid seeming overly identified with the US worldview. Meanwhile, (according to a report dated April 14 in the respected *The Independent* of Britain, based on a telephonic interview with Pickering), both the US and Iran, being no novices in diplomacy, are exploring back-channel contacts, away from the public eye and earshot, to negotiate a deal which would prevent another American inspired descent into military adventure, occupation, and chaos.

Chapter 3

India and The Shanghai Cooperation Organization

ASIA CENTRE BANGALORE AND THE INDIAN COUNCIL OF WORLD AFFAIRS

'India and the Shanghai Cooperation Organization: An Opening to Central Asia'
Proceedings of the Joint Seminar held on

July 16, 2011

Preface

The topic of the July 2011 Seminar of the Asia Centre was '*India and the Shanghai Cooperation Organization: An Opening to Central Asia*'. The seminar was presided over jointly by A.P. Venkateswaran, former Foreign Secretary and Chairman, Asia Centre, Bangalore and S.T. Devare, Director General, Indian Council of World Affairs, New Delhi. The following were the speakers:

Lt General (Retd) R.K. Sawhney	Former Director General of Military Intelligence
Nirmala Joshi	Former Chairperson, Centre for Russian and Central Asian Studies, JNU, New Delhi
B.R. Muthu Kumar	Indian Foreign Service (Retired), former Ambassador of India to Tajikistan, Azerbaijan, and Belarus

The presentations were followed by a question and answer session. The proceedings, which appear on the following pages, have been compiled by N. Ravi, former Secretary (East), Ministry of External Affairs.

Introduction

Lt General Ravi Eipe, Director, Asia Centre extended a warm welcome to the participants and the invitees, and in particular to the Director General, ICWA. The Director pointed out that the SCO is a political group with a strong security and economic focus. He alluded to the West's belief that the SCO had been set up as a counter weight to NATO's growing influence in Eurasia. In 2005, India, Pakistan, Iran, and Mongolia had been invited to join the SCO as observers. Seeing the growing importance of the SCO and its relevance, India had applied for full membership and its application had been well received. It is believed that joining the SCO could be of benefit in many aspects: investment and trade opportunities, energy security, in combating terrorism, and in jointly confronting the challenges posed by the Afghan situation.

Presentation 1: A Strategic Overview

Lt General R.K. Sawhney

Growth and Acceptance of the SCO Established in 2001, the SCO had come a long way and become a significant organization in Eurasia. The conventional notion that the SCO was created as an anti-American move appeared to be changing.

SCO Links with Organizations and States Some experts have argued that stronger EU–SCO links could help stabilize Central Asia, improve its energy security, and strengthen efforts to fight terrorism and drug trafficking. The inclusion of observer states and dialogue partners suggested that the SCO was gradually expanding beyond the Central Asian region into the wider southern Asian region. During the period 2005–07, the SCO had finalized memoranda of mutual understanding with ASEAN, the Commonwealth of Independent States, and the European Economic Community. It had observer status in the UN General Assembly and maintained general contact with ESCAP and UNDP.

Member States' own Views on SCO Although the SCO had gradually evolved to a credible regional group, nothing substantial had been achieved in the economic sphere thus far. The leading members of the SCO were themselves not sure whether it should be something like the EU or like NATO. The rivalry between Russia and China imposed limitations on the SCO, leading to the risk that it might not fulfil the expectations of its members. However, despite its problems and limitations, the SCO's role and influence in the Eurasian region was likely to grow in future for want of an alternative organization.

India and the SCO India joined the SCO as an observer at its 5th Summit meeting in Astana in July 2005. Its admission to the SCO, albeit as an observer, was recognition of its potential role in Central Asia and the contribution it could make to the economic development of the region. In the 2009 SCO Summit in Yekaterinburg, India declared its willingness to play a greater role in Central Asia and its interest in full SCO membership. For India, trade, energy cooperation, and counter-terrorism are the driving sectors in the SCO. Economic cooperation was considered the best way of bringing stability to the region and also of engaging China.

Problem of Connectivity The major difficulty in India's assuming a more active role in Central Asia is connectivity. Pakistan has blocked India's access to the historical route which lies through its territory. The other route which was developed was the north-south corridor from Chabahar and Bandar Abbas through Iran. The use of this facility had declined because of cooling relations with Iran and its disuse reflects the state of the relationship—neglected and with no prospect of improvement.

The Afghanistan Factor Afghanistan has been ravaged by internal and external war for 30 years, beginning with the military intervention by Russia. The US counter-action created the Taliban, leading to a prolonged civil war which ended with the Taliban ruling the country. Afghanistan is still in turmoil and recent announcements of withdrawal by America have not been very helpful, because one did not know what type of withdrawal would take place, and what kind of residual force would be left behind.

The instability is exacerbated by the country's dual identity. The northern half identifies closely with the Central Asian Republics because of the demographic, linguistic, and ethnic make-up that includes Tajiks, Uzbeks, and the Hazaras. Being Shias, they identify with the Iranians. Then there is the southern half which is dominated by the Pashtuns who actually have their roots across the Durand line in Pakistan. Thus Afghanistan is eminently qualified for membership of SAARC as well as the SCO. However, they do not want to become members of the SCO, despite being permanent invitees since 2004. A variety of security challenges—drug-trafficking, terrorism, and extremism—emanate from Afghanistan and so it had become the focus of the SCO's concerns. It was clearly declared at the SCO Summit of Astana in June 2011 that the situation in Afghanistan was one of the 'key sources of threats to regional security and stability'. The declaration stressed the need to pay attention to sorting out the socio-economic issues in Afghanistan.

India's Stake in Afghanistan India had been a strong supporter of a regional solution for Afghanistan involving all stakeholders. There was a similarity in views about instability emerging from Afghanistan. Further, India had meticulously avoided military involvement in the Afghan conflict, and has provided non-military economic aid for development and reconstruction of Afghanistan, and for addressing its socio-economic issues. After the US withdrawal, Afghanistan should not be allowed to become a haven for terrorists and extremists. India favoured the emergence of a neutral Afghanistan where no one nation exercises undue influence, and identifies with the values and perspectives of the SCO on this country.

Membership of the SCO No decision was taken at the June 2009 Yekaterinburg Summit regarding India's membership, though Sri Lanka and Belarus were granted dialogue partner status. The criteria for admitting new members were approved only in the Tashkent 2010 ministerial Summit meeting. According to the statute, to join the SCO a country had to satisfy conditions regarding location, diplomatic relations with SCO members, observer or dialogue partner status, and economic ties with the SCO members. The applicant country must not be under UN sanctions and should not be involved in armed conflict with any state.

A decision to accept a new member to the SCO would need the consensus of all member states. Currently India, Pakistan, and Mongolia are eligible for full membership, but Iran is not, because of the existing UN sanctions against it. Afghanistan and Turkmenistan have not shown any interest in joining either as observers or full members.

Need for Expansion—Intra-SCO Views Some fundamental questions had been raised by China regarding expansion of the SCO. Russian experts have argued that the main reason for expansion is, the SCO is constrained in financing various projects because of a very limited budget. China had promised US $10 billion for projects, but this had pre-conditions. Indian experts feel that with the lack of consensus among member states, it would take not less than two to three years for the admission issue to be resolved.

Challenges Before India as Member of SCO General Sawhney, then, examined the opportunities and challenges India would face in the event of its getting the membership. First and foremost, India would acquire greater visibility in the affairs of the Eurasian region. The SCO would provide an additional forum to engage with China and Pakistan in energy, connectivity, and terrorism issues. India could also progress along these issues with member states. Energy cooperation remained an important issue for SCO member countries, but there were different opinions on how to cooperate within the SCO framework. The signing of a framework agreement in December 2010 to build the Turkmenistan–Afghanistan–Pakistan–India (TAPI) pipeline is a positive aspect reinforced by the support of the Asian Development Bank, the US, and Russia.

Multilateral cooperation is the only way to address the expanding menace of terrorism in the South and Central Asian region. Within the framework of the SCO, India and the member states had much to offer each other in fighting terrorism. China had the problem in Eastern Turkestan, Russia in Chechnya, and India in Kashmir across the Pakistan border. The CAR wants to contain the extremist groups in their own regions.

If India joins the SCO, it will face the challenge of playing a secondary role to China and Russia, which have been leaders since the SCO's inception. India will also have to contend with China's use of the SCO to enhance its own role, not only in the Eurasian region, but also in Southern Asia. In return for granting India full membership in the SCO, China may seek full membership in the SAARC. India will have to analyse the full implications of China's entry into SAARC and Pakistan's membership of the SCO. Sri Lanka's inclusion as a dialogue partner in the SCO also needed to be viewed against the background of China's increasing defence and strategic cooperation with Colombo.

Possibility of Sino–Pak Axis within SCO India would also have to deal with the China–Pakistan nexus in the SCO that would come to the fore in issues such as connectivity arrangements and Kashmir. It is also argued by strategists in Pakistan that the Gwadar port may ultimately help the CAR to actively participate as equal members and help open trade channels through Pakistan and ultimately to India. The creation of a new organization comprising of Pakistan, Afghanistan, China, and Iran and the CAR has been articulated in some Pakistani writings.

Indo–Russian Cooperation Prospects in SCO Today, India–Russia relations need to be viewed in the light of India's increasing ties with US, and Russia's growing economic cooperation with China, which makes it an important strategic partner of Russia. These circumstances could impose limitations on the cooperation that Russia can extend in the SCO framework. While the CARs are interested in India joining as a full member, they are also concerned about getting involved in Indo–Pak rivalry.

Membership not an Unmixed Blessing There are many advantages to India joining the SCO, but it also poses many challenges. In the prevailing state of uncertainty, India needs to utilize its SCO observer status effectively and boost its cooperation at the bilateral level with member states.

Presentation 2: Historical Perspective, Current Developments, and Trends

Nirmala Joshi

Background of the SCO—The Shanghai-5 The SCO, which was formed in 2001, was actually a successor organization to the Shanghai-5, which embodied an agreement between Russia, China, Kazakhstan, Kyrgyzstan, and Tajikistan. When the Soviet Union broke up in 1991, these three newly-independent entities had been involved in the Sino–USSR border negotiations.

Main Purpose of Shanghai-5 The main focus of the Shanghai-5 Agreement was good neighbourly relations. China was concerned about a possible demand by the Uyghurs for special autonomy or even a separate state, even though they were scattered over many places. Hence the constant stress in the SCO deliberations on good neighbourly relations and a peaceful border.

All three new republics lost some territory in the border agreement signed with China but they had no option but to sign as they were powerless to enforce their claims in case of dispute. They have, since, registered this agreement with the United Nations in the hope that in future China does not take out some document from their archives and claim that it is not 126 but 140 hectares!

Growth in Focus of Shanghai-5 By the 1999 Summit of the Shanghai-5, the focus had expanded to encompass regional security in which the emphasis was on fighting what the Chinese called the three evils: religious extremism, separatism, and terrorism. Their objective was that the region should remain peaceful and stable and there should be no change in the situation. This is an ideal which India too supports.

Transformation of Shanghai-5 into SCO in 2001 In the Dushanbe Summit of the Shanghai-5 held in 2000, the scope was extended to include regional economic cooperation. This was important because the Central Asian states were still in the process of transformation and they needed all types of economic support, in the sense of experience and expertise. In June 2001, the Shanghai-5 became the Shanghai Regional Cooperation Organization. Uzbekistan, which had not been part of the Shanghai-5, was made a member of this group. The essence of the SCO remained peace and stability on the common border and this constantly keeps coming up in all the summits even today. Next, the Shanghai Charter was signed followed by a convention on combating religious extremism, separatism, and terrorism. The Regional Anti-Terrorism Structure (RATS) came into existence in 2004 and has been headed by a Russian general. Despite the droll acronym, RATS has emerged as an impressive centre for collecting and collating intelligence information about terrorists and terrorist groups, and drug trafficking.

Highlights of SCO Summits Some highlights of the SCO activities in the last ten years deserve attention. One was the July 2005 Summit in Astana, because it invited India, Pakistan, and Iran as countries with observer status in SCO. The SCO's growth in confidence after 4 years was manifested when it asked the West, particularly the United States, to announce a time-frame for the withdrawal of its troops from facilities in Central Asia. Not only did they ask the US to announce a time frame for withdrawal; more importantly, they also said that they did not want a social model for governance to be exported.

The second highlight was the Bishkek Summit in 2007, at which the border agreements between member countries were raised to the level of a treaty of good neighbourliness among the SCO countries.

At the international level, the One China policy declaring that Taiwan is an inalienable part of China was endorsed by the SCO.

The hope that India would be invited to full membership was not fulfilled at the 2011 Astana Summit. The criteria for membership have been laid down but there has been no further progress. At the security level, it had been planned to create a joint rapid reaction force, but this has not yet happened so that the SCO remains a primarily defensive organization.

Challenges Confronting the SCO

Economic Aspects The economic aspect of SCO is rather weak. A number of declarations have been issued. There is a business council for private entrepreneurship, the development fund, and talks have been held about the energy club and improving transport. But no action is discernible on the ground. China announced a provision of US $900 million as project assistance for the SCO countries, but it turned out to be for bilateral projects.

Russia–China Relations Russia and China are pivotal players and thus far the SCO is useful to both of them as there is an alignment of their interests. However, if differences surface tomorrow, a confident China may spoil the delicate balance within the SCO. The future shape of the SCO will depend a great deal on the progress of the Russia–China relationship.

Multiplicity of Regional Organizations Another challenge which the SCO faces is the surfeit of regional organizations in the area. For example, there is the Collective Security Treaty Organization (CSTO) which is basically a defence alliance, the Commonwealth of Independent States (CIS) which also has similar objectives, the Eurasian Economic Community (EURASEC), and the Quadrilateral Initiative, comprising of Russia, Tajikistan, Afghanistan, and Pakistan. Thus, there are many organizations which have similar or overlapping objectives though not necessarily in conflict with each other.

Broad-Based Approach The SCO will need a broad-based approach to cater to a variety of aims both at the regional and bilateral levels. The presence of more countries in the SCO such as Afghanistan, Pakistan, and India with their experience in dealing with developmental problems can bring expertise in these fields within the Central Asian Republics.

Member States' Views of SCO A leading scholar in Kazakhstan has said that they did not want any Chinese money as it would lead to economic imperialism, and that they would manage on their own. Very recently at the Astana Summit, Kazakh President Nazarbayev had emphasized the need to create a council to deal with issues within the region, because the problems of Central Asia were very different. The Foreign Minister Karayev, of Kyrgyzstan, had earlier said that the SCO is at best a border peace-keeping mechanism. The SCO is conscious of its inability to deal with the problems among its own member countries and they perceive the lack of a proper legal framework as a severe limitation. Whether the CAR is in the process of taking action on these much-needed deficiencies or not, is not known.

Issue of India's Membership India should strive to overcome the challenges to its membership and join the organization because of its immense geopolitical importance for India. Connectivity is a major problem but we cannot wait for the SCO mechanism to become ready for our entry. India would have to be more active at the bilateral level and intensify its diplomatic efforts to achieve its goals.

Future Prospects The SCO, at present, doesn't have the cohesion of a regional grouping. As a Russian scholar has said, it still remains to be seen whether the SCO will remain a discussion club or whether it will become, or surpass, APEC or ASEAN. An important point was that the SCO decisions are not binding; they have to be approved by the parliaments of the respective countries. The current leaders in Uzbekistan and Kazakhstan have been in power for nearly 20 years. The crucial question is how the new leadership in these countries will view the SCO and deal with the future.

Foreign Policy Perspectives

Muthu Kumar, IFS (Retd)

SCO's Rise to Present Status The Shanghai Cooperation Organization emerged out of a simple partnership to resolve the border dispute between China and the four ex-Soviet republics. SCO's agenda today and its activities are attracting international attention. With the exception of China, all are OSCE members and partners for peace with NATO. Russia is a member of the Council for Europe while Kazakhstan, Kyrgyzstan, and Tajikistan are participants. The SCO has not offered participatory facilities to any western country.

SCO's Main Objectives—The Three Evils Notwithstanding the consistently stated position by the SCO, the OSCE and the EU view it dismissively, as an alliance to counter-balance US influence in Central Asia. After 15 years, the group certainly has conducted itself as a regional and international organization striving to build an all-inclusive partnership, characterized by comprehensive development while keeping at bay the three evils: religious extremism, terrorism, and separatist states.

The grouping, since 1996, has taken a step-by-step approach, moving from the bilateral to a multilateral forum, where consensus prevails. Intra-SCO relations have reached the highest level possible—that of a strategic partnership. The cooperation has generated more than 150 agreements, treaties, declarations, and protocols, which constitute instruments that strengthen the organization's consensual partnership. The singular achievement of the SCO, and its precursor, the Shanghai-5, has been its no-nonsense diplomacy and the peaceful resolution of border problems, which came about as a result of pragmatic compromises. All countries made concessions to China, but gained by the establishment of direct road and other transport links, a thriving cross-border trade, and ever-expanding commercial links.

Unfortunately, the SCO members do not have the resources to implement the agreements signed. With the exception of China and Russia, the SCO is a group of poor and impoverished nations. The former, though blessed with rising foreign exchange reserves, have their own domestic compulsions that prevent them from extending full assistance to their poorer partners.

Sino–Russian Competition China would like to wean Central Asian Republics away from Russia's influence, but the priority of Russia's foreign policy is to prevail and hold influence over its ex-Soviet partners. China, therefore, is doing all it can at the bilateral level to entice them with liberal credit lines, totalling over US $20 billion.

Internal Dissension and Conflict Kazakhstan and China also share a dormant mistrust, rooted in the Uyghur issue. Tajikistan and Uzbekistan have not shared good neighbourly relations since 1992. Uzbekistan has also mined certain border districts facing Tajikistan. The animosity between Kyrgyz and Uzbeks is another sad story that hinders cooperation in the region.

Because of the above factors, the SCO is unable to make the most of its potential, and turn itself into an effective international organization. The energy potential of the SCO region is vast. Russia, Kazakhstan, Uzbekistan, and Iran have vast resources of oil, gas, precious metals, and minerals. Russia and Kazakhstan are enthusiastic about the SCO establishing an alternate energy pool as together they hold the largest oil and gas resources outside OPEC. Russia would also like to bring the Caspian Sea reserve into the pool and induct Turkmenistan and Iran as members of the SCO. However, China is opposed to Iran's entry on grounds that there are UN sanctions and that Iran's inclusion may cause the SCO to be perceived as an anti-US forum!

Tussle for Control Although the SCO has a largely Central Asian profile, a disturbing potential threat that looms large as the Uyghur separatists extend their resource base outside the region is of Xinjiang breaking away. The dismantling of the Soviet Union created a power vacuum in Central Asia; China, Iran, Turkey, and the US took measures in turn to fill the vacuum. Russia's persistent assertiveness has dissipated the ambitions of Iran and Turkey, leaving China and the US to vie with it for influence in the region.

Over time, Russia and China have, together and separately, whittled away the interests of the USA; but the countries in the region are still vulnerable to its enticement. Notwithstanding the SCO declaration in 2000, for the US and NATO to leave the region, Tajikistan could not deny itself easy cash and agreed to the US extending its stay; the US also established a military training facility not far from Dushanbe in Karatok. The US is also using an airbase in Kulyab, in the south, whose rent comprises a substantial portion of Tajikistan's GDP. The US has requested recently for Tajikistan to lease the Aini airbase, south of Dushanbe, which was renovated and refurbished by India, at an annual rent of US $160 million.

India's Relations—A History of Non-performance Sadly, India's relations with the region in the past 20 years have been a history of non-performance. Nothing extraordinary has been done and India has squandered away its opportunity. The leaders in the region know us more for our rhetoric, and all say Indian leaders talk very well but nothing more. They only repeat known historical facts but appear to have no goal or focus. With all our goodwill we have not taken Central Asia seriously, though there is much that we can do.

SCO Membership Not Advisable Muthu Kumar, differing sharply with the other speakers, said that membership of the SCO would not help; one's advice would be to stay clear of the SCO. We do not need to join the SCO merely to carry our Pakistan baggage of tension and mutual suspicion to yet another forum. The speaker questioned India's need to spoil the SCO party. It was not a forum for India to be in; India's relevance to the SCO is in her bilateral relations with the members of the SCO. It is still not too late for India to take affirmative action in the region.

Strategic Importance of Afghanistan The situation in Afghanistan is a matter of concern for the SCO. Today, a power that controls this strategic region can monitor the regional nuclear powers: China, India, Pakistan, and Russia; it can counter any threat to the world's energy resource in Iran and the Middle East and it is well placed to thwart the emergence of any other power that could destabilize the region again. Afghanistan's predicament today stems from the United States' strategic plan to control the regions outside the NATO using any pretext. The United States' means of running international relations signals the emergence of a new global sovereignty that aims at the subservience of all nations to it. To this end the United States has placed the region in a state of war since 2001, making Afghanistan the hub. As a consequence, Obama's AfPak policy has also trampled on Pakistan's sovereignty and its fledgling democracy, while democratic principles and human rights remain suspended indefinitely in Afghanistan.

What Afghanistan needs is a complete end to the state of war. The United States and others should discard their flawed geopolitical perception of Afghanistan. While the US decision to start the withdrawal of troops from

July 2011 is a welcome common-sense step towards de-escalation, it could also lead to an intense military campaign against the militants by redeployment of international forces. The combined international force strength will be brought down to the level of early 2009 as the Afghan security forces take on more responsibility to secure the country. The Afghan army strength will be increased to 2,60,000 by 2014 and with experience, Afghan army units are planned to be deployed in medium and low-risk areas. Although the military ingredients exist, it is doubtful whether the combined international forces would be able to contain the insurgency of the militant opposition. From the political point of view, there is no clearly emerging scenario, as Afghanistan could still fall prey to the geopolitical strategy of external powers. Pakistan, meanwhile, faces risks to its own stability and will continue to be a factor in Afghanistan's instability.

While blaming the external forces for Afghanistan's predicament, one must also acknowledge its roots within the country. Afghanistan is a nation of ethnic minorities and no ethnic group can claim pre-eminence over the other. Any initiative to end the war in Afghanistan has to address these internal tensions.

The Way Out of the Afghan Quagmire The way out of the quagmire rests upon a political solution, complemented by a sensitive socio-military strategy worked out by a group of non-combatant nations from the region, namely, China, India, Iran, Russia, Tajikistan, and Uzbekistan. The United States, NATO, and other non-NATO members including Pakistan need to be excluded. The contact group could conduct a dialogue with all the Afghan groups including the Haqqanis, Hekmatyar, and the Taliban, to constitute a national reconciliation commission of 23 members, on the model created by Rabbani, the architect and author of the reconciliation in Tajikistan. Such a commission is very important, because Afghanistan is a nation of minorities and one cannot project Pashtun supremacy alone. A convergence of national interests must be brought about in Afghanistan, exactly as it was in Turkmenistan in 1992, after its bloody civil war.

The UN Security Council mandated the use of international force in Afghanistan; the Security Council could pass another resolution directing a unilateral ceasefire as a first step to halt the war. A new Special Representative with a fresh mandate should then be appointed and establish a UN peace keeping force from non-NATO countries with non-combatant military officers to monitor the ceasefire. A timetable should be included in the Security Council resolution for withdrawal of the US and NATO troops.

The US AfPak Policy Muthu Kumar then dwelt on American policy and actions in Central Asia, which he said were crucial to the SCO discourse. The AfPak policy is an intriguing and deceptive strategy framed by the Obama administration. Overtly, there are two aspects to this; first it asks India to maintain tranquillity on the border, to allow Pakistan to commit its troops to its western frontier to fight terrorism. Second, instability in Afghanistan would have a negative effect and threaten Pakistan's very existence. However, despite tranquillity on the India–Pakistan border, the internal situation in Pakistan has become worse and divisive forces are steadily tearing the country apart. A top US General and erstwhile US National Security Adviser believe that in such circumstances, there could be a fatal attraction for India to settle the Jammu and Kashmir issue. The US strategic engagement of India gains significance from this perspective. There is lack of clarity about the true purpose of the AfPak policy. Several possibilities exist, among which are:

1) It could be an attempt to Balkanize Pakistan and Afghanistan, and create a Pakhtunkhwa and Baluchistan as independent nations;
2) It could be intended to break up Pakistan and take custody of its nuclear arsenal;
3) Its purpose may be to revise the Durand line and redraw borders with Afghanistan;
4) It may be a framework to establish a federative state of Baluchistan and Afghanistan, which would give the latter an outlet to the sea;
5) It could be a strategy to bolster Pakistan as a bulwark and guardian of United States' interests in South Asia;
6) Or, as opposed to all these possibilities, it may be a simple agenda to bring about peace, stability, and prosperity in Afghanistan.

However one may view the policy, there seems to be a better chance of Afghanistan emerging as a stable nation than Pakistan. If the process is linked exclusively to the end game in Afghanistan, there is going to be an escalation in the on-going war within Pakistan. In effect, peace and stability are likely to creep into Afghanistan while Pakistan will encounter divisive forces threatening its statehood. The AfPak policy will commit Pakistan into a subservient military role for its own survival. The United States would, by design, play the catalytic role in the emergence of new nations in South Asia.

Thus, the fallout of the AfPak policy has unpredictable consequences. Given the dangerous scenario on the horizon, India must have a comprehensive strategy in place to deal with the situation, including a split Pakistani army and any other situation arising out of the AfPak policy.

What are the options for India? Given the intrigues and Pakistan's over-emphatic insistence on being an integral player in any peace process in Afghanistan, there is a need to discard solutions proposed by vested interests; direct involvement of United Nations then gains importance.

At the first Bonn Summit it was assessed that redevelopment and reconstruction of Afghanistan would cost US $28 billion, over a period of 10 years. The cost of the Afghan war has far exceeded the level of US $1.3 trillion. When the foreign forces came in, the aim was never to displace the Taliban administration. However, they did throw out the Taliban administration, which could have dealt with development issues, and reconciliation did not happen. The Taliban was not there at the Bonn initiative and neither was Hekmatyar.

Which is the way out of this turmoil? An initiative for national reconciliation is the most needed first step. The Taliban must be on board, since they are Afghans and represent a facet of Afghan politics. They must find issues of national interest where there is convergence, such as the Durand line.

Indian Role in Central Asia It may be flattering for India to think that it has a major role in Central Asia and Afghanistan; but it is in a precarious position. Taking a social scientist's view, the speaker recalled the question framed by the Scottish psychiatrist, R.D. Laing, in the 1960s: 'What do we do, when we don't know what to do?' The answer to this can be found in the words of the 17th century Zen proverb: 'Sitting quietly, doing nothing, spring comes, and the grass grows by itself.'

According to the speaker, this described exactly the current position of Indian foreign policy on Central Asia.

Discussions

Afghan Position on the Durand Line On the Afghan view of an acceptable border with Pakistan, Muthu Kumar clarified that the Afghans were very clear that they want the total annulment of the 1893 agreement on the Durand line. Afghanistan opposed the membership of Pakistan in the United Nations, on the grounds that they did not accept the Durand line as the border. This can only be resolved if access to a seaport is guaranteed for Afghanistan. So a solution would have to be found, which will give Afghanistan an export exit.

Sri Lanka and Belarus in the SCO On a query for the reason for Sri Lanka and Belarus being brought into the SCO, Muthu Kumar replied that Sri Lanka was brought in as a dialogue partner by China, and Belarus by Russia, because Belarus continues to be the scientific laboratory for many things like counter insurgency equipment and so on, for the Russian Federation. The importance of Sri Lanka coming in is to give it a new dimension vis-à-vis India. The Tamil issue can then be brought up as a thorn at will. Although China has welcomed the application of Belarus as a member of the SCO, Russia has opposed it saying that it is not within the region but that it can remain a dialogue partner without being a member. All decisions in the SCO must be by consensus.

Aini—The Big Picture A member sought the panel's view about the big picture on the Indian Air Force's presence at the Aini Airbase in Tajikistan.

Muthu Kumar, in his response, said that the big picture on Aini goes back to 1995; the Tajiks asked India for two helicopters capable of flying at 22,000 feet altitude. Delhi did not accede to this request so as not to disturb Russian sensitivities. Subsequently, there was an offer of the vacant Aini base to India, in exchange for 6 Kiran jets. India dragged its feet for years and lost the opportunity. If India had acquired the use of this airbase, strategic depth could have been gained. It was disturbing that India did not act decisively to take advantage of the strategic opportunity.

Connotation of the term 'Turkic' A questioner commented that 'Turkic' was a very broad term, and wanted to know what it exactly signified. Nirmala Joshi, in her response, said that there was still no historical agreement on the origins of the Turkic people, and whether they are Anatolian Turks who came from Turkey and moved into Central Asia, or vice-a-versa was still not very clear. The Uyghurs claim that they are the original Turkic people who were settled in the Fargana valley and who fled north to Xinjiang when the Turkish invasion began in the mid-nineteenth century.

Views of Speakers on India and the SCO Achala Moulik, former DG, ASI, sought clarification on the differing approaches adopted by the speakers on India's engagement with the SCO, and whether India would deepen its isolation if it stayed out of the SCO.

Joshi expressed the view that India should join. When India is given a chance to be on the inside, we should take it, because India will then have the ability to influence the SCO from within.

Speaking of the American withdrawal, Lt General Sawhney clarified that the number of Afghan forces being raised has come up to 1,70,000 and is increasing. They had raised six corps but it was more of a constabulary and not an army in the modern sense. His opinion was that Afghan officers at the senior rank need to mature a little more. They will require years to mature into a fighting army and till then the US presence will have to continue. The withdrawal will, therefore, be progressively implemented.

We could reap certain advantages by becoming members of the SCO; whether these would actually translate into gains, is something that cannot be predicted.

Acceptance of Risk when Pursuing Strategic Relationships Gonsalves observed that India has no alternative to being there, whether it is SCO, ASEAN, or any of these organizations in Asia, in which we have some kind of a footprint. So it is necessary to take some risks, being willing to take some losses, while putting in some infrastructure. In Afghanistan, it is not a question of military or police; it is a mix of these. What Afghanistan needs is some kind of paramilitary force; it needs an internal structure which will manage the political process of consolidation and economic development.

Humanitarian Assistance A questioner asked what the effect of the humanitarian and infrastructure assistance that India had provided to Afghanistan was.

Muthu Kumar observed that India's humanitarian assistance to Afghanistan was extensive. We had supplied medicines, baby food, edible oil, health biscuits—the list is long—and India has also renovated and reconstructed a children's hospital. Humanitarian aid is an area of strength.

A participant was doubtful whether any benefits would accrue in joining the SCO because despite its charter, the aim appears to be to counter the American influence in the Central Asian region and to prevent the spread of NATO. Also, if India were to be part of an organization which included a China-dominated Pakistan, it was not clear how it would then profit us or serve our interests.

India's Quest for Energy Security and the Shanghai Spirit One member referred to the presence of Americans in the SCO region, an area that has nearly 50 per cent of the world's gas and about 17 per cent of the world's oil, and whether their presence would neutralize our quest for energy security in the same way it did with Iran. Just as Kazakhstan, Kyrgyzstan, and Tajikistan have sorted out the problem with the Chinese, would our membership of the SCO also enable us to resolve the border problem with China? Lastly, is the Shanghai spirit a reformulation of the Panchsheel?

Joshi expressed the view that any initiative on energy security would have to be at the bilateral level. Not having direct access need not be a limiting factor in ensuring energy security. ONGC Videsh Ltd. had recently acquired a block in the Caspian Sea, and also some blocks in Turkmenistan. Punj Lloyd, a private company, is involved in a very big way in Kazakhstan in building pipelines. It is more important for India to have energy presence in the region and get involved in all related sectors.

The Shanghai spirit had certainly been violated by the bases in the CAR. However, it is not just the Americans who have bases in Kyrgyzstan; the Germans have a base in Termez in Uzbekistan and the French have a base in Tajikistan. There is, thus, considerable military presence in the CAR; as Muthu Kumar said, the revenue from these bases is enormous. It helps them manage their economy.

Even though China has settled the border with Kazakhstan, Kyrgyzstan, and Tajikistan, the latter have given up a lot of territory. Whether India should follow that model of conceding territory and then have a settlement of the border is a debatable question. The Shanghai spirit is not quite the Panchsheel, but it does reflect some of the ideas that are there about a peaceful border, non-intervention, and other similar ideas.

Muthu Kumar commented that the Central Asian oil and gas is not a feasible option for India. Its transportation was not economically viable and most of the petro-products (particularly in Turkmenistan) have already been mortgaged to Russia's Gazprom, Luk-Oil, and to China. The concessions ONGC Videsh India has got in the Caspian region is for an oil well that has a capacity of 23 million tonnes annually, which is lower than Bombay high; that is the extent of the concession that we have in Kazakhstan.

As for the question of PRC's problem with India, Muthu Kumar felt that the call was for China to make, because in his view, we were ready to solve the issue. If China had been interested, we could have resolved the problem much earlier. At present we have no option but to wait for China to make that call.

Lt General Sawhney observed that the Americans were gradually finding it difficult to send their material through Pakistan for the NATO troops, and the Americans have started to supply the NATO forces from the northern areas, going through the CAR. This certainly has had the understanding and concurrence of Russia and China, and it does give economic benefit to the Central Asian Republics.

On a point regarding trade, Lt General Sawhney observed that according to research carried out by economists, the total amount of trade of the CIS, Iran, and Central Asian Republics extrapolated to 2020, would come to about US $500 to 600 billion. Even if 20 per cent of that trade were to come through this particular route, it would amount to US $120 billion. This was a substantial sum that would benefit the Central Asian republics and even Pakistan, if it genuinely wanted participation in trade flows. He concluded that, probably at some stage, the economic argument of earning money by giving transit rights would be overpowering.

Regarding border settlements, the General remarked that the Chinese employed arm-twisting methods in reaching settlements in the CAR; the disputes were not settled out of any goodwill or Shanghai spirit. India could not be arm twisted; it had already ceded quite a bit of territory, which it should never have. So, in his view, India could not conclude a border settlement with China for a long time to come.

Concluding Remarks

Sudhir Devare, Director General, ICWA, said that there had been extensive discussion in the Seminar on the issue of the SCO and the need or otherwise for India to join the SCO. The needs of the day being what they were, like-minded countries had evolved coalitions, and bilateralism continued to operate in diplomacy, because it is the main instrument through which the national interest is promoted. It is being increasingly seen that regionalism also reinforces bilateralism, and in many cases helps neutralize conflicts and differences. In the context of globalization and economic integration, or the need to deal with various non-traditional security issues including terrorism, there is a need to address the suitability of regionalism as an approach. India's membership of the SCO must be considered in this context.

As far as Central Asia was concerned, the discussion had brought out that the Central Asian republics and, in particular, the smaller countries among them, had themselves decided to go in for such regionalism. Generally, smaller and weaker nations favour regionalism, while larger nations still like to rely on the direct bilateral approach. Where India stands and what its interests are in this regard were critical questions at this juncture. Whenever India's membership is discussed, an identification of the stakes will have to be made.

Energy is undoubtedly regarded as the USP of this region, plus the need for stability and security in the centre of the world, namely Central Asia. Afghanistan had exacerbated the situation and brought this whole region into the limelight.

Indisputably, there was interplay of major powers in the CAR, with Russia, China, and the US having different interests and objectives. Russia clearly wanted to consolidate its position in its traditional stronghold, China was making efforts to make its entry into the CAR, and the Americans would like to be in Central Asia for a variety of objectives, their strategic goals, access to oil, and so on. India had to see whether there was some convergence developing in these objectives, as for example, seemed to be happening with regard to counter-terrorism. The setting up of the centre for the Regional Anti-Terrorism Structure (RATS) in Tashkent was supported by all these powers. So, to that extent, there would be some commonality of interest with India; but on the main issues, there will obviously be differences between these powers' assessments and those of India.

One thing that can be discerned is that both Russia and the CAR would like to have a kind of integration of Central Asia and South Asia. China, too, though for different reasons, had already invited Sri Lanka as a dialogue partner. He questioned as to where India would stand in this bringing together of Central and South Asia, and queried whether, since Pakistan and Afghanistan are countries that cannot just be wished away, the South Asian region nations should be also called to join this larger group.

Any FTA or comprehensive economic agreement in Central Asia is still a long way off, but as had been observed by Gonsalves, a kind of meshing of regional organizations or the FTAs is emerging in Asia. This was already happening in East Asia, South-East Asia, the Gulf, and North-East Asia; Central Asia is an area which is relatively new and India would have to be part of this larger set up of agreements and arrangements that will emerge in Asia. This would be our strategic perspective with respect to this region.

As for joining the SCO, the question would have to be asked whether these countries want us to be there. Our interest is in the preservation of peace and stability in Afghanistan, for which we have already spent $1.2 billion and have taken the decision to support the Afghan regime. Logically, our support of CAR and the SCO has to continue. So if these interests and considerations are kept in mind, we would have to follow the policy of seeking membership of the SCO, mindful at the same time that our capacity to extend essential assistance to the region would still be circumscribed by considerations of geography and the turmoil that still remains.

Remarks by A.P. Venkateswaran A.P. Venkateswaran, Chairman, Asia Centre, said in his remarks that he would like to convey his gratitude to Sudhir Devare, Director General of ICWA, for having joined up with Asia Centre in periodically arranging such useful seminars. As seminars were but a step in a longer effort, there was a need to keep thinking and to identify what was wrong and where things could be set right. Reviewing the discussions of the day, the Chairman discerned that there was a slight discomfort among members in the audience on our membership of the SCO. There were questions on what India was doing there and quite often, the questioners wanted to know where India stood on various issues. The Chairman observed that, unfortunately, India did not appear to stand anywhere, but seemed to be lying down, and this mindset needed correction. Referring to the remarks on energy security and oil exploration during the question and answer session, the Chairman provided an example on why the ONGC had been unable to use the advantages it had. He recalled that a few years back, Vietnam had given some prime areas to ONGC for offshore oil exploration after withdrawing these areas from the French, despite an earlier commitment made to them; sadly, the ONGC did nothing about it, but simply sold it to a British company after some years.

As for the American withdrawal from Afghanistan, the Chairman said that the Americans had massive air power, and even now much of the killing in Afghanistan was being done by the drones. Concluding his address, the Chairman said that he did not see peace coming soon to Afghanistan, and India would have to be prepared to face tough choices and act on them.

Conclusion

The emergence of the SCO as a vital group in the Eurasian land mass has now been acknowledged by all major powers of the world. The time has now come to address the issue of India joining the SCO. The need for India to be a full-fledged member was generally accepted, though one speaker, a former ambassador to the region, had sharply differing views. Attention was also drawn by the speakers to the fact that China's moves had raised some doubts; China may well link India's joining the SCO to a full membership of SAARC for itself, and this is a possibility for which we have to be prepared with an appropriate response. In addition to Pakistan, China has assiduously wooed Sri Lanka to further complicate India's foreign policy management. At the conclusion of the seminar, the general view was that if India was offered membership of the SCO, it should be accepted without delay.

One positive development is that the focus of the SCO has now turned to Afghanistan. Realization has grown that a peaceful and stable environment there is essential for regional stability in the entire Central Asian region. SCO membership offers a platform for India to cooperate with other members to shape a stable and progressive future for Afghanistan.

India has neglected the Central Asian Republics for nearly two decades and should compensate for this neglect. Our attention seems to be focused on the SCO as an organizational entity, and we have let slip the opportunities to build lasting and fruitful bilateral relationships.

India must engage bilaterally with each of the Central Asian Republics to develop trade, promote energy security, and build closer economic cooperation independent of the dynamics of its bid for the SCO membership. Security cooperation, particularly with Tajikistan, both on the bilateral level and also in the context of Afghanistan, should be pursued with undiluted vigour.

It appears that the US, Russia, and to a certain extent China, have developed a mutual understanding on how to deal with each other's presence in Central Asia, while dealing with the individual nations. While the SCO would undoubtedly help develop closer linkages between Central and South Asia in the broader sense, India must be alert to safeguard its own interests in both the regions from any possible steps by the three big powers.

In conclusion, the seminar has emphasised that while membership of the SCO was important, intensification of bilateral relations with all the Central Asian countries should proceed apace, as closer engagement at the bilateral level will automatically feed into the multilateral level.

Chapter 4

India and Nepal

ASIA CENTRE BANGALORE

'New Realities in Nepal and India's Concerns'
Proceedings of the Seminar
held on

June 19, 2010

Preface

In the last decade, Asia Centre has held three seminars on developments in Nepal, viewed from an Indian security perspective. Two were in April 2006 and August 2008, and the last was conducted on June 19, 2010, on the topic 'New Realities in Nepal and India's Concerns'.

Watershed Events in Nepal The beginning of the century saw violence erupt in Nepal; in June 2001, a massacre ended in the deaths of the king and queen and seven other members of the Royal family. Ultimately, King Gyanendra ascended the throne amidst widespread suspicions of his own role in the tragedy. The new King moved to rapidly concentrate all power in himself, weakening and marginalizing the political parties. In the political space thus created, the Maoists gained prominence and support by violent attacks against the unpopular regime and won the confidence of the common people.

Asia Centre Seminar in April 2006 The seminar in April 2006 focused on the dilemma faced by the Indian Government: as the democracy movement gathered momentum, it became obvious that the people wanted the end of the monarchy. Gyanendra held on to his throne, supported by the Army. In early April 2006, India's options were poised between support for the royalty and backing for the democratic movement. At our seminar, all the panellists concluded that the pragmatic thing to do was to engage the Maoists and support the democracy movement. Some of the panellists also pointed out the contrary view of the US and China, both of whom wished for the monarchy to continue. The seminar conclusions were that India should contribute to the rebuilding of Nepal's institutions, and keep a vigil on possible interference by other countries. There was also the prospect of revisiting the specific questions of an open border, as well as the Indo–Nepal Treaty.

Second Seminar—August 9, 2008 A second seminar on Nepal was conducted in August 2008. Nepal proclaimed itself a republic on May 28, 2008, abruptly terminating the 240 years old monarchy. Just four days before the Asia Centre seminar, on August 5, 2008, the main parties in Nepal agreed to form a national unity government, led by the Maoists.

This seminar brought out a balanced picture of the Nepalese political scene as it was unfolding. As might have been expected with the Maoists at the helm, there was a clear pro-China slant in the preliminary policy statements, but the panel was clear that Nepal could not do without India despite the political statements.

They felt that the revolution had changed Nepal irrevocably, with diversity and empowerment of all segments of the population. Undoubtedly, the new republic would face challenges, which would bring challenges to India, and there would be delicate issues to be negotiated in the light of the historic transformation that Nepal had achieved. Some of the panellists cautioned that there was a potential risk from China. It would also be necessary for us to review our border security and defence cooperation.

Seminar
New Realities in Nepal and India's Concerns

June 19, 2010

A.P. Venkateswaran, former Foreign Secretary and Chairman of Asia Centre presided. The following speakers addressed the seminar:

Hormis Tharakan	Former chief of RAW, Visiting Professor, Department of Geopolitics, Manipal University
Major General (Retd) Dipankar Banerjee	Director, Institute of Peace and Conflict Studies, New Delhi.

Prashant Jha	Political Analyst and Journalist based in Kathmandu
Deb Mukharji	Former Ambassador to Nepal

Introduction

Introducing the subject, the Director, Lt General (Retd) Ravi Eipe, observed that two years earlier, Nepal had been at the cross-roads, with new political forces and equations. This current seminar too, took place at a crucial juncture. There was a political stand-off between the parties and a demand for the Prime Minister (Madhav Kumar Nepal) to step down. It appeared that a new set-up was about to emerge. From a security viewpoint, Nepal is a special neighbour for India in three respects:

1) Its strategic location; 2) The open border; 3) the Gorkha soldiers in the Indian Army.

A summary of the presentations and deliberations recorded by A. Madhavan, former ambassador of India, is provided in the succeeding pages.

Presentation 1: Strategic and Security Concerns

Hormis Tharakan

Resumption of Inter-Party Acrimony On May 28, 2010, in the last hour before the term of the Constituent Assembly (CA) was due to expire, its term was renewed for another year by the agreement of the three major parties. Before the members of the CA got down to the task of drafting the Constitution, inter-party strife resumed. The Maoist demanded that the Prime Minister must step down as promised, within five days of the agreement. But the Prime Minister, his party and the Nepal Congress said that the Maoists should keep their part of the bargain and disband the Youth Communist League, return the properties seized from citizens during the civil war, and integrate the PLA.

The country seems to have gone back to square one. No consensus among the parties appears probable. A sharp division in the Maoist Politburo has surfaced; the chairman of the Maoist party, Prachanda, wants his party to sit in the opposition and carry on the agitation. But the deputy leader, Baburam Bhattarai, wants the Maoists to lead the government, even with another leader who is more acceptable to the other parties than Prachanda. There are numerous aspirants from more than one party for the Prime Minister's post.

This confusion and contention for power have caused apprehension in India and other countries too. To us, Nepal is of vital importance. Instability in Nepal, which is wedged as 'a yam between the two boulders', is of strategic concern to both India and China. Since the historic elections of August 2008, India has been obliged to regard China's growing influence in Nepal with close attention. As B. Raman stated in the last seminar held by Asia Centre in August 2008, China has revealed a Look South policy to counter India's Look East Policy. Till now, India had almost monopolized the strategic space of Nepal. Now, China has become the second player.

Western Interests As regards the US, the UK, and Russia, their primary interests appear to be centred on China, Nepal's proximity to Tibet, its location, and the role of the UNMIN (the UN Mission in Nepal).

This Mission's mandate was prepared with constraints, which some Western critics have attributed to India. Russia has asked for a UNSC visit to Nepal. The UK has an additional interest through its links to Gorkha soldiers recruited in its army.

The focus of current US interest is that Nepal serves as a forum between China and India, which could be adequately used by the US. The US has come a long way from the policy of its previous ambassador, Moriarty, who was a vocal critic of the Maoists during the transition in Nepal from monarchy to a republic. The US Ambassador DeLise called on both Prachanda and Bhattarai after taking over his post. As for Pakistan, it consistently exploits the open Indo–Nepal border by prompting cross-border terrorism into India, infusing counterfeit currency, and in other subversive activities.

The Open Border The practice of periodic joint inspections of the border lapsed after India's Independence. A joint boundary commission was constituted between India and Nepal in 1981 to oversee the border, but it did not meet regularly. Minor disputes arose about the alignment of the border and were generally settled by discussions by the two sides, but some anti-Indian Nepalese magnified these disputes for their own designs. Under the 1950 Treaty, between independent India and Nepal, the border was left open, in conformity with traditional practice. There are now 22 checkposts along the border with only three posts being used for persons belonging to third countries.

The open border facilitates the free movement into India of terrorists, drug and human traffickers, currency racketeers, and spies. Further, it has increased corruption along both sides of the border. At the beginning of this century,

Nepal started deploying its troops on the border. India too has increased the strength of its special border force (Sashastra Seema Bal.)

However, the advantage of the open border is that it facilitates the legitimate requirements of those living near the border on either side. Many Nepalese come unhindered to India and seek to improve their prospects. For Gorkha soldiers and their families on the Nepal side, this freedom of movement is invaluable. These advantages are sufficient to offset the disadvantages.

Nepali and Indian Maoist Connection An important issue to assess is the impact of the Maoist ascendancy in Nepal on the left extremist movement in India. India had suspicions of Prachanda's pro-China leanings. He has acknowledged the positive role that India played during the difficult period of transition in Nepal. He claims that it is wrong to think he is closer to China than to India. We must make an objective and realistic assessment of Maoist intentions without going by preconceptions. Our establishment may lack trust in the Nepal Maoists, but we should not alienate them when their party was returned by the electorate as the most popular one. There is an urgent need to regain the ground that we have lost in Nepal since May 2008.

The Maoist movements in Nepal and India are distinct struggles against the ruling government. For a long time, the Indian left extremists have been calling for a Red Corridor running from the north to south of India. Prime Minister Manmohan Singh had made a significant change in India's Nepal policy by coming to terms with the Maoist party as the majority party in Nepal in 2008. It stemmed from the assessment that the two Maoist movements had no significant links. We should see this as an opportunity to show the Indian Maoists that violence is not the only path to achieve people's power.

After the Maoist party came to power in Nepal, it began cultivating China. Every government in Nepal has balanced its relations with India and China. During the years of the Maoist agitation, China had denied support for the Nepal Maoists, but now has changed tack and is actively helping them since they became the majority party. India must assess if the Chinese moves in Nepal damage Indian interests.

It was a defining moment when the Nepal Maoists chose to take to the parliamentary track, renouncing armed struggle. This shift was severely criticised by the Indian Maoists who clung to their policy of armed struggle against the state. Prachanda and Bhattarai's ideological explanation for the shift in strategy worried the left extremists in India since it undermines the rationale of their revolutionary struggle. The example of Nepal Maoists can serve our government in persuading Indian left extremists to abjure violence.

It could convince pro-left opinion too. But there is a perception among the Nepalese that India wanted the CA to be dissolved when it failed to fulfil the mandate of drafting a constitution by May 28, thus robbing the Prachanda government of legitimacy; and that it welcomed Prachanda's resignation as Prime Minister. The support of all the parties for the extension of the CA's term by one year showed the contrary wish of the Nepalese political class.

Presentation 2: The View from Kathmandu

Prashant Jha

Historic Transition Nepal is a country that is perpetually at the cross-roads, having to make difficult choices. The present situation is complicated by the process of drafting the constitution and the politics of power-sharing. We have to consider factors like the internal dynamics of the various parties, the Terai, and the roles of India, China, and other countries. Nepal is in the midst of a historic transition, from war to peace, monarchy to republic, unitary state to federal state, apart from evolving a concept of citizenship and nationalism more inclusive than one based on narrow identity. The monarchy has been dismantled; state building and nation building are happening together. Drastic democratization of society, with its contestations and conflicts in various political constituencies, suffered ups and downs.

Disagreements on Constitutional Issues May 28, 2010 was a crucial day for Nepal, when the term of the Constituent Assembly was to run out. But at the last moment, the parties came together, avoiding brinkmanship and averted a constitutional crisis by extending the term of the CA for a year. The crisis has been postponed, but it may reappear on May 28, 2011, if the new Constitution is not ready by then. It is not certain that there will be a new Constitution by next May. It means that Nepal's form of government, its legitimacy, and the future of the unsettled relations between the different political and ethnic groups would all be unstable and crisis-prone.

In writing the constitution, the Constitutional Committee must prepare a single text of the draft statute to be debated for public feedback and opinions, to be finally debated and voted in the house, clause by clause. Consensus is lacking on a number of issues.

Form of Government At the core there is a difference between the Maoists and the others on the form of government. The Maoists want a directly elected President who would hold all executive power. The NC prefers the Westminster system of an elected majority party forming a government with a Prime Minister in charge. A few in the Nepali Congress would like to have a directly elected Prime Minister to avoid instability. The fear is that a powerful President would lead to authoritarian rule.

Nature of Federalism The second issue is the nature of federalism, the basis for forming the state. For the Maoists, ethnicity or *jathiyata* is the core basis for the federal units. For the others, it is economic, depending on resources in the different parts of the land.

There are ideological differences too, which block the peace process. The Maoists want each cantonment with a 'dominant ethnicity' to choose its leader from that community. This is opposed by the others. Another debate is on the appointment of judges. The Maoists want to entrust this to a legislative committee, but this may politicize the selection.

Absorption of PLA cadres in Army An important difference is about integrating the PLA cadres of the Maoists into the main army. The Maoists want to keep the PLA almost intact. The other parties are reluctant converts; at best, they want it confined to a few thousand cadres at a lower level, while the Maoists want to induct cadres at the Commander level also. The critics want to keep the army true to its present structure, while the Maoists seek to reform it in line with their programme. This issue goes to the heart of Nepal's future as a state.

Amnesty for Maoist Crimes Another issue is that of ensuring accountability for past crimes like the disappearance of persons during the civil war. This has been thrust under the carpet. The result is the onset of a dangerous culture of impunity, in which violence can be legitimized and tolerated. This engenders militant groups acting independently against law and order.

Maoists in Majority sans Power An important aspect of the crisis is the anomaly in power sharing: the biggest party with the strongest organization has no part in state power. The Maoists have few sympathizers in the bureaucracy and the judiciary, being prominent only in the CA. The non-Maoist parties want the Maoists to be given their due state power only after they undergo a 'course correction': this implies integrating the PLA cadres on acceptable terms, dismantling the Youth Communist League, and returning seized property.

The Maoists contend that all this is a process and not an event. There is a deep trust deficit among and within the main parties. There are several contenders for the posts in these parties, including the Madhesis. Intra-party differences have overridden inter-party differences to vex the nation.

Once the Maoists were in power, they wanted to change the nature of government by placing their men in the bureaucracy and the judiciary. They attacked the media. They even replaced the traditional priests from South India in the Pashupatinath temple with Nepalese priests. The perception grew that the Maoists were attacking institutions in their desire to monopolize power.

Fundamental Intra-Maoist Party Differences The turning point came at the meeting of the Maoist cadres in December 2008, when Prachanda was still the Prime Minister. Bhattarai was for the Constitution to be drafted first, and to continue with the course followed by the party so far. But the dogmatists, led by the veteran Kiran, held that the principal contradiction faced by Nepal was no longer feudalism versus the bourgeois but that of expansionism versus nationalists; he was pointing at India as expansionist. His faction held that the parliamentary path should be given up so that a people's republic could be proclaimed. They would ally with any political elements which recognized the priority of nationalism in pursuing the struggle. But the Kiran line was found unsustainable when the general strike called by the party fizzled out, lacking the people's support. Bhattarai was able to argue that ground realities were not ripe for a revolution. This has resulted in a rivalry between Prachanda and Bhattarai for leadership. The existential question the Maoists have to resolve is this: should they surrender their guns and accept a slow transformation of the polity or revert to civil war and alienate public opinion? Bhattarai wants the party to keep the gains it has won so far and build on them. Prachanda is insecure. This is the core of what is ailing a peace settlement.

Ineffectiveness of other Parties The Nepalese Congress and the other parties have failed abysmally to stabilize the situation and deliver on their promises. Their old and discredited leaders, several of whom lost the elections, have eroded the credibility of their parties. They remain weak mainly because they have not kept in touch with the changes in Nepali society. Among these changes, two are important: first, there is a generational transformation of the population profile, with a majority aged below 25 years; and second, the marginalized communities have begun to assert themselves and seek membership in parliament. It is fortunate that the NC still remains coherent and avoids a dictatorial bias, but factionalism is rampant within.

Indian Role India played a correct role in 2005 by working discreetly to let the Maoists take to the political process. If this decision is being reconsidered now, it is not a good development, since it is better to have the Maoists in the mainstream of political life.

China is engaging all the active groups in Nepal's polity without showing an inclination to intervene and alter political outcomes. They believe in gradually accumulating their political gains in Nepal.

Presentation 3: Indian Interests and Policy

Major General (Retd) Dipankar Banerjee

Two years ago, at an earlier Asia Centre seminar, the issue concerned the future of the Maoist movement. Today, the salient issues are the dynamics of Nepal in the current situation and the challenges to the future of Nepal and South Asia. We have also to analyse developments in Nepal–China relations and how far they impinge on Nepal–India relations. There are challenges of rising nationalism and ethnic differences, and of establishing a democratic process with the people's participation.

Lack of Progress As the deadline for the framing of the new Constitution is only one year, the present respite serves to postpone major decisions. No progress has been made on the essential conditions for peace and stability. There is no road map for the resolution, nor the necessary political consensus for it. The political and economic situation is likely to continue deteriorating. We have to assess India's policy and options in light of this uncertainty.

The Nepal–India Equation Nepal's future is more closely linked with India than with China. We must be sensitive to the feelings of small countries that find it is not easy to live with a strong and big neighbour. Nationalism will gain prominence among them. Let us consider how Nepal looks at India and how we should best interact with it in our interests and strategic framework.

Nature of Current Situation in Nepal We can examine three facets of concern to India, in broad terms. We must assess the nature of present situation in Nepal—whether it is post or pre-conflict.

If it is a post-conflict situation, we can conclude that the victory of the united Maoists—democratic forces over the emerging authoritarian monarchy—was a significant achievement. Only a few years ago, Nepal seemed to be in a state of perpetual internal conflict. Instead, with India's support and encouragement, the conflict was brought to an end and the 12-point agreement was concluded. Now, there is no civil war, which had seemed a continuing possibility. This is no mean success, but there is still no peace settlement or resolution of contradictions.

If however, Nepal is still assessed to be in a pre-conflict situation, it raises the question whether the contradictions can be resolved only by renewed civil war. The question is whether the main players, which is the political parties, will be able to resolve their differences. This seemed unlikely. Therein lies our dilemma. Whether this is a situation where the contradictions can be peacefully resolved without external intervention is not clear.

A Role for India While we recognize that the Nepalese must solve their internal problems, India does have a role in Nepal. Though some Nepalese are unwilling to recognize it, the pre-eminence of India in every aspect of Nepalese life is generally accepted, even if grudgingly. The Maoists will probably lead the groups opposed to India. If the Maoists go back to armed conflict, it will increase India's concerns. What differentiated the Nepal Maoists from the Indian counterparts was their giving up of armed conflict for the democratic path. That is the positive example. But if the Nepal Maoists come to power by successful armed struggle, it would create a negative precedent: the Indian left extremist insurgency fighting against the state may take advantage of it. The possibility of other insurgents linking up with Marxists is a serious concern. There are ideological linkages between the Maoists of both countries. The old objective of forcibly capturing power in the centre, though obsolete and out of tune with the times with the spread of globalization, still appeals to a small section of the people and constitutes a challenge for India.

Difficult Road Ahead Hence, it will be a long and difficult process to stabilize South Asia. Nepal is undergoing enormous changes. Different ethnic groups have gained some share of political representation. But the institutions of stable governance are still lacking or weak. These are formidable challenges. India can learn lessons from the impact of left extremism and apply them to our conditions.

Dealing with China's Role in Nepal We should consider the role of China in Nepal, South Asia, and the world. India–China relations are going well enough now. China's development is proceeding very fast, with spectacular achievements in infrastructure and civil construction. Consequently, Chinese influence will keep growing in South Asia. Without signalling alarm, we should cooperate with China wherever it is in our interest to do so. China is expanding its presence in South Asia and setting up Confucius Centres in various cities. It is an observer in SAARC. These actions need not cause us concern, but we should be careful to uphold our long-term strategic interests and safeguard security. In this period, when nationalist sentiments are getting more prominent in Nepal, we should take care not to interfere in its internal developments and adhere to a strict policy of non-intervention.

Nepal's Stability is in India's Interest It is for the people of Nepal to find their own solutions to their domestic problems. At the same time, we should be aware that it is wholly in our interest that Nepal should be stable, secure, and economically better developed. The monarchy is discredited and gone, but there is nothing to take its place. The economy is in disarray. Ethnic consciousness is aroused, but there is no agreement on how to accommodate the aspirations of the different communities. Nepal is not a failed state. Its institutions are intact, though weakened. The Nepal Army remains under democratic control and is capable of securing the state.

India's interest at this juncture is to promote the rise of a peaceful Nepal, stable and prosperous, living at peace with itself and its neighbourhood.

Suggested Policy Thrusts

Indian policy should be framed to secure this outcome.

1) This can be achieved by facilitating the transition to a stable democracy within a Constitution that satisfies a majority of the Nepalese people. India can offer such guidance as is acceptable to them.
2) Nepal would arouse Chinese concerns if there is any sign of support to unrest in Tibet and Xinjiang. Nepal must take care of this sensitivity. It could be enabled to identify itself with South Asia, seek the larger group of the SCO and other organizations like BIMSTEC.
3) Nepal should be part of a resurgent South Asian economy. We have to facilitate Nepal to this end by encouraging a dynamic regional development in SAARC. Nepal is an important neighbour for India. We should, therefore, actively promote our bilateral economic cooperation with that country.

Presentation 4: India and Nepal—A Political Overview

Deb Mukharji

New Elements in the Nepal Situation Other countries of South Asia were subject to colonialism with all its disadvantages, but in the process they moved ahead with the rest of the world. In Nepal, the civil institutions were not allowed to take root, either under the Ranas or under the monarchy. A feudal aura, the *huzur* mentality of subservience, was deliberately ingrained in the people by the elitist sections wielding power. But there were some successes, such as when the media played a vital role in thwarting the King's attempt to take over the state. The *Janandolan* of April 2006 was the first sign of the people claiming power in Nepal and the end of the *huzur* mentality. A new self-confidence in Mades and rising expectations of the hitherto deprived classes became evident. With the insurgency, the *Janandolan II*, and the end of the monarchy, not one genie but a host of genies has been let loose. These genies, such as the rising expectations of the people, cannot be put back into the jar. What has emerged is not a 'new Nepal' but a Nepal of new aspirations, which have to be addressed.

A distinction must be made between the people of Nepal and the politics of Nepal. If we do not consider the people and their aspirations, we cannot come to grips with the current stand-off. When the Maoists adopted the democratic path to power, they gained votes beyond their own expectations in the elections. In a way, they have had difficulty in handling their success. The Maoists are the only party with an agenda which has the people's support, but they do not have a credible roadmap. In their list of 40 points, about 35 should be acceptable to most social–democratic sympathizers.

The recent contradictory statements by rival Maoists regarding multiparty democracy have indeed clouded the issues. The call for 'people's democracy' and comments by some Maoists have been confusing and roused suspicions.

The elections to the Constituent Assembly were a mix of the 'First-past-the-post' principle and Proportional Representation (PR). In the former mode, the Maoists would have got 30 per cent of the votes and 50 per cent of the seats; in India, this would have given them an absolute majority. The PR system brought down their share of seats. In quality of representation and as a reflection of the people's will, the Maoists gave a substantially larger representation to women, youth, and the depressed classes (*janajati*.) It is surprising that this unique revolution in South Asia has gone unsung. The Maoists have given representation to marginalized elements, while other parties have mainly fielded members from the elitist Brahmin and Kshatriya castes.

The political classes have, at least, managed to step back from the brink, but there is little to unite them, and the polity is unmanageably fragmented into 22 parties. While the other parties seem bereft of any vision, some of the declared Maoist objectives have raised genuine concerns. As for the future, there is some concern about a right-wing reaction. If that happens, Nepal may be back to square one. The reactions of the Nepal Army are a matter for speculation, but it is no longer a continuation of the Royal army.

Nepal's India and China Policies As regards India and China in Nepal's foreign policy, the professed 'equidistance' cannot be taken as applicable to every situation. The Nepalese understand that geographical imperatives do not permit equidistance. Though some politicians have played the China card, we should be aware of India's inherent advantages and avoid being paranoid about Nepal–China ties. When we react to issues, we should make it clear that our initiatives are intended for the people of Nepal and not for any particular interest group. Irritants, there will be, in trade and transit arrangements. Our economic projects have had considerable impact, and lately, India has gone into the Nepal countryside to place projects. True, the management of river waters has become hostage to the political classes in Nepal. But there is a growing body of opinion that cooperation with India can benefit Nepal, as Bhutan's example has shown. Nepal has its experts and we should avoid acting as if we know better and leave it to the Nepalese to arrive at a political decision in cases of this kind.

People-to-people contacts are substantial, but India should encourage greater interaction with the increasingly assertive civil society of Nepal. Of course, some Nepalese are hyper-critical of India, but this sentiment should not be overstated as anti-Indianism in general. In remote places, there is no trace of it. It is explicable as the psychological complex of a much smaller neighbour country, especially among some political sections in Kathmandu which use it as a low-cost diversionary tactic. A similar situation prevails in Bangladesh.

Conclusion India's basic interest in its Nepal policy is the welfare of the country; everything flows from it. We must refrain from involvement in Nepal politics, which may benefit some politicians, but not the two countries. In conclusion, we must take note of a recent highly critical article by Manjushree Thapar, whose father was Nepal's ambassador to India. In it she has blamed the Indian establishment for political manipulation in Nepal in alliance with the non-Maoist parties, and warns that the clock cannot be turned back.

Discussion

Effectiveness of Non-Government Welfare Institutions Mukharji said that there were major projects from previous years, like the East–West highway and small projects funded by private agencies, such as clinics. Gifts like ambulances for clinics do generate goodwill and help the people. An arts centre with fine exhibition facilities had been built with both private and governmental funding.

Effect of Royal Massacre Akbar Khaleeli asked if the massacre of the royal family at the palace in Kathmandu in June 2001 had changed the politics of Nepal. Mukharji replied that the 'aura' of the King had gone, with Birendra being considered the last king. The end of monarchy was a jolt, but the belief grew that it was not the permanent definition of the Nepal state. For some, the king was the incarnation of Vishnu and he was suddenly gone when the country became republican. Prashant Jha added that after the royal massacre, Gyanendra destroyed the traditional legitimacy of the monarchy by attempting to take over complete power.

Chinese Threat to India through Nepal A member commented that the Chinese support and funding for Maoist activities had enabled them to gain the high ground, making India vulnerable to invasion through Nepal. In reply, Prashant Jha explained that China, under Deng Xiaoping, had given up involvement in revolutionary movements elsewhere. Contrary to the questioner's impression, China had supported the Nepal monarchy right to the end. It has now enhanced its connections in view of the Tibetan situation, from which it wants to insulate Nepal. The Nepal Maoists are not Chinese agents, but an autonomous movement within Nepal. The Nepalese do not consider the Chinese devious, but rather, some Nepalese blame 'the devious brahminical mind'.

Indian Assistance to Nepal Major General Banerjee added that India had given aid worth Rs 120 crore to Nepal and endowed 1500 scholarships per year. These have had a reasonable impact, though, of course, more could be done. Chinese influence in Nepal is growing and will grow further with the cultural centres they are putting up in the country. The Maoists, having come into the power structure in Nepal, want Nepal to have an alternative to India as support. When India stopped its military aid to Nepal, China supplied US $1 million to it.

A Negative Lesson A member said that the Nepal Maoists had fought the Nepal army and security forces and even blockaded Kathmandu. This is a negative lesson which the Indian Maoists may prefer to learn from. He asked what would a Maoist government's policy be, regarding issues like China, Gorkha recruitment, or the open border. Tharakan agreed that the Nepal Maoists had come to the negotiating table after fighting for 10 years, but they had chosen the electoral path after concluding that revolution had failed because of their not taking part in the parliamentary system. As for India–China relations, we know that it is not the open border with Nepal that the Chinese consider an invasion route.

A member argued that in Nepal, the Maoists have won the elections but cannot hold on to power. Indian Maoists could see this as a negative example ascribable to the parliamentary route.

General Banerjee responded that the Nepal Army was a professional one that has contributed troops to the UN peace-keeping operations for a decade. In the civil war it had been the Nepal police forces which had been countering the Maoists. The Maoists never won militarily, though they indulged in an enormous number of violent activities and killings. Local support for the Maoists was due to the political parties losing their credibility and legitimacy.

Hindu Kingdom Mukharji clarified, in response to a question that Nepal was known as a Hindu kingdom, that it did not follow that they favoured India. The Nepalese are religious but not communal: they are liberal and accept other faiths like Buddhism and Islam. It is Indians who kept thinking of Nepal as a Hindu kingdom.

Hydel Power Generation A questioner suggested that India and Nepal could fruitfully develop Nepal's huge hydro-electrical potential to mutual benefit. The Chairman, Venkateswaran, explained that the Nepalese are firmly against India utilizing their rivers for generating electrical power to be sold to our country.

Madhesi Issue In response to a query about the Madhesi problems, Jha said that Madhesis constitute about a third of the population, living mostly in the Terai. Many have kinship ties with Indians living in Bihar and Uttar Pradesh. Until recently, Madhesis were regarded as a 'fifth column' from India, since the Nepalese nationalist identity had been dominated by the hill-nativist elite. The Madhesi movement seeks to redefine Nepal nationalism in a more inclusive way and to claim equality in citizenship. Their increased electoral representation has brought them into the political space as an emergent force. The Maoists constitute the other new political force. At present, the political landscape is fragmented and the state is weak, with organized crime from Bihar and adjacent Indian areas crossing over into Nepal with ease.

Khaleeli intervened to remark that the present transition in Nepal is neither 'pre-conflict' nor 'post-conflict' but 'in-conflict'. He cautioned that Madhesis, if suspected to be aligned to India, could cause problems for us. India should avoid alignment with any particular group in Nepal, and be firm against cross-border terrorism from the Nepal side. The rest should be left to the Nepalese. If the state is destabilized, the fallout will spill into India.

Concluding Remarks The Chairman, Venkateswaran, in his concluding remarks observed that the seminar had been very useful and informative. Our problems are largely created by ourselves. He cited Sardar Patel's letter to

Nehru in 1950, warning of India's weak northern borders, which needed to be strengthened in defence against infiltration and vulnerability to a possible Chinese advance. Conflict cannot be ruled out in our world, which is far from the utopian idea of One World expressed by Wendell Wilkie's book of that title in 1943. In such a situation, we should strive to make India a strong and cohesive nation without impinging unnecessarily on others.

Conclusion and Suggestions

As of July 28, 2010, Nepal remains in an unstable transition between governments, with one month gone out of the Constituent Assembly's extended term of one year. The front runners for the post of Prime Minister are the Maoist party leader Prachanda and the Nepal Congress Vice-president Ram Chandra Paudel, with the former well in the lead at the poll by members of the CA on July 21.

Even a new government is unlikely to resolve the ideological differences between the Maoists and the older parliamentary parties. Prashant Jha had thrown light on the disarray among the political parties, but there were also the hopeful signs of the Maoists functioning within the democratic framework and the inclusion of hitherto marginalized groups like the Madhesis. The possibility that the revolutionary faction in the Maoist party will initiate another futile 'people's war' must be reckoned with. Perhaps this can be precluded with India's support to Nepal's development.

The China factor in Nepal has also to be reckoned with, and though Chinese influence in Nepal will increase, India must be confident of its own standing as a benign neighbour and participate with the Nepalese in efforts to increase the people's welfare through government-sponsored or private projects.

Among the measures which the government can initiate are:

1) **Survey of Projects** A survey of the most-needed small-scale projects in places outside Kathmandu in order to set up welfare schemes with Indian aid, and an independent assessment of the performance and utility of the existing Indian aid projects in Nepal.
2) **Detailed Study Of Nepal** A detailed and comprehensive study of Nepal, in all its aspects, to create a database for all agencies that deal with Nepal.
3) **Visits to Border States** With the Home Ministry, the MEA could send personnel to the Indian states adjoining Nepal (UP and Bihar), in order to be better informed of all aspects of the situation on the ground.

4) **High-Level Visits** India could boost Nepalese pride by one or two high level visits when the time is right.
5) **Studies on Trade and Economy** Initiate studies on trade and economy with a view to improving Indo–Nepal economic and commercial relations.
6) **Sponsored Studies** There is a need to encourage more discussion of Nepal–India relations in forums located outside New Delhi and the main universities. The average Indian's knowledge about Nepal's history, culture, socio-economic problems, and ethnic diversity needs to be raised. The MEA could sponsor special in-depth studies about Nepal and publicize the results to address the lack of knowledge about Nepal. Ph.D. aspirants in the humanities could be given special topics concerning Nepal (and our other neighbours) for their dissertations.

Chapter 5

India–Bangladesh Relations

ASIA CENTRE BANGALORE

'Developments in Bangladesh and India's Security and Economic Challenges' Proceedings of the Joint Seminar held on

February 6, 2010

Introduction

Two seminars were held on Indo–Bangladesh relations, one in September 2005, when the BNP was in power and the ties had dropped to a low ebb; and the other in February 2010, when a new regime under Sheikh Hasina of the Awami League had come to power, with winds of change for the better.

The major highlight of the first seminar was the Indian dilemma in dealing with Bangladesh: should our policy be guided by our security, political, and economic interests rather than by the pursuit of nominally congenial good-neighbourly relations, which may prove transitory anyway? The speakers explained all the friction points in our bilateral dealings, and the particular problems arising from the unfriendly, unhelpful attitude of the present BNP coalition led by Begum Khaleda Zia. They also made it amply clear that Bangladeshis had yet to find a national identity distinct from their shared Bengali high culture and Bengali language with India.

Bangladesh's poverty and economic backwardness, compounded by high unemployment, natural calamities, and a polity dominated by the armed forces has made the country vulnerable to Arab Islamic propaganda; to the detriment of its traditional tolerance towards the Hindu, Christian and tribal minorities, as well as the cultural pride of its people. Dependence on foreign capital and technology has weakened it. India has a major interest in its stability, democracy, and relatively secular policy, though radical Islam funded from West Asia will continue to make inroads into its social and educational system and alter its national identity.

'Developments in Bangladesh and India's Security and Economic Challenge'

February 6, 2010

A.P. Venkateswaran, former Foreign Secretary and Chairman, Asia Centre presided. The following speakers addressed the seminar:

Brigadier Sumant Chatterjee	Research Scholar, USI of India, Editor, *South Asia Security Trends*
Sreeradha Datta	Director, Maulana A.K. Azad Institute of Asian Studies, Kolkata
B. Raman	Former Additional Secretary, Cabinet Secretariat; Director, Institute for Topical Studies, Chennai
Veena Sikri	Former Ambassador to Bangladesh

This seminar on Indo–Bangladesh relations, with special attention to the security and economic aspects, turned out to be very timely and useful. It was held shortly after the January 2010 visit of Sheikh Hasina, the Prime Minister of Bangladesh, which had generated a welcome breath of optimism after the strain on the relationship when Khaleda Zia was in power. The four panellists were experts drawn from different areas of experience—an army officer who had formerly served as Defence Adviser in our High Commission in Dhaka, a research analyst and author from the IDSA, a senior former officer of RAW and prolific writer on security issues, and a former High Commissioner to Bangladesh, with academic experience.

They covered various aspects of the complex bilateral relations with somewhat different emphasis, but markedly convergent focus on certain specifics: 1) the need for India to understand and relate to Bangladesh's problems and constraints with sympathy, and the consequent obligation to help Bangladesh to develop its economy and its infrastructure, so that the demonstrable benefits rebound to our advantage; 2) the importance of security issues affecting our national interests, which we cannot compromise upon, whittle down, or set aside, but must insist on safeguarding against encroachment; and 3) the merit of cultivating a variety of leaders, political parties, and opinion-makers, so that India gains a wider base of goodwill and support from the people, without exclusive reliance on a few leaders who recognize the common interests which the two countries share in all spheres of activity and geopolitics.

Presentation 1: A Military Perspective

Sumant Chatterjee

Bangladesh today presents a picture of stability and progress. It is accepted as a Muslim-majority nation that has taken strong measures to fight terrorism by cracking down on Islamist extremist forces as well as Indian insurgent groups operating within its territory. Bangladesh has also successfully weathered the global financial downturn and maintained a growth rate of 5–6 per cent per annum in recent years.

Centrality of Army in Bangladesh's Polity Historically, the Army has always been an important player in the country's political life, starting from the Liberation War in 1971, when the Mukti Bahini was formed to fight the Pakistan army. But many of the Bengalis in the old Army were caught on the West Pakistan side and returned (as 'Repatriates') to Bangladesh only two years later. There was always a strain in the BD armed forces between the 'Freedom Fighters' and the 'Repatriates', since the former were given two years seniority above the latter.

To understand the ethos of the Bangladesh military we must keep in mind the following factors:

1) It was originally part of the Pakistan Army and even today uses the same regimental names and proudly keeps its trophies. They still have strong links with the old army and celebrate ceremonial occasions regularly and with pride.
2) The officers come from urban surroundings, and the soldiers from the rural areas. Bangladeshi society looks up to the Army officers. Their standard of living is much higher than that of average citizens.
3) There has always been a division in the ranks between the Freedom Fighter recruits and the Repatriates. The older generation of officers is retired or retiring shortly. But there are divisions along political lines. The armed forces being highly politicized, many officers join politics after leaving the Army. A fair number of retired officers become MPs.

4) Like their Pakistan counterparts, the armed forces consider India as the main enemy and greatest national threat. Being almost surrounded by Indian territory, this phobia is understandable.
5) All their training and exercise manoeuvres are modelled on India as the target. They refer to India as the 'Foxland'.
6) Their military strategy focuses on blending conventional and unconventional operations of the kind that defeated the Pakistan Army in 1971. China is deemed their ally and the Siliguri Corridor is Foxland's vulnerable point that can be severed. They consider our North-East as their backyard and would like to prevent its integration with India. This is the rationale for their support to Indian insurgent groups from the North-East. For this reason, the Army is generally against giving transit and port facilities to India and opposes any gas pipeline from Myanmar to India through Bangladesh.
7) This mentality has also nurtured the expansionist dream of 'Birat Bangla'.
8) Similarly, Bangladesh has turned pro-China and pro-Pakistan in order to counterbalance India. But in the past, China has not come to aid Pakistan in India–Pakistan conflicts.
9) Bangladesh has made recognized contributions to UN Peace-keeping Operations, which are growing. Now, it is the largest contributor of defence service personnel (about 10,000). The Army is very proud of this status. It has given it a *raison d'être*, apart from its defence role against Indian domination. The Bangladesh Peace-keepers are the second largest foreign exchange earner for the country, next to the export sector of ready-made garments. Officers may get three or four UN mission postings in their career, which not only helps them financially, but also broadens their vision and knowledge.
10) Culturally, the people cherish their strong roots and bonds with India, especially the Bengali language. This cultural pull can sometimes be stronger than that of religion.
11) They admire and also envy Indians for the progress we have achieved, our religious freedom, and the relative freedom of womenfolk from old domestic restrictions, our higher education facilities, cultural diversity, and democracy, despite its problems. Bollywood is another great attraction. Bangladeshis like to visit India for its medical facilities and for pilgrimages. Their children are encouraged to opt for higher studies

in India rather than the West. Their marriage customs are carried over from Hindu customs, and many of their names have Hindu roots.

India's Strategic Concerns India's eastern flank is vulnerable and lacking in security and connectivity. Insurgent groups in the North-East are still active. China's revived policy of confrontation and claims to large parts of Arunachal Pradesh, its build-up of supply lines and air bases in Tibet, close to the border with India, are matters of grave concern. The poor development and connections in the region continue to help the insurgents. Development depends on greater connectivity with the North-East, and the route is through Bangladesh. The older rail and sea routes are not available for use.

Presentation 2: A Politico–Economic Survey

Sreeradha Datta

Economic Difficulties The economic situation in Bangladesh is very difficult. Despite the global economic meltdown, the country has maintained a growth rate of about 5.9 per cent per annum. But, this will be difficult to sustain. On the energy front, there is a huge gap between supply and demand for power (4000 MW as against 5500 MW). India can come in strongly to meet this deficit. On the trade front, Bangladesh relies on its export earnings from garments, pisciculture, and remittances from abroad, sent in as savings. Remittances account for some 80 per cent of the earnings in foreign exchange. Though the two countries issued a long joint communiqué after Sheikh Hasina's visit to India (in January 2010), this issue was not addressed in it. India should be sensitive to the problems of the neighbour country and take a unilateral approach to offering help.

Hasina's Unpopularity Rubbing off on India Another aspect that we have to remember is that the political rivalry between the leaders of the ruling party and the main opposition party is hurting Bangladesh. Instead of factoring in the Opposition, Sheikh Hasina has marginalized it in a small-minded way, for instance, by framing the budget without any consultation with it. This has a bearing on our bilateral relations, considering that in Bangladesh, the preponderant foreign policy issue is India. The Bangladeshis feel that India has neglected their country in our foreign policy framework, and that, but for insurgents from the North-East finding shelter there, India would have downplayed its relevance even further. In truth, few Indians know much about Bangladesh or care for its problems or understand the importance of developing better relations with it.

Generous Gestures—Zero Tariff? Bangladeshis, being emotional people, set store by timely gestures India can make. It is true that China is similar to India in running a huge trade surplus with Bangladesh. It is also true that the Bangladeshis loudly complain of the deficit with India when any bilateral issue comes up, but hardly grouse about China's highly favourable trade. We do import Bangladesh goods without duty, but there are still about 248 items on 'the negative list'. A zero tariff on all the items would perhaps cost a small fraction of our overall trade surplus. It can generate invaluable goodwill for India. Bangladesh responded warmly when the Foreign Minister Pranab Mukherjee visited Dhaka in 2007, during the Caretaker regime, and raised the quota of duty-free imports from Bangladesh garments from 2 million pieces to 8 million.We have a problem in raising the quota higher. Educational cess is charged by our side, and this falls under State jurisdiction in our constitution. It would be ideal, though futuristic, if South Asia could team up in export promotion for the garment industry, using Pakistani high quality cotton, Indian accessories, and Bangladesh skilled labour.

India's Unfulfilled Promises It is important for India to deliver on promises of support. After the devastating cyclone which hit Bangladesh, India had agreed to rebuild 221 villages. Nearly three years on, India has not yet begun construction work. The affected villagers are deeply disappointed. We must understand that there is a huge interaction at the level of the peoples of the two countries. Bangladeshis look to India for medical and educational facilities. Our problem is to improve on effective and timely delivery.

Illegal Migration—India must Mitigate Problem Finally, the illegal migration from Bangladesh is a perennial issue which neither side is able to tackle. The sociological and economic causes of the continued migration patterns need to be properly and objectively assessed. Given the great density of population in Bangladesh compared to the surrounding regions in India. Given the growing demand for domestic and semi-skilled labour in urban India, the phenomenon will persist despite any administrative controls by Bangladesh, for which it has neither the means nor the will. Any mitigation practicable must come from our side.

Presentation 3: Security Challenges

B. Raman

Reality of Anti-Indian Constituency in Bangladesh We have to constantly keep in mind the reality of a surviving anti-Indian constituency in Bangladesh.

We cannot quantify the strength of this group, but we cannot dismiss it lightly. It is an important constituency nurtured by Pakistan and Islamic fundamentalist organizations and charities from Saudi Arabia, both directly and via Pakistan.

We should not be carried away by our satisfaction over Sheikh Hasina's return to power, into minimizing the strength of anti-Indian elements. They may have lost the last elections but their street power and their ability to create instability remains. Sheikh Hasina knows this but believes that the common people want a better life, which will be facilitated by cooperation between Bangladesh and India.

She understands that the anti-Indian mindset of some sections cannot be eradicated but that it can be prevented from harming better bilateral relations, when the benefits of cooperation are demonstrable. The criterion which we must constantly keep in mind is of Bangladesh's perceptions of good results from improved bilateral relations.

There have been some good gestures by India towards Bangladesh: a credit-line of US $1 billion, an agreement to supply power, water-sharing, and so on. But anti-Indian elements project such gestures, not as generous ones, but as quid pro quo for security-related concessions made by the Bangladesh government. They allege that Sheikh Hasina has signed a secret security treaty with India.

India's Security Concerns

Support to Terrorist Groups India has vital security-related concerns in Bangladesh: the sanctuaries given to Indian insurgents and indigenous ethnic terrorist groups like the United Liberation Front of Assam (ULFA) in Bangladesh, the activities of Islamic terror groups like the Muslim Liberation Tigers of Assam (MULTA), the Independent Liberation Army of Assam (ILAA), and the People United Liberation Front (PULF).

Support to ISI-backed Terrorist Groups In addition, we have to contend with the activities from Bangladesh territory of pro-Al-Qaeda groups of Pakistani origin with ISI backing, such as the Lashkar-e-Taiba (LeT), the Harkat-ul-Jihad-al-Islami (HUJI), and the Harkat-ul-Mujahedeen (HUM), and gun-running into the North-East from or via Bangladesh.

Government of India cannot but spell out clearly our serious concern over such issues to the government of Bangladesh, regardless of the party in power there. Some of our concerns date back to Partition. The Naga and Mizo insurgencies were prolonged till 1971 due to their use of sanctuaries in Chittagong Hill Tracts in East Pakistan. Likewise, the ULFA and other insurgencies have been supported from Bangladesh territory. Governments in Dhaka have been ineffective in countering pro-Al-Qaeda groups. Collateral issues like illegal migration, gun-running, fund flows, and counterfeit currency (of Pakistan origin) are serious challenges which we need to take up with the powers in Dhaka.

Illegal Migration Causes Demographic Distortions The illegal migration of Muslims from Bangladesh into Assam and West Bengal (which can potentially make Assam a Muslim-majority Indian State), the funding from Wahabi charity organizations in Saudi Arabia to fundamentalists in the Bangladesh–India region, and the ISI's use of Bangladesh (and Nepal) for pumping counterfeit Indian currency into India.

Security Issues not Dependent on Ruling Party It is a mistake to assume that such security issues become more manageable when the Awami League is in power in Dhaka and more serious when the BNP or the Army is in power. The gravity of the issues has remained, regardless of the leader in power. The only difference is that, during Sheikh Hasina's current term as Prime Minister, there is a desire, which seems genuine, to address India's concerns. But Sheikh Hasina has repeatedly failed to translate the desire into effective and concrete measures, perhaps out of fear that the opposition would use them to discredit her as an Indian stooge or because there are persistent anti-Indian, pro-Pakistan elements in Bangladesh's intelligence and security establishment thwarting her. Of course, Khaleda Zia does not even have the desire to soothe Indian concerns.

Will Sheikh Hasina's current term see a genuine change in this regard? Would her greater self-confidence now embolden her to act more vigorously against those who threaten not only India but also Bangladesh itself? Examples of positive actions in the last year may be noted. Arabinda Rajkhowa of the ULFA may have fallen into the hands of Indian security agencies due to Bangladesh pressure on him when he was ensconced there. Investigation and prosecution of persons indulging in gun-running under the Khaleda Zia government, disabling of a plot by the LeT to attack the Indian and US diplomatic missions in Dhaka, pressure against one or two Mujahedeen persons in Bangladesh, forcing them to cross into India and fall into the hands of the Indian security forces.

Hasina Alone Cannot Remove Anti-Indianism Despite such positive steps, Sheikh Hasina is cautious enough to ensure that she is not seen as rushing into full-throttled cooperation with India in security-related matters. In the observations she made while in New Delhi, she drew a subtle distinction between cooperation with India against the international terrorism network, which posed a threat to both the countries, and action against indigenous organizations such as the ULFA, which posed a threat to India and not to Bangladesh. To cite her remarks as reported in the *Times of India* of January 14, 2010, when she was asked about the anti-India mindset in her country, she replied: 'Perhaps that may remain. I cannot change that. But common people want better lives and if results are achieved in India–Bangladesh co-operation, these sentiments will not work.' A bane of India's Bangladesh policy has always been that our policy-makers tend to put many, if not all of the eggs, in the basket of Sheikh Hasina and her Awami League. The importance of building bridges of understanding with non-religious political elements such as those in the BNP, even if they are not well disposed towards India, is not realized. Unless we build such bridges, there will always be strong opposition in sections of the political and public opinion in Bangladesh to any meaningful cooperation with India in security-related matters.

India Seen as Hegemonic by all Neighbours In our relations with our sub-continental neighbours, we are always unfortunately seen as a big power with hegemonistic tendencies. We have failed to project ourselves as a huge market, with an increasingly prosperous middle class which can absorb much of what they produce. How to make them see us as a highly attractive market and not as a repulsive power? Can a policy of unilateral gestures in trade-related matters help in creating a demonstration effect? This is another question which needs to be addressed by this seminar. Our recommendations should be forward moving and not backward-looking.

Presentation 4: Strategic Analysis

Veena Sikri

Indian and Bangladeshi Interests Sikri observed that Bangladesh being a significant neighbour of India, we should understand our strategic perspectives and Bangladesh's interests in our relations with that country. First, India wants a stable, peaceful and prosperous Bangladesh. Its location is sensitive. If Bangladesh is 'India-locked', our North-East is also Bangladesh-locked, as one Bangladeshi pointed out. Second, we want to see that Bangladesh territory is not used against Indian interests. Third, we want access to the North-East states through Bangladesh. We want Bangladesh to be cognisant of Indian interests and concerns. For instance, the illegal immigration of Bangladesh nationals into India, totalling about 29 million (in some estimates) and the cattle smuggling for slaughter which prevail from India do impinge on our interest, and need to be dealt with cooperatively.

Water Resources Water resources are important for Bangladesh, which, though richly endowed with rivers, must cope with its downstream location, with the waters flowing down from India. People have a phobia about India using up too much of the water flow. This grievance has been stoked from its pre-Independence days.

Trans-Border Movement The border being impossible to police and fence off, trans-border movement of people cannot be adequately controlled. Our Border Security Force (BSF) is regularly blamed by Bangladesh for killing its villagers and civilians. Such shooting of suspected intruders occurs mostly at night, when it is not possible to distinguish between innocent civilians and smugglers or criminals. But this is a huge grievance which needs to be addressed.

Commonalities in Interests These apart, there is a great commonality between the two neighbours. Bangladeshis are keen on democratic governance, and India too wants to deal with an elected government there to ensure peaceful change. Democracy is linked with pluralism and secularism, which we subscribe to. They deeply resented the repression they had to endure from West Pakistan's military rule. They have endured two periods of their own military rule even after Bangladesh became independent. In 1991, democracy was restored, in deference to the pressure of public opinion. In 2007, when Khaleda Zia was ousted from office, the change of government could be called an internationally inspired military coup. The people welcomed it, but elections were held the next year because the people wanted democracy, not army rule, though the Army did achieve some reforms in governance.

Investing in People, not in Leaders Sheikh Hasina should be seen not as pro-Indian, but as a staunch nationalist. She supports what is in their interest, that is, for democratic secularism and the ending of terrorism. Hers is a mandate given by the country's youth. She has to deliver on her programme of objectives. Her Indian visit should be seen in this context. India is not investing in Hasina as a leader, but in the people. That should be our yardstick.

Utilizing the Regional Framework Indo–Bangladesh relations must be placed in the regional context. Sheikh Hasina may be criticized by opponents who sloganize her visit to India 'a sell-out'. We have to convey that both sides have won. If India gains more connectivity to the North-East via Bangladesh, the latter can also use it to promote trade with the North-East states. Giving Bangladesh direct access to Nepal and Bhutan also helps the small countries and the North-East states to access Chittagong port. The opening has great potential for development and prosperity in the whole sub-region and furthers our Look East Policy. In this context, the 'BIMSTEC' grouping is very relevant. It will not get blocked by Pakistan's antipathy to India. Bangladesh should be supported in its bid to be the seat of the secretariat. It could take up and present initiatives regionally rather than bilaterally, much to the benefit of the participants and readier acceptability.

India should rely on people-to-people relations growing well. It is not right to regard the Bangladeshis as 'ungrateful'. When more direct contacts are established or facilitated, they feel genuinely touched.

The Migrants Issue—India shares Responsibility Dealing with illegal migrants from Bangladesh is not solely their responsibility. There is a security issue here, because insurgent groups like ULFA recruit new militants from the illegal entrants. There is tacit encouragement from our country to Bangladesh labour coming in to help in domestic employment, construction enterprises, and so on. Further, such immigrants, eventually being given voting rights, are used as vote-banks by our politicians. The issue of cattle smuggling is also contaminated by sectional Indian interests encouraging it for profit. We may note that, technically, cattle entering Bangladesh is not 'smuggled in', but something for which a duty is levied and paid. The demand for hides in India also contributes to the unsavoury network of interests which span both sides of the border. But in India, we have contrary interests which oppose the slaughter of cattle for food or leather, complicating a reasoned solution.

Recommendations

The speaker concluded with three recommendations:

Joint Business Ventures We should encourage the business community and the corporations to promote economic cooperation through joint enterprises with Bangladesh counterparts. This can be a very productive area.

Agriculture Another important area is agriculture. Bangladesh is endowed with fertile soil which can be cultivated for three crops a year. But the productivity of land is very low. India can impart its experience and technical knowledge to raise the output of food and other crops in Bangladesh.

Military to Military Links India should actively encourage closer professional links between our defence forces and those of Bangladesh in training and institute periodic consultations.

Discussion

Several interesting questions were raised in the discussion period.

Legitimization of Covert Cattle Trade To a question whether the trade that underlies the covert cattle smuggling problem could not be legalized, Sikri replied that it could be legitimized only if Indian states accept the reality of supply and demand factors and remove the ban on cow slaughter. It was deplorable that the current practice of the Indian parties in this trade involves maltreatment of the animals.

Social Indicators A view was expressed that Bangladesh had registered a respectable performance in both economic and social indicators. We should promote more cooperation in the garment sector for our mutual benefit.

Sikri responded that the improvement in social indicators has been mainly due to the work of NGOs, of which several had become suspect. One foreign NGO, for instance, was found to be covertly running an ordnance factory. In family planning, though some NGOs have done good work and there are no social taboos which impede its propagation, it is found that the birth rate in Bangladesh is again going up. The improved social and economic indicators have to be sustained over a longer term.

Connectivity—a Double-edged Sword A member of the audience asked if the connectivity we seek through Bangladesh to the states in the North-East is not a 'double-edged sword', in the sense that it may also help to legitimize Bangladesh-based militants using the new opening for their subversive actions against India.

Sikri agreed that it was difficult to exclude all misuse of the connectivity, but the advantages outweigh the danger, which we should try to minimize by vigilance.

China in Bangladesh The same member asked about China's involvement in Bangladesh and the steps India could take to limit it. Can India and Bangladesh cooperate towards this objective?

The former ambassador replied that in economic matters, under the new Bangladesh government, India expects a level playing field, such that Indian tenders for contracts and projects are not excluded for political reasons. There are big opportunities for securing contracts in infrastructure projects like the railways, with India having offered assistance of US $1 billion.

Cooperation in Energy Sector B. Raman reverted to the important issue of connectivity, which can be both favourable and unfavourable in its consequences. Since energy has priority for us, we should effectively persuade Bangladesh to let India, at least, explore the gas potential it enjoys, seeing that its government may award contracts to an American company. The Bangladesh refusal to permit a gas pipeline from Myanmar to India had an unhappy consequence for us: that Myanmar contracted to build a pipeline from Arakan (the origin of its gas reserve) to Yunnan in China. This is galling to us because the earlier prospecting was done by a consortium in which India was a partner. We should not romanticize our relations with any country when our national interests are at stake. It is true that connectivity is 'a double-edged sword', as was observed. India should aim to have a double option in case Sheikh Hasina loses power. Our government should not be over-dependent on her regime.

Sikri observed, in this context, that India should develop its own option, by building a pipeline through Indian territory (the Siliguri Corridor), albeit at a higher cost, but avoiding the need to pay transit and other charges annually to Bangladesh.

Conclusion and Suggestions

The seminar was both timely and instructive, with a common motif emerging; namely that India should be more aware of Bangladesh as a neighbour state, potentially a partner to be trusted in developing the entire Eastern region of India or a danger if its people, defence forces, and government turn emotionally or conspiratorially antagonistic towards India.

Importance of Bangladesh Bangladesh is too important and strategic a neighbour to slide off India's foreign policy radar. Its location next door to West Bengal makes Bangladesh crucial for the integration of the states in the North-East of India, which deserve a sense of fuller participation in the life and economic advancement of the Indian Union. Bangladesh, too, will benefit immensely from the expanded opportunities of a regional approach which encourages more enterprise, more investment, and more exchange among the countries and Indian States of the Eastern part of the subcontinent.

Follow-Up on the Hasina Visit India must earnestly follow up the leads offered by the bilateral talks and agreements during Sheikh Hasina's visit to New Delhi in January 2010. The positive and optimistic mood of the visit can be easily reversed or vitiated if the expectations on either side are disappointed by indifference, negativism, or bureaucratic obstacles. The main areas for India to act with a broad mind of helpfulness are economic, commercial, and technical; while, reciprocally, for Bangladesh, it is in the area of mutual security, in apprehending and frustrating externally directed jihad-terrorists, insurgents from the Indian side who have sheltered in Bangladesh, and 'wanted' criminals on both sides.

Military Cooperation Since the military continues to have an influential role in Bangladesh polity, both direct and indirect, India should step up its initiatives for professional and practical exchanges between the two defence establishments. We should allow time for some proposals to mature into acceptability by the other side, but if it is convinced of mutual regard and benefit, the way will be opened.

Bangladesh Foreign Relations In foreign policy, Bangladesh's contacts with China, Pakistan, the US, Myanmar, Russia, the EU, apart from Nepal, Bhutan, and South-East Asian countries must be a priority for us. If we find any security-related move that affects our interests, we should take appropriate action immediately, engaging Dhaka firmly but with traditional diplomacy. Regional groups present different problems and chances. Bangladesh has been active as a member of SAARC and is keen to play its part in BIMSTEC. India could discreetly consult and support Bangladesh when there is a converging interest. India could also support the initiative to locate the Secretariat of BIMSTEC in that country.

Tackling the Trans-border Traffic Issue Admittedly, there are no easy solutions to be sought in a short time for the pending problems of Bangladeshi migration into India, which is partly due to economic disparities, and the smuggling of cattle, drugs, and the trafficking in women and children. But these issues must be tackled, with greater responsibility being accepted by the Indian side. We cannot afford our border security to be cast in the role of enemies and killers by the common folk on the other side.

Chapter 6

India–Myanmar Relations

ASIA CENTRE BANGALORE
AND
THE INDIAN COUNCIL OF WORLD AFFAIRS

'Winds of Change across Myanmar: Strategic Implications for India'
Proceedings of the Joint Seminar
held on

June 9, 2012

Introduction

A seminar on 'Winds of Change across Myanmar: Strategic Implications for India' was held on June 9, 2012 at the IAS Officers' Institution in Bangalore. The seminar was jointly conducted by the Asia Centre Bangalore and the Indian Council of World Affairs, New Delhi, and was presided over by A.P. Venkateswaran, Chairman of Asia Centre and former Indian Foreign Secretary. The following distinguished speakers addressed the seminar:

Sanjay Pulipaka	Fellow at the Maulana Abul Kalam Azad Institute of Asian Studies (MAKAIAS), Kolkata
K. Yhome	Fellow of the Observer Research Foundation (ORF), New Delhi
General (Retd) V.P. Malik	Former Chief of the Army Staff
Eric Gonsalves	Former Ambassador and Secretary in the Ministry of Foreign Affairs
Rajiv Bhatia	Former Indian Ambassador in Myanmar

The presentations were followed by a question and answer session. The proceedings of the Seminar and the discussions that followed have been compiled by Arun Vishwanathan, Assistant Professor, International Strategic and Security Studies Programme at the National Institute for Advanced Studies, Bangalore and are given in the succeeding pages.

Opening Remarks by the Chairman The Chairman, Asia Centre, A.P. Venkateswaran, welcomed the speakers and the audience. He remarked that they had, before them, a distinguished panel of speakers. The subject matter was of special importance, as even before India became independent, we had the first Asian Relations Conference. There was emphasis on Asia, but somehow, after independence, despite the Non-Alignment movement, the focus shifted away from the Cold War to the big powers, with the unfortunate result that India gave less and less attention to our neighbours. The realization that our neighbours are more important to us than any big power farther away has become even more important now.

The subject of the day was Myanmar, with whom we had not had substantive relations over the past few decades due to various reasons, although at one time as Burma, it was part of British India.

Introduction of Speakers Vice-Admiral R.N. Ganesh, Director Asia Centre, informed the members that the seminar was being jointly conducted by the Indian Council of World Affairs (ICWA) and the Asia Centre Bangalore. He welcomed Malika Jain, Deputy Director of the Indian Council of World Affairs, who attended as the representative of the Director General, ICWA. The Director then introduced the speakers of the day.

Presentation 1: India Myanmar Relations—An Overview

Sanjay Pulipaka

Myanmar has witnessed rapid political changes in the recent past. The President, Thein Sein's government, which came to power after 2010 elections, initiated wide-ranging political reforms. By-elections were held in April 2012 and Aung San Suu Kyi's National League for Democracy (NLD) won a landslide victory. As a consequence of these developments, Myanmar, which had been treated as an international pariah until recently, witnessed a flurry of visits from various heads of state. The Indian Prime Minister, Manmohan Singh, held wide-ranging consultations with people from across the political spectrum during his visit to Myanmar. The governments of both countries have identified priority areas to enhance the relations between them. India is working to recalibrate and enhance its engagement with Myanmar.

India–Myanmar Relations: A Mixed Bag

India and Myanmar have strong historical ties. However, in colonial times, the British brought Indians to run the administrative apparatus in Myanmar and, over time, people of Indian origin became prominent in the economy as well. Myanmar had a substantial presence of People of Indian Origin (PIOs) before the Second World War. The resentment, then, grew among the Burmese that their employment and business opportunities were shrinking because of these 'outsiders'.

India and Myanmar signed a Treaty of Friendship in 1951 which committed them to 'everlasting peace and unalterable friendship'. In the early years, there was some similarity in their foreign policies, but the imposition of a military dictatorship in Burma in 1962 and the subsequent 'Burmanization' policies caused relations to break down. Myanmarese foreign policy diverged from India's with Myanmar withdrawing from the Non-Aligned Movement in 1979. But the need to combat the insurgencies in North-East India and in Northern Myanmar prompted the leadership on both the sides to stay engaged.

During the 1980s and early 1990s, India strongly supported the movement for democracy in Myanmar. Aung San Suu Kyi was given the Jawaharlal Nehru Award in 1993, causing anger in Yangon and a freeze in relations. The exchange of visits by senior foreign ministry officials in 1992 started a shift in India's Myanmar policy, and from the mid-1990s, India adopted a more nuanced approach to its relations with Myanmar, because of security, ethnic, economic, and geopolitical considerations.

Security and Economic Imperatives

Insurgencies and Ethnic Politics The realization that it needed cooperation from Myanmar to combat militancy in the North-East prompted India to engage the military regime. Insurgents from Nagaland and Manipur operated from across the border and the Indian government coordinated with the government of Myanmar to flush out militants.

Political Space for Ethnic Minorities While tackling insurgencies is a significant issue, there is also a need to reflect on other aspects such as the conceptualization of a political space along the border regions of India and Myanmar. There are cognate ethnic groups along the India–Myanmar border, some of whom have been demanding independent homelands.

Development of Northeast India India has been making efforts to enhance economic interactions with Myanmar and other South-East Asian countries as a part of the Look East Policy. According to Directorate General of Foreign Trade (DGFT) statistics, India's Trade with Myanmar in 2007–08 amounted to approximately 0.24 per cent of India's overall international trade. At the moment, we have a negative balance of trade with Myanmar. It should be noted that the trade figures between India and Myanmar do not reflect the true picture, as sometimes, trade is carried through Singapore in light of the artificial exchange rate of the Myanmar Kyat. Nonetheless, there is no denying the fact that India–Myanmar trade performance is below par. During the Indian Prime Minister's visit, there has been significant emphasis on issues relating to border areas. India is involved in developing infrastructure projects in Myanmar such as Kaladan multi-modal project and other oil and natural gas projects.

Promoting Democracy

As India scaled up its engagement with Myanmar, there was growing criticism that India has bartered its principles at the altar of the realist approach. India's engagement with Myanmar has been multi-dimensional, and it has been active in the realms of education and business training. India has set up several institutions such as the Myanmar–India Entrepreneurial Development Centre, the India–Myanmar Industrial Training Centre, and the Myanmar Centre for English Training. These institutions enhance capacities of the citizens of Myanmar in various fields such as entrepreneurship and basic skills required for industrial growth. In the recent past India has been training journalists from Myanmar, which few countries can claim credit for.

Approaches to Promoting Democracy There are two approaches to democracy promotion. There is the political approach, which focuses essentially on elections and procedural dimensions of democracy. And then, there is the developmental approach, which focuses on the pre-requisites of democracy such as plurality of civil society organizations and the capacities of the human resources to facilitate smooth transition processes. India's policy has been to adopt the developmental approach towards democracy promotion.

Treatment of PIOs The treatment of PIOs in Myanmar is an issue that needs to be handled with care. In contrast to the salience of the same issue with Pakistan, with Myanmar major shifts in relationships were negotiated without too much of an impact because relations between India and Myanmar never became hostage to the issue. For instance, during the recent Prime Minister's visit, media coverage pertaining to the PIOs in Myanmar has been sparse. It appears that there is some closure on Indian side on this issue. In Myanmar, the fear is still very real that 'outsiders' are usurping jobs and economic opportunities. This can be seen from the recent legislations that are being contemplated in Myanmar. As India seeks to engage with Myanmar, it must factor in such anxieties.

Increased Number of Political Players Second, unlike before, India will have to engage numerous actors. It will have to engage the military and also the members of the newly created parliament and the executive. At the moment, there are three major groups in Myanmar. The first is the Military and its political party the Union Solidarity and Development Party (USDP), the second is Daw Suu Kyi's National League for Democracy (NLD), and third is the group of ethnic parties which has emerged during the 2010 elections. Some of these parties have performed well in spite of severe constraints. The Shan Nationalities Development Party (SNDP) is emerging as a major political party. There are indications that the ethnic parties are planning to form an alliance at the national level and it is important that India keep an eye on the evolving ethnic politics in Myanmar, given the ethnic overlap in the North-East border region.

The China Factor Third, China has made strong in-roads into the political and economic landscape of Myanmar. Not only has China developed substantial networks (formal and informal) within Myanmar, but more importantly, the China–Myanmar border is extremely porous and some armed ethnic groups in Myanmar reportedly enjoy a comfortable relationship with China. If China–Myanmar relations deteriorate in the coming years, then China will be able to incite the rebel groups in Myanmar to protect its interests, with a deleterious impact on the security situation in the North-East, again given the ethnic overlap. On the other hand, the movement towards a more participatory political system of Myanmar represents a challenge for China in ideational terms. There is a belief that China is not merely supporting authoritarian countries for resources, but is also exporting the idea of separating democracy from capitalism (staying autocratic). Myanmar's successful evolution as liberal democratic country will have a widespread effect.

New Economic Competition in Myanmar Fourth, because of economic sanctions, India had found it relatively easy, thus far, to attract the attention of Myanmar's decisionmakers. With many countries either lifting sanctions or suspending sanctions, India will have to compete with many other powerful countries to promote Indian interests in Myanmar.

Opportunity to Scale up Democracy-building Assistance Finally, India can immediately scale up its democracy-building assistance to Myanmar by enhancing capacity building activities through Election Commission of India's new training institute 'India International Institute of Democracy and Election Management (IIIDEM).'

Presentation 2: India–Myanmar Trade including Border Trade—Overview and Prospects

K. Yhome

Introduction

The first section of this presentation provides an overview of India–Myanmar trade relations since independence of the two countries in the late 1940s. The second section deals with opportunities and challenges in India–Myanmar trade relations in the context of recent changes in Myanmar. This section also poses a couple of theoretical propositions with the hope that it will generate debate and discussion.

Trade Ties: An Overview

Early Trade Practice One of the first trade agreements between the two countries, signed in 1950, allowed the indigenous hill tribes of both countries living within 40 kilometres of the border to conduct trade through barter system. This informal trade, in the form of *melas* and *bazaars*, are organized even today, under the supervision of district administration and the para-military forces.

Nationalization Policy The nationalization measures initiated by the previous government under U Nu and Ne Win in the 1960s had a harsh impact, forcing over 200,000 Indian nationals to leave Myanmar.

After this, there was a general decline in trade between India and Myanmar, although several trade agreements were signed. The decline was caused by various factors which included: 1) Improvement of food production in India; 2) Economic policy of the Ne Win government in Myanmar; and 3) the emergence of new rice markets elsewhere.

Phase of Improvement Following General Ne Win's visit to India in January 1970, the two countries signed a trade agreement in the same year to expand trade and economic relations, and there was a steady increase in the bilateral trade for several years. After 1983, there was again a sharp increase in India's imports with a purchase of 3 million tons of Burmese rice besides pulses, timber, and gemstones. But India–Myanmar relations reached its nadir in 1988 as a result of India's strong position against the Myanmar military's brutal suppression of the pro-democracy uprising.

Impact of Look East Policy The Look East Policy in the early 1990s paved the way for improvement in relations with Myanmar's military regime and efforts were made to promote bilateral trade. Since then, India–Myanmar bilateral trade grew steadily through the 1990s to reach a level of US $570 million in 2005–06, US $920 million in 2006–07, and US $1.3 billion in 2010–11. India is now the fifth largest trade partner of Myanmar after Thailand, China, Hong Kong, and Singapore; the 4th largest export destination for Myanmar, and the 7th largest source of imports into Myanmar.

In October 2008, the United Bank of India signed a Memorandum of Understanding (MoU) with three Myanmar national banks to facilitate trade. In addition to this, a Bilateral Investment Promotion Agreement (BIPA) and a Double Taxation Avoidance Agreement (DTAA) were also signed in 2008. In the 4th JTC meeting held in New Delhi on September 27, 2011, both sides agreed to set up a Joint Trade and Investment Forum including both businessmen and government officials, which would meet along with the JTC.

Border Trade

As part of India's Look East Policy, the first formal border trade treaty was signed in January 1994 and border trade was officially opened on April 12, 1995, in which only 22 items were identified for barter trade, which was later increased and two more trading points opened.

India and Myanmar border trade is estimated at US $13.73 million in 2009–10. This figure would be much higher if informal trade, which flourishes at the border, is taken into account. A comparison of Myanmar's border trade with its neighbours in the same period will give a perspective on where India stands.

Country	Bilateral Trade	Border Trade
China	2.9 bn$	1.4 bn$
Thailand	3.6 bn$	275 mn$
Bangladesh	185 mn$	18.4 mn$
India	1.4 bn$	13.7 mn$

Border Trade below Potential India's border trade with Myanmar lags behind even Bangladesh, and is only 1.3 per cent of Sino–Myanmar border trade. China's border trade with Myanmar is equal to India's entire bilateral trade with that country.

Several issues have been raised by the governments of the North-Eastern states:

1) Conversion of Border trade to 'Normal Trade'—this was decided at the Joint Trade Committee meeting in 2008.
2) Increase in the number of items under barter trade mechanism.
3) Poor infrastructural facilities and trade facilitation measures.
4) Transit facility to India by Myanmar for movement of goods to other ASEAN nations.

Recent Initiatives

As far as trade ties are concerned, the recent visit of Prime Minister Manmohan Singh to Myanmar, has laid the foundation for strengthening and expanding trade between the two countries. Recent initiatives between India and Myanmar include the agreement to expand their economic cooperation, broad-base their trade basket, set a US $3 billion bilateral trade target to be achieved by 2015, and the construction of the Kaladan Multimodal Transit Transport Project by 2014. These steps are expected to transform trade between North-East India and Myanmar.

The MoUs on border area development and establishing of border 'haats' across the border between Myanmar and India during Prime Minister Singh's visit underscore the importance of the role of the local population, giving them a stake in the improvement of the bilateral relationship between the two neighbours.

The MoU on establishment of Joint Trade and Investment Forum will further strengthen interactions between business communities of the two countries. Both sides agreed to set the Forum in the 4th JTC meeting in 2011.

Transportation and Connectivity The other significant step taken during the Prime Minister's visit was in the field of transportation and connectivity between the two countries that will facilitate trade. The trilateral highway between India–Myanmar–Thailand has been given a major boost with India and Myanmar agreeing to make it a reality by 2016. Earlier, the Joint Task

Force on Trilateral Highway among India, Myanmar, and Thailand was revived. The decision to repair and upgrade bridges and roads would finally help to establish trilateral connectivity from Moreh in India to Mae Sot in Thailand, via Myanmar.

The steps taken to facilitate 'business friendly-banking transactions' through the establishment of a representative of the Union Bank of India in Myanmar and 'currency arrangement' to allow payments in local currency will remove major problems faced by traders between the two countries.

During the Prime Minister's visit, India and Myanmar have also agreed to have an MoU between Reserve Bank of India and Central Bank of Myanmar to allow payments in local currency.

Myanmar's Finance Measures Myanmar's recent economic reforms will also help bilateral trade between India and Myanmar. As part of the economic reforms, President Thein Sein's government has overhauled the complex exchange rate system in April 2012 and Central Bank of Myanmar has set a new exchange rate of 818 Kyats per 1 US dollar. In May 2012, a new investment law was finalized. Under the new law, foreign companies are allowed to set up in Myanmar without local partners. Earlier, foreign companies were required to partner with a local company and the multiple exchange rates were major source for problems.

Hangover of the Nationalization The 1960s nationalization policy of Myanmar had a deep impact on the business community in India. For many years it created a mental block for Indian businessmen to do business in Myanmar. This feeling seems to have gradually been overcome by the Indian business community.

The Way Ahead—Leveraging strengths

Sub-Regional Groupings India needs to leverage its strengths in Myanmar. It shares long land and maritime boundaries with Myanmar, and both have been involved in a number of regional cooperative frameworks with neighbouring countries, including the Bay of Bengal Initiative for Multi-Sectoral Technical and Economic Cooperation (the BIMSTEC), the Mekong-Ganga Cooperation and the Forum of Bangladesh, China, India, and Myanmar (BCIM). These sub-regional groupings have been established with the intention of strengthening relationships and to promote development and mutual benefits. They aim to integrate systems and allow free flow of goods, services, investment, capital, and skilled labour. In addition, with the implementation of India–ASEAN FTA and India's Duty Free Tariff Preference Scheme for LDCs, expectations are high that these initiatives will boost bilateral trade.

Indian Diaspora and PIOs There are a large number of people of Indian origin in Myanmar. According to the 1983 official census of Myanmar, the number of PIOs in Myanmar was a little under half a million and the stateless PIOs about a quarter million. A section of Indian businessmen in Myanmar have been pushing the two governments for increased economic relationship. Indian businessmen obviously want to exploit the opportunities offered by Myanmar and should be helped by India to further strengthen trade ties between the two countries.

Revisit Old ways of Thinking There is a need to revisit some of the old ways of thinking. 1) Give consideration to 'Constituent diplomacy', which is the 'participation of regional and local governments in foreign policy and affairs'. According to the constituent diplomacy paradigm, the provincial governments have a prominent role in the making of foreign economic policy. 2) The second notion is, to consider if there is a need to expand the civilian space over military and the legal space over illegal. The basic point of argument here is that all key stakeholders should play an active role in the process of foreign policy making, thus giving them a stake in regional diplomacy, as these decisions directly impact them.

Relook at 'Borderland Discourse' Apart from removing the restrictions and improving infrastructure, there is a need to relook at the whole borderland discourse which is dominated largely by the 'security' paradigm, where the civilian space is marginalized. The role of the local population needs to be expanded in all border activities.

Conclusion

The importance of trade as a component in India–Myanmar relations will continue to grow. India's increased interest in trade with ASEAN nations and East Asia will continue to push India to strengthen ties with Myanmar for greater trade links. For India, trade ties are seen as one of the major factors that drive its relations with Myanmar, and for Myanmar, it is important because it also helps in reducing its dependence on China and Thailand.

Presentation 3: Past, Present and Future of Indo–Myanmar Relations from the Perspective of India's National Security

General (Retd) V.P. Malik

Introduction

India and Myanmar share a 1,600-kilometre long land border with four of India's North-Eastern states.

Myanmar has a land border with four other countries in South and South-East Asia, including China. One-third of its total perimeter of 1,930 km forms an uninterrupted coastline along the Bay of Bengal and Andaman Sea. During Second World War, Japanese forces invaded Myanmar. They were able to reach Imphal and Kohima on land, and were able to make their presence felt in the Bay of Bengal before they were forced to withdraw by Indian forces.

Early History

In the 17th century, several Meitei rulers from Manipur would raid Burmese areas right up to the Irrawaddy River. And when the Mandalay Empire under King Bodawpaya became strong, it annexed Manipur in 1814 and part of Assam in 1817. It was the second largest empire in Burmese history, but also one with a long, ill-defined border with British India. The breadth of this empire, however, was short lived. Myanmar lost Arakan, Manipur, and Assam to the British in the First Anglo-Burmese War in 1824–26.

Myanmar was colonized by Britain following three Anglo–Burmese Wars (1824–1885). In 1886, British made it a province of India. This arrangement lasted until 1937 when they decided to administer it separately. Myanmar achieved its independence from the British rule on January 4, 1948.

Post-Colonial Period

India's relations with Myanmar, which started on a cordial note in 1948, went into a headlong dive when the latter came under the revolutionary council headed by General Ne Win in the early 1960s. His relentless persecution of 'resident aliens' (immigrant groups not recognized as citizens of the Union of Myanmar) led to an exodus of some 3,00,000 Burmese Indians. The uneasy Indo–Myanmar relations were exploited by secessionist Naga, Manipuri, and Mizo groups to establish ethnic sanctuaries and training camps in Myanmar, across the mountainous and heavily forested porous border. Large numbers of Naga insurgents, in hundreds, would go to Yunnan (China) for training and supply of weapons and equipment.

Cross-Border Movements A few important points need to be noted when we consider cross-border movement of insurgents along the Indo–Myanmar border.

1) The writ of the Myanmar Government in North and West Myanmar is weak. Myanmar armed forces (the Tatmadaw) do not have the capacity to take proactive military action (here and elsewhere) to put down insurgencies in the manner we can do.
2) Despite large scale deployment of regular and para-military troops inside Arunachal Pradesh, Nagaland, Manipur, and Mizoram, and better surveillance along Indo–Myanmar border, it is extremely difficult to eliminate cross-border movement of small groups of secessionist elements.
3) India and Myanmar have traditionally allowed tribals from both sides to travel freely up to 16 kilometres and purchase necessities from local *haats* as per an old treaty.
4) The pernicious *Inner Line* permit regime has now become an obstacle in proper integration of Border States in our North-East.

China–Myanmar Relations in Recent Past

China and Myanmar have had several border disputes dating long before the British annexation of Myanmar. The last border dispute culminated in 1956, when People's Liberation Army invaded northern Myanmar. That was repulsed. A border agreement—along the extension of McMahon Line—was reached in 1960, which enabled substantial improvement in relations between the two countries. In the absence of any other regional power, Chinese influence in Myanmar increased substantially. Many Sino–Burmese were influenced by the Cultural Revolution in China and began to wear Mao badges. In June 1967, due to increasing number of ethnic Chinese students supporting Mao by carrying the Quotations from Chairman Mao books, large scale anti-Chinese riots broke out in Myanmar. Shops and homes were ransacked and burned. The Chinese government started a war of words but no other actions were taken. The anti-Chinese riots continued till early 1970s.

Cessation of Support to Myanmar Communists After some time, China withdrew support to the Communist Party of Myanmar and began to supply weapons and equipment to the military junta in exchange for greater access to Myanmar markets. As a result, the military junta of Myanmar became even more reliant on China for their high level of power.

I must also state that during this period, partly due to post-1962 China phobia in India, and because large scale military invasions across international borders were still considered possible, India's intelligence and security agencies used to take Chinese military threat through Northern Myanmar quite seriously.

India's Myanmar Policy Shift

Ideology to the Fore—Security on the Back Burner In the next two decades, due to Myanmar's long years of stringent military rule and isolation, and our own ideology-based policies, Yangon drew more close to Beijing for political and economic support and for military weapons, equipment and training. China developed road communications, and trade links from Yunnan (China) into North Myanmar. That caused a heavy influx of Chinese immigrants (approximately 1.5 million) and their socio-economic influence, right up to Irrawaddy River. India's secessionist groups from North-East India continued to operate from their safe sanctuaries in North-West Myanmar. Gun-running and drug traffic from the Golden Triangle into North-East India by land and sea routes increased substantially. During this period, India's security concerns took a back seat and ideology took the front seat. As the only economic and defence hardware partner, Beijing got a huge strategic and economic advantage over India.

*Change to **Realpolitik*** The credit for changing the ethics-based policy to *realpolitik* in Indo–Myanmar relations goes to the governments of P.V. Narasimha Rao and Atal Bihari Vajpayee. They realized that without diplomatic relations and cooperation with Myanmar, it would be impossible to control insurgencies and bring about stability in our North-Eastern states, or to pursue India's Look East Policy. Besides, the fast growing balance of power and influence of China in India's immediate neighbourhood and South-East Asia, our long term political and economic interests required a constructive policy in the East. By now, encouraged by China, Pakistan too had established military-to-military contacts with Myanmar and began to supply some arms and ammunition. These imperatives made it necessary to engage with the Myanmar military regime. India's national security concerns thus guided New Delhi's *realpolitik* and change of attitude towards Yangon.

Border Trade and Drug Trafficking Control Agreement In March 1993, Foreign Secretary J.N. Dixit visited Yangon and signed a bilateral agreement to control drug trafficking and border trade.

Military Diplomacy

Paving the Way In 1999, several proposals on Indo–Myanmar cooperation were under consideration but there was limited progress due to lack of political contacts. The Prime Minister, Vajpayee, and National Security Advisor (NSA) Brajesh Mishra then decided to utilize military diplomacy to supplement India's foreign policy. Shyam Saran, Ambassador (and later Foreign Secretary), proposed to the Myanmar military government that General Malik, then Chief of Army Staff and Chairman, Chiefs of Staff Committee, have a 'quiet' meeting with General Maung Aye, then Vice-Chairman, Government of Myanmar, Deputy C-in-C, Armed Forces, and C-in-C, Myanmar Army. This would lead to his inviting Maung Aye and some Myanmar ministers (mostly military officers) for a meeting with ministers from India.

Indian Military Delegation flies to Mandalay On January 5, 2000, General Malik left for Imphal in an Air Force aircraft along with a small tri-service delegation. They were received at Mandalay by Maung Aye and almost the entire Myanmar cabinet (mostly Generals). Shyam Saran, the Ambassador, was at hand.

Personal Discussions with General Maung Aye Over the next 48 hours, besides a formal meeting, dinner, visit to nearby military institutes (in Pyin Oo Lwin), and local sightseeing, the Indian Army Chief had several one-on-one discussions with Maung Aye. They discussed the need to enlarge Indo–Myanmar military cooperation to include greater border contacts, passing of real time information and coordinated operations against insurgents on both sides of the border. He also apprised him of training programmes and military equipment that we could offer. The need to expedite planning and implementation of civil projects, already accepted in principle by our two countries, and widening diplomatic exchanges were also discussed. Maung Aye and his colleagues did not speak about China but their keenness on increasing civil and military ties with India was quite apparent.

Return Visit by Myanmar Delegation On January 8, the respective delegations in separate aircrafts flew to Shillong via Gauhati. The Air Force gave a guard of honour to the visiting Vice-Chairman of Myanmar. Maung Aye and his delegation met the Union Minister of Commerce and Industry and the Union Minister for Power, and civil officials from several ministries who had flown in from New Delhi.

Coordinated Action against Insurgents When Maung Aye left Shillong, the Indian Army gave him a map marked with locations of hostile Naga gangs in North Myanmar and asked him to get them raided by Myanmar Army. A fortnight later, these camps were raided and destroyed. When the insurgents attempted to run across the boundary into India, they were ambushed by our troops and suffered more casualties.

Formal Visit to Myanmar In April 2000, the Indian Army Chief was invited by the Government of Myanmar; this time more formally. He met the Chairman, General Than Shwe and other leaders. Their cooperation by this time had extended well beyond insurgents' cross-border activities. It included mutually beneficial infrastructure projects, offer of seats in Indian technical and military institutions, participation in Indian Navy's Exercise Milan in the Bay of Bengal, border trade, and several other diplomatic issues.

Coco 'Elint' Base On this occasion, General Malik also raised the issue of the much rumoured Chinese surveillance base in Coco Island (just North of Andaman and Nicobar Islands in the Bay of Bengal) to monitor Indian Naval as well as ISRO and DRDO missile and space launch activities. This was firmly denied by Maung Aye. He offered him a visit to the Coco Island, if he wanted to go.

Need to Counter China's Growing Influence On the delegation's return, the Army Chief informed Vajpayee that notwithstanding national or international unpopularity, the Myanmar military regime was likely to remain in the saddle for many years. China had gained marked socio-economic influence, particularly in North and North-East Myanmar. Unless we made efforts, this influence would extend to the West of Irrawaddy River and in the South. The Myanmar Government was keen to improve relations with India in the fields of economic development and technology, which ought to be reciprocated.

The Nuclear Threat

In 2007, Russia and Myanmar signed a controversial Nuclear Research Centre deal. According to some reports, this Centre was to comprise a 10 MW light-water reactor working on 20 per cent enriched uranium-235, an activation analysis laboratory, a medical isotope production laboratory, silicon doping system, nuclear waste treatment and burial facilities. This report was followed up by some more reports in 2009 that Myanmar, with assistance from North Korea, was working to develop nuclear weapons by 2014. This became a major cause of concern for the world, particularly in India. Later, these reports which had originated from two high-ranking defectors settled in Australia, were found to be baseless. Incidentally, Myanmar is a member of the International Atomic Energy Agency (IAEA) since 1957, and a signatory of the nuclear non-proliferation pact since 1992. The military junta had informed the IAEA in September 2000 of its intention to construct the Research Centre.

Present Relations

In the last 12 years, despite criticism from several domestic and Western quarters, Indo–Myanmar relations have travelled a long way. A steady stream of high level civil and military visits from both sides has enhanced dialogue and trust, and also created mutually beneficial opportunities.

Infrastructure Projects India is involved in a host of infrastructure and energy projects in Myanmar. It has built a 160 km long Tamu–Kalewa–Kalemyo Road across the Manipur border. It is building a 1200 MW hydel project on Chindwin River. Besides, it has provided high speed data link to many cities. Indian firms are working to develop Myanmar's railway network, including supply of coaches and locos. The Kaladan Multimodal Transit Transport Project and the Rhi–Tiddim projects now under the anvil, and will, when completed, have a major economic impact in the region. It can transform India's North-East and bordering region. Development of Sittwe port will allow our North-Eastern states to access the port and reduce India's transportation dependency on the security sensitive Siliguri corridor.

Naval exercises Early this year, Myanmar was part of a 14-nation joint naval exercise with India in the Bay of Bengal aimed at combating piracy and terrorism. The stability of Straits of Malacca remains a key concern for the economies of Asia–Pacific including India and Myanmar. China too, remains worried about the US naval presence in the region. It views its trans-Myanmar Shwe pipeline project as a possible solution to its Malacca dilemma.

The Future

Insurgency—The First Priority From the national security point of view, India's first priority is to work jointly with Myanmar to settle ethnic insurgencies in India's North-East and North Myanmar. This was stated in the joint statement issued after the Indian PM's meeting in May 2012 with Thein Sein. They reaffirmed their commitment to fight terrorism and insurgent activity, which included the commitment that the territories of either country would not be allowed to be used for activities by terrorists and insurgent organizations against the other. In this context, security cooperation between the two countries needs to be upgraded by establishing more frequent border meetings, actionable information sharing, joint patrolling (when necessary), and cooperation on border management. Economic and social development in the region will pay security dividends for India as well as Myanmar.

Myanmar Ceasefire Agreements with Ethnic Groups The Myanmar government has been able to negotiate ceasefire agreements with most groups. Its negotiations with various groups address the issue of an inclusive political architecture. The inclusive political structure would be helpful for India's national security concerns.

Further Scope for Security Cooperation India and Myanmar should also enhance cooperation in maritime security, particularly in combating piracy, terrorism, gun-running, and for security of respective island territories. This would require bilateral and multinational arrangements and training. India, being the largest nation in the region, can take the lead to extend assistance for this purpose to Myanmar's naval and coast guard establishments. This would help check further expansion of Chinese maritime activities in the Bay of Bengal.

Energy Security Myanmar has 2.54 trillion cubic meters of natural gas reserves and the largest copper mines in Asia. India's public and private sectors investing in Myanmar's undeveloped secondary and tertiary sectors like educational, telecom, and healthcare systems will enable binding relationship that can change the economic character of North-Eastern India.

India Need not Attempt to Supplant China in Myanmar In the General's reckoning, there was little chance of India becoming an alternative to China in Myanmar. It would be in India's interest to focus on areas West of Irrawaddy River, and South, to strengthen bilateral relations through 'trade and investment links, development of border areas, improving connectivity and building capacity and human resource'. Through interdependent social and economic relations we need to make Myanmar sensitive to our security requirements and neutralize Chinese influence in this region.

Coordinated Approach in Multilateral Forums Considering that the ASEAN countries are not very comfortable with the idea of enhanced cooperation in defence and security due to the China factor, India and Myanmar can coordinate their approaches on the issue of cooperation in ASEAN, in which India has summit level relations, the ASEAN Regional Forum, ASEAN Defence Ministers' Meeting (ADMM+), BIMSTEC, and SAARC, where Myanmar has an observer status.

Conclusion–The Benefits of Pragmatism Since independence, India has tended to neglect its East, within and outside its national boundaries. In the West, despite irrational hostility towards us, we have maintained a comprehensive diplomatic dialogue with Pakistan's military dictators. In the East, despite historical and cultural relations and important geo-strategic interests, India shied away from a substantive dialogue with military rulers. It needs to be reiterated that strategy and diplomacy in international relations is based not on sentiments but the art of possible and the advancement of national interests. Kautilya had stated,'When the interests of the country are involved, ethics are a burdensome irrelevance'. India is now on the right side of history, and pragmatism displayed in the 1990s may bear fruit and reduce the gap between *realpolitik* and sentiment. Another lesson that India has learnt from this experience is the utility of military diplomacy to supplement our foreign policy endeavours.

Presentation 4: Myanmar Relations and the Look East Policy

Eric Gonsalves

Gonsalves, the Ambassador, began by thanking the Chairman for the opportunity to present his view at the meeting today. He said that he would be talking from a broader perspective as he was also the Convenor of the Indian Group of the BCIM. His talk would be a commentary about our Look East Policy, about which he felt we talk a lot but do very little.

Gonsalves recalled that when he had been a Secretary, he was able to get an invitation for India to the ASEAN dialogue, but that did not materialize. In retrospect, the prospect of India becoming a genuine dialogue partner in 1980 was bleak, as first, it would put us in a cold war context between Indo-China and South-East Asia. Secondly, the state of our economy did not give us the capacity to be a dialogue partner. However, 10 years later when Narasimha Rao became the Prime Minister, he initiated the Look East Policy (LEP) and we became a dialogue partner with ASEAN.

The Speaker felt that we had been slow to respond to changes. India had been making big statements and has not acted on them. There has been an inexorable march by China through and down into South-East Asia and we have not either measured it or coped with it.

Against this backdrop, the speaker and a few others responded to an invitation from the Yunnan province of China to set up the BCIM forum in 1999. The initiative was slow to take off; initially it was mainly a low-key talk shop. This is blamed on India's insistence on keeping its presence on

Track II, though actually there was lack of clarity on the part of the Chinese, who felt this would be better done by an intra-government organization. The Indian establishment, which preferred BIMSTEC, was always suspicious about Chinese intentions. Connectivity is the key to regional cooperation and development across the region, but is still seen by some as inimical to India's security. He recalled that Ambassador Ranganathan, had worked very hard to get the BCIM Forum organized in its initial years. After toiling for a decade, at the forum's last meeting in Kolkata, the forum members are beginning to see some of the possible results of what they could do.

In South-East Asia, India has to be able to work partly with and partly in competition with the Chinese. There is no choice. The countries there are so dependent economically on China, that they do not want to be in a position to make a choice between India and China. None cares to take sides in a Sino–India rivalry as China gives these countries markets for their goods, projects, loans, and so on. However, recently these countries are beginning to realize that the Chinese support comes at a price. It has recently shown itself as a somewhat predatory neighbour, and the region would like to encourage some balancing factors. That should be made into our opportunity.

The speaker expressed conviction that engagement with China was a necessary engagement. It would not be a totally negative engagement, nor would it be a totally positive engagement. But it illustrated the new paradigm of security which we needed to understand. In earlier times, building borders was seen as the best way of ensuring one's security. This is not so today in the interdependent world where one has to deal with one's neighbour. He felt that India is slow to react again as cooperation and cross-border facilitation are not easily reconciled with state interests and security concerns.

Gonsalves continued that the Chinese did want to be the dominant power in the region, but their thrust was broad-based and they placed considerable emphasis on economic penetration. They had successfully used exports of cheap manufactured goods, raw material imports, and joint projects for this. Their growing military capacity is taken seriously. Lately they have also begun a drive using soft power. North-East India is in their sights. But more than only increasing defence capacity, India has to buttress its position there with more stable political regimes and establish much greater economic capacity that would be able to repel the Chinese economic onslaught, and project its economic prowess into South-East Asia and even into South-West China. This would require the fast-forwarding of connectivity in that whole region. Transport links into Myanmar to ASEAN would also connect inevitably to the neighbouring areas of China, and there is reason to believe that they would not be unwelcome there, as those provinces do not relish depending solely on the routes via Chinese Pacific ports, as for centuries they relied on the ports at the mouths of the Irrawaddy and Ganga Rivers.

For the future it was doubtful if we had any alternative to cooperating and competing with China in this region, and elsewhere in the world. To do this it would be useful to look at the experience from the European and ASEAN experience. To put aside deep mistrust in Europe and between ASEAN and Indo–China, the countries involved opened up to each other while also maintaining and upgrading their own security and intelligence apparatus. The Helsinki and ASEAN processes of detente, said the speaker, have lessons for us.

On our Eastern border we had to expand infrastructure, connectivity, and economic cooperation, while at the same time ensuring security, mainly by upgrading intelligence rather than relying on more massive force deployments. The new paradigm will be more complex than those we have used till now.

ESCAP has already gained international approval on paper for a Trans-Asian road and rail network. It is far from implementation. Wherever we wish to connect, Myanmar territory has to be crossed. Projects could be bilateral or multilateral.

The Sittwe–Kaladan project to provide port access for our North-East is an example of the former and needs to be expedited. The Tamu–Moreh road to Mandalay and the old Stilwell road from Pangsau Pass to Myktina and thence to Mandalay and Kunming are examples of the latter.

Gonsalves said that there was an urgent need for dynamism and drive in implementation of policies, giving the proper priority to national interests over populist politics. Policy paralysis is more marked in external relations. There has to be coordination between the Centre and the states for proper implementation. Our vision of future commerce cannot be based on barter and border trading of local produce, but we have to embrace concepts such as Most Favoured Nation relations.

A basic need for the LEP is a robust endorsement from the Eastern region including the West Bengal government, and the urgent build-up of the economy and the infrastructure in the North-Eastern states. The States need to understand and take on their share of the massive effort that will be needed. The recent experiences in preparing for the BCIM Forum in Kolkata gave no ground for optimism.

The situation in Myanmar has changed radically now and many avenues have opened up with the PM's visit. The economies of India and Myanmar are so complementary that there is almost a text-book case for cooperation. They have surplus energy which we can help develop and extract. As an electricity grid is developed across our North-East, Bangladesh, Nepal, and Bhutan, we can envisage weaving many forms of energy across the region to mutual benefit. Myanmar could benefit from parallel development of water resources too, as a lower riparian state. The speaker mentioned a number of areas where there was potential for cooperation in agriculture and food processing. Collaboration in manufacturing, IT, and other services should also be considered. Education and health and other social and cultural sectors could be fruitful sources of cooperation.

Presentation 5: India–Myanmar Policy Recommendations

Rajiv Bhatia

Introduction

Bhatia began by thanking the Chairman, Asia Centre, and ICWA for designing this event and the panellists for the rich feast of analyses, ideas, and concepts which have thrown a lot of light on this very complex subject.

The speaker said that the fact that Aung San Suu Kyi (Daw Suu Kyi) is an important player in the entire debate and in strategizing about Myanmar is often overlooked in the drive to be objective. *Realpolitik* is crucial and its importance cannot be overstressed, but as human beings we still believe that there is a place for values, principles, and ethics, and this cannot be overlooked.

When viewed in the context of the failures of Myanmar's army and its generals to solve the problems of the country and its people, keeping these values and principles in mind becomes more important. Also, the entire change happening in Myanmar began with the current President Thein Sein meeting Daw Suu Kyi on August 19, and developing a certain accommodation which has unleashed the ongoing changes in the country.

Transition in Myanmar

The primary reason behind the ongoing transition in Myanmar is the fact that the thinking in Tatmadaw (Myanmar's military) changed. Bhatia said that to understand the current change, we had to remember that unlike Ne Win, subsequent generals never wanted to remain in power permanently. Even Than Shwe and his top Generals saw themselves as a transitional authority. The problem was that the manner in which the generals wanted to bring in change was not amenable to the political class.

Thus, when the Road Map to Democracy was announced in 2003, Myanmar's Foreign Minister said it was a seven-stage road map but it would not take seven years; but in reality it did take seven years to allow democracy to come in. The younger Generals began to feel from 2006 onwards that Myanmar's prosperity and economic power had taken a huge hit. This was also the time around which the US began opening up to Myanmar. After the Obama administration took over, there was a series of consultations beginning in 2009 and early 2010, which laid the foundations for the US Secretary of State Hillary Clinton's visit to the country.

Slowly, a *modus vivendi* emerged that if Myanmar wanted to get out of its economic morass and also address its fears of excessive dependence on China, the way to go forward was to open up to the West. The easiest way to do this, the Generals realized, was to make use of Daw Suu Kyi who had been under house arrest for 15 of the past 22 years. Thus, in essence, the change Myanmar is seeing today is the result of a triangular understanding between the Myanmar's generals, the NLD of Daw Suu Kyi, and Washington. Thus, when Obama decided to send the US Secretary of State after consulting Daw Suu Kyi, it signalled a momentous shift which had been successful because there had been sufficient dialogue and understanding between all the three parties involved in the process.

As a result of the change, the western media, especially, draws the conclusion that everything is changed and hunky dory, and democracy has arrived; this has resulted in a rush of VIP visits to Myanmar. But if we ask whether democracy has really arrived in Myanmar, the answer is 'No.' Real democracy would have been if the NLD had been given power in 1990 when it had 80 per cent seats in the Parliament, which was never convened. Today, the NLD has only 6 per cent seats in the Parliament; this was a very peculiar kind of power-sharing. Very clearly, change was taking place as per the script written by Tatmadaw. And this script did not seem to involve full-blooded democracy, but a 'managed' or 'guided' democracy.

The speaker said that another question we needed to ponder is how would the 2015 elections be: would they be like the 2010 elections in which the NLD were not allowed to take part? Or more like the by-elections of 2012 in which the NLD was allowed to take part and Daw Suu Kyi swept the polls, getting 96 per cent of the seats? But whether the military would have the gumption to organize completely free and fair elections was a big question. Thus, it was safe to say that the transition was not over yet.

India's Myanmar Policy

The development of India's Myanmar policy can be viewed in five phases: 1988–91, 1991–99, 2000–11, and the latest (current) stage.

First Phase (1988-91) The first phase was very clearly India's pro-democracy phase.

Second Phase (1991-99) In 1991, Daw Suu Kyi was awarded the Nobel Prize and India's congratulatory message was elaborate and warm. But by end of 1991-1992 Narasimha Rao was in charge, and the visit of the Director General of the Myanmar Foreign Office to New Delhi reciprocated by the Foreign Secretary Dikshit's visit to Myanmar. This signalled the beginning of the engagement with the military.

The beginning was tentative as there was and still is a strong lobby in India which was pro-democracy. On one hand, we entered into a border trade agreement but, on the other hand, gave the Nehru award to Daw Suu Kyi.

Third Phase (2000-2011) From the year 2000, though India did not give up its dual track policy, under that garb it started focusing on engaging the military.

Current Phase (2011 -) Now, starting with the end of 2011 with the Prime Minister's visit, we were seeing yet another phase of India's Myanmar policy. The present attempt is to deal with the military and do everything possible to take the relationship forward. It was also very important to remember that for the first time, an Indian Prime Minister had gone on record and said 'the People of India stand ready to support a stable, democratic, and prosperous Myanmar.' This is a good policy to adopt as it neither turns a blind eye to the prospects of democracy, nor does it unnecessarily annoy the military, which would remain in power.

Prime Minister's Visit

With regard to the Prime Minister's visit, it has two important aspects. First was the statement in which he singled out Myanmar to stress that it had a special place in India's Look East Policy. Secondly, he also said that Myanmar could play the role of a bridge between India and China and between South Asia and South-East Asia. Though, at the operational level we might still run into some troubles, the words of the Prime Minster would be very useful in guiding India's policy forward.

Though the Prime Minister's visit has come after a gap of 25 years, it should not be seen as an indicator of neglect of India's relations with Yangon—the visit should be viewed from the point that it arose from a conscious decision—was timely, carefully designed, and produced substantial gain. The long-term impact of the visit, however, will depend at least on three factors: First, the fate of

President–Suu Kyi relations; second, New Delhi's ability to operate in a more competitive environment; and third, our ability to deliver on commitments made to Yangon.

In the bilateral context, both political and economic facets are important and deserve to be studied carefully. Regional dimensions are both multiple and complex. A few pointers:

1) The full potential of sub-regional cooperation needs to be appreciated and exploited through existing mechanisms, especially BCIM and BIMSTEC.
2) The implications of Myanmar enjoying a special place in our LEP must be spelt out and understood more widely.
3) So far, LEP has been managed with very little reference to our North-East region and our relations with Bangladesh and Myanmar. It is time, as pointed out during Manmohan Singh's visit, to refocus and integrate them.
4) In the larger context of US–China 'strategic contest', it is imperative for India to be clear-headed about its policy. New Delhi wants regional cooperation, but we should have alternatives in case China does not play by the rules and seeks dominance. We should have a credible insurance through a network of relationships, our own necklace of diamonds against their string of pearls!

Policy Options and Recommendations

Looking to the future, it is important to begin an annual bilateral summit with Myanmar at the political or institutional level. A joint commission should be set up at Ministerial level. The provincial leadership should be brought in appropriately. Parliament should be engaged more proactively. It is also important to discover an ideal formula to deal with the Suu Kyi phenomenon; this would be crucial for the future of bilateral relations between New Delhi and Yangon.

In the defence and security sphere, it would be important to nurture ties with Tatmadaw through clear-headed action, not words. A realistic measure of the problem of cross-border insurgency and its contributing factors had to be taken. The Regional Border Committee should be utilized fully. It is also important to craft a strategy to address maritime challenges in Bay of Bengal, especially near the Myanmar coast.

On the economic front, it is imperative to focus on implementation and on motivating Indian corporate to play a greater role. Other actors like media and strategic community, civil society, and wielders of soft power must contribute to re-building of relations with Myanmar and the region instead of leaving everything to South Block.

Bhatia ended with stating his view that finally in order to take our Myanmar policy forward, it would be crucial to coordinate thinking and action with select partners in ASEAN and the West.

Discussions

The following points were brought up during the discussions:

The issue of the relationship between the Military and Aung San Suu Kyi is most important. If the relationship worsens, it will definitely have an adverse impact on the current transition that is going on in Myanmar. The recent foreign trips by Daw Suu Kyi have not been particularly liked by the military elite.

It is important to see the current opening up by Myanmar as a process and not an end in itself. The process will go on until the 2015 elections and the role that the military plays then.

The Myanmar nuclear issue also came up for discussion, but it was pointed out that Myanmar as stated by its Defence Minister during the recent Shangri-La Dialogue, is not interested in nuclear power, weapons or any related technology.

Conclusion

India and Myanmar have a long history, which is not to say that they have always been cordial or friendly. During the Colonial period the British used Indian administrators to manage Burma as a province of India, and this certainly did not make the Indians very popular in that country.

India's relations with Myanmar underwent several changes after the early post-Independence years. Both countries were partners in the non-aligned movement and acted in close concert in international matters. A chill descended on the relationship with the 1962 military coup in Burma and this was followed by a long period of stagnation in India's relations with that country.

India did not endear itself to Myanmar's junta by its active support to the democracy movement in Myanmar. We chose the moral high ground, which, of course, did nothing to promote our own interests and only propelled Myanmar into the Chinese embrace. Myanmar returned the favour by supporting insurgency in India's North-East.

In the early 1990s, a welcome dose of pragmatism was added to our Myanmar policy and relations gained some positive energy. There has, however, always been the feeling that more can be done to exploit the potential that exists in a wide spectrum of areas—trade, technical cooperation, cultural relations, infrastructural aid, and military cooperation. Our past policies have resulted in our being strategically outflanked by a major inimical power and this situation must be redressed.

Recent changes in Myanmar have far exceeded the expectations of even the most optimistic observers. Myanmar has a civilian President after a long time, and steps appear to have been initiated to ease the military grip on the polity. It would be hasty to welcome the advent of true democracy in Myanmar—to quote Daw Aung San Su Kyi—'The world loves a happy ending, but there is a long way to go.'

Whatever the pace or success of the transition, there is a clear need for India to remain ahead of the curve in what might be the beginning of a major transformational process; we must assume a leading place in Myanmar's foreign policy calculus. Western leaders who were on the brink of imposing additional sanctions on Myanmar are now vying with each other to patch up relations with Naypyidaw. India cannot afford to merely follow the West's lead. Myanmar is of great strategic significance to us for a number of reasons, the chief of them being the need to strengthen the North-Eastern ramparts.

The measures that need to be taken are not difficult to determine. Primarily, these relate to increasing the bilateral trade by both widening and deepening the commercial relationship. There is also great scope for undertaking major projects in infrastructure, the manufacturing industry, and in medicine and pharmaceuticals. Our cultural ties and interaction can be increased to bring the countries closer.

Defence relations are of particular importance in the Myanmar context. Both countries are plagued with insurgencies and cooperation in this area will be of mutual benefit.

As with other smaller neighbours, there is little knowledge about Myanmar or interest in that country in the Indian media, cultural, or business circles. The speakers have all made several eminently implementable proposals in their respective presentations. What is needed is for India to get down to the task in all earnestness, and not be outflanked at our own doorstep, of which there is a definite risk.

Chapter 7

India–US Relations

ASIA CENTRE BANGALORE
AND
THE INDIAN COUNCIL OF WORLD AFFAIRS

'Emerging Realities of Indo–US Strategic Relations:
A Cost Benefit Analysis'
Proceedings of the Joint Seminar
held on

September 25, 2010

Introduction

Asia Centre, Bangalore had held a previous seminar on the 'Changing Contours of Indo–US Relations: Challenges, Risks and Opportunities' on June 3, 2006, in the context of the nuclear deal and the agreement between the two countries to upgrade the bilateral relationship to a many-sided strategic partnership. In the four years since then, international developments have changed some expectations of this entente and its advancement. Some of these changes are China's rapid rise as a major power, the global recession, the continuing war in Afghanistan, and the difference between the Obama and Bush world-views and policies concerning India.

The Director Asia Centre Bangalore, Lt General Eipe, welcomed the speakers and introduced the subject of the seminar. He said that at the seminar on Indo–US relations three years ago, there had been a sense of optimism about the possible benefits of the new partnership that had been formed between the two countries. However, these expectations have not been fulfilled. This seminar was intended to take stock of current realities and assess where India should go from here, and what changes needed to be addressed.

This chapter covers two events on Indo–US Relations. A joint seminar held by Asia Centre and ICWA at Bangalore on September 25, 2010 on 'Emerging Realities of Indo–US strategic Relations: A Cost Benefit Analysis' and the special Annual Lecture of Asia Centre by Shyam Saran on 'Evolving Indo–US Relations: Ensuring Mutual Benefit in a Balanced Partnership'.

The Seminar was co-chaired by A.P. Venkateswaran, Chairman of Asia Centre and S.T. Devare, Director General of ICWA. The guest speakers at the seminar were:

N. Krishnan	Former Permanent Representative of India to the UN headquarters, New York
General V.P. Malik	Former Chief of the Army Staff
Ronen Sen	Former Ambassador of India to the USA

A summary of the presentations and deliberations at both events, recorded by A. Madhavan, former ambassador of India, follows in the succeeding pages.

Presentation 1: A Strategic Overview

N. Krishnan

Extremes in Perception The US embassy in New Delhi exudes optimism on the prospects of the bilateral relationship; the prevailing sentiment in India is however one of disappointment. When considering Indo–US relations, it seems difficult to avoid the extremes of euphoria based on too rosy a prospect and doubts and fears combining to form a dire prognosis.

The Root of the Problem The root of the problem is the term 'Strategic Partnership', which is misleading, holding out a perspective of long-term policies and actions by both sides in manifold areas, including foreign affairs and defence. It also suggests a partnership in global as well as bilateral issues. Apart from the basic asymmetry of power between the two countries, there is also a basic lack of convergence in our respective regional and global interests, policies, and strategies.

Post-Cold War Changes in US View of India The end of the cold war changed world politics, and along with them, Indo–US relations. Paradoxically, Pokhran 1998 while upsetting the non-proliferation applecart, also sparked a rethinking of India's position in Asia and the world order. Indo–US relations received a major boost. When Obama became President of the US, his immediate priorities and preoccupations were different, but now we see a shift to more active engagement with India. Though India is not billed as a counterweight to China, the new thinking raises India to a major role in Asia. Our record of democratic values, promotion of human rights, and freedom is lauded. What is new is the liberalization of our economy, the opening up of our market, and our higher growth rate in GDP.

From Estrangement to Partnership When President Bush came to India in 2006, he saw India becoming 'one of the major centres of global power' and the US intention to develop 'a strong, forward looking relationship' with India. In the Obama administration, Secretary of State Hillary Clinton has said that in view of the large convergence of fundamental values between the two countries, Americans were 'laying the foundation for an indispensable partnership.' From the Indian point of view, opening up relations with the US across the board would be very welcome, even if the US is no longer the sole superpower.

US–India Nuclear Deal—the Core Issue The nuclear deal became the core issue of the strategic relationship for many. The obstacles encountered during the negotiations reflected the basic problems that beset the growth of Indo–US relations. Similar difficulties came up during the passing of the Nuclear Liabilities Bill by our parliament. The UPA government seemed to show more anxiety to heed the concerns of foreign suppliers than to protect the interests of the Indian public. The Left parties alleged that changes in the draft bill were being made under American pressure.

Main Concerns

Implicit Linkage with NPT When the Americans welcomed the advent of India in the civilian nuclear market, they saw its enrolment into their version of the non-proliferation framework, which is different from the NPT, which India has clearly rejected. In this version, the US wants India to observe the non-proliferation regime, but remain excluded from the nuclear weapon power status of the NPT. India has scrupulously refrained from proliferation activity, though not in the NPT. In contrast, some NPT members, including nuclear weapon states, have violated its requirements. India has accepted controls up to the level of the NSG and the MTCR, and had passed the WMD Act; there was, therefore, no need for further commitments. Krishnan wondered whether we had walked into a self-made trap which inhibits our autonomy in regard to our nuclear arsenal. Another worry was that in upholding non-proliferation,

India might be pressured to act against certain countries against its will. India might be asked to sign up for American policies like the PSI and CSI, agreements which are outside the UN, but inspired and enforced by the US.

Pressure to Side with US in Foreign Policy The next concern is the US promoting India as a major player, expecting that India would accept the 'responsibilities' going with that status, and readily take the appropriate decisions when required. In other words, India would not be allowed to shun objectionable decisions and abstain, as was evident when the US pressed us to vote with it on Iran at the IAEA meetings. The Indian vote appalled many of us. Though the Government denied it, veiled warnings by influential Americans suggested that India voted under pressure. The PM is right when he says we do not want a new nuclear-power in our neighbourhood, but we became such a power without bothering about our neighbours. When the US invaded Iraq, we declined to join it. But the next time there is such a move, the US may expect India as a strategic partner to sign up alongside.

US and Indian Visions of 21st Century Global Order Condoleezza Rice's Foreign Affairs article (2005) had spoken of a global balance of power structured around the US, Japan, Russia, the EU, China, and India for stability. It is questionable whether India would accept such a structure which leaves out Africa and Latin America. The American perspective for the new world order is different from the Indian perspective of a harmonious and peaceful world order, which gives importance to bio-diversity of humans, the plurality of peoples, and cultures and values as well.

Secretary of State, Hillary Clinton, has spoken of 'a new global architecture' and declared that 'the US can, must and will lead in this new century.' The State Department further said that India could play a leading role in the regional architecture which the US hopes to build, so as to address issues more effectively. Krishnan queried whether the new architecture meant issue-based global agreements that would result in global issues being kept out of the UN. He said that one was left uneasy, as the US has the leadership capacity and the power, but not always the wisdom.

India's Aspirations and US Support of Pakistan The partnership with the US will not make India the sixth nuclear weapon power and permanent member of the UNSC like the P5. For the present, India should aim to be a regional power with a voice in world affairs. A major obstacle is Pakistan and its capacity to unleash trans-border terrorism. The US role is crucial. Its continued military support to Pakistan and the mollycoddling of its Army and ISI tends to nullify all efforts to persuade Pakistan to desist from this policy. The US AfPak policy assigns a primary role to Pakistan and thereby tends to sideline India.

Pressure and Conditionalities in Technological Cooperation We should ensure that we do not come worse off in our growing economic, trade, and technology agreements with the US. With the civil nuclear liability bill that the parliament has passed, India showed the courage to do what it felt right. Unlike the US, which expects to export its equipment, India does need foreign investment and technology, but in seeking American participation we should beware of pressures and conditionalities. There is still work to be done on securing access to high technology and to revise the Entities list they use to bar important Indian units from such access.

Presentation 2: Defence Issues

General V.P. Malik

Introduction

Strategic relations with the US must be based on enduring, long-term logic in our national interest. The areas of convergence should outweigh the differences in our expectations. There is much to be gained from defence cooperation, but this is contingent on its being embedded in the larger context of bilateral relations, including political and economic ties. In a strategic dialogue, we need not focus on short-term deliverables or tactical issues, but problems on too many fronts can deflate the strategic balloon. This talk is mainly on defence issues, with some observations on geo-strategic issues.

Unipolarity instead of Anticipated Multipolarity Though a multi-polar world order was foreseen by many, no such state has come into being. Power may be more dispersed today, with each pole having greater influence in its region, but there are difficulties in that influence being transformed into power. Despite its relative decline, the US continues to be the sole superpower and will remain so for long.

The AfPak problem Stability in Afghanistan can be achieved through a reconstruction and development process. The US has a more limited objective: to ensure that the Taliban or the Al-Qaeda do not use Pakistan–Afghanistan territory to carry out terrorist attacks. To achieve this, President Obama seems keen to take over the country with a coalition of forces, including the so-called moderate Taliban, which would explain Pakistan's added importance. He appears desperate to get out of the war in Afghanistan.

The US President seems to appreciate India's development programmes in Afghanistan but not its strategic interests, which go well beyond his outlook. India wants a stable, democratic, and strong Afghanistan; it is unclear how these differing objectives can be strategically adjusted.

China Both India and the US have a problem with China. China has managed to carve out strategic space for itself and thus develop significant leverages. Chinese military modernization and its opaque policies and intentions have already created suspicions in many countries. While India's economic relations with China may be improving, its security relations are worsening. China's strategic relations with Pakistan, its influential relations with other South Asian countries, its 'string of pearls' strategy in the Indian Ocean, the unresolved border issue, and its assertive attitude on Jammu and Kashmir and Arunachal Pradesh are becoming a major concern for India. The Sino–Indian relationship cannot and should not be seen in a purely bilateral framework, but in the broader context of Asian regional security. The state of US–China relations will have a major bearing on India's relations with the US, China, and on Asian stability. India would be uncomfortable with close relations prevailing between the US and China, although tension between them is not easy for us to manage. Similarly, China will never be comfortable with any American administration promoting India as a pillar of new Asian balance.

BRIC Prospects as a Strategic Bloc The foursome (Brazil, Russia, India, and China) may be useful only on soft issues such as trade, WTO, and climate change. Mutual wariness between Russia–China and India–China are strong impediments to the emergence of the four-nation group as a strategic bloc.

Climate Change and New Technology The US and India have divergences on climate change and clean energy issues. Military establishments are investing hugely in Researchand Development (R&D) for newer, cleaner, and greener technologies. India hopes that they will not be classed as 'dual use technologies' that would be denied to it.

Defence and Military Cooperation

Military relations are now better than they have ever been, but they have not achieved results at the desired strategic level. India's engagement with the US in defence started in 1991. The relationship has developed in slow stages through the 'Agreed Minutes on Defence' in 1995 involving the defence departments of both countries, the 'Next Steps in Strategic Partnership' and the 'New Framework for the US-India Defence Relationship' in 2005.

'New Framework for US-India Defence Relationship' The New Framework has set up an institutionalized framework, and states that in pursuit of the shared vision of an expanded and deeper strategic relationship, the defence establishments of the two countries will:

1) Expand capabilities in counter-terrorism, anti-WMD proliferation, rapid disaster response, and peacekeeping operations.
2) Conduct joint exercises and collaborate in multi-national operations and in missile defence.
3) Conduct exchanges on intelligence and defence strategy and transformation, and continue strategic discussions at senior levels.
4) Expand mutual trade in defence and increase technology transfer, co-production, R&D, and a framework of technology security safeguards.

The Agreement is a road map for 2005–15, and under it the Indian army has participated in 18 exercises since 2006.

Mutual Benefits The scale and level of these exercises are politically insignificant, but there is scope to raise the level. The Indian military can gain from the US in areas such as Combined Arms training, Information Warfare, and advanced surveillance and stealth technology, and on measures to counter cyber-terrorism and anti-IED mechanisms. Likewise, our navy and air force can learn from their experience, for instance on submarine rescue operations.

We have invaluable operational experience in all types of terrain, sub-conventional war, ethnic conflict management, and international peacekeeping. Indians have vast experience in non-combat operations like aiding civil authorities in maintenance of law and order, disaster relief, humanitarian assistance, and maintenance of essential services from which the US military could benefit.

Defence Procurement and Industry—The Crux of Cooperation The crux of Indo–US cooperation is in defence procurement, dual-use technologies, R&D, and our defence industry. It is important, in view of our lack of a credible defence industry, which is an unbearable weakness in our security infrastructure. In the last few years there has been some improvement in defence trade through foreign military sales. It has the advantage of procurement of modern equipment through governmental deals, but the disadvantage is the US insistence on separate agreements for spares with the manufacturers, which makes them the exclusive vendor. There are doubts about the reliability of the

US as suppliers after the delay in supply of certain spares. Major purchases like attack helicopters, transport aircraft, and ultra-light howitzers have been stalled by the US demand that India sign technology safeguard agreements with certain stipulations. The US cite their domestic laws for their insistence on these agreements, which provide for fitment of certain equipment on the platforms we buy with conditions that we have found unacceptable. This has also threatened the transfer of other crucial equipment, some of which affect the already purchased P-8I Poseidon maritime and C-130J Super Hercules transport aircraft.

The growing distance between India and the US on these agreements is causing frustration on both sides. Last year, India reluctantly gave in to an End-User Monitoring Agreement, but rejected US proposals for a Logistics Support Agreement and Cross-Servicing Agreement that would allow the US forces ready access to Indian logistics.

US Focus on Sales, Not Technology Transfers In the field of research and development, the dual use technology issue remains the litmus test by which healthy relations can be measured. Unless some regulations are waived by the US, high-tech cooperation does not appear possible. Ten years ago, India was importing 70 per cent of its weapons and equipment. But today the imports on a cost basis have climbed up to 77 per cent.

The DRDO, Ordnance factories and the Defence PSUs promise a lot, but deliver little. Hence, the Services suffer critical equipment deficiencies over long periods. We expected that the US defence industry would be able to transfer some latest technologies and help us establish the much-needed industrial complex. Such collaboration now appears to be a long way off. Off-the-shelf sale and purchase do not build long-term partnerships. However, it must be stated that the blame for the lack of progress cannot be laid entirely at Americans' door. The US companies find it hard to collaborate with India's DRDO ordnance factories and public sector undertakings due to the bureaucratic stranglehold, decision-making delays, and differences in work culture. They prefer to work with more efficient and profitable private sector firms. Several revisions of procurement procedures and off-set policies notwithstanding, the playing field is not level. We are trying to encourage the private sector to invest with foreign collaboration. But there are huge vested interests within the government and, therefore, very little progress on the ground is being made.

Naval Cooperation The Indian Ocean region faces several security threats that endanger maritime peace and stability. They include the smuggling of weapons of mass destruction (WMD), organized crime, trafficking in human beings and drugs, poaching in territorial waters and the EEZ, environmental degradation through oil and radioactive spills, maritime terrorism, and piracy. Almost 70 per cent of the world's natural disasters occur in the Indian Ocean region. The tsunami disaster relief and Lebanon refugee evacuation operations have shown the benefits of working alongside other navies.

Improvement in Naval Cooperation Exercises with other friendly navies enable us to gain operational and doctrinal expertise, share conceptual and practical experiences, improve inter-operability, and enhance our own maritime domain awareness. Starting in 1994, USN–Indian naval cooperation has grown with the participation of advanced surface ships, submarines, and long range maritime patrol aircraft in joint exercises. During Operation Enduring Freedom in 2002, the Indian Navy escorted 24 US high-value vessels to the Straits of Malacca , at the request of the US, to support the international war on terrorism.

Current Indian-Foreign Navy Exercises India's position astride the shipping lanes of the Indian Ocean, which has over 100,000 ships transiting through annually is unique; it was only natural that the maritime states dependent on these sea lanes of communications should befriend our navy. Over a period of time, the Indian Navy has begun exercising with the navies of Britain (Konkan series), France (Varuna series), Indonesia, Oman, Russia (Indra series), Thailand, Singapore (Simbex series), and the US (Malabar series).

Incremental Increase in Maritime Cooperation In the complex strategic scenarios that we may face, India prefers a cooperative model of regional security and is willing to work with all friendly countries for it. Freedom of navigation is important for India, the US, Japan, and countries in South-East Asia. Though the Indian Navy has gained much from its maritime cooperation with the US, the pace of maritime cooperation is incremental.

Conclusion

The current level of strategic partnership is clearly not a strategic alliance, as many people perceive. India cannot afford to compromise its strategic autonomy and let this partnership dilute strategic relations with other nations. It cannot allow the emergence of a situation when India is perceived as a hedge against China, or accept the US policy of ensuring peace between India and

Pakistan through a 'military balance.' To realize its potential, India has to play an independent role and cooperate or compete on issues with other nations depending upon its national interests.

The Indo–US strategic partnership is still evolving. At present, it seems that political sensitivities, lack of total trust, bureaucratic and procedural hurdles, and some short-sighted domestic policies in both countries are stalling this process.

Presentation 3: Emerging Realities

Ronen Sen

Introduction

Sen began by commenting that the title of the seminar was topical, as the realities of the changes in Indo–US relations have not yet been comprehended. The term 'Cost-benefit analysis' was also apt; both sides should respect each other's expectations and work for each other. We perhaps expect more from the US than from any other country. We complain about arms supplies to Pakistan by the US, but never take up the larger supply of arms by China to Pakistan. We expect the US to stop China's nuclear cooperation with Pakistan but hesitate to take it up with China.

India-US Connections Fundamental Rights in our constitution derive from the US Bill of Rights. There are many connections of this kind. F.D. Roosevelt had great sympathy for the Indian freedom movement. It was only in the aftermath of the Cold War that there was a period of benign neglect of India by the US. While Clinton did not know much about India initially, George W. Bush had long had a fascination for India. President Obama is a very different man from Bush; he likes to seek all views, but prefers to make his decision final.

Rather than seeking to see the US–India relationship in isolation and restricting the discussion to the US, we should be aware of the world context. Sen said that he would not answer questions concerning American perceptions, but only about his perceptions of the US.

The Nature of the Alliance As both General Malik and Krishnan had pointed out, this is not a 'natural alliance' or a 'strategic alliance'. It should be a long-term partnership to be strategic, and basing it on shared values and concerns would not be enough. It is not just intersecting interests. The criterion of 'cost-benefit' must be applied in both directions. For us, the US is our biggest export destination; we enjoy a favourable balance of trade. This bilateral trade has added to our high-tech and created upper-end jobs in India. Our students prefer the US to the UK. The US is a country which offers advantages to professionals, and our NRIs have done well there as physicians and academics. Hence the people-to-people interaction is high and valuable. The Tarapur stand-off (after Pokhran I) and the Bangladesh War (1971) mark the lowest levels in our bilateral relations. The divergence over Bangladesh has been removed. We did not 'sell' the nuclear deal well within India. It is far too technical and legalistic, hence difficult to put across to the people.

Importance of Nuclear Deal The nuclear deal is important. Let us recall that a single-country exemption was made from the prevailing restrictive international regime expressly for India. On the controversy that arose, it is necessary to remember that the US legislation is supreme only within the US, and that it does not apply to an international agreement, which is what the nuclear deal has become after approval of the exception in India's favour by the NSG.

The Supplier Liability Issue We should also be aware that other countries with which we have nuclear dealings are also concerned that their suppliers should not be made liable for indefinite damages, on account of reactors or equipment related to nuclear trade which they have supplied to India. Russia's aid in the Kudankulam project had encountered this difficulty; it was explicitly stated that subsequent legislation would not be retrospectively applied to that project. The US–India nuclear deal was alleged to be favouring American corporate interests though, in fact, the two firms concerned have substantial Japanese corporate shares and are not exclusively American-owned.

Importance of Considering Indian Interest The third aspect is that nuclear liability should not be seen only in the international context, but more pertinently, in India's interest. India is not going to be a perpetual importer of reactors. We have commitments to other countries too. We require the technology. We have to reconcile our commitment to US with international commitments. Other nuclear supplier countries will benefit more than the US from our deal. We aim at a 70 per cent offset of liability. Across the board, the costs of production will be driven up by insurance costs if India legislates for the indefinite liability of the supplier. Even Indian firms which will be suppliers of equipment have expressed serious reservations about the liability factor being moved to the suppliers and not the operators. This will be a deterrent in the sourcing of much needed equipment.

Without being too legalistic, we should debate our overall interest on nuclear energy issues. India will remain outside the NPT. Bush made the US the first country to recognize India as having a military nuclear (or strategic) programme. The clear-cut separation of civil and military facilities was needed to fix accountability and responsibility on the personnel involved.

India and Anti-Proliferation The Proliferation Security Initiative or PSI was introduced by the US in 2003, in a drive against proliferation by states and non-state actors of Weapons of Mass Destruction. It was a convention accepted by more than 90 countries to interdict the transfer of such weapons and related materials. India was prepared to join it as a core member, but we lost interest when no core group was formed. It was an arrangement among the countries in favour, not an international agreement. In fact, India was the first country to stop a North Korean ship which was bound for Libya, carrying cargo of a suspect nuclear nature. We would interdict a suspect vessel even without the PSI, if it is in our national interest.

CISMoA and Logistic Agreements—Indian Drafts About the CISMoA issue, which General Malik spoke about, the original draft was ours, not that of the US. The Logistical agreement was also our draft. But our side became excessively wary when the US agreed with our suggestion.

Address Central Command on AfPak Issues While the Pakistan army is dealing with the US Central Command, we are not. Pakistan's military is in policy making. The speaker queried why we were not talking to the Central Command at an institutional level on these issues. This was considered at high levels, but our side felt that the US would not agree since Pakistan would have objected.

Background to Vote on Iran Sanctions As for Iran, US did not figure in the first draft decision to vote on sanctions under the IAEA. The Iranian President had gone out of his way to mention India specifically to object to the US–India nuclear deal. It was a campaign against us. There were a series of other reasons, and we went along with the IAEA draft. It was only later on that the US Congress got into the act and a controversy arose on India's vote on this resolution, being alleged to be a submission by us to US pressure.

Successes in Modifying US Posture On the CTBT and Kashmir issues, we got the Americans to make changes. Before his Indian visit, Clinton was more insistent on equivalence for Pakistan and India. He was urging Obama to mediate on Kashmir.

Obama's Moderated Approach on China Unlike his predecessors, Obama began by trying to accommodate Chinese concerns, including their demarche that he should not meet the Dalai Lama on the latter's visit to Washington. He had even mooted the idea that China could work with the US to lessen Pakistan's concerns. But now he is moderating this approach and moving away from it to express American concerns. India and the US have an opportunity to boost their dialogue on China. Kissinger was perhaps right in holding that in triangular relations, the US should aim to have better relations with the other two countries than the other two had with each other.

Discussion

Comments by Co-Chairs

Comments by Chairman Asia Centre A.P. Venkateswaran, Chairman, Asia Centre recalled that he was serving in the Indian Embassy, Washington during the Emergency in India, when the Americans had no good word for India or Prime Minister Indira Gandhi. America is, in its own eyes, a beacon of liberty, though its history contradicts that claim. The US was the first to drop atom bombs on cities (Hiroshima and Nagasaki.) President Truman wanted this to be a warning to the Soviets. Russia developed the atom bomb and managed to test it too; China followed. India congratulated China on going nuclear, but when India conducted its nuclear test, China condemned it. These are facts of life. Power is amoral; it does tend to corrupt. Venkateswaran then invited the DG, ICWA, to make his comments on the seminar.

Comments by DG, ICWA S.T. Devare, Director General, Indian Council of World Affairs, commented that they had heard comprehensive presentations from varied viewpoints. The title of the seminar said a lot and calls for our perceptions of the future course of the bilateral relationship. We think of it as bilateral from our own viewpoint, but our other relationships are also important. As Sen said, the US made India the only exception in the NPT regime and the NSG resolutions. The US claims our maximum attention, and will remain in our focus as a superpower, but India has well-nurtured and important relations with some countries, which we have to consider.

Comment on Cost–Benefit Assessment Regarding cost–benefit, we have to determine whether our core interests have been protected and advanced by the US relationship; we need peace and security in our neighbourhood, concerted action against terrorism which cuts across boundaries, energy security, and advanced technology. We have to see how far this relationship helps us in these core areas. We have high expectations from the US, but it is the common refrain that some are not fulfilled.

US Insensitivity to Indian Concerns There is a feeling that we have been let down by US; outsourcing is facing intervention, H1B visa fees have been inordinately hiked, the 'entities list' has been retained with a few deletions, export controls continue, and in general, there is insensitivity to our concerns. But India can take these into account while not being worried by what the US will do, if we cultivate our own strategic autonomy and space effectively. For instance, our relations with Russia are very important for us, since we still obtain a variety of defence materials from there, and this trend will continue. We must develop our strategic options. Is our strategic space impinged? We can take a leaf from China's book. China started from 1970s to seek US partnership, with the Nixon visit to China (1972.) Though the two countries had serious differences, the Chinese dealt with the US with maturity and confidence. India is a rising power, as the IT sector shows. The younger generations in India are prepared to take on the world. We need a different prism to look at the world. We should take a more balanced view of the concerns bedevilling India.

The Chairman Asia Centre then invited comments and questions from the audience.

Constancy of Ties with US In response to a member's comment that it would be wrong to assume constancy in ties with the US, Ronen Sen said that no country is more diverse than the US in races, languages, urban and country economies, in federal polity, and groups within the Congress. This meant that any serious issue had to be delicately handled so as to carry the diverse interests with us. We had to tackle a broad spectrum of basic issues with the US, ranging from 'dual use' technology denied to India to issues like the 'Entities list', the Missile Technology Control Regime, and the Nuclear Supply Group, where we had to take care to cover the concerns of group interests like those of the Australia group. Secondly, we had to deal with differences in the Senate, the House of Representatives, and various States of the US. On the nuclear deal, the Indian Americans of all parties supported us, which was most encouraging.

Impact of US Actions on Muslims A lady member emotionally complained against the invasion and occupation of Afghanistan by Russians, and the human rights violations they committed against the people. Secondly, why should Iran not have nuclear power when others have it? Why should the US object to it? The Americans have roused the anger of the Muslims. Thirdly, the US invaded Iraq and even hanged Saddam Hussein. Muslims all over the world are very disturbed by these violations.

General Malik responded that there was truth in what was said, but it might not be whole truth. In such matters we had to see the compulsions of both sides. As for Iran's nuclear policy, nuclear weapons have grown in numbers, and the fact is that no one wants others to have them though they themselves may have them. China, the US, and India too, oppose nuclear proliferation.

Regarding Iraq, some European countries opposed the invasion of Iraq; once the US went in, their opposition was muted, and now the question was how to resolve the situation in post-war Iraq and Afghanistan. We should not go too much into history since events were happening fast, but look ahead and draw useful lessons.

Khaleeli remarked that it was not easy to understand how deeply it has affected millions of Muslims. George W. Bush was one of the least popular presidents of the US, but if, before the election, he had bombed Iran, he would have been elected. Khaleeli's view was that for a country like India, bilateral relations can be tactical and regional. In our region, if we had trouble-free relations with China, we would be relieved of our major concerns, being left only with the Gulf area and Pakistan to deal with. China is a global power; we could have a deal with it. Pakistan is not a global power, it is not a nation. West Asia is a region of vital interest for us. Iran is most vulnerable. India should repair its relations with Iran as well as Iraq. Together we should be able to deal with any inimical power that intrudes in this region.

Reluctance of Indian Entrepreneurs in India Ravi commented that many Indians had studied in the US after passing through IITs and IIMs, and settled there, but very few of them had returned to set up manufacturing enterprises in India. He asked why our people were so reluctant to take advantage of the liberalized Indian economy to set up enterprises in, for instance, food processing and plastics and castings, which were promising lines.

Sen responded that first, he fully empathized with what Khaleeli said. If we looked at ourselves before looking at the US, we would have to admit to a lack of sensitivity. The result of the US going into Iraq was the opposite of what it intended. US actions in the Arab-Israeli stand-off have benefited Iran more than any other country. Secondly, he would agree with Khaleeli that an American attack on Iran would have ensured a Republican victory in the US election. It was true that US profiling of certain kinds of visitors with beards has been deplorable. On Iran, India could have done more to maintain good relations. He was sure, however, that Iran would acquire nuclear weapons; we had to deal with reality on this issue. It was Persia, an old and proud civilization, not Iran, which we had to reckon with.

Regarding N. Ravi's question, Sen said that we were indeed trying to facilitate the return of NRIs in the US to set up enterprises. Actually, there has been a good deal of Indian investment in Britain, and also in the US in recent years. It was not just one-way investment in India. The strength of industry in Germany, the US, and other Western countries was in small and medium scale enterprises, and we too could do it.

US Ambiguity In response to a member's question of US ambiguity on issues of concern to India, Sen replied that as ambassador to the US, he never raised the issue of US arms and other aid to Pakistan with the government. They should determine what is in the US interest. Nor did he raise the issue of India's membership of the UNSC, because it went against our self-respect. We could transform the reality of India into a country that deserved to be invited in.

Disincentives to Investment in India An entrepreneur who had returned from the US commented that some NRIs were returning to India, but the Indian tax system was a serious disincentive. In his company's case, for instance, an extra 12.5 per cent tax had been levied because they were creating a new technology which had not been allowed.

Sen agreed that many NRIs were willing to come back, but unfortunately we had not encouraged them. There were needless hurdles and little coordination among the departments concerned. Most of the difficulties were related to the states, and there were different regulations in the various states. We had to tone up the whole process of enabling NRI investors to set up enterprises in India. They were not asking for preferential treatment or favours. We had to understand that the innovative potential is now with key scientists in universities and institutes, whose main income is not the salary but the rewards of their research work in cutting-edge technologies, their Intellectual Property Rights, outside governmental networks, and integrated with firms for commercial advantage. Our IITs are good at training talented people, but engage very little in research work. We must go in for R&D in a big way and get commercial linkages to research work right, along with industrial applications too. The potential is tremendous if we undertake the reform of education and research.

Indian Protectionism General Malik remarked that he was, of course, pro-Indian. But he had to point out that we were today protesting against protectionism in the US, without addressing our own. The defence PSUs and ordnance factories are producing obsolete goods, and despite government attempts to reform the system, very little is achieved. China has established its capabilities, but India is unable to do it. We can learn from China. But we refuse to learn. We do not have capabilities to build capacities.

On India's quest for permanent membership of the UNSC, C.V. Ranganathan recalled that when he organized the heads of mission conference in Paris at P.V. Narasimha Rao's behest, there had been much discussion on the subject, which was topical at the time. But at his instance, the Prime Minister put an end to the discussion by asking what the Indian envoys would advise India to do once we were in the Security Council. The discussion thereafter returned to the subject of India, the EU, and the Maastricht Treaty!

Regarding the US and China, Sen noted that there was great interdependence of the two economies, or rather, an increasing US dependence of China today. It raised an important point: what could we do for the US?

On the issue of sovereignty over the South China Sea, India could take more initiative and strengthen the ASEAN stand. As a move for broader and cooperative maritime security, both the US as well as China could be involved in the discussion. We could use our drafting skills in such an initiative. Regarding AfPak, we could work for a regional arrangement of all the neighbours of Afghanistan to secure an independent, neutral, sovereign Afghanistan. Regarding the US, our envoys must be careful not to arouse inflated expectations. On issues involving Muslims, India should not be seen on the wrong side.

No Financial Game-Changer for India A member observed that China holds trillions of dollars of US treasury bonds which gives them a commanding position in dealing with the US. India has always sought legitimacy and played by rules. The US respects those who respect themselves; we ask for respect for playing by the book. If the panellists can think out-of-the-box, what is the one thing they would have India do as a game-changer?

S.T. Devare's response was that India–US trade amounts to US $40 billion per annum, while China–US trade tops US $400 billion. China has American lobbies working for it. India had first to develop its strength and economy; US pressure groups would then play for us, without any browbeating or protestations of abiding by rules on India's part.

A member's comment was that it was true that the US was comfortable dealing with dictatorships. We are strong in principles, but torpedo them in our procedures. In the 21st century, it was not governments but civil society that would be decisive. In Indo–US relations, India wants US technology and the US wants our markets. If India keeps growing, governments would be less important than the people in both countries.

General Malik observed that if we did not get the needed technology now, we would have to pay a bigger price for it later. The Chinese had established their base and let the foreign firms' profit, but now reap the benefits. We have failed to do what China has done.

Collaboration with Universities for Research Commenting on the tardiness in response, R. Sen narrated how in one instance, he had sent a proposal for research collaboration with a university and got no response for two years. Meanwhile, a Chinese delegation had visited that institution in California and finalized the proposal in two weeks. Secondly, we should be more pragmatic, like the Chinese after Deng took charge. They got every technology available around the world, recognizing the important fact that in modern systems, no country can act alone, but only in combination with several suppliers of components. This is so in nuclear reactor technology too, where the turbo-generator can be Russian and the control system German. The Chinese are now going in for competitive bidding for the procurement of components or systems.

Role of Domestic Politics A question was raised about the effect of domestic politics on decision-making in Indo–US defence matters. The questioner asked whether India would have resolved the differences with the US on CISMoA and logistical support if a political consensus had prevailed in these matters.

General Malik agreed that it was a valid question. Decisions were easier to reach when there was a consensus in the government. Now that a political consensus is lacking among the parties, it has become much more difficult. He had asked the Raksha Mantri, once, why we could not close down our antiquated ordnance factories and PSUs and sell them off, and upgrade the rest. He said that in the current situation of a coalition government, the move would be impossible.

US Diversity Venkateswaran commented that there was a projection that by 2020 the population of the US will be largely non-white, with Hispanics, blacks, Asians, and others outnumbering the whites. He wondered what impact this would have on America—whether the whites would accept the changes and treat the others as equals. He recalled that after the emergence of South Africa with the ending of apartheid, he had had the chance to ask President Mandela if the whites had accepted the new reality. He replied, 'We have all the positions, but the whites have the power.'

R. Sen responded that in both India and the US, realities are changing. There is recognition in the US that the ethnic composition of the people is changing markedly. The debate has started; people are coming to terms with it. In Arizona, immigration from Mexico and Latin America is a live issue; there could be local conflicts. In Alabama, they fly both the US flag and the Southern Confederate flag on a building opposite the Governor's office. There was no doubt that the prejudice against Obama was partly racist. His popularity was definitely down. He had raised unrealistic expectations among the people; he was vulnerable because of the number of jobs lost by Americans. On issues like the closing of Guantanamo prison, he had disappointed his followers. His Nobel Peace Prize made it worse for him because the US is still caught up in the war against the Taliban in Afghanistan.

Conclusion

Concluding the discussion, S.T. Devare said that they had had a rich and constructive discussion; the subject of the Indo–US relationship was very important and timely in view of the Obama visit in November. The discussion showed that we need clarity on both sides about our expectations. We had seen that technology is our dire need; we should get the best technology even if it is more expensive. India can build the relationship on a more enduring footing. Our discussions had provided a valuable input and ties in with interaction in civil society, supplementing governmental discussions.

SPECIAL ANNUAL LECTURE

'Evolving Indo–US Relations: Ensuring Mutual Benefit in a Balanced Partnership'

Shyam Saran

Introduction

The Chairman Asia Centre, A.P. Venkateswaran introduced the speaker, Shyam Saran, in warm words, lauding him as one of the most outstanding Indian diplomats he had worked with. He described Shyam Saran as a pragmatist and a patriot. It is easy to be led away to exalt other countries as superior. But Saran keeps Indian interests firmly in mind in his work with other countries.Obama's visit to India in early November gives added relevance to this lecture. India is forging a new relationship with the US which, despite signs of decline, is still the most powerful nation in the world. While making new friends, India should not forsake old friends, among whom Russia figures prominently. India has to look to its own interests with courage, refusing to be cowed down by any power seeking to threaten its security. India should also be wary of enemies from within who could betray it to gain favour with external powers.

Lecture by Shyam Saran

The last time I spoke at Asia Centre (in 2006), it was on the Indo–US nuclear deal, in the negotiation of which I was concerned. It was a difficult interaction, since many of you had serious doubts if the deal would be conducive to a balanced relationship between India and the US. We concluded the nuclear deal because it would benefit India, enlarge its diplomatic space, and increase its energy security. The current lecture too, concerns India–US relations and again I find strong sentiments doubting the prospects. The subject is topical in view of Obama's imminent visit to India. It will be an important visit and he will have a difficult time, since constant comparisons would be made with George W. Bush's successful visit in 2006, after the nuclear deal was settled. Obama will have one advantage, such as, that in the meantime, India–US relations have broadened with increased trade, technology, and investment, and also widened in non-official areas. There are some 90,000 Indian students in the US; the Education Initiative is on the anvil to give more density and content to the interactions.

A Practioner's Perspective As a practitioner rather than a theorist, let me give you my perspective. In diplomacy we should avoid labelling other countries as friends and adversaries, but pursue our national interests without becoming prisoners of the past, even with a former adversary who can bring benefit to us now. Why deny ourselves the benefit to our country from such a policy?

There has been a significant change in our international perspective. What was the change due to? Between 1960 and 1990, India had a strategic partnership with the Soviet Union, though ideologically the two countries were far apart and we had more in common with the US in that respect. The strategic glue was the mutual antipathy we shared with the Soviet Union due to the perceived threat from China. This has changed in one very important way. During our 30 years of our partnership with the Soviet Union, none of the military ware and technology we obtained from it was available to China. Now, with the collapse of the Soviet Union and the end of the Cold War, the relations between Russia (the successor state) and China have changed: Russian arms sold to India now are also sold to China. This has altered the strategic aspect of the relations. When we consider which major power shares our sense of threat and challenge from China now, it is only the US; both India and the US see China in an adversarial situation. Therefore, if we look at what India needs to do to maintain our room for manoeuvre, so that our diplomatic space does not shrink because of the rapid emergence of China as a major military and economic power, a long term strategic relationship with the US becomes critical in our foreign policy framework. But this does not mean that we must forgo the advantage of working with China in areas where our interests coincide.

Need for a Long-Term Relationship We have to look for a long-term strategic relationship. The US used to look at India through a cold war prism as a country on the other side, and hence denied us high technology through the NPT regime and the Nuclear Proliferation Act, and so on. We do not deny that history. But circumstances have changed. In 2004–05 we started the dialogue with the US; it was about the strategic perspective ahead in the next three decades or so. The nuclear deal was a consequence of this dialogue (in which I had talks with a senior academic and diplomat-adviser, Phil Zelikow, who had also worked with Condoleezza Rice). We were clear that India would not be part of any containment ring around China. Since then, the economic interdependence of the US and China has increased. Similarly, our own relations with China were intended to normalize bilateral relations in the common interest. The US understood that India will play a leading role in Asia, which could tally with American ideas and wishes, but also be independent. For instance, in Myanmar, India is working with the generals and not supporting Aung San Suu Kyi; in Nepal we have our own interests. China is rising, but India is rising too, adding to the complexity of international relations, which must be managed with nuanced diplomacy. Both sides saw there was a parallel thinking in this perspective, though we did have serious differences. They were sharp enough on Pakistan, Iraq, Afghanistan, and several other issues. Overall, however, there is a strategic vision we can share and prospects for the two countries working together over the next two or more decades. The nuclear deal would not have been possible without an understanding of this convergence of the long-term relationship.

The Change in the Relationship What has changed in this relationship, since 2005, is that the clarity which obtained then has become blurred now. The US now faces practical compulsions regarding its relations with Pakistan and China. For example, as seen by both sides, we need closer relations with Japan, ASEAN, and Australia, a forum where we could discuss and exchange our perceptions of the emerging landscape in Asia. The Chinese became agitated by this initiative. They charged us during bilateral talks with India having become part of an anti-China alliance. Our response was that we had a right to consult others, just as China consulted its partners in forums like the Shanghai Cooperation Organization. Our discussions, we explained, were not directed against any country. China cannot have a veto on the countries India can consult, just as we do not have a veto on which China consults. But the US, the prime mover of this consultative initiative, changed its approach to China, not wishing to confront it. The US had encouraged Japan to stand up to the Chinese, but held it back, much to Japan's dismay, because the Americans found they needed China's support to restrain nuclear North Korea and Iran. Japan had been as concerned about China's assertive manifestations as India was. For tactical reasons, during Bush's time, this trimming of sails was done by the Americans. Later, with the situation in Afghanistan worsening, Pakistan gained increasing salience in US calculations. It has become far more important in the last two years. Such is the backdrop of the strategic picture, where tactical pulls make matters more difficult for us. We have to assess which way America will go, as it is being exacerbated by the economic and financial crisis facing it.

Two Trends in American Thinking There are two trends of thinking in the US. One (prevalent in both the State Department and the White House) is that the Americans must accept that China has permanently changed the balance of power by its very speedy rise. This implies that the US and the world have to accept this reality, which is not merely tactical, but strategic as well. Signs of this trend were apparent during the first year of Obama's accession as president, when concepts such as 'G-2', about the US and China working together for a stable world order, were current. The second trend of thinking is that China is the new adversary that the US must face. This perception impinges on a whole range of US interests, with the implication that the US has no option but to confront China. In doing so, the US should advisedly seek other countries which share this convergence. A sign of this trend came when Secretary Hillary Clinton refused to accept China's declaration that the South China Sea was one of its core concerns. It is not clear which line is winning in the US. When Obama comes, we should assess from the talks which line is dominant. This perception will have huge implications for our foreign policy.

The Afghanistan Challenge The second challenge is Afghanistan. What will happen to Pakistan? Here too there are two trends of opinion among US policy makers. The first is to give priority to dealing with the Taliban insurgency, to defeat which the US should keep Pakistan on its side and neutralize its harmful potential. But the US should not hesitate to hit Pakistan if its interests warrant the action, like increasing the 'drone' attacks on specific targets in North Waziristan. The second line is for the US to do everything possible to settle Afghanistan and leave, even if this involves some collateral damage to India. There is little sensitivity on this score. One expression of such a policy is Blackwill's advice that the US should cut its losses in the southern part of Afghanistan, redeploy troops in the North, and stay on with a military presence in Afghanistan to harass the Taliban-controlled areas. It is seen as essential for the US in order to have some influence in Central Asia, including a deterrent presence with Iran and Russia and even China. This school wants to minimize the damage to the US but retain influence in the region. It is not clear which line is winning. On the evidence we have, including our Prime Minister's talks with President Bush, my sense is that Obama wants out. The main reason is the heavy financial burden at a time when the US is stretched. This has huge implications for us. If the US is leaving Afghanistan, in a sense in defeat, India must assert its presence in the region from now on. Without such a presence, India would face great danger from both Pakistan and Afghanistan. If the US retains its presence in Afghanistan and is looking to destabilize southern Afghanistan under Taliban control, it has implications for Pakistan. There is a strong Pakhtun movement in the area. Even the Taliban never accepted the Durand Line border. Some Americans consider it a way to fix Pakistan and to make things difficult for it if it does not cooperate fully with the US, an implicit threat of using Pakhtun irredentism.

Advantages of Good Relations with US Such is the backdrop for Obama's visit. This said, there is a huge area where we can work closely with the US in technology and in buttressing our international profile and diplomatic efforts. Many partner countries of the US take the cue from the US. Hence, it is an advantage to have good relations with the US in diplomatic initiatives. For instance, US allies like Japan and Germany follow the limitations on technology transfers which the US decides on, and if this situation is changed in our favour, the others will be likely to follow. Lastly, if we look at the next three decades or so, the US is one country which has the proven ability to bounce back from a reversal of its fortunes, thanks to the tremendous concentration of brain power it enjoys (some of it from India); it is still the chief source of cutting-edge technology in the world, generating the maximum number of innovations among advanced industrial countries.

So, it makes sense to link up with the US. We should keep our ears and eyes open, as we could be impacted by US decisions in key strategic interests. We should not hitch India to the US, but make independent assessments of the situation affecting us in our best interests. We should have more diversified relations with other major powers, including China. With China we should work on issues having potential or existing convergence with our interests, such as climate change (at the Copenhagen Summit this became prominent) and on trade. We need to adopt more nuanced policies. It is not clear if we can develop a strategic partnership with the US like the one we had with the Soviet Union, though it seemed possible in 2005.

Formulating the Indian Approach What we can do with the US depends on both countries, each pursuing its interests, without the other complaining. The problem is not the US but how India deals with the US. Owing to India's rapid rise we have more diplomatic and strategic space than we ever had. The problem is that we do not know how to leverage this advantage. We are not comfortable with the exercise of power. We should be rather cold and calculating in diplomatic practice, not carried away by any sentimental idea of constant friends. We can package our policy attractively. We should be aware of the ground situation at all times, without overblown rhetoric on 'natural friends', but safeguard and promote Indian interests always.

Discussion

Three Questions

1) **A.P. Venkateswaran:** We have heard a very impressive speech from Shyam Saran, who has set forth his views candidly and without equivocation. Can we ask what the phrase 'India should stay engaged in Afghanistan' implies in military or political terms?

2) **N. Ravi:** The Soviet Union collapsed as a communist state in four decades, and more recently capitalism was shaken to its roots, with wrenching disruptions in the economies of many countries, including Western ones. China seems to have escaped rather lightly and Japan is stalled in a plateau. The US opened its markets to countries in their stages of advancing development. How will China deal with the US at this stage?
3) **Peter Sinai:** Obama faces the prospect of the Democratic Party losing seats in the Congressional elections to be held prior to his visit to India. If so, he will be weakened and cannot do for us as much as Bush did. Do you agree?

Response by Shyam Saran

In Afghanistan, India has its options. It is not an either/or situation about the US presence or departure from there. India is in touch with all the political forces and keeping contact with the northern groups that had figured in the settlement earlier. Secondly, there are other countries that are also disturbed by the prospect of a Taliban-dominated Afghanistan, such as Iran (a largely Shia country) and Russia too. Russia had kept a distance till now in view of their earlier unhappy Afghan experience. After Prime Minister Putin's visit to India earlier this year, we saw that Afghanistan is now at the top of their agenda. They fear that a Talibanized Afghanistan would be a breeding ground for terrorism, which would be directed at Russia also. Others like the Uzbeks and the Tajiks also fear the export of terrorism to their countries.

China's attitude is ambiguous. It counts on Pakistan as its client state to safeguard its interest (in Xinjiang.) But India has contact with several countries in the region which will gladly work with us. We should be up-front with the US if the latter's Afghan policy has adverse implications for India. Then we should feel confident to press our own interests and options. India may not send troops to Afghanistan and put 'boots on the ground', but we could send arms to trusted partners, as we did to the Northern Alliance. It is important for us to think of these contingencies. If the Americans leave, it is not the end for India. Ours should be an independent presence, not a derivative one. We had refused to join the International Security Assistance Force (ISAF), a good decision. We should do our job independently, without being seen as an appendage of the US. Today, India is unblemished by any taint of being part of the ISAF. Goodwill is our leverage.

Regarding China, as I said, there is an important difference in thinking about China's rise in the US establishment. Some influential scholars see it as a permanent change in the balance of power to which the US must adjust itself. Despite the global economic crisis, there does not seem to be any collapse or marked deceleration in China's rate of growth. It is a firm upward curve, according to this school of thought. The US must come to terms with it. The counter view is that China's economic development is caught up in a complicated supply chain from raw material source to finished product and the markets for it, mostly in the US and Europe. It is true that the decline of the US and the West will affect China's markets, but it is not serious so far. The Chinese are taking precautionary measures to sustain their growth momentum by expanding heavy infrastructural investment in its less developed western regions, from the coastal to the interior, in a clever strategy. China is not invincible, but it has done a pretty good job of looking after its interests with more agility than others (including India) and adjusting to changes.

Regarding the US Congressional elections, Obama will probably come to India after facing bad results in them. But he would be eager to look for success with India. We should play along with this.

A leader can make a difference to the policy of a country in its relations with another country. At the margin, the personal involvement and commitment of a leader like Bush could favour improvement. We should capitalize on this aspect. We should stop looking at ourselves as demanders, a mindset of the past. We can nudge the US in the right direction and tell them how we see India in the world scene.

Questions

1) **C.V. Ranganathan:** It was after President Bush recognized India as a strategic partner that other countries began to take India seriously as a rising power. India should take the initiative to develop a regional approach on Afghanistan, involving Central Asian countries also, so that we are not excluded from any settlement that is attempted by others and from the development of Afghanistan. What programmes should we undertake to this end?
2) US recovery depends on China's domestic situation, to some extent. It is vital that we should exchange views with the US on our interests and perspectives regarding China. India should not be isolated, but ensure that other countries like Japan and Australia could also be consulted.

3) The US has often been fickle in its partnerships with other countries, using and manipulating them for its own interests to prevail. With the nuclear deal, India is locking itself into a commitment with a fickle partner. The Americans could later renege on the supply of components and materials. Have we put India at risk? What is India doing to safeguard its interest?
4) Regarding the two trends of opinion in the US which the speaker mentioned, what about the trends within the Indian government? Which trend will the government follow?

Shyam Saran

1) Regarding Afghanistan, India has already taken some initiatives to consult others. We have had talks with Iran recently. With Russia too, we have discussed the Afghan situation when Putin came earlier this year. It is important that we should maintain our own independent sense of Afghanistan and our interests there, to convince others. The situation can be detrimental for us if the Taliban–Pakistan nexus is established. India should be a major actor; we should not to be excluded. Government is acting on this basis.
2) It is true that the US economy depends to some extent on China's domestic situation. The US recovery will come in time, when they cut down their fiscal and trade deficits.
3) The US may be 'fickle'? Strong powers tend to be ruthless and manipulative when they consider it necessary. India, too, should be hard-headed when it is strong enough to press its interest. We should not lack the confidence to say no to the US, if their view goes against our basic interest. We can tell the US what we can and cannot do. For example, they wanted us to agree to the separation of our civil and defence nuclear facilities. Not only that, but they wanted the separation to apply to our personnel handling the facilities as well. This we firmly told them was unacceptable. In negotiations, one should be flexible and seek compromise solutions where needed; it is a matter of give and take. Using the interdependence with the other partner to one's advantage is a matter of skill. The Indo–US nuclear deal involved our dealing with 45 members of the Nuclear Suppliers Group. The deal was not exclusive to the US. So it does not lock us in with the US, but opens up a choice of partners for nuclear cooperation. India has the technology to set up and run nuclear plants. We have enhanced it through this deal.

4) As for the question on trends in thinking in our government, I am no longer with the government. But in my experience, we have, in our Prime Minister, a leader who thinks strategically, looking at the prospects 15–20 years ahead for India in relation to the US, China, and other major powers. It is not always possible for him to put his policy in practice, because there are serious constraints. He has a longer term strategic vision, perhaps for the first time a leader in India has such a vision.

Question from Audience

Iran and Pakistan have agreed on the supply of Iranian gas to Pakistan by a pipeline. Should not India join the project in order to benefit from the gas supply?

Shyam Saran: In my view, it would be bad for India to go into this project because the pipeline has to come through Pakistan. Why should we expose ourselves to this risk? If we want to keep the ball in play, that is fair enough, but to sign for this project would be a big mistake.

Questions from Audience

1) Will China become expansionist?
2) Secondly, why cannot we 'fix' Pakistan and its bluff? Why do we have to harp on our shared culture, and so on, when they are obviously so different from India?
3) The US and China have serious differences over China's alleged currency manipulation to keep the Yuan undervalued against the dollar, so as to boost its exports unfairly. A currency war with China has been spoken about. The Chinese hold two trillion dollars of US treasury bonds and other assets. If they begin to dump the bonds, will it not impact on the US economy and India's too? India has some hedging options in business interests; in our trade with the US the balance is in our favour. Are we in talking to the US about this?
4) **Alan Nazareth**: The US pressed India to vote against Iran at the IAEA. The Prime Minister and Bush had established a personal link. But was it necessary for the Prime Minister to say in Washington, shortly before the end of Bush's tenure, that India loves him? This, when certain assurances had been given on the nuclear deal by the US; but its State Department wrote to the US Congress that the assurances were political, not legally binding.

Shyam Saran

On China's strategy: China is still a developing country. It has still some way to go to become an advanced country. The Chinese have wisely begun to develop their underdeveloped western part with massive investment in infrastructure. China's strategy is the accretion of its economic and military power over a longer period. It aims to build an economic/security architecture in the Asia Pacific region, not by occupation of territory, but by having a veto on any move by others against its interests. In this region, China aims to be at the top in economic and military terms, to be the dominant power in it. This will affect India, if China's growth restricts our access to key resources. We have already seen signs of China using its hard power, when it acted against the Australian mining firm, Rio Tinto. India has to counter this drive by another strategy: India is for a loosely structured, open, and inclusive arrangement to give more credibility to global power. China will need access to more resources; it is bent on cornering them to become incrementally more advanced. If our access to resources is restricted, it will be a very serious concern for India, since in the coming decades we would be importing 90 per cent of our oil requirements and a large percentage of our coal also. China's ambition is to be equal to the US as a world power and to be treated as equal by the US. Maybe this is too high an ambition.

India must move in areas of greater interest for us. In the Indian Ocean area, the Chinese do not have a strong presence now, though we may not retain the edge for long. I believe that the biggest challenge to India is from China.

On nuclear policy, India's position was that our own uranium resources were too limited and could only support some 10,000 MW of electric power generation over a limited period even if we have all our mines working, which is not the case for various reasons. After the nuclear deal, the world nuclear market has opened up for India. We are able to buy uranium from countries like Kazakhstan, Uzbekistan, and Namibia. Our nuclear reactors have a maximum capacity of generating 700 MW of power. The world benchmark is 1700 MW. Different kinds of reactor technology will be available to us. We have to go in for more powerful reactors than those we operate. We have the infrastructure and the skilled manpower to fit in well with the expansion. There is no alternative to a rapid development of nuclear energy, even as we develop other sources of energy with new technology.

On the entities list of the US, the situation has eased for India, but there are, still, 13 of our institutions, scientific establishments and firms on that list. We expect that this entities list will be removed or reduced. There is now no licensing requirement for India to import from the US a large number of much needed components. This will be reflected in a rapid increase in the bilateral trade in technology. Countries like Germany and Japan will also be able to supply some of these components to India, now that the US is removing its restrictions on Indian imports of high tech.

On personal relations at the top level: it is not the main factor, but at the margin good relations do make a difference, as we saw when Bush himself intervened to clinch the nuclear deal when it got blocked during the negotiation of a difficult clause, which India could not accept.

ASIA CENTRE SEMINAR
'Emerging Realities of Indo-US Strategic Relations: A Cost Benefit Analysis'
and
LECTURE BY SHYAM SARAN
'Evolving Indo-US Relations: Ensuring Mutual Benefit in a Balanced Partnership'

A Summary

Introduction

The two events covered by this report provided an informative background prior to the visit of Barack Obama to India. The seminar took stock of the pluses and minuses of the bilateral relationship in the current context; the lecture a month later was an assessment by Shyam Saran, a pragmatic 'practitioner of diplomacy' who favours building up a long-term strategic relationship between the two countries. The discussions during both the events raised concerns relating to the degree of trust which India could repose in the US as a reliable supplier of technology. Some sceptics held that the unequal nature of the partnership would oblige India to go along with American preferences despite any reservations we may have on particular issues.

Arguments in Favour of Close Relationship with the US

The main points made by those *in favour* of a closer, long-term strategic partnership between the two countries are summarized below.

1) **India Needs US Technology and Investment** The US appears to be a superpower in decline, struggling to break out of the economic recession, which it triggered in 2008; but it is likely to remain the leading economic, military, and political power in the world during the next few decades, being also the leading source of technological innovation. India badly needs high technology and heavy investment in infrastructure to improve its productivity in industry and agriculture. India must also raise about 400 million of its poor people to minimum standards of living and provide profitable employment for its youth. India is an energy deficient country which cannot sustain its recent high growth rates without assured sources of energy, for which a conspicuous increase in nuclear power production is the obvious way forward. For these purposes, India would stand to benefit from closer relations with the US.
2) **Advantage of Cultivating Relations** With Indo–US relations already spreading across many sectors and with interactions at the non-governmental levels adding density to the cooperation, there is great potential advantage in cultivating this bilateral relationship and taking it to a higher level.
3) **Convergence of Interests in Asia** There is a distinct convergence of strategic interests in Asia between India and the US, which could be strengthened. It covers diverse areas, notably China.
4) **Partnership to Discourage Possible Chinese Adventurism** The dynamic rise of China since 1980 has been sustained and has not slowed down much due to the global recession. China and the US are locked in mutual economic and financial interdependence, with China having an edge over the US as creditor and supplier of desirable consumer goods at low prices. But the two major countries are basically adversarial, with China ascending and the US declining. China has lately become more assertive in its claims to parts of India and to exclusive rights in the South China Sea. Its modernized military has moved to sophisticated levels of technological capability in land, sea, air, space, and cyber warfare. China's long-cultivated friendship with Pakistan has shown an unmistakable thrust against India. China's prospecting for oil and gas in seas surrounding its own neighbours, combined with naval patrols hint at menace. The US is also becoming chary of China's ambiguous and opaque defence strategy. But the US refrains from a confrontational

approach to China since it needs China's help and cooperation to reverse nuclear proliferation by North Korea and Iran. The geopolitical unease provoked by China is shared by India and the US. Neither country wants their partnership to point at China as an adversary, and both are for the present independently intent on quiet diplomacy to reach a *modus vivendi* with China. But it is reasonable for India and the US to share their perceptions and concerns in order to dissuade any adventurism by China, asserting its claims unilaterally regardless of other countries' rights.

5) **Pre-empting Unfavourable US–Pakistan–Afghan Arrangement** The US is trying to extricate itself from a messy military situation in Afghanistan, which is threatened by the resurgence of the Pakistan-supported Taliban. India is concerned to protect Afghanistan as an entity free from terrorist-related forces, and re-established as a viable, independent, and neutral country. The US has become tactically over-dependent on Pakistan's military to facilitate a compromise with the Taliban on a post-civil war power-sharing regime in Afghanistan, so that the American forces can go back, leaving a reduced permanent military presence there. While this contingency puts India out of reckoning for the US–Pakistan managers of an Afghan future, we must plough our own furrow, preferably with US power and understanding behind us, and prevent any anti-Indian arrangement which Pakistan wants to impose there.
6) **Joint Strategy to Protect SLOCs** The Indian Ocean has opened up new channels for Indo–US naval strategy and cooperation in protecting the vital sea-lanes from the Persian Gulf to Malacca, China, and Japan. The US has shown a strategic interest in teaming up with our navy to safeguard the sea lanes from being dominated by China and by piracies from the Somali coast.
7) **Leveraging the Indian Diaspora** The US has built up excellent institutions of higher learning and research which continue to attract Indian talent. The Indian–American community in the US has become politically more active and should be kept involved in India's plans for rapid development, as also to further our national interests in America. We should cultivate these openings for increasing goodwill and understanding. The ancillary benefits in educational initiatives, cultural exchanges, tourism, civil aviation, shipping, and scientific research are opportunities not to be spurned.

8) **Cooperation in Combating Terrorism** Though the fight against terrorism is among the most important concerns which unite the two partners, there is a divide due to the American practice of giving priority to countering terrorist groups attacking them, and ignoring or minimizing those attacking India, out of undue solicitude to Pakistan. Despite this serious lacuna, India and the US must cooperate more intimately in their professed common aim of eliminating terrorism as a threat to civil society everywhere. The sharing of timely intelligence is particularly vital for the Indian government in this regard.

Arguments against Close Relationship with the US

The main points adduced *against* India seeking a closer bonding with the US are:

1) **Divergence in Interests** The US is a global power with multiple interests, which do not mesh with India's priorities. For example, its policy towards South Asia is heavily conditioned by its AfPak strategy that marginalizes India and favours Pakistan's ambition of installing a pro-Pakistan, Indo-phobic regime in Kabul. Afghanistan–Pakistan would then become a dangerous source of terrorists and Islamic extremists bent on wresting the Kashmir valley from India and wrecking the national integrity and secular fabric of India. We cannot rely on the US to stabilize Afghanistan as a neutral and pluralist country, with India doing its best for the Afghan people's benefit through economic and social development.
2) **US Pakistan-reliant Strategy outweighs Indian Ties** Pakistan has leveraged its strategic geographical location on the one hand and its dangerous disarray as a cohesive state on the other to blackmail the US into giving it substantial military and financial aid, notwithstanding its equally munificent donor and patron, China, and to the detriment of Indian interests. No Indian partnership with the US is likely to change this strategic advantage that the US and China have conferred on Pakistan for their own reasons.
3) **Frictional Issues** There are a number of frictional issues between India and the US. The nuclear deal may have opened India's access to imports of uranium and more modern nuclear reactors from abroad. But the conditionalities imposed on civil nuclear cooperation by the US, one of which is the prevention of fissile material storage for our

strategic nuclear reactors, along with a ban on nuclear testing to improve the explosives we have stored, will push India into the status of a pale protégé of the US, rather than a regional power. In military and space technology too, India will continually be obliged to depend on American goodwill to obtain limited upgrading. Irritants like Obama's disfavour of the Indian IT industry in Bangalore and the hiking of visa fees for H1B visa applicants have disappointed Indians. In international diplomacy, India would lose some of its independence of judgement on issues where the US is set on building a strong consensus. This will cramp our style in taking our own line on issues like climate change, disarmament, reforming the UN, the World Bank, the IMF, and the WTO.

4) **Asymmetrical Relationship** It is widely understood that President Obama has rejected the Indophile premises of the logic which had, earlier, prompted President Bush to sponsor a closer strategic partnership with India. Obama has, however, subsequently endorsed the idea that the US should make India 'an indispensable partner.' It is possible that, during his visit to India, Obama will remove or reduce some of the frictional irritants in our relationship, like the 'entities list' and the licensing requirement for some high-tech exports to India. He may also give a hint of support to India's permanent membership of the UNSC, though this should not be on our list of priorities. Even so, the basic asymmetry in the relationship and the undisclosed terms on which the US promises to befriend India over the longer term should be carefully considered.

It is therefore apparent that there are eager proponents, as well as sceptics and pessimists, in determining if India and the US can craft together a long term strategic partnership. Much will depend on the discussions between the two sides during Obama's visit to India in early November of 2010. Bilateral and global issues will be discussed with a fair degree of understanding of mutual constraints. There are plausible arguments for working for modest agreements on specific issues and a quest for convergence in long-term strategic interests.

Chapter 8

India–Russia Relations

ASIA CENTRE BANGALORE

'India–Russia Relations in the New World Order: How Can Ties Be Strengthened to Mutual Benefit?'
Proceedings of the Seminar
held on

December 11, 2010

Introduction

A.P. Venkateswaran, Chairman, Asia Centre and former Foreign Secretary presided. The following speakers addressed the seminar:

Ravi Neelakantan	Former Secretary (East), MEA
Vice-Admiral (Retd) R.N. Ganesh	Former FOC-in-C Southern Naval Command
Madhav Palat	National Fellow, Institute of Advanced Study, Shimla
Kanwal Sibal	Former Foreign Secretary

This seminar on Indo–Russian relations, with focus on political, security, and economic aspects, turned out to be very timely and useful. It was held just before President Medvedev's visit to India in the third week of December 2010. The four panelists were experts drawn from different areas of experience: a historian, a naval officer who had trained and served in Russia, and two

Foreign Service officers, one of whom was later the Foreign Secretary of India. The seminar analysed comprehensively all aspects of India–Russia relations in the new world order and discussed measures that should be taken to further strengthen existing ties for the mutual benefit of both countries.

Lt General Ravi Eipe, Director of Asia Centre, outlined the subject of the seminar prior to introduction of the speakers. There have been significant developments in the recent past that have impacted on the world order. Russia, because of its energy reserves, has been able to improve its economic position significantly. India has also made impressive progress economically and there are compelling reasons for the two nations to further strengthen existing ties to mutual benefit. This seminar is also well-timed as the Russian President Medvedev is visiting India on the December 22, 2010.

The Indian armed forces owe a lot to the erstwhile Soviet Union, which helped India in building a modern fighting force. A majority of our weapon systems are of Soviet origin. India has always been supported in times of need by Russia, particularly during the 1971 conflict with Pakistan. While it may not be possible to restore ties to the old level, they can certainly be further strengthened in areas where there is a convergence of interests.

The summary of the presentations and the discussions that followed have been is given in the succeeding pages.

Presentation 1: India–Russia Ties in the New World Order

Ravi Neelakantan

Neelakantan began by stating that he had had the unique opportunity to have dealt with Russia in the late 1970s, late 1980s, and late 1990s, and into the 21st century. India passed, during the latter part of this period, through the process of economic reform, emerging as an IT destination, and engaging with a variety of challenges to achieve high levels of growth for wealth creation and distribution. Russia passed these phases through its misadventure in Afghanistan and managed the break-up of the Soviet Union while adjusting to the emergence of the erstwhile republics as independent countries. During this time, 10 'oligarchs' literally ruled and bled Russia. They converted state assets to private assets and then extended loans to other state assets. When these state assets were unable to pay back the loans, these oligarchs took over the state assets and bled them and nearly ran the Russian economy into the ground. No investments were made in the energy sector, as these peoples' objective was to make money by any means. Then President, Yeltsin, appointed Putin as the Prime Minister and some order returned to Russia. During the same period, India was also moving forward. We had moved out of the licence raj and wealth creation was not looked down upon. The Y2K episode created a positive image of India as a problem-solver.

Russia, under Yeltsin, had turned towards the West and relations with India deteriorated. After Putin was appointed Prime Minister, governance began to stabilize in Russia. The rising prices of oil also shored up the Russian economy and Putin began a series of reforms in the country.

The first decade in the new millennium after these wrenching experiences, saw significant developments emerge in the defence and bilateral political sectors. The orders for the advanced Su-30 MKI fighter aircraft revived an entire industry that was on the verge of collapse. The strategic partnership of 2000, signed during Putin's visit to India, further stabilized relations between the two countries. Russia tempered its 'look west only' policy by opening out to countries in Asia also. The rupee–rouble method of trade, which had characterized relations during the Soviet times, gave way to dollar trade, causing some upheaval in the early stages. Bargaining by India for better deals resulted in an agreement to permit third-country avionics to be incorporated in the Su-30 aircraft. The earlier buyer–seller relationship has been altered somewhat to India's benefit.

Russia is still a leader in nano-technology, micro-electronics, biotechnology, and space technologies, apart from its strength in manufacturing high-end weapon systems. Russia and India can also cooperate in the area of energy, steel, and telecom. A 5-million tonne steel factory is being established near Bellary with Russian technology. India has the potential to enter the Russian market with automobiles, consumer goods, and the traditional tea, coffee, and leather goods. Russians are keen to learn English and India has a vast knowledge industry specializing in such areas. This could be gainfully exploited. But overall business to business relationship remains at a low level considering the potential.

One area which has huge potential is the Central Asia. The CIS countries all had and have good memories of India. If we can create a physical access to these states, then with Russian collaboration, this burgeoning market can be exploited. Russian language is spoken in these countries, so joint Indo–Russian ventures have good possibilities of succeeding. Many of these states have an energy surplus, and even if we cannot transport energy to India because of geography, we could help these states to swap their products in accessible markets on a sharing basis. Another area of assistance that India can provide is in the sectors of healthcare and education. While the old and existing relationship with Russia must be nurtured, the focus of future India–Russia relations must lie in the immense potential that is available in the Central Asian region.

Presentation 2: Indo–Russian Military Cooperation

Vice-Admiral R.N. Ganesh (Retd)

Newly independent India had a somewhat disorganized military structure due to the partition of assets. Most weapon systems were received as reparations after the Second World War. There was no coherence in type and capability, and it was quite difficult to create viable fighting units around these obsolescent weapon systems. India was able to get some weapons of war from the West, but with Pakistan joining the SEATO, there was reluctance on the part of the Western powers to arm India. USA delivered F-86 Sabre jets to PAF and later followed up with the F-104 Starfighter, tilting the balance heavily in PAF's favour vis-à-vis the IAF. India's request for Sabres and F-104s were turned down as was the sale of British Lightning and Swedish Viggen fighters. It was in this environment of denial by the West that India turned to the Soviet Union. The Soviets were more than willing and they immediately offered the MiG-21, then a state-of-the-art interceptor, and Indian armed forces started taking a definitive shape around the systems provided by the USSR. The USSR also benefited from the fact that India, as the leader of the Non-aligned Movement (NAM), could facilitate its relations with other emerging democracies and countries. The cooperation and support provided by USSR during the 1971 war with Pakistan is well-chronicled and there are not many instances of such close support elsewhere in the world. It wasn't always roses all the way when dealing with the Russians, as they followed a strict hierarchical 'need to know' system, and it took much time to clarify doubts or know more about the systems being negotiated. The terms and conditions of the deal were very beneficial to India as payments were based on the rupee–rouble parity system. When India, seeking some sea-denial capability, requested for a submarine, the British offered us a vintage one built in 1933. When India requested the USSR for a second-hand submarine, they offered us 4 brand new ones, which later became the force around which Indian Navy's submarine capability was built. The availability of modern weaponry from the USSR enabled the Indian military to plan their 'force architecture', and a serious effort began to build a modern fighting force, rather than the earlier practice of window-shopping for what was available. The Soviets also assisted in setting up huge military–industrial complexes like the ones at Vishakhapatnam for the navy and at Ojhar for the air force. The PAF received F-16 fighters from the USA, again tilting the balance against the IAF. This resulted in a watershed event in India–Russia military ties, in that they upgraded to a strategic level. Marshal Ustinov on a visit to India, offered the MiG-29 air superiority fighters and also the nuclear-powered submarine, 'Chakra', and by 1982, Indians were in USSR training on these two potent weapon systems.

The collapse of the Soviet Union seriously affected the Indian military. Spares became unavailable and the serviceability state of Indian weapon systems dipped to very low levels. The Soviet system of manufacturing various parts of a weapon in different locations and then integrating them at another also resulted in much confusion. Russia's foreign sales agency 'Rosoberon' hiked prices arbitrarily and this led to many difficult situations. The period 1990–93 marked a low in India–Russia military ties. The Russian President Yeltsin's 'look west' policy sharply affected relationships. Putin's arrival on the scene restored some order. An Inter-governmental Commission for Military Technical Cooperation was formed with the Defence Ministers of both countries as co-chairmen. This resulted in scrutiny of projects at the highest levels and the situation improved considerably. Many deals, including the carrier Gorshkov, 1000 T-90 tanks, Brahmos missile, Mi-17 helicopters, and Il-76/78 for AWACS and FRA missions were signed. The deal for licensed production of Su-30MKI was also signed. The value of the India–Russia military deals is US $10 billion for this decade, and will increase in the next.

There will, of course, be challenges for the India–Russia relationship in the coming years. India has strategic partnerships with both the USA and Russia. If the future brings these two powers into an antagonistic state, what will be Indian position? Then there is the Russia–China–India triangle. In the past, 40 per cent of Russian arms production went to China, though it has reduced drastically at present. For strategic reasons, Russia has forged close ties with China. China is a huge market for energy and Russian Siberia is a vast energy resource region. If India and China confront each other, Russia will have to deal with a tricky situation.

Many talk about reviewing India–Russia relations, forgetting that even after Pokhran-II, Russia went against world opinion to transfer nuclear reactors to India. In the strategic realm, Russia has assisted India in creating second-strike capability. Russian help has been crucial in all our military ventures. Here, a question needs to be asked. For 50 years, we have been producing aircraft under licence, but except for the yet to be operationalized LCA, we have not been able to produce a quality fighter or even a transport aircraft. Our attempts to produce an engine for the LCA are also floundering despite sinking in large resources.

Today 75 per cent of our air combat capability, 90 per cent of tanks, 40 per cent of ships, and 80 per cent of ship-borne weapons are of Russian origin. While diversification of military hardware sources is a desirable aspect, it has to be done in a planned and deliberate manner. While we forge a stronger relationship with the USA and try to stabilize our ties with China, India's interest lies in building a strong strategic relationship with Russia.

Presentation 3: The Best Russia for India

Madhavan K. Palat

There has been much discussion about 'unipolarity', 'bipolarity', and 'multipolarity' after the collapse of the USSR and the emergence of a weakened Russia. Unipolarity presumes USA as the single pole with a submissive Russia, whereas bipolarity would have a hostile Russia reminiscent of the cold war period. At present, Russia is not in a position to challenge the USA. Multipolarity would have US as the main pole with other groupings as separate poles. So unipolarity and multipolarity have a peculiar symmetry with acceptance of the US as the primary power. India is not a 'pole' at present, but hopes to be one. Both India and Russia accept unipolarity without saying so. Russia is more autonomous than European states. This status is called 'democratic' and ideologically satisfies all.

As Russian politics and the international position evolve, a continuity can be discerned in the past 30 years. From Gorbachev to Yeltsin to Putin, the difficulty has been how to manoeuvre between Russia, Europe, and the rest of the world and also become an arbiter of world politics without the costs of the cold war. A modern version of the Gaullist approach can be discerned.

Putin has been able to stabilize internal politics and maintain consistency in international posture. Russian internal choices have oscillated between two extremes. The first is an extreme, uncritical Westernism represented by Yeltsin's 1st term. This was also the worst phase of Indio–Soviet relations. The Russian policy was to accommodate NATO to the extent possible. The attack in Bosnia and then Kosovo hurt and humiliated Russia. It felt that WW2 enemies and cold war enemies had ganged up against it. NATO expanded into what were earlier Soviet fiefdoms, like Czech Republic, Poland, and Hungary followed by the Baltic states in 2004. The trend continued after Putin took charge in

1999. He accepted the abrogation of the ABM Treaty in 2001. He opened up Russian airspace to the US after 9/11, and also allowed the setting up of bases in Central Asia. Despite all these major concessions, there was no reciprocity from the West. Then a series of 'colour revolutions' began in Georgia, Ukraine, and Kyrgyzstan. The US also tried to challenge the CIS grouping by the formation of GUAM comprising Georgia, Uzbekistan, Azerbaijan, and Moldova. Later Ukraine was also included.

The other extreme end of Russian policy was to show some challenge to the west by forming regional groupings. Putin also tried to form a grouping of Germany, France, and Russia in the aftermath of the Iraq invasion, but again this did not take-off. The Shanghai Cooperation Organization (SCO) formed in 2001, comprised Russia, China, Kazakhstan, Kyrgyzstan, and Uzbekistan. It focuses on cooperation to contain security threats to the region, threats from Islamic militancy, terror, separatism, narcotics, smuggling, organized crime, and the like. It was not meant to be a military alliance, yet its members are committed to providing military assistance to each other in case of attack by terrorists and secessionists, and it has conducted military exercises from 2005. Similarly, the CSTO, formed as early as 1992 to organize the Soviet space under Russian leadership, is a military alliance. Azerbaijan, Georgia, and Uzbekistan refused to participate and departed in 1999, but Uzbekistan returned to the fold in 2006, when the US was damagingly critical of its role in the Andijon crisis and the president, Islam Karimov feared a 'colour' revolution in his country. The CSTO acted as a shield against the US in this case and it emboldened him to expel the US from the Shanabad military base. Primakov had conceived of it as a means to integrate the Soviet space; but its weaknesses were evident, and Putin, consistent with his general policy of not reverting to the past, has merely used it as an instrument for extending Russian influence in the former Soviet space, and if possible beyond into the SCO, but not to reconstitute the Soviet space. The third such initiative, not yet an organization, is the trilateral between Russia, India, and China, which essentially, merely meets to discuss possible areas of cooperation and to define its limits. It has repeatedly made clear that it is not directed against the US and that it does not seek to alter the current international order. All this indicates Russia's desire to integrate into multilateral structures without posing any challenge to the USA.

The reason it is taking Russia such a long time to integrate is that it was not completely defeated at the end of the cold war, the way Germany and Japan were, and therefore it cannot totally integrate in the manner Japan and

Germany were forced to. Russia is not like Britain and France, who were on the winning side, but were defeated, and therefore integrated and subordinate to the US.

A strong and assertive Russia might revive the antagonisms of the cold war era and India will be placed in a position which we do not wish to be. A weak Russia integrated into the western ambit may take positions regarding our immediate neighbourhood not in India's interest. What would suit India is a Russia domestically more developed and economically more advanced, and therefore, capable of making its choices better. Russia and China can only collaborate up to a point as they have too many challenges and tensions between them. In Central Asia, USA and Russia can never have the same viewpoint as Pakistan's adventurism in that area is unacceptable to Russia. So there will be a great divergence between the West and Russia regarding Central Asia and that aspect is an aspect of convergence between Russia and India.

Presentation 4: Survey of India–Russia Relations

Kanwal Sibal

Outlining the Relationship There is a need to outline India and Russia's points of convergence, the foundations of the relationship, and the structures in the international order that makes the relationship valid. Since the end of the cold war USA was able to dictate to the world, but then it made some awful mistakes like in Iraq. There was general concern in countering this form of US unilateralism and saving the international community from the mistakes made by the USA. This domination has now ended and the notion of multipolarity has lost its pressing urgency. It was in that period that the concept of Russia, India, and China trilateral dialogue was mooted. China was reluctant and India was not too enthusiastic, but Russia pushed ahead. Initially there was some concern in the West, but after the 2nd meeting, it became clear that this was not a front against USA. There was also a summit level meeting of RIC but not much of substance was discussed. Russia realized that the India–China arm of RIC had problems. So the idea of BRIC, with Brazil as the 4th member was put forward. Russia assessed that a large South American country's presence would take the heat off the India–China imbroglio. It also served Russia's objective of starting a fresh initiative in Latin America. Now there is the RIC and the BRIC with the latter being more active. The basic weakness in RIC is that, despite the current concerns in USA about China 'rising' and becoming more assertive, there is little scope for major changes in the US–China relationship. There is a 'financial fusion' between US and China. The trade deficit that US runs with China is larger than the total external trade of India. China has also invested $900 billion in the US Treasury Notes. And manipulating from behind are the US corporations whose interests are entrenched in China. Putin, on his part has tried to come closer to USA but has been rebuffed despite the many concessions made by Russia. In February 2010, Putin spoke against USA for not accommodating the legitimate concerns of Russia. We Indians have our own transformational relationship with the USA. Our leadership is careful not to send any negative signal to the US even when we are provoked. So we will not do much about RIC. A plan to give an economic dimension to RIC did not succeed.

Terrorism and Religious Radicalism The other point of convergence with Russia is terrorism and religious radicalism. Russia is very sensitive to the situation in its South. It sees the frontiers of its defence against religious radicalism on the borders of Afghanistan. Russia considers Tajikistan and Uzbekistan as the buffer zone. Both these countries have had religious problems and Russia is suspicious of the US trying to weaken it and divide it internally, through Islamic fundamentalism. Lately, however, the Russian focus has shifted to drug trafficking from Afghanistan–Pakistan region. Russia has a massive social problem in that drug-habit that claims 30,000 Russians annually. But Russia is not putting the problem in a wider perspective and, thus, a problem arises between India and Russia. While many world leaders directly point to Pakistan's culpability in terror activities in India, Russia is very cautious while making statements concerning terrorist activities against India. Russia is also hedging its bets on the fallout of a US withdrawal from Afghanistan. It has formed a group of four countries, Russia, Pakistan, Tajikistan, and Afghanistan, to deal with the power structure that may emerge in Afghanistan. This contradicts its earlier talk of working with India and Iran to deal with a Taliban that is sharing power in Kabul. All this encourages Pakistan to think that they have succeeded, with Turkey, in excluding India. The USA has agreed that India has legitimate developmental role in Afghanistan, but Russia, despite knowing about religious radicalism, thinks otherwise. It sees no role for India, but a central role for Pakistan, after the US troops withdraw.

Defence Relationship India–Russia strategic defence relationship has matured over time, and today, a high percentage of our military hardware is from Russia. During President Medvedev's visit, the design agreement for the fifth generation fighter aircraft (FGFA) is likely to be signed. This will be a huge defence deal with India planning to acquire 300+ of these combat aeroplanes. As regards the 126 MRCA selection, there is unlikely to be any political fallout if Russia does not win. Ideally, it would suit India to deal with Europe in this case. Americans may be persuasive, but we have had bitter experiences with them earlier. Their interoperability conditions and very stringent transfer of technology regime makes dealing with the US a risky affair.

Nuclear Technology As for nuclear technology, Russia has been very cooperative with India. Its decision to supply enriched uranium for the Tarapur reactor came in for criticism, but Putin honoured his word and took the flak in the NSG. But the Russians also see themselves as pillars of CTBT and NPT and keep nudging India to fall in line. Medvedev's visit will also indicate Russia's stand on our civil nuclear liability law, but if they take the lead and we make progress on Kudankulam 3, 4, 5, and 6, then it will be a high point for our bilateral relationship.

Russia's Strength in India's Interest A strong Russia is in India's interest. After the collapse of the USSR, the USA stepped in to the void and dictated terms to the world. Now, a declining America is witnessing the rise of China. If Russia enters the equation forcefully, the greatest impact will be on China. The talk about G-2 will wind down. It should be remembered that there are some inherent long term tensions between Russia and China. The current collaboration between the two results from Russia being rebuffed by the West. Russia under Putin developed a multi-vector concept and the Asian dimension is a by-product of Western pressure. If Russia succeeds in normalizing its relations with NATO in an acceptable way, and the new European security architecture that Russia has proposed takes off, then there are bound to be changes in the way Russia views China's rise. Russia is aware that China is becoming a huge behemoth right next to them and Siberia is wide open. Russia is keeping China engaged, as is India, to limit unpredictable behaviour on China's part. The more one gauges China, the lesser the chances of conflict.

Russia has major problems too. Its population is declining by 700,000 every year. Incentives to the European Russia to reproduce more are not working, while the Muslim states have increasing population. This will change the religious demographic composition of Russia.

India's absence from the UNSC permanent membership restricts our options of greater bilateral cooperation with Russia. Russia and India have lost a lot of ground in bilateral relations. India has every interest to have strong forward-looking relationship with Russia, but Russia has to reorganize and give itself the capacity to reach out to a rising India with expanding needs.

Discussions

In the ensuing discussions, some members presented their views while others asked questions from the speakers.

A lady member commented that it had been a scintillating seminar and thanked all speakers for their brilliant presentations. Her question to Palat was that Russia had gone through many turbulent periods, but each had thrown up a great man and leader who had raised Russia from chaos to preponderance, and this had been happening for the past 900 years. Palat replied in the affirmative about Russia having gone through many troubled times until the war of the 17th Century between the Orthodox and the Catholics. There were no innocents or guilty in this game. Russia has enormous resources and, after Germany, is the only great power to confront the west. After WWII, of the six great powers, four were knocked out and now, after the cold war, Russia has been knocked out. Five centuries of growth has now been reversed.

Arvind Seetharaman asked if there was any one facet where Russia was dependent on India. As a follow-up, he asked as to what role India could play in the Shanghai Cooperation Organization (SCO).

Sibal replied that Russian dependence was only in the defence sector, because even now 25 per cent of Russian arms sales are to India. Though at one time China was buying 40 per cent of the Russian weapons output, it has virtually dried up now. But Russia will not acknowledge this dependence. In fact, they still think they are doing India a favour. It is also equally true that Russia is the only country that will help India build up a genuine military industrial capability. The 5th generation aircraft and the permission for India to receive military signals from GLONASS navigation system are examples of Russian cooperation.

As regards the SCO, there is very little that India can do. India has observer status at SCO. Our problems are with terrorism and drug-trafficking from the Afghanistan–Pakistan area. The problem is that the perpetrator of our problems, Pakistan, is also an observer at the SCO.

Manmohan Reddy asked if India can act as an equal to Russia. He narrated an incident when the Chief of Bureau of Sukhoi asked the visiting head of HAL what the HAL had brought to the design table—there was silence. The design bureau chief himself said that India can bring only money to the table, implying that India had nothing to contribute to the 5th generation fighter programme. Sibal clarified that in the design agreement, specific requirements of India are a twin-engine twin seater FGA and the fly-by-wire system will be of Indian design.

Jairam quoted US author Richard Haas stating that the dawn of the age of non-polarity has arrived, where what counts is purely economics and commercial interest.

Sibal said that it is too early to write-off the USA. In 15–20 years, a clearer picture will emerge, till then USA will remain the dominant, pre-eminent power and they will be the principal pole. In an age of globalization, countries do not have to make ideological choices, they have multiple options. India has problems with China, but when it comes to WTO or climate change negotiations, we are on the same side.

Palat added that economics can never be isolated from other aspects.

The Chairman added that money tries to buy power, but power commands money. So the race is not over yet. He agreed with Sibal about polarity. He stated that if the North Pole from our earth is taken away, the other pole will also fly out of orbit. The world order has to find some kind of accommodation resulting in stability.

Nazareth from the audience said that the roles of USA, Russia, and China have been commented upon when talking about Central Asia, but there was no mention of Turkey. Many countries in the region speak the Turkish family of languages. Huntington had stated that if Turkey was not allowed into European Union, it would abandon secularism and become the leader of the Islamic nations in the region.

Sibal answered that the collapse of the Soviet Union happened when he was the ambassador in Turkey. There was great euphoria in Turkey as if they would recover their lost brothers and Turkey would dominate this strategic hinterland that had opened up, and become a player on the global scene. They sent many delegations to CIS countries trying to discover similarities and commonalities. There was a plan to persuade these countries to abandon the Cyrillic script and adopt the Turkic script. But what Turkey wanted never happened. Turkish companies are active on the construction front and the consumer goods market. Turkey has realized that it has reached the limits of its influence. Turkey is energy dependent, but has not been able to harness the resources from Central Asia, except from Russia and Kazakhstan. So Turkey does not have any role to play in the most important resource for economic progress of Central Asia. There is very little we can leverage from Turkey's presence or influence in that area.

Palat added that when Turkey was the head of the Ottoman Empire, and there were many pan-Turkic movements, it never volunteered for leadership of the Turkic speaking people.

Shankaran said that in the globalized world, no country had friends or enemies. Only two things matter, one is resources and the other is a market. She stated that the ascendancy of India and China could be attributed to their huge markets.

In his summing up, the Chairman stated that all four speakers had articulated their views very well, done splendidly, and the subject of Russia would be our abiding interest. When the Russians started their Revolution in 1917, it was a great human experiment to see if a new kind of human being can be created—a system where everyone would have the right to develop. It went wrong and folded up. The greatness of the movement cannot be denied. Russia has given up its Asian Republics, but in all these Republics the population is literate because of communism.

Russia has stood by India through good and bad. Both countries are in the process of change, but a strong bilateral relationship between the two is mutually beneficial and good for a stable world order.

Chapter 9

China's Defence Modernization

ASIA CENTRE BANGALORE

'China's Defence Modernisation: Implications for India'
Proceedings of the Seminar
held on

October 24, 2009

Preface

Asia Centre conducted a seminar on October 24, 2009 on the topic 'China's Defence Modernisation: Implications for India'. A.P. Venkateswaran, Chairman of Asia Centre, presided. The following speakers addressed the seminar:

D.S. Rajan	Director, Chennai Centre for China Studies
R. Nagappa	Professor, National Institute of Advanced Studies
Air Chief Marshal (Retd) Fali Major	Former Chief of Air Staff
Srikanth Kondapalli	Professor in Chinese Studies, Jawahar Lal Nehru University, New Delhi
C.V. Ranganathan	Former Ambassador to China and France

The following summary of the Seminar proceedings was prepared by A. Madhavan, former Ambassador of India and member of the Asia Centre.

Introduction

Mutual Mistrust The deep-rooted mistrust between India and China stems from a divide that relates not only to the unsettled border between them, but also to the strategic sphere where Indians perceive Chinese moves to constrict our influence in the region. For its part, from the time of the Dalai Lama's flight into India in 1959, China still suspects India of designs to detach Tibet from the Chinese republic in collusion with other powers, despite India's acceptance of Tibet as part of the PRC. In recent times, China has stepped up claims to Arunachal Pradesh as Southern Tibet.

Building Relations in other Areas Both countries have for several years set aside their irresoluble differences and strengthened relations in other areas, especially trade and economic, reaping mutual benefits. They have tinkered with Confidence Building Measures to mitigate the bitterness of the border dispute, with scant success. They have found convergence to forge a common approach on global issues like climate change.

Aim of Military Modernization China's defence modernization is of a piece with its overall strategy of catching up with the US and surpassing it by the mid-21st century as the world's premier power. However, India cannot ignore the implications for its own strategic perspective of China's modernized military.

Indian Response to China's Growing Strength China's rapid, all-round progress has created a marked asymmetry between India and China in the military sphere, with little prospect of the gap closing. Without racing to match the Chinese military strength, India can accelerate its own economic and technological growth and modernize its own military. Indian diplomacy should strengthen a multipolar network for warmer bilateral and regional ties to counter erosions of our strategic space by Chinese activities. Such was the consensus that emerged from the seminar and the discussion.

Need for Modernizing Indian Defence The five experts who spoke at the seminar covered China's defence modernization in detail, citing China's 2008 White Paper on defence. China's defence budget is far higher than India's. India's defence should have higher priority in order to modernize, without which, the present *modus vivendi* with China will be fragile. Our defence production needs radical reforms with a mix of state-managed and private defence industries.

China is not merely modernizing its defence forces; it is expanding its military capability quantitatively; it is fast acquiring maritime power projection capability. Driven by its need to secure the sea lanes in the Indian Ocean for its energy imports and to back up its claims over a vast EEZ in the South and East China Seas. It is building more nuclear and diesel submarines as well as surface combatants, including aircraft carriers, developed long-range cruise missiles, and is working to acquire port facilities at key locations on its extended sea routes. In aviation, China has indigenously improved on Soviet planes to match US fighters, and built bombers to carry medium range terrain-hugging cruise missiles. China has become a leading space power, with counter-space war capacity and accurate killer-satellites. In ground forces, the PLA has been sharply reduced in personnel but much improved with modern weapons and electronic aids for 'informatised' (or cyber-dimensional) warfare.

Presentation 1: Upgradation of Chinese Forces—Implications

D.S. Rajan

Growth of China's Military Power The assertion in the official White Paper on 'China's National Defence in 2008' that China will never seek hegemony or engage in military expansion now or in the future, is regarded by the world with scepticism, given the lack of transparency in China's military actions and plans. The US, Japan, and India are among the countries that are concerned that the military balance is shifting, with far-reaching implications.

The speaker covered two topics: China's land and naval forces and the territorial disputes between China and India.

Defence Modernization Defence modernization is part of the 'four modernizations' programme of China dating from 1978. The 2008 White Paper offers clues to Chinese policy as to its security concerns and the stages of defence modernization intended to meet them.

With increasing international interdependence, China believes that the risk of a world war has lessened; the Asia–Pacific region is relatively stable, and tension has reduced with Taiwan. The negatives are conflicting claims for territorial and maritime rights, the consolidation of regional alliances by the US and 'containment of China from outside and sabotage by separatist and hostile forces inside'.

'Two Incompatibilities' President Hu Jintao, in 2008, had referred to 'two incompatibilities' in China's preparedness: 1) between military capabilities and the aspiration to win local wars, and 2) the level needed to defend expansion of national interests. China wants to fill the gaps.

National Defence Strategy

Upgradation of Strategy Three objectives are mentioned in the White Paper, in its 'National Defence Strategy for a New Stage in the New Century': 1) 'Informatisation' for modern defence, 2) upholding national security and unity, and 3) coordinated development of national growth with the armed forces. The modernization is planned in three stages; by mid-century the modernization plan should be accomplished, that is, China should catch up with the advanced powers. The PLA is charged with the 'historical missions' of consolidating the Party leadership, safeguarding China's expanding national interests, and maintaining world peace. The military should be capable of defending the borders, win local wars in conditions of 'informatisation', pursue nuclear strategy under the 'no first use' principle, maintain security, including maritime, space and cyberspace, carry out counter-terrorism tasks, and develop military operations 'other than war', as in countering Somalian naval piracy.

Increase in Defence Budget The Chinese have upgraded the technological levels of defence by moving from land wars of attrition to 'informatisation' of main battle weapon systems, for example, rapid detection, target location, and precision strikes. They are now more transparent in their budgeting. They show a 15.9 per cent annual increase in defence expenditure in 1998–2007. China's military budget for 2008 is US $57.2 billion, an increase of 17.6 per cent from the previous year. The US estimate of China's defence expenditure is between US $97 and $139 billion.

Modernization of Military Technology and Organization The Taiwan issue will remain important in China's defence posture. China intends to improve services level capabilities by a modern integrated network. It has obtained advanced weapon systems from abroad, augmented the scope and technology of its defence industries, and conducted reforms in military doctrine and organization. The DF-31 and 31A intercontinental missiles, its anti-access denial capability through advanced cruise and anti-ship missiles, its anti-satellite weapon test in January 2007, all show a significant augmentation of strategic capability. Such moves indicate that China has factored in contingencies beyond Taiwan, such as conflict for resources in disputed areas. The Airborne Early Warning and Control and aerial refuelling programme are plainly intended for operations beyond the South China Sea.

Though China, as yet, lacks long-range power projection, it plans to extend its reach, as evidenced by its aircraft carriers, nuclear submarines, and space-based surveillance system. It will also use counter-space and cyber warfare against technologically superior enemy forces.

Land Forces

China's land forces have evolved from the infantry-based level to Electronic Counter Measures (ECM) wings for joint operations with the army, navy, and air force. The Army has shifted its focus from regional defence to trans-regional mobility. The Army is downsizing itself and acquiring aviation and missile capability for integrated joint operations and long distance manoeuvres on the borders. The main responsibility is to deter any outside intervention in a possible conflict across the Taiwan Straits. The aim will be a multiple layer offensive system for land, sea, air, and cyber operations.

China's Navy and Power Projection in the Indian Ocean

Transformation of Navy for Oceanic Capability The PLA(N) has moved from coastal defence, to offshore defence, to an oceanic capability. It is to be equipped with a new generation of weapons, large surface combat ships with ballistic and cruise missiles, amphibious forces, and long-range aircraft. Its sub-surface fleet is to acquire modern conventional as well as nuclear submarines with cruise and ballistic missiles. All this confirms China's ambition to become a naval power with a global reach. Two further hints of maritime ambition may be noted. 1) an airport and sea port on Mischief Reef in the disputed Spratlys, and 2) military bases, starting with a test base in the South China Sea to protect China's commercial interests.

Energy Security and Role of Chinese Navy

There is a shift in naval focus from the Taiwan Straits to the Indian Ocean Sea Lines of Communication. But China's navy is not yet capable of protecting the sea-lanes from West Asia to the South China Sea. Hence, China is forging alliances and political arrangements with the rim lands of the Indian Ocean and building port facilities. But the ports of Gwadar, Chittagong, Sittwe, and Hambantota may also be viewed as potential facilities for the Chinese navy, if the 'String of Pearls' theory is valid.

Sino-Indian Competition

China believes that India could impede this drive and block outside entry to the Malacca Strait, which is vital for China's imports.

A retired senior Indian official has said that with the possible instability in key areas like Hormuz, it is useful for the major powers to form a collective security arrangement to safeguard the flow of maritime trade. A 'concert of Asian powers' is conceivable.

Sino–Indian Territorial Dispute

China has been territorially ambitious. At various times it has claimed Nepal, Sikkim, Bhutan, NEFA, and Ladakh; even Assam and the Andamans are claimed to have been historically parts of China. No border claim is allowed to lapse, though some, such as the South China Sea dispute, the Senkaku issue with Japan and the border dispute with India are allowed to lie dormant, to 'await a suitable climate for solution.'

Both China and India perceive the boundary issue as complex, but have been ready to develop bilateral ties, looking beyond the dispute. China's stand is that its borders, as in 1912, the end of the Qing period, were ignored by British India in the Shimla Convention of 1914. China consequently rejects the McMahon Line, and claims all of Arunachal Pradesh, calling it 'Southern Tibet'. India, however, regards the McMahon Line as the *de facto* border with China.

Chinese claims in Sikkim, intrusions along the border, and the fulminations about Arunachal and warnings in the state-controlled Chinese media have all vitiated the atmosphere of bilateral relations. At the diplomatic level, however, China has maintained correctness; the inference is that hawkish elements in the PLA and the Party are influencing its policy towards India. Tibetan unrest weakens China's claim of sovereignty in that province and also its case in the border negotiations with India.

Strategy for India

As part of its strategic posture vis-à-vis China, India should:

1) Engage China bilaterally and globally while protecting its own strategic interests, which include Indian defence modernization in parallel with China's.
2) Strengthen its relations with Japan, Vietnam, and South-East Asian nations for strategic deterrence against China, and should use its relationship with the US to balance China's military rise but without entering into treaty alliance with the US.
3) Affirm its core interests while dealing with China. Its recent protest against China taking up infrastructure projects in Pakistan Occupied Kashmir is a right move in response to China's anti-Indian statements. Indian leaders could also consider meeting the Dalai Lama as a religious leader.

4) Continue border talks with China indefinitely. Zhou Enlai, in 1960, had proposed a border settlement roughly on the basis of mutual accommodation: Chinese acceptance of a line close to the McMahon in the East, and an Indian acceptance of Chinese claims in the West (Ladakh and Aksai Chin). Such an accommodation could be reconsidered by both sides.

China's Future Strategic Posture China wants to advance towards 'peaceful development', and is unlikely to act to the detriment of its need for international stability and a 'favourable neighbourhood'. The question remains whether with its modernized military power projection, it will act more aggressively. To quote Harry Harding, a China scholar: 'Beijing may not resort to military means to settle issues, but will use its growing resources to shift the overall balance of power in China's favour, especially in Asia; such a shift is already taking place.'

Presentation 2: Missile and Space Modernization

Rajaram Nagappa

Impressive Strides In the recent past, China has made impressive strides in science, technology, industry, and policy, apart from military modernization. The approach is long term; a conscious effort to think far ahead in conceptualization, planning, and implementation.

A Clear Pattern A clear pattern can be discerned from an analysis of the growth of Chinese military aviation. It started with licensed Russian production in the 1950s; the stoppage of technology with the break Sino–Soviet relations in 1960s forced a self-reliant approach; this was followed by trial and error learning, mastery over quality control problems—all of which led to a rich bank of self-acquired knowledge and capability. The window to the West was opened up in the 1980s, resulting in an economic boom and exposure to new technologies. The collapse of the USSR caused a cash-strapped Russia to part with state-of-the-art technologies and expertise and a cash-rich China exploited it to the hilt. Today, China boasts of Generation-4 type of indigenous aircraft capability and is no longer dependent on imported know-how. A high level of maturity and capability is evident in their missile development efforts, spin-offs into space efforts and a natural follow-up relating to militarization of space.

Defence White Paper—2008

A good place to start is the latest White Paper on National Defence. The 6th white paper for 2008 was released on January 20, 2009. It gives an overall picture of China's national defence covering the security environment, national defence policy, and defence expenditure and arms control. Exclusive chapters are devoted for the 2nd Artillery Force, army, navy, and air force and science and technology. The key words are 'Mechanisation' and 'Informatisation.' The white paper outlines a time bound programme covering:

1) Military mechanization and advancement in informatization by 2020;
2) Strengthening the military by means of science and technology;
3) Defence industry reforms;
4) Chapter XI of the white paper deals with 'Science, Technology and Industry for National Defence.'

Military needs will be the drivers of the science, technology, and industry with spin-offs into the civilian domain. This approach will clearly create a highly coordinated system involving R&D, academic research, and industrial production and training with civilian partnership. Major policy changes are underway to promote the transformation of defence industry enterprises into joint stock enterprises, diversification and specialization-oriented restructuring. Simultaneously, while retaining state control over weaponry and equipment research and production, the non-public sector is allowed to compete for research and production projects. Some specific research areas are mentioned in the white paper and give an idea of the thrust and priority accorded to them. They include: Digital simulation and hardware-in-the-loop simulation facilities, advanced experimentation and demonstration facilities (to aid higher design capability and R&D success rate), precision manufacturing, and so on.

The white paper stipulates China's policy of 'no first use' (NFU) of nuclear weapons. It is stated that in peace time, the nuclear weapons of the Second Artillery Force are not aimed at any country. The important point is that since 1990, the conventional missile force is also under the command of the second artillery force. Unlike the nuclear force, which is primarily deterrent in nature, the conventional artillery force is primed for offensive operations.

Missile Development

Development of Ballistic Missiles China started development of ballistic missiles based on Russian technology transfer in 1957. By the time of the chill in Sino–Soviet relations in the 1960s, the Chinese had evolved enough institutions and personnel who could engineer larger capability missiles. At that time each Chinese missile was target-specific: the DF-2 for Japan, the DF-3 for US bases in the Philippines; the DF-4 for Guam; and the DF-5 for continental USA. All these missiles used earth storable liquid propellants and DF-5, the largest, could carry a 3,000 kg warhead to 12,000 km.

Solid Propellant for Missiles In the early 1960s, China realized the operational superiority of solid propellant missiles over the liquid counterparts. But hampered by technology-related issues and upheavals caused by the Cultural Revolution, the project took long to fructify. In November 1981, a successful flight test was achieved; a launch from a Chinese nuclear submarine took place seven years later. The DF-21(3,000 kms) and DF-31(8,000 kms) are land-based; JL-1 and JL-2 are the submarine launched versions. With this the reach of the Chinese missiles is truly global.

Of specific interest to India are the shorter range M-9 (supplied to Pakistan) and M-11, which target the North and North-East of the country; the DF-21 can penetrate deep into the southern regions of the country.

Cruise Missiles Terrain-hugging cruise missiles, such as the US Tomahawk, used extensively in the 1991 Gulf War have the outstanding advantages of low cost, stealth, long range, and accuracy. They can be launched from various platforms—land, air, ship, or submarine. Impressed by this, China went all out to procure, assimilate, and develop this technology. The DH-10 is a 1,200+ km range land attack cruise missile. The range of this weapon increases when launched from an aircraft. Some observers believe that the Chinese H-6 bomber can launch the DH-10 missile. Cruise missiles are designed for radar avoidance and low level flights. They can be carried over the Himalayas by air and launched from air to be guided along the terrain.

The global positioning system (GPS) is essential for accurate navigation by aircraft, ships, submarines, and missiles. China has operationalized its own GPS navigation constellation, the Beidou system.

To summarize:

1) China's ballistic missiles are capable of reaching targets anywhere in the world (except for parts of South America).
2) The later missiles are solid-propellant based with higher range and improved CEP (Circular Error Probable).
3) China has a large number of improved versions of M-9 and M-11 missiles with a CEP of less than 50 metres.
4) The DF-21 can cover all parts of India.

5) Long-range cruise missiles are being developed on priority.
6) China has put in place its own satellite based navigation system.

Chinese Space Activities

Aims of Space Activities The aims of the Chinese space activities are:

1) Explore outer space and enhance understanding of the Earth and the cosmos.
2) Utilize outer space for peaceful purposes; promote human civilization and social progress, benefiting the whole of mankind.
3) Meet the demands of economic reconstruction, scientific and technological development, national security and to raise the scientific standards of the Chinese people and to protect China's national interests and rights, all leading to a comprehensively strong China.

Satellite Programmes China has launched more than 70 satellites since 1970 for a variety of missions. China's early missions included recoverable space capsules. They would have, therefore, acquired early mastery in technology for recovering objects from space-mission management and thermal protection material development.

China has used the booster of the DF-5 ICBM in their very successful Long March (CZ) series of launch vehicles, which can place 9.5 tonnes in Low Earth Orbit and can be used for both unmanned and manned missions. China initiated its manned space flight programme in 1992 and has long-term plans for a manned space laboratory and space station. It has established space tracking, telemetry, and command network as well a deep space network.

China has used its launch capability as an exercise in soft power. Some initiatives in this category are:

1) Offer of launch services at attractive rates. Customers have included the US, France, and Sweden.
2) It has a joint development programme of Earth Remote Sensing satellites with Brazil. Two satellites have already been launched and two more are planned.
3) It has promised US $222 million in funding to Pakistan for space research. In 1990, China launched Pakistan's Badr-1 satellite.
4) China has active MOUs with Iran, North Korea, Mongolia, Pakistan, and Thailand on Cooperation in Small Multi-Mission Satellite Project and Related Activity.

5) It has promoted the Asia Pacific Space Cooperation Organization. Besides China, Bangladesh, Indonesia, Iran, Mongolia, Pakistan, Peru, and Thailand are members of the Organization.

With the space capability described above, it is clear that China aims to be a major space power. A 2004 article in the People's Liberation Army Daily asserted that 'Information dominance cannot be separated from space dominance. We can say that seizing space dominance is the root for winning the informatised war.'

Counter-space capabilities

In an Anti-Satellite Test (ASAT) conducted on January 11, 2007, China destroyed an old weather satellite with a DF-21 missile. While there was world-wide criticism of the widespread debris caused, the fact remains that this was a major technical achievement and China had broken no international law in the process. As part of the overall counter-space strategy of China, this was a clear signal to the US against its attempts at space domination. US technology and conventional forces are superior to those of China, but the US relies totally on its space-based assets in war—especially the C4ISR (Command, Control, Communication, Computers, Intelligence, Surveillance, and Reconnaissance) component. If this superiority is to be overcome by a relatively weaker power, space denial to blunt the C4ISR will be an obvious strategy.

In counter-space capabilities China is concentrating on:

1) Space objects surveillance and identification systems (investments in optical telescopes, laser-tracking devices and large phased array radars).
2) Kinetic energy weapons.
3) Small satellites.
4) Directed energy weapons (ground-based high and low power lasers).

Side by side, China is also pursuing with Russia diplomatic initiatives for prevention of the weaponization of space. In successive white papers, China has maintained that space should be used for peaceful purposes and opposed its militarization. In the Conference on Disarmament, it has proposed draft resolutions to the UN General Assembly on the Prevention of an Armed Race in Outer Space (PAROS) and is an advocate of the draft treaty on the Prevention of Placement of Weapons in Outer Space and the Threat or Use of Force against Outer Space Objects.

Information Warfare

China has stressed informatization with Chinese characteristics in successive white papers. The 2002 White Paper noted the addition of outer space and the 'information sphere' to the established land, air, and sea battlefield spaces.

High bandwidth connectivity is an obvious priority; a 2002 report showed that the cable network spanned 20,000 kilometres in Western China in 2002 and a million kilometres in 2006. In 2002, Gen Dai Qingmin published his concept of Integrated Network-Electronic Warfare. He postulated that Information Warfare, of which Network Warfare and Electronic Warfare are parts, has several forms aimed at enabling a country to use its own networks while denying the adversary the use of his networks. At another level, it prevents the adversary from acquiring or forwarding information. At the extreme end, information warfare includes the physical destruction of technical means. The essence is to achieve the functional effect, which in most cases should result in messing up the enemy's decision-making process.

China is known to have carried out attacks on US, Indian, Japan, and Taiwan computer systems as part of its information warfare practice. The aim of the exercise was to disrupt critical infrastructure like banking, power supply, and telecommunication networks in the target countries.

China's Defence Budget

During the years 1988 to 2007, China's defence expenditure rose at an average of 14 to 16 per cent. In actual terms, the defence expenditure in 2006 was about RMB 298 billion (US $43 billion) and is pegged at RMB 418 billion (US $60 billion) for 2008. The US DOD estimates are much higher—twice or thrice as much—than the figures given out by the Chinese. China's GDP is high, and in 2007, its defence expenditure amounted to 1.38 per cent of the GDP (US $3,675 billion). India's defence budget in contrast, was about 2.38 per cent of GDP; however, in real terms this amounted to only US $23 billion.

Conclusion

China Second only to US China is ahead of India in many technology disciplines and aims in the short run to be second to the US, and in the long run equal or overtake the US. It is in the process of charting out S&T roadmaps up to the year 2050 in 18 key sectors, which include energy, space, marine science, material science, information technology, nano-technology, water resources, and hydrocarbon resources. China's stated defence budget is more than double India's defence budget of US $23 billion (but half when expressed as a percentage of GDP). What India needs is a focused approach and to build on the strengths it already possesses. The other day, Roddam Narasimha, in his talk on 'India and World Science', mentioned that 10 years ago, Indian aeronautics was ahead of China. The situation is totally reversed today.

Corrective Measures for India India needs to assess the impact of development in China on many issues and evaluate appropriate counter-measures. Investment in situational awareness tools is a must and will require sizeable investment in sensors and tracking equipment. The Agni missile variants provide for adequate deterrence in terms of capability—the logic of a well enunciated policy of deployment with conventional warheads as an offensive tool may be worthy of debate and consideration. Either way, India will have to step up its production rate of missiles and warheads. India has lagged behind in development and deployment of subsonic long-range cruise missiles and must take urgent corrective steps.

Critical technologies required for counter-space strategies need to be prioritized and taken up for development. India must develop small satellites, which can play a major role in time to come, as well as an independent launch capability in this regard. There are a host of associated technologies and launch services, as well as enhancement of the industrial sector and issues of private sector participation to be addressed.

In the areas of missiles, space, counter-space, and electronic warfare, we have established the basic capabilities but need to coordinate and prioritize our development, not only to meet the challenges confronting us, but to devise counter-measures of our own.

Presentation 3: A Strategic Review

Air Chief Marshal (Retd) Fali Major

National power is increasingly determined by economic and technical power rather than military might. Economic strength is fundamental and sustains all other aspects of power, but it must be protected by military strength. The importance of economic strength is evident in the development of Russia, China, India, Japan, the US, and the EU.

Conflict is endemic to human life. The past three millennia have seen 14,500 wars, with only 270 years of peace. It is utopian to hope for a peaceful, harmonious world. India awakened to its destiny as a regional power only after independence. It has gained respect and influence as the world's largest democracy, with a sound economic and technical base for development. Asia has become the global engine of growth. All the major powers have a presence and stake in it. Economic growth has galvanized Asian military capabilities.

Asia will still be racked by conflict, instability, and terrorism, but India as a vibrant, resurgent nation with resources can assume a greater role in world affairs. India and China are neighbours, the largest democracy jostling with the largest autocracy in the same region. China envisioned the differences decades ago to create a strategic space for itself. India has experienced the Chinese provocations beginning with the assertion of control over Tibet, the huge border claims, the 1962 aggression, right down to the latest moves of opposition to India's membership of the UNSC, the criticism of the Prime Minister's visit to Arunachal Pradesh, the claim to Tawang, and the accelerated pace of military modernization. All this has provoked anger and hostility in India.

But instead of hyping China as a power too formidable to rival, we should focus on what India can do. Despite turbulence and uncertainties, we live in exciting times with challenges which should provoke a fitting response. Despite cynical and pessimistic forebodings, we must credit our armed forces. They have by no means ignored China's defence developments and modernization. India too has been adding to its defence strength, though at an admittedly slower tempo. All armed forces continuously modernize, reform, and improve their infrastructure, personnel, and combat readiness, following similar paths. India is no exception. Modernization is inevitable, since equipment becomes obsolete and doctrines must change with technology and the security environment.

Armed forces must prepare for the capabilities of other powers, not their intentions. India faces a dilemma regarding Chinese intentions when China is in overdrive in defence modernization. We must assess how far their capability matches their display of might and organization in parades and ceremonials.

China's Air Force has surely made huge strides in capability, but no air force can rely only on a technologically sophisticated inventory. Neither funding nor technical progress will be sufficient to provide it. China's buzzword of 'informatised warfare' should not stun us. The Chinese are not targeting only India, but other powers too. In space technology, India certainly needs to speed up its programme, since other countries are already taking up slots in the satellite world above us.

India should focus on the entire spectrum of possible threats, not limit plans to one country or two, since new power centres emerge along with conflict zones. For too long India was Pak-centric in defence preparations, neglecting China's ascent.

It is hard for a country to build up adequate capability, but no country can acquire a full range of capability all at once. It is good that India has finally started a capability-based approach to defence policy. It has begun to modernize its military assets. Notably, there is a change from the policy of dissuasion (of the perceived threat) to active deterrence. This has infused urgency in the whole exercise. Further, we are into a systematic, nuanced programme spread over three plan periods, with no funding constraints and full government support. If successful, it should advance Indian defence by a few generations.

The underlying causes of Sino–Indian differences will remain unaltered. Despite the hazards of prediction, it is reasonable to envisage that future wars will not be long-drawn out world wars. But violence of many kinds will remain, and conflicts of low level, border wars and regional wars, are always likely. India may even have to initiate a limited and calibrated conflict to defend or assert its interests and demonstrate its will. Our planning takes such contingencies into account.

A key question in defence preparation is whether doctrine drives technology or *vice-a-versa*. Do we have to go into conflict situations with what is available or do we demand the technical improvements by enunciating a newly felt need. It is doctrine that should dictate the technical levels of preparation. If there is a perceived gap in capability, the military planners should ask for a technical 'fix' and the process will lead to the approved design and the product. India needs this process, along with a robust core of R&D to make it timely and effective. India is over-dependent on governmental support, the DRDO (which has performed quite well), and public sector defence industries. To go beyond the current level of transferred technology under licensed production, we must involve the private sector in defence industry. Technology gallops ahead, and armed forces should not only absorb new technology, but also manage the old equipment resourcefully until it is superseded.

Another issue is that technology for weapon systems should be reinforced by building up the capability of personnel through training, induction of new technologists, and specialization. Older personnel need retraining. China too has followed the same route.

If it is a race with China, India may be slower, but that is partly due to China being an autocracy. The quest for technological advantage must continue. Defence must generate force multipliers, both tangible and intangible. The latter kind depends on the quality of personnel and strong doctrines. More can be achieved with less in men and materials if the quality is superior.

Asymmetric warfare means that an armed force must prevail over an adversary with greater numbers.

India's strategic perspective is strengthened by its civilizational memory, its composite culture, benign approach to other countries, moral principles, and the wide acceptance it commands in the comity of nations. India must demonstrate its soft power backed by economic and military capability.

Presentation 4: Implications of China's Rise

Srikanth Kondapalli

China's rise began with its reform process in 1978. It is propelled by an obsession with the GDP; from a high of 12 per cent, this parameter has slowed down to 8 or 9 per cent per annum. It is reckoned that one percentage point up or down involves an increase or decrease of 20 million jobs. Unemployment creates serious problems for the Communist Party and the state.

China's GDP has shot up to US $4.4 trillion, the third largest in the world. India's is reckoned to be US $1.2 trillion. According to a Goldman Sachs estimate, in terms of GDP, China will be the largest economy worldwide in 2027. The global balance of forces will move from the West to the East. China is using its rise to good effect to gain bargaining space in negotiations and appreciation as a responsible stake-holder in world affairs. There is even talk of a G2 (the US and China) to manage difficult global issues. India does not welcome this since it may erode the diplomatic gains of the US–India nuclear deal and strategic partnership under George Bush, along with the prospect of India being accepted as a major power.

China has expanded its naval reach in the Indian Ocean in order to safeguard its energy flows through these important sea-lanes. The Indian Navy is also becoming more active in this area, with exercises and improved relations with the littoral countries, especially in the arc from Bandar Abbas to Malacca. China believes that the Indian vision is tactical, not strategic, whereas the Chinese vision has been strategic since the Nixon visit in 1972. It is to acquire comprehensive national strength, evolve both hard and soft power, and become the manufacturing hub of the world. China today would rank fourth in a scale of ten major countries. India may be at the sixth position, but will take long to reach the level of China in all-round development. Hard power, that is economic and military power, remains important in world standings. China manufactures for export, with foreign trade valued at US $2.2 trillion, or nearly 60 per cent of its GDP. Therefore, keeping the sea-lanes safe is a priority for China, which implies that its navy has been given a more important role now.

During the global financial crisis, China was worse hit than India; being more dependent on foreign trade, it suffered from reduced demand from the West, mainly the US. China's domestic consumption amounts to only 21 per cent of the GDP. This aspect makes the sustainability of China's growth problematic, whereas India can sustain its growth rate better. In China, the economic crisis led to industrial unrest. India is a relatively more stable society.

An important point is that China has the ability to transfer funds within the defence budget more smoothly than India. The army has been downsized from a strength of 4.5 million to 1.6 million. Further demobilization is planned. With the increased defence budget, the per capita amount available per soldier is higher than in India. The retirement age is set at 62 years. China's armed forces will have a younger age profile with more new recruits joining. China can be flexible in disbanding or amalgamating the units in the forces. China aims at a coordinated and integrated set of modernized and trained armed forces which are 'lean and mean' and reliably available in theatres as and when required. The military regions have been reduced in number while the mobility of units has been greatly increased.

Reforms have also been carried out in the Western and the Eastern theatre command forces. Rapid Response Forces have been set up, 20 units already posted. They can move from one point to a target point speedily. The implication for India is that the lead time our side can expect at a given battle front is much reduced. The Indian army has hitherto believed that the Chinese across the border posed a low level threat, because it would take three to four months before it could mobilize and be combat ready, but that expectation has to be revised in view of the Chinese military reforms. India and China at present maintain broadly similar troop strengths along the border. The Chinese military regions of Chengdu and Aksai Chin are ranged against our side. In Tibet, there are perhaps about four lakh Chinese armed personnel.

Quality upgradation is the main line of reform. The Indian side used to count on its capacity to inflict heavy damages on the adversary in a conflict. But the Chinese have significantly increased the combat capacity of their army, making up the leeway. India, perhaps, has the better air force.

China proclaims the principle of 'No First Use' of nuclear weapons. But we cannot be sure when the nuclear threshold may be passed. At present, the phase of confrontation is rated as a sub-sub-conventional phase, but there have been many violations by them of the Line of Actual Control, publicized by the media and acknowledged by the army.

China studies the weaknesses and strengths of the adversary. It found a weakness in the US satellite array, and then showed its capacity to knock-off a target satellite. The Chinese must be noting India's weak points. Bangalore, for instance, is both a weakness and strength, thanks to its IT success. Some of the software developed there goes to China. The Chinese have invested US $54 million in India in key sectors of use to them. Elsewhere too, they choose investment opportunities in the energy sector and other sectors which can help them to advance as a world power.

In the area of anti-terrorism, China and India have attempted joint exercises. On our side, there seems to be a difference between the Ministry of External Affairs and the Ministry of Defence in assessing the feasibility of joint exercises with China, the former being more sceptical. In Confidence Building Measures, the two sides have so far probed the possibility of conflict prevention, but not trust-building. Joint air exercises are unlikely, since China does not want to invite Pakistani suspicions. Though both India and China have a common interest in fighting terrorism, China is unwilling to accept the Indian contention on 'cross-border terrorism' from Pakistan. At best, there can be some sharing of intelligence on terrorism.

In sum, China's rise does pose a challenge to India. It has assessed that India is tactically focused on South Asia, whereas its own focus is strategic. China's policy will be to confine India to South Asia. It is for us in India to break these constraints by an equally strategic vision, which we should realize in stages.

Presentation 5: The Way Forward

C. V. Ranganathan

The outgoing naval chief, Admiral Sureesh Mehta, in a speech before his retirement, drew attention to the asymmetries between China and India in economic, military, technological, and other areas of development. The India–China comparison has bred an Indo-pessimism which needs to be resisted. Such an outlook does not take into account the vast differences between the two countries in their historical experience, cultural traits, their chosen paths of development, and the systemic differences in the instruments of political governance and the opportunities which each of them availed of amid changing international situations.

This apart, there are features which belong to the realm of political psychology which are noteworthy in the India–China comparison. In spite of spectacular economic growth and the international influence which it has brought China, certain basics of China's party—state relations and the approach of the leaders of the CCP in statecraft and strategy—have not altered much since the founding of the PRC in 1949. This is mainly to be seen in China's approach to sovereignty and political power. All its rulers, since 1949, have been committed to putting China in a position to determine its own destiny. All have identified China's independence with the material power of the ruling political organization, and all have considered and developed China's ideological mind-set as instrumental to that goal.

China's sovereignty is manifest, almost tangible. A state's independence is meaningless unless its government can act as it sees fit. But since economic interdependence has become a priority after globalization began in earnest, Chinese leaders seek ways to influence whatever advantage there is with the potential to influence. This situation calls for an exceptionally vigorous and far-reaching foreign policy. Wherever China's interests are at stake, that is, almost everywhere, China must be present. This implies that China must not only have a robust enough economy to supply its needs and a powerful enough military to resist outside pressure; China must also work to cultivate an international system that is not inimical to its internal political order and its broader objectives.

Viewed in this light, the difference diminishes, with the Indian public having its own parallel idea of sovereignty issues, the pursuit of Indian national interests, the threats thereto. The entire globe is seen as being connected to India, with international interdependence the ruling principle. The difference, however, is marked in the capacities which China and India have built up. The asymmetries in turn lead to a lack of trust.

In China, a new generation far removed from the difficult times of the 1950s has come to the fore. The younger Chinese people have been brought up on a diet of nationalism bordering on chauvinism. They have been acutely schooled in sovereignty issues, territorial integrity and Chinese honour. These factors impact on India. The Tibet issue is contentious, and parts of India where Tibetan spiritual connections were present have influenced the border question.

The Chinese type of robustly defined sovereignty and territorial integrity is interpreted to mean that threats can arise to the nation, not merely from hostile acts by adversaries, but also from fundamental contradictions, or even conflicts of interests with other countries. These include opposing social systems and ideologies as well as disputed economic interests, territorial, or ocean rights.

Another aspect of asymmetrical relationships is that the smaller side has more at stake, which makes it more attentive to the contentious issue. The larger side runs lower risks in the relationship. But more attention from the smaller side need not mean a better understanding, because it tends to exaggerate the risks as well as expectations and opportunities. The larger side tends to underplay them. The insensitivity of the larger power can amplify the paranoia of the smaller, and lead to tension and the erosion of public support. Difference in capacities creates a situation of different expectations, even in a stable relationship. The larger side expects deference from the smaller, while the smaller expects respect for its autonomy of judgement in pursuing its own interests.

Closer economic, trade and investment links do not by themselves solve the security dilemmas, for example, in the Sino–Japan relationship, the Sino–American and the Sino–South Korean relationships.

Another aspect of China needs to be noted. One can distinguish between power, defined as the capacity to achieve set purposes, and 'impact', defined as the effect on others. China has a great deal of impact that is often perceived as power.

China's relations with countries neighbouring India, with the exception of Pakistan, are not so much to dictate outcomes as to prevent others (India mainly) from undertaking activities that threaten China's core interests. As regards India's relations with major powers and groups, China has yet to adjust itself in particular to the Indo–US relationship.

Regional constraints on China should not be overlooked. In East Asia, there are three main ones: North Korea's nuclear and missile capability, the Taiwan issue, and the future course of Japan. In South-East Asia, China has unresolved maritime and territorial issues. In the economic field, China's imports from the region to feed its finished goods exports could be problematic. China needs to increase its domestic consumption levels to sustain its growth rate in future. India has been welcomed by some of these countries to take on a bigger role for the Indian Navy, which China does not favour.

Among China's problems is the rise of fundamentalism manifested in ethnic unrest (in Xingjian.) In Central Asia, while China has forged relations with the republics, a favourable balance will depend on Russia's military might and China's economic clout. These republics, aware of balancing, are also inclined towards the US role in the region.

For us in South Asia, regional security or insecurity is perhaps the biggest issue in bilateral relations with China. The friendly and positive statements by the two governments need to be translated into action. Air Chief Marshal Fali Major's remarks set the right tone of self-confidence and the case against pessimism in the Indian strategic community.

The area from the Irrawaddy to the Hindu Kush faces many different kinds of perils of the unconventional kind: terrorism, smuggling, drug, and arms-running, criminal activities, human trafficking, and aggressive messianism.

The permeability of borders has blurred the barrier between regional security complexes—India and China. They both have to watch the situation in the neighbourhood to maintain their own domestic stability. These interests go beyond the traditional power plays. The internal stability of neighbouring states becomes an important factor in the maintenance of regional security. Cooperation and dialogue between India and China has not gone beyond the purely declaratory level. The principle of interdependence is challenged by regional contexts where internal policies have serious external consequences.

A wide gap needs to be bridged in India–China relations vis-à-vis South Asian security. Similar security interests are not always approached as common ones. The low level of cooperation in security matters is because, as an objective, it is ranked below the wish to maintain diplomatic, economic, and military dominance vis-à-vis another state. This applies to India–Pakistan and India–China relations.

In conclusion:

1) India must work on China not to allow Pakistan to make Afghanistan an exclusive area of Pakistani influence, and not to allow the exclusion of India from the developmental progress in Afghanistan. To resolve the Afghan problem, a grouping of India, the US, the EU, Russia, China, Iran, and the Central Asian republics could be mooted.
2) We should continue the mature handling of the border question.
3) Both countries could intensify their military-to-military relations and start confidential talks between them to prepare for the acceptance of a reasonable, defendable, and maintainable boundary.
4) The two countries should work towards a broader Asian collective security scenario.
5) They should work towards joint India–China infrastructure projects in transportation (both rail and road) in Myanmar and other countries.

Discussion

The first question during the discussion period was asked on China's probable strategy of hacking the key computer and communications networks of the other side in future skirmishes. The Chinese are investing in key industries and services in India with such networks in mind. What can India do to counter this strategy?

Kondapalli replied that Chinese strategists had begun working on futuristic scenarios of 'unrestricted warfare' even from 1995. The concept includes domains like electromagnetic fields and paralysing enemy networks. Pakistan is also studying techniques of hacking and other methods, for example, in the University of Changsha in Hunan. The hacking of our websites at BARC, the MEA, and the MOD was possibly by the Chinese. To avoid this danger, the US is deliberately experimenting with systems avoiding computer networks. Since the Indian armed forces have not yet adopted full-spectrum networking, they are relatively immune from serious damage to their systems in a conflict involving the sabotage of networks.

Venkateswaran pointed out that in diplomacy, reciprocity is a recognized principle and that India had allowed Chinese technologists to train in institutes like Infosys, without Indian trainees being able to find similar opportunities to train in China.

A question was asked about the likely outcome of the Prime Minister's meeting with his Chinese counterpart in Thailand on October 24 (the day of this seminar). Ranganathan replied that he was baffled by the outburst of media hostility displayed on both sides in recent weeks due to bilateral tensions. He hoped that both governments would show maturity to safeguard their common interest in and desire for improved relations. Indians, he thought, were swayed by Western literature on the rapid rise of China, but the Chinese on their part were making the mistake of acting insensitively, in a way reminiscent of their attitude in 1962.

A lady member argued that India was too defensive in using its cultural legacy to gain more recognition and prestige. In Arunachal Pradesh and Ladakh, where our archaeological and cultural togetherness could be highlighted, the Indian government, she thought, was being over-solicitous to respect China's concerns over Tibet. Ranganathan agreed that it was a valid point. India should spend more on cultural diplomacy and opening more cultural centres abroad. Indian assistance in developing countries is well appreciated, especially in Afghanistan. He added that corporate industry and the private sector should do more to supplement governmental efforts. Another lady commented that India should invest in public relations and highlight its accomplishments over the ages and also its current problems.

Air Chief Marshal Major said that any PR exercise must be backed by performance. In our effort to catch up with China's defence capability, we must modernize. We are not relaxing, but asymmetries will remain. It is futile to go into an arms race, but we can reduce the asymmetries.

Jayaramu expressed the view that in dealing with China's military modernization, we have to take the route of diplomatic negotiations, through confidential dialogues, and private level exchanges over an extended period. If necessary, India should also 'play the America card.' We should find out what the young Chinese feel about India, whether they are intent on conflict with India or want to be at peace with us. We should not take on the Chinese in the technological and military fields. A former military officer recalled the heroism of our jawans and JCOs against the PLA in the 1962 border engagements. In 2009, we are far better equipped and prepared, but does the experience of border negotiations with China hold any lessons for India now?

Ranganathan agreed that following Rajiv Gandhi's visit to China in 1988, there was an understanding that the unresolved border issue be set aside and that discussions be held on other bilateral issues. This approach has paid dividends. The boundary being undefined, we have to manage our patrols along the border with care and delicacy. Without crossing the disputed Line, our patrols should go up to the LAC in its commonly accepted sections and defend it. We should uphold our rights within the LAC and assert them, as they do from their side.

Kondapilli explained that in the 1914 talks with British India, the Chinese envoy disputed, not the McMahon Line, but the British move to divide Tibet by marking an Inner Line and an Outer Line. Natwar Singh, in his recent book of memoirs, has said that Zhou Enlai accepted the boundary as marked by McMahon, with some alterations, but wanted another name for the Line. But in 1986, the Chinese made a specific claim to Tawang as part of China.

Concluding the discussion, the Chairman observed that China's borders today are very different from what they were 2000 years ago. So also, are India's borders. But China was an aggressive power which incorporated large areas, while India was not a predatory power. It was Nehru's mistake, when the territorial conflict began in the 1950s, to declare that our army would expel the Chinese from the border areas on the Indian side which they had encroached. China overran some of our border pickets, and withdrew to the present Line of Actual Control. If the Chinese soldiers had stayed on in the Eastern sector, they would have been snowbound and trapped by the winter. They had no rail and good road communications in Tibet at that time. A decision was taken by Delhi not to use the IAF to isolate the Chinese forward positions. India should stand up to China and not act in a subservient manner. China will respect us only if we do so.

The issues with China need to be taken up seriously, not hysterically. Deng Xiaoping began the Four Modernizations policy in 1979 after China was humbled in a military conflict with Vietnam, which exposed the outdated weaponry of the Chinese and resulted in large casualties for the PLA.

China has indeed made great advances in industry and agriculture, and other fields. It is a dictatorial regime, a regimented society with its own weaknesses and problems. China wants to be the first in everything, but its growth has become lopsided, with reliance on exports and a relatively low level of consumption. To meet the possible threats from China, India should undoubtedly strengthen its defence forces and the infrastructure to sustain it.

Conclusion

The speed of China's military modernization and reforms, powered by a determined CCP and PLA command, has alarmed sections of the Indian strategic community, because it has been accompanied by escalation of anti-Indian statements, hostile moves and signals in the Chinese media. The climate of India–China relations has also been vitiated by the overblown anti-Chinese articles and talks by some Indian commentators. Memories of Chinese perfidy in 1962 have contributed to a mood of pessimism about India's chances of deterring any Chinese encroachment of our strategic space. Though China and India are bracketed as the rising powers of Asia in Western discourses, Indians are sceptical of India ever equalling or rivalling China's current status as a leading world power.

A cooler examination of the present situation shows that China's concerns are related to certain factors and circumstances affecting India: 1) the suppressed unrest in Tibet and Xingjian reveals that China does have problems of unresolved ethnic and class divisions; 2) the loyalty that the Dalai Lama commands among Tibetans and the reverence accorded to him in Tawang have discomfited China; 3) India standing fast by its decision to allow the Dalai Lama to visit Tawang as a Buddhist leader is a diplomatic reverse that the Chinese cannot brook. India's protest against China undertaking development works in Pakistan Occupied Kashmir and its refusal to accept the validity of Chinese visas on separate sheets stapled on to passports by Indians from Kashmir has demonstrated that India will not give up its rights to conciliate China.

On the other hand, China has also gained in strategic terms. The US–India partnership has been attenuated in President Obama's first year, when the US finds itself at a distinct disadvantage in its negotiations with China on key issues like Afghanistan, Pakistan, North Korea, and Iran. The weakening of the US and the parallel enrichment of China had altered the equation. The US being grossly indebted to China is a potential geostrategic earthquake that obliges the Americans to be solicitous to Chinese concerns. India cannot afford to overlook the fact that China and Pakistan have a rock-firm alliance of mutual convenience which the US is obliged to accept, though there is a sinister side in its nuclear and missile transactions; and though it is adversarial to India, which the US would wish to retain as a trusted partner.

China is emboldened by its Indian admirers and friends who use our free media to canvass Chinese views. We need not agree with those who believe that India has been outflanked by Chinese strategy of containment, but it would be a blunder to disregard the stunning advances in China's military modernization. This should impel our leaders to modernize our armed forces rapidly and urgently, integrating them under a single overall command, and upgrading our missile, anti-missile, and space capabilities. Deterrence rather than a forward policy needs to be the guiding principle.

Suggested Measures Some suggestions for consideration and action by the concerned ministries and departments of the Government of India are:

1) Take advantage of China's genuine interest in preventing a disturbance in the conditions for peaceful development.
2) Strengthen the convergence of interests between India and China to set aside irresolvable issues for a better time, and to strengthen bilateral ties, economic, commercial, and other.
3) Encourage close consultations on global and regional issues where both have similar or same positions, such as climate change.
4) **Defence Modernization Plan** Prepare a national plan to modernize every part and wing of India's defence. Particular attention has to be paid to formulating new military doctrines to meet the threat of border incursions and aggressive patrolling, as well as threats of aggression from sea and air. This exercise has to run parallel to continued negotiations on the border issues, with an eye to possibly more effective CBMs, and in the longer term, a renewed 'package' solution which can gain acceptance in parliament and among the main political parties.
5) **Attention to Development of Navy** Special attention should be given to the Indian Navy in its role as a guardian of the Indian Ocean sea lanes between the Gulf and Malacca. Parallel with this, we may encourage navy-to-navy visits, exchanges, and understandings with China.
6) **Aerospace** Our aircraft fleet needs to be thoroughly renewed with new technologies like pilotless drones (UAVs) as well as upgraded fighter planes (initially to be imported at a very high cost, unavoidably.) We must make up the leeway in cruise missiles and missile capability. We

must enlarge our ISRO and space programme for defence purposes assertively. The use of small satellites and counter-space war strategies needs more national attention.

7) **Enhance Diplomatic Arm** The diplomatic arm has also to be strengthened, so that China does not find congenial ground to sow anti-Indian sentiments in India's neighbourhood. India can gain more friends in the region by enlarging the economic space we have already created, so that our neighbours can share the opportunities we open up for development and improved technologies.
8) **Trade with China** Indians would also benefit from such a drive. In our trade with China, we should consciously reduce the raw material export components and increase the value-added components. We can go by reciprocity rather than look for short-term gains from cheaper Chinese consumer goods and services.
9) **Possible Diplomatic Initiatives** India should put across in all forums and foreign offices the realities and risks of China condoning Pakistan's proxy terrorist war against India. India must influence the US to deter Chinese activities against India, though Obama seems to be relying on China to stabilize South Asia under a misguided view of regional realities. Russia and the EU are also important powers which can help to ensure a safer regional environment for India.
10) The Indian leadership must eventually prepare the parliament and public opinion for a national consensus on negotiating the border with China with some flexibility, since a securely delimited border will remove one serious issue which has bedevilled bilateral relations.

This seminar was an effective means to find a reasoned and informed understanding of China's military modernization, and the deficits on the Indian side which must be addressed without delay. The details of China's defence strategy, and the conviction that India must pursue its own defence modernization without desperation or hype, came out clearly from the five presentations and the discussion afterwards. The role of diplomacy in cooling down bilateral tensions and reducing areas of disagreement was also a running theme of the seminar.

Chapter 10

India–Pakistan Relations

ASIA CENTRE BANGALORE

'Whither Pakistan? Emerging Realities and Measures to Safeguard India's Security Interests' Proceedings of the Seminar held on

May 30, 2009

Introduction

Asia Centre Bangalore has conducted three seminars on the situation and developments in Pakistan in 2005, 2009, and 2011 as part of its periodic review of the regional political and security situation.

India–Pakistan relations have a long and acrimonious history, beginning with the accession of Kashmir to the Indian Union. Pakistan has initiated four major wars and maintains a continuous warfare by proxy, using fanatical irregular troops and terrorist mercenaries. The continuance of poor relations is in large measure attributable to the dominant status of the Pakistani military in every sphere of national activity.

Despite this grim background there is a realization in India that it needs peace and stability in the region and cannot let itself be mired in conflict. Despite all negative factors, therefore, successive Indian governments have persisted with the peace process.

A.P. Venkateswaran, former Foreign Secretary and Chairman of Asia Centre presided. The following speakers addressed the seminar:

Captain Alok Bansal, IN	Research Fellow at IDSA, New Delhi
M.K. Bhadrakumar	Former Ambassador to Uzbekistan
S. Gopal	Retired Special Secretary, Cabinet Secretariat
Lt General Satish Nambiar	Former Deputy Chief of Army Staff

The presentations and deliberations were recorded and summarized by A. Madhavan, former ambassador of India.

Lt General Ravi Eipe, Director of Asia Centre introduced the subject of the seminar. He observed that the present period is one of flux, with developments which aggravated the Taliban challenge to Pakistan as a state. It affected India too, and we should assess possible Indian responses. Pakistan nurtured the Taliban to gain a strategic asset in Afghanistan, but now it is posing a threat which can destroy Pakistan itself.

In countering the Taliban, Pakistan was attacking selected factions. Its military planning was centred on India as the main and constant adversary, with Kashmir as the main focus. But in the face of the new challenge from within, questions abound: whether Pakistan would reset its priorities or cling to its anti-Indian ones, whether there were serious fissures in the Pakistan Army regarding their anti-Taliban policy, and whether Pakistan was sincere in its cooperation with the US in its AfPak policy. Its nuclear weapons were a major concern for all nations.

That the US has asked China to help Pakistan in its crisis of stability indicates an alignment of the US and China as regards Pakistan's future. How would it affect India?

Presentation 1: The Crises in Pakistan

Captain Alok Bansal, IN

Pakistan faces four major crises.

State of the Economy The economic crisis, arising from a large deficit in reserves of foreign exchange, has been tided over due to three relieving factors: 1) Liberal foreign aid by the West and the IMF. Significantly, not much aid has come from the OIC or even China. 2) Lower oil prices have given Pakistan a respite from the depletion of its foreign exchange. 3) Due to recession, many overseas workers who had been laid off have returned to Pakistan with their savings. The overall economic picture, however, remains grim. Agricultural output in sugarcane and cotton has lagged because of structural problems and limited irrigation. The textile industry, which employs most factory workers, has declined along with exports. The trade deficit is 9 per cent, the fiscal deficit 7.4 per cent, and the inflation rate is 20 per cent. With lower investment now and lesser remittances, Pakistan faces deficit from high defence expenditures.

Sectarianism The Two-Nation Theory which propounded that Muslims cannot coexist with non-Muslims is an ideology of exclusion. It also excludes some sects in the Islamic fold, since there is no unanimity on determining who is a Muslim. Even among the Sunnis, there are sub-divisions. Deobandis clash with Barelvis, and among Shias, Athna Asharis consider Ismailis apostates. Sectarianism has risen to crisis proportions with the increase in violence between the various Islamic factions.

Rising Ethnic Aspirations This trend is evident after the elections of February 2008. The nationalistic aspirations of the Baloch people constitute the strongest challenge to the Pakistani state identity. Sindhi nationalism has also risen but has been checked by the PPP government in Islamabad. Sindhis oppose the influx of Pashtuns into Sindh. Mohajirs are trying to link up with Sindhis and Balochis; they are in the forefront of opposition to Talibanization and the movement of Pashtuns into urban Sindh. Besides this, there is an emerging Seraiki nationalism in Southern Punjab after the last elections. Pashtun nationalism is latent, but has failed to consolidate itself as a counter to Islamic fundamentalism.

Talibanization This process dates back to 1947, when Pakistan began promoting an all-inclusive Islamic identity, subsuming the different ethnic identities. The Taliban was promoted in order to facilitate a pro-Pakistani regime in Kabul in quest of 'strategic depth'. Attempts to accommodate Taliban representation eased the spread of the movement from South Waziristan to North Waziristan, and from there to other parts of FATA, NWFP, and lately to Punjab and Karachi. The Taliban has joined the sectarian war against Shias. The current operations to defeat Talibanization are unlikely to solve the problem. Three million people have been displaced. Most are unhappy with the military operations. The refugees are also exacerbating ethnic tension. The Taliban has succeeded in rousing a fear-induced psychosis among the people. State authority is eroding faster than anticipated. Of the two possible developments, Lebanonization or Balkanization of the country, the former could be catastrophic for India and should be prevented, even at the cost of seeing Pakistan balkanized or fragmented.

Presentation 2: A Security Assessment

S. Gopal

Trapped in History The people of Pakistan are trapped in history and history is trapped in them. It was created as a separate nation on the basis of religion, a state that has been functioning on the principle of hostility to India. It has fallen victim to the very fundamentalists whom the state used for terrorist attacks against India. Pakistan's nuclear weapon capability renders the situation more serious. More than 60 years after Independence, half of which under military rule, it remains a feudal society where ryots fall prey to fundamentalist propaganda.

Ineffectual Civilian Governments Civilian governments have been transitory, weak, and corrupt; they were from the feudal class mostly. Benazir Bhutto's regime, with her husband Zardari involved in money laundering, was notoriously corrupt and arraigned by Swiss authorities and EU investigators, apart from the Pakistan government itself. Lack of social infrastructure drove people to despair and bred the jihad mentality. During military rule, a clique of politicians, businessmen coveting state-owned land, and armed forces elements amassed wealth and entrenched their privileged status.

Rise of Islamic Radicalism Islamic radicalism found fertile ground. Pakistan's most difficult and explosive issue is social and economic inequality. With no state-aided education, the poor seek *madrassas* to educate their children. There are about 20,000 *madrassas* in Pakistan. They are free-board Koranic schools that propagate militant Islam, turning out about 2 million teenage boys a year from the rural areas. In result, a joyless and stern Saudi-inspired revivalism (Wahabi) dominates the lower middle classes. With training dominated by memorizing medieval texts, they are attracted to militancy as a career. It was General Zia ul-Haq who began using Islam as an instrument of state policy 25 years ago. Sectarian differences were aggravated to the disadvantage of Barelvis and Shias, who were treated as non-Muslims. Even in the relatively liberal Pakistan Punjab, the fundamentalist line taken up by the Taliban has begun to make inroads into the legal system.

Mujahedeen Diverted to Kashmir After the Soviet withdrawal from Afghanistan and the US receding from the scene, the region was full of jobless mujahedeen. Many were guided towards Kashmir, the ground for the ISI's proxy war. Al-Qaeda, urged by Taliban, financed and trained Islamist youths, especially those with anti-Shia mindsets, in Pakistan and Bangladesh. It had penetrated Kashmiri and Pakistani groups active in Kashmir in the 1990s in order to target India. Al-Qaeda branded India along with the US, Russia, and Israel as enemies of Islam. After the Taliban seized Kabul in 1997 with Pakistani help, they had set up common training camps in Afghanistan.

Taliban turned against Pakistan After the US intervention in Afghanistan in 2001, the militants moved to Waziristan where they re-established bases. Lal Masjid in Islamabad became a symbol and transit facility. More than 100 militant Islamists were captured from Lal Masjid, but later released by the Musharraf regime in 2008 under media pressure. They have dispersed to other provinces to plot their revenge for the Lal Masjid attack. There were suicide attacks on an army mess, an ordnance factory and the police in the capital.

After the 9/11 attack on the US, the American 'war on terror' ousted the Taliban regime in Afghanistan, but the remnants of both the Taliban and Al-Qaeda found shelter in the border region of the NWFP in Pakistan. The US bullied Pakistan into joining the war. Pakistani fundamentalists joined hands with the Afghan Taliban and stymied General Musharraf's efforts to remove them from Pakistan. Army action inevitably cost civilian casualties and displacement, making the Musharraf regime more unpopular. He was himself targeted in assassination attempts. The army was not motivated to fight Taliban militants in the early stages. Thus, the Zardari government gave in and approved the agreement of the Taliban and Tehrik-Nifaz-i-Shariat-i-Mohammadi with the NWFP government for imposing the Sharia law, a reactionary code which allowed atrocious punishments by the tribal militants on helpless victims for minor transgressions in their perception. The militants defied the constitution and federal judiciary to enforce their law.

Dependence on Foreign Funding Pakistan banked on the support of the US and the West during the cold war for its weaponry and finances. It is again allied to the US, which sustains it in the war on terror. On April 17, 2009, the US, Japan, and allied countries pledged more than US $5 billion to stabilize Pakistan's shaky economy and help it in the anti-Taliban drive. The US has already pledged US $1.5 billion per year in aid for the next five years. The IMF has also committed US $7.6 billion to rescue Pakistan from its balance of payments crisis. Interestingly, only US $900 million out of about US $10 billion in aid to Pakistan since 9/11 has gone to its development expenditure, the bulk of it having been channelled to the military.

Spread of Terrorist Strongholds The urban terrorists are mostly Punjabis from the South. They belong to groups training for jihad in Kashmir. When General

Musharraf curbed these groups, they turned to Al-Qaeda and the Afghan Taliban in FATA. Thus, the terrorist network now stretches from Bajaur in the North to Karachi in the South. It comprises at least 17 foreign nationalities and includes Punjabis, Pathans and Afghans.

Military in Control despite Civilian Government Civilian governments in Pakistan have been transitory. The military, the top bureaucracy, and the intelligence services have been the permanent features of the state. The civil government enjoys little autonomy. The military is unlikely to relax control of 'structural' missions involving Afghanistan and India and nuclear weapons. The army chief of staff has command and control of the intelligence services, though the ISI is formally answerable to the prime minister.

The Nuclear Threat Reports of Pakistan expanding its nuclear arsenal are most disturbing, since it can fall into the hands of Taliban or a fundamentalist government. Pakistan is increasing its plutonium capacity. It has dispersed its nuclear weapons in the country to reduce risks. Jihadis are using the internet and other means to gain control of the arsenal, perhaps co-opting sympathetic ministers. But the Army has confidently declared that it is secure against seizure.

Joint Action Needed as Both Countries under Threat Pakistan and India both face a terrorist threat and mutual conflict. The attitude of the Pakistani people is worrying. Until they free themselves from Wahabi inspired violence which envelopes the country, the threat to Paksitan's stability will continue. India needs a dialogue with the Pakistan military and the liberal sections of society, to disabuse them of any threat from our side and to convince them of the urgency of joint action by both countries against the common danger. But the adversarial attitude to India by the Pakistani establishment and the military is a serious obstacle. India has to keep its defence strength alert and ready to face possible conflict.

Presentation 3: A Strategic Overview

M.K. Bhadrakumar

Continuance of Military Domination The Pakistani power structure shows little evidence that the return to democracy means the supremacy of civilian government. The permanent establishment remains in place: namely, the military, top echelons of the bureaucracy and the intelligence agencies. The army continues to be in the driver's seat on foreign and defence policy, internal security and nuclear policy. It is a fallacy to look for 'rogue elements' within the ISI or assume that it is 'a state within a state.' It is under military control and serves as the military's instrument. It may have operational freedom but it cannot act against military interests. The military functions as a coherent organization without factions.

Among the political parties, the PML and the PPP still remain acutely polarized. Islamic parties are handmaidens of the establishment. We should not exaggerate the influence of the civil society.

The military's corporate interests are to preserve its political and economic prerogatives it enjoys as the vaunted custodian of the state.

Military Support for Jihad The military will probably continue to support militant groups that serve Pakistan's regional interests. It will deal harshly with groups that threaten the nation's territorial integrity. Clearly, it will not tolerate secessionist tendencies. It believes the jihadi groups that serve its interests are ultimately subject to its control.

The military's animus against India will not diminish. It sees the situation through an anti-Indian lens, and has a deep-rooted suspicion about India's intentions. This has been compounded by fears of US-Indian collusion or strategic alliance, acute insecurity over India's arms purchases, suspicion over perceived Indian influence in Afghanistan and Indian meddling in Pakistan's domestic scene. Such fears will grow, and are a compelling reason why the military will not give up its reliance on jihadi groups in the foreseeable future.

The military perceives the Taliban as a strategic asset, especially in the event of American forces abruptly quitting Afghanistan. Quite apart from the growing Indian presence in Afghanistan, Pakistan has legitimate interests in that country.

US Priorities The US's priority is to expand its leverage over Pakistan, given the American dependence on Pakistani cooperation in the Afghan war. Obama has proffered a new civil and military aid programme, to strengthen Pakistan in the medium term. He has also shown extra willingness to accommodate Pakistan's regional perceptions and legitimate concerns such as restraint in recognizing India's pre-eminence in the region, greater attention to Indo-Pakistan tensions, persuading India to resume 'the composite dialogue' with Pakistan, and more room for Pakistani interests in Afghanistan by urging India to lower its profile there.

Furthermore, Obama is encouraging other states like China, Saudi Arabia, and the EU to help stabilize Pakistan. The US invitation to China in this regard has far-reaching implications.

While the US has misgivings about the Pakistani political elite in dealing with the Taliban crisis and its capacity to rise above sectarian politics, it depends overwhelmingly on the Pak military to deliver and is quite unlikely to impose conditionalities in its military aid. Finally, the US will not follow a containment strategy towards Pakistan as 'the epicentre' of international terrorism, as some Indians hope.

Stalemate in Afghanistan As for Afghanistan, there is a stalemate: the Taliban cannot capture power, nor can NATO defeat it. Defence Secretary Robert Gates has said that the Afghan Taliban has the upper hand now. The US, facing a war-weary public, is unlikely to push for unqualified victory. The major NATO powers have no wish to increase their force contributions. So the US must conduct the bulk of the fighting.

The 'surge' strategy involves increasing pressure on the Taliban in southern Afghanistan and pushing the militants eastwards to the Pak border, while the Pak military applies the squeeze from the other side. Alongside, a 'political track' will hammer the 'irreconcilables' while segregating the 'reconcilable'. This is similar to the pattern of 'the Awakening' strategy in Iraq, which built up a 'bottoms-up' approach province by province.

Afghanistan—Multiple Strategies, Uncertain Outcome Meanwhile, there is a separate track, unacknowledged by the US, for negotiating with the hard-line Taliban leaders like Gulbuddin Hekmatyar. Hamid Karzai, the President, pursues his own contacts with the Taliban. The outcome of the different strategies is unclear. The Saudis, the ISI, and British intelligence are all involved in them. Obama has mentioned regional initiatives, but there are uncertainties over US–Russian relations. Both Russia and China oppose NATO expansion in Central Asia. The US–Iran standoff is in animated suspension. Indo–Pakistan tensions have spilt over into the Hindu Kush. Geopolitical energy rivalries complicate the picture.

India's Concerns Among the adverse factors are that the US policy is a replay of past approaches, relying on military aid to enhance its leverage with the Pakistani army. Such aid boosts Pakistan's military capability. It is premature to assume a basic change in the mindset of the Pakistan military. Since the priorities of the Pakistan military and the US diverge, the efficacy of the AfPak strategy is doubtful. Deeper US involvement in the region alienates Pakistani opinion and generates more militants: a core issue which the US disregards. The Afghan war has a bearing on Pakistan's stability: the longer it goes on, the greater the turbulence in Pakistan. A creeping 'Islamisation' or radicalization in Pakistani attitudes and lifestyles is noticeable, and ethnic divisions are surfacing in Pak society. Balkanization of Pakistan will be catastrophic for Indian security. This may prompt the US to address its increasing need to intervene in Indo–Pakistan relations in order to appease the Pak military. The US wants a roll-back of Indian presence in Afghanistan, and may accommodate Taliban representatives in the Afghan power structure despite Indian opposition. Ambassador Richard Holbrooke has sought China's help, which could augur a Sino–US understanding concerning the region. Pakistan is being drawn into Western alliances such as NATO and OSCE. Obama's policies belie Indian expectations of being recognized as the pre-eminent power in the region, and a *de facto* 'hyphenation' of India and Pakistan is apparent in US policies. This, with the broadening US–China ties during the current global economic crisis, puts paid to any Indian role as a 'balancer' in the emerging international system.

The plus factors for India are: Pakistan's response to terrorism is under international scrutiny, which could lessen ISI activities against India. If the US succeeds, Pakistan would be stabilized, its military would become less anti-Indian in focus, and also sever links with militant groups. The Pakistan military, when increasingly involved in fighting Taliban militancy in the border area, would be less liable to foment tensions in Jammu and Kashmir.

India needs to energize its moribund regional diplomacy. Relations with Russia and Iran have lost their élan. Greater attention should be paid to the Shanghai Cooperation Organization (SCO). India has much in common with its members in combating terrorism, religious extremism, and separatism, apart from promoting regional stability.

India should factor in China's increased strength in the last two decades. India must engage China constructively on regional issues like Pakistan, Afghanistan, Sri Lanka, and Nepal instead of being fixated on the dubious theory of a Chinese 'string of pearls', which was floated by an American analyst. Chinese policies need not be seen as centred on isolating India in the region.

Presentation 4: Whither Pakistan?

Lt General (Retd) Satish Nambiar

General Nambiar's presentation was based on three aspects: Pakistan's identity crisis, its religious indoctrination, and the role of the army. He then outlined Pakistani developments as viewed by the West, China, and South Asian countries, with his observations on Indo–Pakistan relations.

Pakistan's Identity Problem General Nambiar began with the observation that Pakistan began by defining itself negatively as 'not India.' It is an Islamic republic with varied ethnic stock: Punjabis, Pashtuns, Kashmiris, Baluchis, and so on, with their Muslim identity in common. This explains the reluctance of the Pakistan Army to deploy forces on the western front, since it would go against its *raison d'être*. In the course of three decades, Pakistan has sought to exchange its South Asian identity for an ersatz Arab–Islamic one. As Pervez Hoodbhoy, the Pakistani physicist, has written, the stern ethos of Wahabism is replacing the gentler faith of the Sufis and saints. It frowns on all forms of innocent pleasure and wants to control the education system.

Madrassa Indoctrination Islamic radicalism or extremism is spreading fast in schools, both urban and rural. Liberals worry that this *madrassa* indoctrination will breed a generation unfit to coexist with anyone outside its own kind. Islam is for them a complete code of life. This mindset becomes paranoid about threats to Islam everywhere. It will produce human drones which could be detonated at a command. Since religion is a touchy matter, nobody wants to criticize this abuse of children by mullahs.

The Pakistan Army The Pakistan Army is professional, and proud of its traditions and work culture. It continues to reflect the feudal structure of Pakistani society. It is comfortable with being detached from governance, being aware of the multiple problems which are now the responsibility of the civil administration. But it will mark lines to bind the political leaders, particularly as regards cooperation with the American coalition in Afghanistan. It knows that the US and NATO forces will eventually withdraw from Afghanistan, leaving the field to be dominated by Pakistan for it to gain 'strategic depth' vis-à-vis India. For the Army, this makes the Taliban a strategic asset, though the Pakistani Taliban is another matter.

Whether the revanchist army mindset after the 1971 defeat by India will abate when a new generation takes command is a speculative matter. Much depends on the tussle between the moderate and extreme elements and also on the degree of 'Islamisation' of the Army. One American expert has stated that the risk of an Islamist takeover is a myth invented by the Pakistani military to consolidate its hold on power. It is the Army that has made use of Islamic organizations for its goals, not the other way round.

Pakistan's Usefulness to the US All regimes in Pakistan have exploited the role of a link between China and the US. It was predominant during the 1980's when the US was pitted against the Soviet presence in Afghanistan.

The US accorded favoured treatment to Pakistan even in nuclear matters by condoning the deals facilitated by A.Q. Khan with China and other countries. Currently, though Pakistan is designated as the epicentre of international terrorism, Pakistan receives special favours, as the US needs to combat Al-Qaeda and Taliban. This American line is unlikely to change and must be factored into our security calculations.

China's Support of Pakistan China has consistently supported Pakistan since the 1960s as a hedge against the rise of India in the region. We have contributed to this effort by always hyphenating India with Pakistan on political and military matters. The Sino–Pakistan relationship is 'an all-weather' phenomenon which will last. China is beholden to Pakistan for providing the bridge to the US that enabled the latter to recognize it and endorse the 'One China' policy. This is another vital factor in our security calculations regarding Pakistan.

Pakistan is seen by our other neighbours as the only country that can challenge India's military strength, especially as it has nuclear weapon capability. So they tend to gang up with Pakistan to counter Indian regional dominance. With China becoming an observer in SAARC, the situation is worse for India.

Continue Efforts despite Pakistani Animus India needs to initiate moves for improved relations with Pakistan, with some international help, but we must bear in mind the following: 1) Significant sections of Pakistan's leadership still believe in the notion of 'the unfinished agenda of Partition', of which the Kashmir issue is a manifestation; some Pakistanis even believe that they are destined to rule over India. We cannot ignore this security threat. 2) The Pakistan Army is still smarting from its defeat in 1971 by India and the loss of credibility in the Kargil misadventure. We have to assess whether it will be able to move out of its revenge mentality under General Kayani. 3) India's success in consolidating its democracy and in socio-economic development is viewed with envy by some Pakistanis.

For the immediate future, we can at best expect an adversarial relationship rather than one of enmity. If democratic governance takes stronger root in Pakistan, and economic growth brings more benefits, the relationship could become more tranquil and stable.

Discussion

In the lively discussion that followed the four presentations, several issues and questions were raised. The main ones are given below.

Engaging China is Beneficial It is better to 'engage' China rather than to go for a stand-off. China has had some moderating influence on Pakistan: for instance, in the aftermath of the Lal Masjid action. Sino-Pakistan relations should not be interpreted as being always directed against India. China in its quest for oil and gas from Kazakhstan has a strong interest in regional stability. The so-called 'string of pearls' theory which Western commentators have projected to show up China's naval ambition to dominate the Indian Ocean should not guide our viewpoint.

Use of Soft Power Eric Gonsalves intervened to say that India should make better use of its soft power in our neighbourhood. He believed that China should not be regarded as a monolith. There are possibilities of building up improved trade and understanding, as for instance through the 'Kunming initiative', in which he had taken part. A lady member suggested that culture could be used as a bridge between India and Pakistan, since it is a human softener that can improve mutual understanding.

Gas Pipeline When a member mentioned Iran's projected pipeline, Captain Bansal said that Jundullah, which is Pakistan-based, is dead set against the Shias. It is a militant group exacerbating sectarian relations within Pakistan, where the Baloch people are mainly Shia. Sectarian violence could endanger the proposed gas pipeline from Iran. Bhadrakumar dwelt on the geopolitical tussle between the West and Russia or China for control over the new and planned energy pipelines out of Iran and Central Asia. Iran is a key factor for the Nabucco project of the EU in its quest to diversify its energy sourcing away from Russia. Russia's Gazprom has offered to contribute to the financing of the Iran gas pipeline to Pakistan. Russia wants Iranian gas to be channelled eastward rather than westward, as the US and the EU wish to see. Khaleeli added that the Iran gas pipeline is a very important project and that India's opposition to Iran at the IAEA is an adverse move which Iranians will not forget. He agreed that in Pakistan it is the Army that is of greater consequence than either Zardari or Sharif. He also spoke of the Wahabi antagonism to Sufis, but believed that the latter could be militant, if provoked.

Refugee Influx from Pakistan Unlikely Another member raised the possible refugee problem from Pakistan across the Indian border, which was discounted by Captain Bansal. He added that Pakistan's immediate economic difficulty has been assuaged by Western aid, and that a growth rate of 2.8 per cent has been forecast for the economy.

No Call to Support US Campaign in Afghanistan It was unlikely that the American call for India to join the anti-Taliban campaign would be taken up by us. Gopal pointed out that India has a stake in Afghanistan and is engaged in its development and the build-up of its infrastructure. But India has no call to support the US campaign in Afghanistan. He added that terrorist cells acting from Bangladesh posed more serious problems for us.

Summing Up Ranganathan wondered why Islamic authorities have not condemned terrorism in the region in a more forthright fashion. Regarding Sino–Indian relations, he agreed with Bhadrakumar that the two countries have intersecting interests, which should be managed and developed by interaction rather than left to fester. China and the US were engaged in discussions on sharing maritime vigilance which could benefit others too. He thought the US request to China for helping Pakistan rather naive. India, he suggested, should engage with China, but carefully and watchfully.

Summing up the discussion, the Chairman, Venkateswaran, pointed out that the US drone strikes in Afghanistan and Pakistan result in 'collateral damage', not only in terms of killing civilians, destroying property and driving out native people, but also in political terms, provoking anti-American passions. When Obama became president of the US, there was a glimmer of hope for a saner policy, but he too is obliged to depend on the CIA, which has used torture in deplorable forms against prisoners. In truth, he concluded, the West continues to retain power and influence in our entire region, while the governments have a semblance of being in charge.

Summary and Conclusions

The seminar comprehensively reviewed the salient recent developments in Pakistan and their consequences for India.

The withdrawal of the Soviet Union from Afghanistan left the Mujahedeen available for re-deployment by Pakistan against Kashmir. The US-led invasion of Afghanistan once again mobilized the Mujahedeen, this time against the US and NATO forces. The speakers have clearly brought out how Pakistan's induction into the US war on terror caused the Pashtun Taliban to turn violently against the Pakistan state, thereby not only endangering Pakistan, but also threatening regional stability. Pakistan is severely strained by the rift among its ruling classes: the Army, the civilian government, and the mullahs.

US drone attacks stir anger and hatred in Pakistan against Americans. The anger is hardly mitigated by the billions of dollars that the US is pouring into Pakistan's Army and government. Pakistanis are resentful that their country is being bamboozled into fighting America's war when the US has treated it shabbily.

For the US, the objective of retaining Pakistan as an ally in its war against the Taliban and Al-Qaeda overrides all other considerations: the blatant misuse of massive aid, Pakistan's duplicity in 'shadow-boxing' with Taliban militants, or its sponsorship and direction of terrorist groups like the LeT and the JuD which target Indian cities including the attack against Mumbai in November 2008. Further, the US under Obama has taken up the Pakistani cause for a negotiated bilateral settlement of the Kashmir issue, and sided with Pakistan in asking India to thin down its forces in Kashmir and reduce its presence in Afghanistan. Ominously for India, the US has recently urged China to join it in funding and materials for Pakistan which will obviously be directed at India instead of the Afghan Taliban.

Meanwhile, Pakistan's nuclear arsenal and its security have triggered urgent concerns in the US and among major powers. The nuclear weapons may be safeguarded from Taliban and other raiders, but Pakistan's bravado about increasing its nuclear weapon capability and its indulgence to A.Q. Khan as a popular hero have alarmed American experts.

China's policy towards India is a mix of belligerence and calls for mutual accommodation. The seminar speakers favoured wary engagement, since both countries want the subcontinent to be a stable and peaceful region, and since both can well expand their economic cooperation while reserving the disputed issues for longer term solutions.

Since this seminar at the end of May, developments in Pakistan and Afghanistan have confirmed its main conclusions, but also thrown up new trends which need our careful attention. The Pakistan Army has lately been more active against the Taliban militants, who were threatening to take over Swat valley and parts of South Waziristan. The Afghan Taliban now has a Pakistani branch, the TTP, with its leader, Baitullah Mehsud still active. This linkage against India that was initially encouraged by the Army and the ISI has boomeranged on Pakistan in a series of terror attacks in Army strongholds like Islamabad and Lahore. The Army has belatedly realized that the Taliban, if unchecked, will turn against the state and its institutions.

What policy should India adopt at this juncture? Paradoxically, India's global prestige as a democracy and as a potentially buoyant economy has gone up, while its international profile has gone down because of its perceived diffidence in safeguarding its interests as a regional power. India needs international support, without over-reliance on one power or set of powers.

This calls for diplomatic energy in presenting the dangers of Pakistan's resort to terrorist groups, without being fixated on Pakistan's obduracy, as Indian diplomacy has bigger tasks in the region.

Pakistan is on course to self-destruct, unless the Army can rein in the militants. Pakistan wants India to resume the suspended 'composite dialogue', though the periodical reassertion of the Kashmir issue and its inability or unwillingness to dismantle the terror camps are serious impediments. The solution however, is not to close the door on discussions. At the summit of the SCO and BRIC at Yekaterinburg in Russia in mid-June, President Zardari and our Prime Minister resumed bilateral contact, but the onward move from there to negotiations depends on Pakistan's ability to deracinate jihadism from its soil.

The Army and the ISI have a decisive role in Pakistan. They may be more amenable to US persuasion than to negotiations with India or other nations. Indo–US relations need to be re-established under Obama. India must impress its point of view convincingly to the political and military centres of power in the US, so that it does not leave India to clear up the debris of misadventures in the 'AfPak' terrain.

Chapter 11

India and The Indian Ocean

ASIA CENTRE BANGALORE
AND
THE INDIAN COUNCIL OF WORLD AFFAIRS

'Is the Indian Ocean ceasing to be Indian?
Current Realities, Challenges and Opportunities for India'
Proceedings of the Joint Seminar
held on

February 26, 2011

Introduction

A seminar on the theme 'Is the Indian Ocean ceasing to be Indian? Current Realities, Challenges and Opportunities for India' was held jointly by the Asia Centre and the Indian Council of World Affairs in Bangalore on February 26, 2011.

The seminar was presided over jointly by A.P. Venkateswaran, former Foreign Secretary and Chairman, Asia Centre, Bangalore and S.T. Devare, Director General, Indian Council of World Affairs, New Delhi. The following were the speakers:

Mohan Guruswamy	Chairman and founder of Centre for Policy Alternatives, New Delhi
B. Raman	Director, Institute for Topical Studies, Chennai
Rear Admiral (Retd) Raja Menon	Author and Strategic Analyst

The presentations were followed by a question and answer session. The summary in the succeeding pages of the presentations and the discussions that followed has been compiled by Vice Admiral R.N. Ganesh (Retd).

Lt General Ravi Eipe (Retd), Director, Asia Centre welcomed the participants and the invitees. A special welcome was extended to the distinguished guest speakers and to S.T. Devare, Director General, Indian Council of World Affairs, who had consented to co-chair the proceedings.

Adverting to the seminar, the Director said that India has a dominant position on the shore of the Indian Ocean that bears its name. Yet historically, we have been a continental power, because all invasions of India have occurred overland from the north and we were more concerned about land threats. India has had a seafaring tradition but seems to have neglected a maritime role.

In the last two decades, there has been a marked change in our outlook and strategic orientation. The size and reach of our Navy has grown steadily and the world has started to take notice of India's new naval capabilities, particularly when they saw the Indian Naval response to the tsunami of 2004. The focus of this seminar is to see how we can achieve our rightful place in the Indian Ocean and diminish the influence of outside powers like China, and at the same time assuage the misgivings that other regional states may have.

Presentation 1: An Economist's Strategic Overview

Mohan Guruswamy

Economic Importance of the IOR to India

With the advent of oil and the rise of India and China, the sea lanes of communication (SLOCs) through the Indian Ocean became very important–90 per cent of the world's oil—70 per cent of China's, 80 per cent of India's, and 90 per cent of Japan's oil passes through this ocean. Large merchant navies of all major countries traverse this ocean, within 400 miles of the Indian coast. India imports the most from the US, then from Saudi Arabia, and the third UAE. The US tops India's export list, with the UAE second.

An analysis of India's foreign trade figures will show that India has a great dependency on trade with the Middle East. Presently the region ranks third in terms of India's bilateral trade, after China and the USA. The UAE is also important to India as a means of indirect trade. For instance, India's direct bilateral trade with Pakistan is under US $12 billion, but this figure increases several-fold if the indirect trade through Dubai is taken into account. India's non-oil trade with the UAE rose from US $13.6 billion to US $15.4 billion between 2007 and 2008. India's major exports are petro-products, jewellery, machinery, textiles, and cereals. From the UAE, India imports crude oil, petro-products, electrical machinery, and iron and steel.

Saudi Arabia too, occupies an important place in our foreign trade. Last year alone, Indian investments in Saudi Arabia touched 4 billion dollars. India's imports of Saudi Arabian oil are vital to the Indian economy.

Trade with the Middle East is critical for India to balance its trade. Our imports are expected to rise to US $460 billion in the next two years. The foreign trade deficit will increase in the next two years with rising oil prices, and is predicted to reach US $200 billion, which will be almost 10 per cent of the Indian GDP. This is obviously an untenable situation, which makes trade with the Middle East extremely important to India.

Competition for MENA Trade

There is a growing competition for trade with the Middle East and North Africa (MENA) region between China and India, driven by their soaring energy demand and aggravated by the oil price rise. Together, China and India account for 20 per cent of the global GDP. The MENA region has 10 per cent of the world's population. 82 per cent of oil comes from here, and 40 per cent of our manufactured goods, 17 per cent of our machinery exports and 12 per cent of food and beverage products are exported to this region. More importantly, these are all value-added exports which enhances the benefit to the trade balance. According to the latest figures, 37 per cent of India's trade and 41 per cent of China's is directed towards this region, and these figures are rising.

Another important trading partner is Iran. Indo–Iran trade crossed US $13 billion last year—a rise of 80 per cent over the previous year. If one takes into account third-country exports via the UAE, this figure becomes US $30 billion. India and Iran have recently signed an agreement to increase their bilateral trade to US $30 billion. Iran has responded positively to Indian politico–military initiatives and has joined the Indian Ocean Naval Symposium, an Indian initiative for regional maritime cooperation.

Criticality of Indo–Iran Trade

Iran and Saudi Arabia are the most important sources of oil for India, which imports 16 per cent and 18 per cent of its oil from these two countries. But the special aspect of the oil trade with Iran is that Indian refineries export large quantities of refined petro-products to Iran, which gets 40 per cent of its refined products from India. Obviously this has a positive impact on the balance of trade and offsets the oil price rise to a significant extent. India has also invested US $5 billion in Iranian oilfields. The demand for oil and gas in both China and India is rising. Last year China's demand was up by 20 per cent and that of India by 15 per cent.

With this level of dependency in such a vital and strategic sector as energy security, India has to be extremely wary of US pressures to curtail trade with Iran and impose an embargo on oil trade with that country. India has to be guided by its own strategic interests in this matter.

Uncertain Future in West Asia

While Indo–Saudi trade is booming, there is an element of uncertainty in the future. The Middle East is in turmoil, and about two years ago there was a Pentagon paper that postulated a scenario based on the Shia–Sunni divide in which Iraq was split and a new independent state of Najaf was formed. Added to this is the current political set-up in Saudi Arabia where a few thousand privileged members of the aristocracy blatantly exploit the country at the expense of the majority of the population. These are not wholly unrealistic scenarios and the situation will present a dilemma for our diplomacy. We have to look after our own national interests, and in this crisis in Saudi Arabia and the Middle East, our interests are best served by keeping quiet.

China and the Indian Ocean

I give no credence to the so-called 'String of Pearls' thesis. India cannot be blockaded by any 'String of Pearls'—these days no country can blockade another—a Chinese blockade is thus out of the question.

Implications of China's Myanmar Pipeline

Sittwe and Gwadar, however, are important for other reasons. From Sittwe in Myanmar, China is building a pipeline to upload 22 million tonnes of oil to Kunming, from where Szechuan and Yunnan will get their energy requirements. These pipelines go through five rebel areas in Burma. There already is an existing parallel that we have to look at carefully. The People's Liberation Army supplies work teams and are building tunnels in Gilgit and Baltistan. Armed PLA units are deployed to provide protection to the workers there. Sometime or the other the rebels in Myanmar will demand rent for the pipelines passing through their territory, and will blow it up if denied. So the PLA will come to protect the pipeline in Myanmar sooner or later. An Indian pipeline from Sittwe to Kolkata is also planned, and Indian and Chinese agencies will be alongside each other; there will undoubtedly be confrontation and conflict. Ultimately Indian forces will also have to go there to protect our assets and people. So there will have to be a Chinese base in Sittwe to protect the port and the Chinese installations. They have a gas field also sanctioned at a place very close to Sittwe. So I believe that the Bay of Bengal, more than the Arabian Sea, is going to be the cockpit of military competition—not commercial, but military competition.

Gwadar—a Commercial, not Military Challenge

South Block does not seem to have appreciated the risks in the East, but continues to be focused on Gwadar. The Indian military are focused only on Pakistan. Gwadar is not going to base a single Chinese naval ship—if that were to happen, the Western navies would play havoc with them. The intention in Gwadar is for it to become the Chinese entry point into MENA. This will be the special manufacturing and export zone for Chinese trade with MENA, that challenges Indian trade primacy with the region, and its aim is to ensure that Indian goods are replaced by Chinese goods. Our government appears to be busy with other things, but unless we make special provisions for SEZs for MENA, Gwadar will become China's Hong Kong in the Indian Ocean, and will capture the MENA market. We have to meet this commercial challenge from Gwadar. It is Gwadar's rich commercial potential that makes Pakistan so sensitive to the threat of secession of Baluchistan, and is the reason why they keep making accusations about India playing a nefarious role there. Looking ahead, the US already has contingency plans for an independent Baluchistan consisting of the present Baluchistan with Sistan in Iran conjoined to it.

In the respect of this region, I like to describe India as a Western Union Economy. It thrives on 'invisible' remittances from UAE—our seven million workers there send back 21 billion dollars a year; this is almost half the total annual remittances into India, which amounts to about $52 billion. The much vaunted IT industry doesn't send much money home to India—I have a favourite saying—'Nerds don't remit!' It is the Middle East from where our money comes. We need peace and stability in this region, and we need to craft a policy focused on protecting India's interests there—a policy specially designed for the 'Western Union economy.' In the meanwhile, the IOR countries spend US $7–12 billion a year to combat piracy that causes a total annual loss of US $500 million. The expense is disproportionate and we need a more imaginative diplomatic policy and military policy to deal with the situation.

Presentation 2: India and the Indian Ocean

B. Raman

India's Eroding Influence in Sri Lanka

The main security threats to Indian interests in the Indian Ocean area arise from three factors—first, the gradual erosion of the Indian political influence in the area; secondly, the increase in the Chinese presence in the area; and thirdly, the uncontrolled activities of the Somali pirates.

Nowhere is the erosion of Indian political influence more evident than in Sri Lanka, where, despite our assistance to the Government of Sri Lanka in its successful counter-insurgency operations against the Liberation Tigers of Tamil Eelam (LTTE), we have not been able to protect either the interests of the Sri Lankan Tamils or the lives and livelihood of Indian Tamil fishermen, who have been at the mercy of the Sri Lankan Navy.

Our repeated pleas for finding an early political solution to the grievances of the Sri Lankan Tamils and for stopping attacks—some of them brutal and fatal—on Indian Tamil fishermen have had no impact on the Government of President Mahinda Rajapaksa. Rajapaksa, while pretending to be sensitive to Indian interests, has been ignoring them without any fear of the likely consequences. India's core interests in the region to the south of India have been repeatedly ignored by Rajapaksa.

Our dilemma in Sri Lanka underlines the hard reality that having a strong Navy alone would not be sufficient to make our core interests prevail in the Indian Ocean region. In the absence of courage and political will, our Navy will not be a powerful arm of the State ready to go into action if our core interests are threatened, but mere oceanic curios, exhibited in public and admired, but not feared.

Situation in Island States

The negative state of affairs that we are confronted with in Sri Lanka today could be repeated in the Maldives, Mauritius, and Seychelles in the years—if not months—to come if the Indian political leadership is not more assertive in protecting Indian interests in these island countries.

Fortunately, in the Maldives, the Indian interests still prevail despite an increase in political and economic contacts between China and the Maldives. The Government of Maldives continues to look up to India for strengthening its capacity for meeting threats to its security, which presently mostly arise from non-State actors such as Pakistan-based jihadi elements and the Somali pirates. It is still attentive to Indian interests in the area.

So is the case in Seychelles. Despite the Chinese offer of help to Seychelles for strengthening its anti-piracy capabilities, which it has accepted, the Government of Seychelles continues to be as receptive to Indian offers of assistance and cooperation as it was before.

However, one has reasons to be concerned over recent developments in Mauritius since the visit of President Hu Jintao of China to Port Louis in February 2009. During his visit to Mauritius, China announced low-interest loans and grants, totaling over US $270 million for various projects including modernizing and expanding its airport. He said that trade between the two countries had increased by 11.7 per cent during 2008 to reach US $323 million. The Mauritian Prime Minister, Navinchandra Ramgoolam, said that the two countries had discussed further assistance to improve transport in the island's capital.

Hu pledged to speed up the construction of the China-funded Economic and Trade Zone north of the capital. Known as the Tianli project, it will be the largest single foreign-funded project in Mauritius creating about 40,000 jobs. Between 1972 and Hu's visit in February 2009, the total value of the Chinese assistance to Mauritius amounted to US $117 million. Fresh assistance extended since then has crossed US $1 billion—an almost ten-fold increase.

Economic and Trade Zone

The 521-acre economic and trade zone is an important part of China's Africa strategy. It aims to convert Mauritius into a 'Singapore' for servicing its projects, where the corporate headquarters of Chinese companies operating in Southern Africa are expected to be located. Since Mauritius does not have enough skilled workers to meet the requirements of the Chinese-aided projects, it has allowed China to bring its own nationals to work in these projects. As a result, about 50 per cent of Mauritius's foreign labour force could be Chinese. There could be more Chinese than Indians working in Mauritius. The corporate city being built by the Chinese will compete with the Ebene Cyber City constructed with Indian assistance. Huawei, the Chinese IT company, reportedly operates from the Cyber City. It provides financial services to Chinese companies in Southern Africa.

In an article titled 'China makes foray into Mauritius', published in January 2010, the *Financial Times* of London wrote that China's state-led approach to foreign investment was muscling India aside in its traditional 'backyard'—by investing US $700 million in a special economic zone in Mauritius—to service Beijing's expansion in Africa. Ramakrishna Sithanen, the vice-prime minister of Mauritius and minister of finance, said that China's 'different approach', which forcefully combined business and government interests, was in contrast to India's more fragmented style. He said his government's relationship with Beijing was so strong that he was able to call on the personal intervention of Hu Jintao to sort out problems. China's participation in Mauritius is a key part of the island's diversification away from a sugar cane and tourism economy into logistics, information technology, and financial services.

Having seen the gradual erosion of the Indian political influence in Sri Lanka, we are now seeing similar erosion in Mauritius. It used to be under Indian cultural and economic influence. It continues to be under the Indian cultural influence, but the economic influence is more and more Chinese. As the Chinese economic influence grows, so will its political influence. In protecting one's core interests, it is the economic and political influence that matters and not the cultural influence.

Chinese On-shore Presence in IOR

The gradual decline in our political and economic influence in the Indian Ocean region has been accompanied by a steady increase in the Chinese onshore presence in the countries of this region, mainly for helping these countries in developing their infrastructure—an airport and an economic and trade city in Mauritius, a commercial port and an international airport in Hambantota in Sri Lanka, expansion and modernization of the Colombo port, and road and rail repairs and construction in others parts of Sri Lanka. There is a major project to build a new port at Kyaukpyu in Myanmar, and pipelines to connect Kyaukpyu and Yunnan so that gas and oil locally produced or imported from West Asia and Africa could be moved to Yunnan without having to pass the Malacca Strait. China is also constructing a rapid rail system connecting Yangon with Yunnan. Talks are on with Bangladesh for Chinese assistance in the modernization of the Chittagong port and for connecting the rail systems of Bangladesh and Myanmar. China is the largest foreign investor in Myanmar today, with the total value of investments already touching US $3 billion. China has two assets which India will not be in a position to match in the foreseeable future—its vast cash reserves and its vastly superior infrastructure construction skills. There is a hunger for the development of infrastructure in all these countries, and China is their first choice for expanding and modernizing their infrastructure.

Even the best of Navies with a vast reach in the Indian Ocean region will be only of limited use in the absence of commensurate political and economic influence in the countries of the Ocean region. In building up its onshore presence and influence, China has taken a head-start over India. The Chinese Navy still cannot match and will not be in a position to match the off-shore presence of our Navy in the Indian Ocean area, but Beijing's onshore presence and influence will pose increasing challenges to the Indian political leadership and diplomacy.

No Evidence of Chinese plans for Bases at Present

Periodic reports of a speculative nature regarding a Chinese interest in the acquisition of military and naval base facilities in the Indian Ocean region have not been corroborated. They have been developing a robust military supply relationship of a strategic nature with Pakistan, Sri Lanka, and Myanmar. One can see the beginnings of such a relationship with Bangladesh too. There is no evidence at present that these relationships form part of a well thought-out strategy to acquire a permanent military presence in this area. Their willingness to enter into military supply and capacity-building relationships with the countries of this region is a tactical move to strengthen their economic and political influence.

They project their moves as inspired not by a larger Indian Ocean strategy to undermine the Indian influence, but merely as responses to requests for assistance received from the countries of this region. Whatever the purpose of these moves, the net effect will be an undermining of the Indian influence.

Current Chinese Pre-occupation

The present Chinese focus is on the Pacific. Their efforts are concentrated towards building a strong Pacific presence for their Navy and Air Force so as to be able to counter the US presence there and achieve parity with it. Building an equal Indian Ocean presence is not yet part of their short or medium term strategy. I do not visualize a Chinese threat to the naval presence of the US and India in the short and medium terms.

Compared to their Pacific naval strategy, there is very little debate in China on the contours of an Indian Ocean strategy. Their interests are presently focused on protecting the security of their energy supplies and keeping Pakistan propped up as a credible threat to India.

PLA (Navy)'s Entry into the Arabian Sea

The entry of Chinese naval ships on anti-piracy patrols into the Indian Ocean region and the Gulf of Aden has not created any adverse reactions in the region or in the West. The Chinese concerns over the growing threats from the Somali pirates to their ships and crew are accepted by the countries of the region and the West as natural. The regular anti-piracy patrols undertaken by ships of the Chinese Navy in this area, without causing any regional concerns, have enabled the Chinese Navy to familiarize itself with operating conditions and difficulties in the waters of this region, build up Navy–Navy relationships and offer Chinese assistance in capacity-building.

Should their anti-piracy forays be used as the initial building block for a long-term Indian Ocean strategy? The Chinese are avoiding any open discussion on this question, lest they give rise to unnecessary concerns in the region about Chinese naval assertiveness in the Indian Ocean region, as a follow-up to their assertiveness in the Pacific. Occasional voices are heard from the community of retired Chinese naval officers on the need for a naval base in this region to meet the logistics and rest and recreation requirements of their anti-piracy patrols, but such voices have been discouraged by the government and party leadership to prevent undue concerns. A long-term Chinese naval strategy for the Indian Ocean region is not yet evident.

Need for Composite Strategy

In working out an Indian strategy for the Indian Ocean region, the political, economic, and naval aspects have to receive equal attention. So too must the aspect of the Indian and US Navies cooperating with each other to maintain their present primacy in this region. Working out a national Indian Ocean Region strategy should go hand in hand with working out a joint Indo–US strategy to safeguard their interests in the Indian Ocean region.

Presentation 3: US, Chinese, and Indian Strategies in the Indian Ocean

Rear Admiral (Retd) Raja Menon

The 'Glorious Years'

It is customary to refer to the days before the advent of Europeans into our region as 'glorious' and 'peaceful.' In many respects they were indeed so. The Indian rulers of that time encouraged free trade and the state did not intervene in commercial dealings. There was equality of treatment. While it is true that there were periods when Indian influence spread across the eastern oceans, the Arabs were the better sailors. What Indians were good at was in financial services. Trade was conducted through complex transactions involving craftsmen, agriculturists, ship owners, and merchants, and there was a need for some equivalent of today's instruments of commerce such as insurance and letters of credit which cover the risk taken by the various parties. This is where the Indians came in, and the Chettiars of the South became exceedingly wealthy as a result.

Cotton textiles were the monopoly of India—India virtually clothed the world. When the Europeans came to the east in search of spices, they had little to offer in exchange except gold and wool. There was a limit to the amount of gold that could be absorbed by the Asian countries, and wool was of little use to them. So the Dutch set up factories in the Coromandel, bought textiles here, sold it in the East Indies and used that money to buy spices, making huge profits at every stage.

Current Pattern of Trade

It is obviously impossible to go back to those days because all our trading partners now are extra-regional—China, the European Union, the United States, and so on. But it is possible to rejuvenate trans-border trade—the best example is trade between India and Pakistan. The current pattern of trade between India and Pakistan is absurd—Indo–Pakistan trade totals about US $1.8–2.4 billion, whereas the indirect trade between these two countries through Dubai is about US $11.5 billion. When the subject is raised with Pakistanis, one finds that there is a total lack of interest. The reason for this is that there is a large number of families from both countries which profit from this indirect trade and cream off about 15 per cent of the profits both ways. These families act in nexus; hence Pakistan is not interested in changing the system that is lucrative to the rich and the powerful. We need to have something that is irreversible.

The Present System—Dominance of the US

If we cannot go back to the old system, we need to understand the existing one. Whether we like it or not, we have to accept one fact—the strongest power in the Indian Ocean is the US. The US is the dominant world power, so it has to be the most powerful everywhere. It is of little use saying that the US is extra-regional and that it is not an Indian Ocean power. The United States has huge infrastructure in the region—command facilities in Bahrain, equipment for two armoured brigades in Kuwait, and equipment for one Air Force wing in Saudi Arabia. It has ships pre-positioned in Diego Garcia, loaded and ready to sail on expeditionary missions. The US has agreements with Singapore, Saudi Arabia, Masirah, and Bahrain for the use of the air, naval, and military bases there when needed. They are here in strength, and we need to understand why.

Understanding American Strategy

The answer lies in a kind of round-robin reasoning. As somebody famously put it, 'If the Middle East was known for vegetables or flowers, the Americans wouldn't be there.' So the obvious reason is oil. The world economy runs on oil from the Middle East; for global stability there has to be stability in the oil trade, which calls for the existence of some sort of regulatory system. This is the core of the US strategy—to prevent oil instability by assuring regime stability. If a regime were to be attacked in the Middle East, there is a big risk of it choosing the 'Samson option'—if it goes down, it will take others down with it. So the US guarantees regime stability, paying the regimes huge amounts of money which they can't spend anywhere else except in the US—on education, imports, luxury goods, contracts, and so on. It offers package deals, making available hi-tech equipment, the newest military technology, and the latest fighter aircraft. The Saudi army and navy budgets, for example, are the same as India's. When asked about their support to such regimes, the US says they also support other countries even when they don't have oil, like Jordan. But actually they support Jordan because of close relations between Jordan and other royal families in Saudi and the Middle East, which serves to strengthen US influence. Whether we like it or not US is the dominant power, so its interests are dominant.

The US is fighting a war on terrorism at a huge cost of money and blood. We need to understand its views; whether we agree or not is a separate matter. It is often said that terrorists have no address—but they don't live in the clouds either. They have to live somewhere. The only country that can risk harbouring a terrorist is an emirate. The word 'emirate' has a specific connotation when used in technical jargon. It is not what you or I think is an emirate. In their understanding, an 'emirate' is a state where the only law that applies is the law of the Book. It is forbidden in that state to elect a legislature, because all the laws that the emirate needs are already there in the book, and there is no room for any more laws. So you have an emirate and if you have more than one emirate you get a caliphate. This may seem unrealistic but this is the jargon. One can have a terrorist leadership taking shelter in an emirate, and it has been seen that an emirate does not always have to have the same boundaries as the host country. In a sense, the emirate is like a cancer; just as a body cannot get rid of a cancerous organ, so the host country cannot get rid of the emirate. Today, there is no question that there is an emirate around Quetta and the areas that adjoin Afghanistan, and neither country can do anything about it. The US view is that if the cancer is dislodged from here it will only go somewhere else, and the prime possibility if they are ousted from the AfPak region is Yemen and perhaps Somalia after that. That is the American view and they are going to fight to prevent this happening. Put plainly, their view is 'We are the dominant power and these are our interests, and you have to ally yourselves to secure our interests. Whatever we can give in return we shall. That's the deal.' One of the things they give in return, they say, is the SLOC system and the global commons, which they will regulate in the common interest.

The Entry of the Black Swan

Let me draw an analogy between the situation in the IOR and the opening of Tchaikovsky's famous ballet 'Swan Lake'. To start with, all is idyllic and joyous, with birdsong and sunshine. Tranquility is rudely disrupted when the Black Swan, Kaldun, makes a dramatic entry and dominates the stage with his ominous presence. China is the Kaldun in the Indian Ocean, and it has jumped on the Indian Ocean stage. By 2017, the main user of the Indian Ocean will be China, as opposed to Japan today. China's view is that it cannot accept a situation where it will be the prime user and the US continues to be the dominant power in the IOR. The reason is that they feel the US will strangle them at the Straits of Malacca —China's so-called Malacca dilemma. There are those who try to persuade them that this not so, that their fears are baseless; there are others like me who see no reason to relieve their sense of unease.

Chinese Strategy in the Indian Ocean

To combat this fear the Chinese have a grand strategy. This actually consists of two sub-strategies. First, most of China's oil comes from West Africa, and not from Saudi Arabia any more. So China thinks that it will take its oil through Gwadar and Sittwe and avoid the Straits of Malacca . That way it would have a huge pump house on-shore to pump oil over the land route. Actually, they can only transport about 15 per cent of the oil overland, but this is what they have decided. So China has come down the Himalayan region and occupied all the northern littoral of the Indian Ocean as far as it can.

The PLA(N) in the Indian Ocean

There are voices in China who ask why they haven't sent the PLA Navy to the Indian Ocean. But the PLA Navy cannot survive in the Indian Ocean without tactical air cover round the clock. So in the second part of the strategy, China has decided that it needs a base: this would meet both requirements—the logistic base for PLA ships, and the pump house. But it is not working out because China is expanding too fast. China's energy requirement is going to quadruple along with their GDP, which has made them go into Africa in a huge way to secure energy to fuel its growth. There is a significant Chinese presence in Sudan, Kenya, Ethiopia, Tanzania, Zanzibar, Angola, the Congo, and Cameroon and so on along the Africa littoral. They are in every coastal African state. China has invested US $120 billion and sent about half a million Chinese in Africa: 120 thousand in South Africa, 20 thousand in Sudan. This is reminiscent of the East India Company, when Flag followed trade. There is a growing opinion in China which questions whether with so many of its people in Africa they can be left undefended, but no other country does that. The biggest users of the Indian Ocean trade routes are the Japanese, but they don't want to come to the Indian Ocean. India has oil interests in Kamchatka, but India does not say that we have to send Indian destroyers there. The explanation for the difference in the Chinese approach is simple—because we believe in the global commons and they don't.

The ideal place for the Chinese to come in the IOR would be East Africa. They are trying to obtain bases in Mauritius and Seychelles, but it is questionable whether they can get it. Can these small island states risk becoming belligerents on the side of the Chinese, and face the ire of both India and the EU? This is the problem the Chinese would face.

China's Pace of Development

In considering the growing presence of China in the region, we have to remember the sheer size of that country. China is a five-trillion dollar economy—we are at US $1.4 trillion. And they are going to double, maybe quadruple in the foreseeable future. So what is the problem for a US $20 trillion economy to have a navy with 6 aircraft groups and 34 SSNs? That can happen in 14 years. The sheer pace of development that the Chinese can achieve is something that we need to imprint on our minds. Their strategy is that they need to not just progress; they have to hurtle along if they want to avoid internal discontent. For that they need to soak up resources and this will make them turn up in the most unlikely and unexpected places. There are way-out scenarios—they have bought the national debt of Iceland, and nearly that of Greece. They may go to the Mediterranean. One must expect out-of-the-box courses of action when one is confronted with a nation that is hurtling from a five to a US $20 trillion-dollar economy.

Conclusion—India's Options

Lastly, what are our options? It would be nice to say we believe in sovereignty and we need to stand on our own feet. There is nothing wrong with that from a strategic point of view, but there is a great deal wrong with it from an economic point of view. It is prohibitively expensive. The Indian Navy's share of the defence budget has been going up by 0.5 per cent year after year (today it is at 17.8 per cent), which does not make it look as if we want to stand on our own two feet. We could land up in a 1962-like situation, when Nehru wrote to plead for assistance from Kennedy. But we can't afford to go broke trying to stand on our own feet. The Americans tell us that we must alleviate China's sense of insecurity by allowing them to work in a rule-based system and join the world, by guaranteeing them the use of the global commons. But people like me say 'not on your life—we've got problems with the Chinese.' There are diplomats present here who know this. The Chinese always take every opportunity to deny us entry in multi-lateral forums, or any status in international organizations. There is a diplomatic offensive on here. The 1962 'Status quo in the East for Aksai Chin in the West' option is no longer on the table. The PLA has remodeled itself completely, and by 2020, the Chinese army which already has 3 airborne divisions will get 3 more air mobile divisions. The restructured Peoples' Liberation Army is hugely helo-based and is not a territory-occupying army. It is a political lesson-teaching Army. That is a strategy for which I don't think we are preparing for. And if we are not preparing for it in the mountains, we had better have a hold on the jugular in the Indian Ocean. If there is one aspect of our naval development that will do it, it is nuclear attack submarines, or SSNs. They are the most terrifying prospect for anyone going to sea, because the SSN attack is undetectable, and the Commander at sea does not know where it is going to come from.

India needs to think carefully. The last thing we need is full-blown ultra-nationalism and rhetoric. We have to see where diplomacy can fill in to complement military capability and where military capability can fill in when diplomacy cannot get results.

Discussions

Global warming

Manmohan Reddy also raised the broader question of the effects of global warming. The rise in sea temperatures off East Africa has resulted in depletion in the fish catch, causing great hardship to the Somali fishermen. This, according to him could be behind the rise in piracy in that area. Admiral Menon responded that global warming would have a strategic impact, but of a different kind. It would cause the shrinking of the Arctic ice cap, which would have two effects: it would expose currently ice-covered reserves of oil and gas to exploitation, and secondly, it would open up the Arctic route for navigation. This may not be so evident seeing it on a conventional map, but in great circle terms, the distance from South America to China is greatly reduced by following an Arctic route. And the Chinese have huge investments in Venezuela and Argentina. They have shown interest in this and have already sent ice-breakers to operate in the Arctic 'for practice.' This also lends some significance to the Chinese presence in Iceland.

US–Chinese competition over Gwadar

Sowmya Sitaraman referred to the competition and confrontation between the US and China over Gwadar, and asked what India should do about it. Raman responded that in his view, Gwadar would never be a naval base. Although the Chinese had built a beautiful port, there are no roads and rail connections to it which Pakistan which was supposed to provide. A Japanese journalist who had visited Gwadar had told Raman that there were no signs of any military infrastructure and hardly one or two ships had visited the port. The Pakistanis had asked the Chinese to take over the responsibility for the infrastructure also, but the Chinese have not shown interest. There is a view that the US should take over Gwadar as the logistic port for NATO troops in Afghanistan. So the Gwadar situation is unclear, and the Chinese are having second thoughts about the wisdom of this investment. We should not be surprised if the US and China come together on this issue in developing Gwadar. If Gwadar ultimately becomes a naval base in 10 or 15 years, it will pose a threat to us, and we must prepare for it.

Investing in 'Soft Infrastructure'

A second point raised by the same questioner was that since India was unable to match China, it may be advantageous for India to invest in soft infrastructure—cultural ties like theatre, music, and even Bollywood movies. Responding to the question, Raman said that a country had to decide what kind of infrastructure it needed to create that would be of relevance in case of a future conflict. Investing in Bollywood-like initiatives would not be of any use to us in a strategic context. If we want to be a power, we have to think in strategic and military terms. We have not done anything in that regard; if tomorrow there is a conflict with China, we will find ourselves totally unprepared.

Strategic Linkage with United States

Jayaramu from Bangalore University remarked that the presentations by Admiral Menon and Raman had demolished his impression that we were in a comfortable position with respect to China; if India cannot 'take on' China, why not go further and tell the USA that together we could take on the Chinese in the Indian Ocean?

Secondly, all speakers had talked of the lack of political will to act to protect our strategic interests. He said that RAW, the MEA, and other government agencies should explain the gravity of the situation clearly to the government. Asia Centre should send a resolution to the government, to the Prime Minister, and the *Raksha Mantri* declaring that the situation was serious, and that they should either take it seriously or make way for others to do it.

The Chairman intervened to say that everything that was discussed here was indeed sent to the government agencies concerned. It would seem that currently the government was busy attending to many things and so national security was not getting the attention it merited.

Admiral Menon observed that the current scenario was one of a three-cornered relationship—India, US, and China—where none trusts the other two. Today India is superior in the Indian Ocean. Whether it would be true twenty years from now, one could not say. He felt that perhaps the MEA was hedging its bets, in the prevailing atmosphere of absence of implicit trust. There has been some talk of a 'G-2' grouping, which would be nothing but a strategic power and influence-sharing arrangement between the US and China. One thing was clear. Although China is bigger than us, the cost of making things very uncomfortable for China in the Indian Ocean would not be all that much for us, and could be done.

Raman commented that if the questioner's earlier belief in our capabilities vis-à-vis China had been changed, that was the good part of such seminars, which served to make us think and re-examine issues afresh. He continued that the US itself was not clear in its mind about its strategy concerning India. The latest US national military strategic document by Obama has several paragraphs devoted to China but just one sentence about India. He felt that it would take a long time to convince the US that India has an important role to play.

Economic Aspects of the India–China Equation

Mohan Guruswamy offered three comments:

1) Countries do not grow at the same time. India was probably 20 years behind China, and the Indian economy would grow behind China's. But we should know that projections indicate that the Indian economy would quadruple by 2020, from the current US $1.6 trillion to over US $5 trillion. It would reach US $40 trillion in 2040.
2) Whereas the Chinese growth rate had started to come down, the Indian economy is still on the ascendant—this is not due to any brilliance in economic management but because of other factors such as demographics. India's growth rate would be around 10–11 per cent next year, 12 per cent in 2013, and maintain that rate for 20–25 years. Citibank released a report which predicted that the Indian GDP would reach US $90 trillion dollars (at Purchasing Power Parity) by 2050, and would be the largest economy in the world.
3) At present, China's economy depends heavily on its favourable balance of trade with the US, which it is utilizing to buy up energy resources globally. But if the US achieves Obama's recently announced target of reducing the trade deficit to zero in 5 years, it will neutralize China's 150 billion dollar reserve.

Need for Patience and Resilience

Guruswamy emphasized that we need to have the capacity to hold on when things are not going our way, and to exploit conditions when they turn favourable to us. For instance, the US fought China in 1952, but sided with China and egged it on to attack India in 1971 (this was learnt from recently declassified records of conversations between Nixon and Kissinger.) India must take advantage of the current US–India coalescence. If we can have the steadiness and wisdom to bide our time, it will go well with us. Guruswamy declared that he was optimistic that India was poised on the brink of brilliant economic progress.

Export Growth and India's Economic Profile

N. Ravi proposed that some incentive system could be started by the Indian Government for the security and education of the families of expatriate workers. He also asked on which sector should be selected as the export growth leader since our trade deficit is a major problem.

In his answer Guruswamy pointed out that 65 per cent of the population in India is engaged in agriculture, but they produce only 18 per cent of the GDP. He commented ironically that India has achieved a post-industrial profile, dominated by the services sector without having industrialized. 61 per cent of India's investment comes from Mauritius. The origin of this money is ambiguous and unidentifiable. It could be Dubai money, or it could be from certain shady politicians. Foreign direct investment has reduced every year because investors are deterred by the corruption and red tape here. Even the Tatas and others are investing abroad. Without investment in Indian industry, our exports will continue to remain a trickle and we shall remain at the current low levels. We need to take measures such as creating special SEZs, and not allow economic policy to be dictated by party politics.

The workers of Kerala do a great service to the country by remitting US $11 billion every year, but are treated shabbily when they come home. Major attitudinal changes are undoubtedly needed, but building schools abroad is not a solution. Schools need to be built in India where there is a crying need for them. Sixty per cent of Indian children do not have access to schools. We need to look at it holistically and not export just because we want to export.

Putting China on a Pedestal

Air Chief Marshal Major was critical of our tendency to put China on a pedestal in all forums; we overplay China's predominance. India may be behind China by a decade, but we are not what we were in 1962.

The Air Chief Marshal said, in the era of globalization, all oceans and water bodies are mere transit routes. Protection of its own littoral was obviously the responsibility of a country but to say that somebody is building a port in Gwadar and that is going to affect us, is being very defeatist.

Military Importance of Indian Ocean and Navy

Guruswamy replied that he would answer perhaps in an indirect way. Picking up from the remarks of ACM Major, he said that the importance of the Indian Ocean and the Indian Navy is that, whereas the Chinese are stronger in the north, their vulnerability is in the Indian Ocean. He agreed that two or three SSNs would be a major asset that would keep everybody at bay for a while. China's outlook was bad. India is going to be the biggest country in the world in a few decades and our population would stabilize only in 2060. By that time, China is going have a larger number of old people and the dependency ratio, which is the ratio of the non-working to the working population, would rise to

60 per cent by 2050. India's demography is very good, as a younger population is essential for progress. The bad news, he said, is that the 'BIMARU' states are growing rapidly, but the stabilization in the population is happening in the more forward states. These states are paying a huge price for the backward states.

Remarks by S.T. Devare, Co-Chairman

Devare said that the Indian Ocean consists of several sub-regions, each with its own specifics which demand separate assessments and a differentiated policy approach. Also, the Indian and Pacific Oceans form a continuum and have a mutual influence on each other. There is no reason why Indian ships should not go into the Pacific region. We have to build relationships with the countries of the region. India can build sufficiently strong relations with South-East Asian countries, which are all wary of China. None of them have defence agreements with China, whereas they have no qualms about entering into defence cooperation agreements with us.

It is the same with East Africa. It is true that the Chinese are expanding their trade and commercial ventures there, but we have capabilities in many areas in which these countries look for our assistance.

There is one diplomatic instrument—regionalism, which the countries of this region are quite amenable to—that we can still use. India took the lead in establishing the group called the Indian Ocean Association Rim-Association for Cooperation (IOR-ARC), which consists of 18 member states including Australia and South Africa. Not much has been achieved because Australia and South Africa lost interest. That was more than a decade ago and their perceptions of India have now changed. India is chairing the IOR–ARC meeting this year, and there is scope for many initiatives. These are small building blocks. We may not have the financial resources that China has, but not everything can be bought. The countries in the region regard China differently from the way they look at India. That is the strength that we have in this part of the world. The region can again be our ocean if we can formulate a plan of action and implement it after strengthening the right mechanisms, involving both governmental as well as corporate resources. The record of Indian investments in Indonesia, Australia, and East and South Africa holds out much promise for the future.

Concluding Remarks by Venkateswaran, Co-Chairman

Venkateswaran said that he fully agreed with the remarks of the Director General, ICWA. India has a unique position with all the countries of this region. When ASEAN welcomed Vietnam, it was because Vietnam was the only country to have defeated China repeatedly. India is not looked at with fear; that is a good thing. Maybe India is not regarded with as much respect as China is, but that will come with time, as we progress.

Our cultural contacts with Asian and African countries are much closer, and our customs and practices are more acceptable than Chinese customs and habits in the region. People say that we are moving forward much slower than China. Things will change, as in the case of Bihar. Bihar was considered to be a basket case at one time, but there has been a remarkable sense of security and forward movement since a change in the leadership occurred in Bihar. So, one must appreciate changes in the situation and not remain trapped in past views.

I, for one, am full of hope that we shall move forward, irrespective of what happens in Delhi. Let us all make our own little contribution and move forward.

Conclusion

Indians are inordinately proud of the fact that the Indian Ocean bears the name of their country. Yet historically, we have been sea-blind and except for a brief period in the 11th century, have never been a maritime power of any significance. This neglect of sea power resulted ultimately in the colonization of India from across the seas.

Trade and Energy Security

The Indian Ocean continues to be a major factor in India's overall strategic scenario in the modern era. Most of India's vital interests come together in the Indian Ocean region, foremost among them being trade and access to energy resources. As clearly brought out in this seminar, India's trade with the Middle East is of crucial importance in the management of the mounting trade deficit. In addition, this is the region on which India's energy security directly depends. India must maintain good relations with its trading partners in this region, prominent among which are Saudi Arabia, Iran, and Dubai. Other Middle Eastern countries are important for the number of Indian workers who earn their livelihoods there, and remit significant amounts to India by way of foreign remittances. India's relations with these countries must therefore be driven by enlightened self-interest and cannot be subject to pressures from extra-regional states that have their own strategic priorities.

China's Economic Expansionism

The Chinese are quite evidently looking to accelerate their GDP growth rate to three to four times the current level in the next two decades or so, when they will then attain predominant world power status. With its rapid economic expansion westwards, China is acquiring oil and strategic material resources and assets in almost every African country; it has done this outside of the global market system, and prefers to own the source rather than follow international trade practice. China's presence in the IOR has increased correspondingly, and with the growth in their economic ties, their political influence with the countries of the region is bound to increase. With this situation, there is a probability that at some time in the future China will feel the need to defend its huge investments and assets, which in turn will pave the way for its military presence in the IOR. China has challenged India's economic and strategic influence in its own back yard, and India has been slow in its response.

India's Security Perspective

India's immediate security perspective is dominated by the hostile and volatile relationship with Pakistan. The most serious issues are Pakistan's involvement in cross-border terrorism and its covert support to and instigation of militant insurgency in the North-East. Pakistan's acquisition of nuclear weapons capability has given its military leadership the self-assurance to carry out hostile cross-border acts (via the sea as in 2008) with the confidence that the United States will rush to prevent a potential nuclear flare-up.

With China, the border dispute continues to be virtually the sole area of discord. This could however be a surface assessment; it can be argued that in reality, China sees India as an ideological threat because of its success in pursuing its developmental goals without sacrificing its democratic ethos. The Chinese position has hardened with the modernization of the PLA, now almost complete. In the course of its economic campaign, China has built ports in Sri Lanka and Pakistan and roads in Pakistan and Myanmar. It is going ahead with the building of oil pipelines from the latter countries to the Chinese heartland. Though these pipelines can never match sea-borne oil transportation, they indicate China's determination to reach the Indian Ocean and to areas of vital interest to India.

There is no indication that South Block has given due attention to the steps taken by China to modernize the PLA, which is transforming six divisions from conventional infantry units to airborne divisions. The military lessons learned from our bitter experience of 1962 may well have to be revised drastically in the face of this transformation.

The maritime scenario is somewhat different. China has to perforce transport its energy and strategic mineral requirements through the Malacca, Sunda or Lombok Straits, and this has created a perceived vulnerability that the Chinese are apprehensive about, their so-called Malacca problem. Because of this vulnerability, the naval equation is the only one where the PLA(N) is at a disadvantage, as it cannot operate autonomously in the Indian Ocean without integral air cover, which is not likely to be available to it in the near future. Speakers at the seminar have suggested that India can take advantage of this situation by deployment of a relatively small number of nuclear attack submarines in the Indian Ocean, which will serve as an effective counterpoise to any gains made by the Chinese in the North.

Relations with Countries of IOR

India's relationships with the other countries of the region have stagnated, or cooled considerably. There are two reasons for this: first, India has in recent times been so engrossed in its pursuit of a strategic relationship with the USA that it has not given the smaller regional states the attention that it should have. The second reason is that India has been either unable to match the vigorous and focused campaign by China to dominate economic ties with the countries in the Indian Ocean region. In Sittwe, Myanmar, Hambantota, and Mauritius, India has been outdone by China; this was due to inattention rather than a lack of capability, and resulted in the decline of Indian influence in the region. Our efforts to improve the state of relations with IOR countries need to be intensified, taking advantage of existing forums such as the Bay of Bengal Initiative for Multi-Sectoral Technical and Economic Cooperation (BIMSTEC) and the Indian Ocean Rim-Association for Cooperation (IOR-ARC).

Maritime Terrorism and Piracy

The rise in piracy in the North-West Arabian Sea has resulted in the increased presence of warships of extra-regional powers and legitimized the presence of Chinese naval units in the Indian Ocean. India has not joined the Western (NATO) Task Forces but is taking independent action to combat piracy. There is scope here for cooperative regional effort, and the issue can be discussed in a suitable forum such as the IONS.

Need for a Comprehensive Policy for IOR

To sum up, India faces three kinds of challenges in the region. The first is economic, with the Chinese vigorously working to displace India in its economic ties with the countries of the IOR. The second is a security challenge, with China and Pakistan in active strategic collusion against India. The third is the task of enhancing our influence the Indian Ocean region. There is an urgent need to formulate and implement policies and plans to meet these challenges, if the nomenclature of the Indian Ocean is not to become a historical oddity.

Chapter 12

India's Look East Policy

ASIA CENTRE BANGALORE

'Impediments to India's Look East Policy—Suggested Remedies'
Proceedings of the Seminar
held on

September 22, 2007

Introduction

A.P. Venkateswaran, former Foreign Secretary and Chairman, Asia Centre presided. The following speakers addressed the seminar:

C.V. Ranganathan	Former Ambassador to China and former convener of the National Security Advisory Board
D.S. Rajan	Former Director, Cabinet Secretariat, GOI, current Director, Chennai Centre for China Studies
Vice-Admiral (Retd) P.J. Jacob	Former Vice-Chief of Naval Staff and former member, National Security Advisory Board

This report, written by Meera Baindur, a doctoral research scholar at the National Institute of Advanced Studies, Bangalore, summarizes the presentations and the discussions that followed.

Presentation 1: 'India's Look-East Policy: Visions and Reality'

C.V. Ranganathan

The Idea of Asia as an Entity The former Ambassador to China C.V. Ranganathan began with a quote from Nehru's *Discovery of India* (1944), where he foresees India becoming the centre of economic and political activity in the Indian Ocean area, from South-East Asia right up to the Middle East. Other visions of Asian unity such as Ho Chi Minh's statements to build Asian unity in 1945, the Asian relations conference and the 18-nation conference on Indonesia as well as the Bandung conference in 1955 were inspired by many factors that brought Asian nations together. Important among these was the rise of consciousness of Asian identity, nationalism, and culture in a postcolonial context. India's Look East Policy was thus a recent successor to earlier visions.

Factors Influencing Asian View of India

Sino-Indian Estrangement Speaking of Asian perceptions of India in South-East Asia from the late 1950s to the early 1990s, Ranganathan pointed out that from the late 1950s there had been a long estrangement between India and China, culminating in the boundary conflict in 1962. There was an improvement in Sino–Indian relations after Rajiv Gandhi's visit to China in 1988, which contributed to better relations between India and its South-East Asian neighbours, whose comfort level with India increased with the trend of improving relations with China.

Close Indo-Soviet Relationship The other major factor that influenced South-East Asian perceptions was the Indo–Soviet Union relationship. The Soviet Union's occupation of Afghanistan and India's ambivalent attitude to this event as well as the pro-Vietnam attitude after Vietnamese defeat of the Pol Pot regime in Cambodia, reinforced perceptions that India was a partner of the Soviet Union.

Initiation of Talks with ASEAN Officials The contribution of A.P. Venkateswaran in his capacity as Secretary in MEA to initiate diplomatic talks with his counterparts in Singapore and other South-East Asian states helped in improving matters. The Cambodian crisis was used by ASEAN to establish its political identity as an international political grouping, and as a player on the international stage. Other factors which helped were Gorbachev's ascendancy and his welcome initiatives towards China and South-East Asia.

Effect of Post-Soviet and Recent Developments After the breakup of the former Soviet Union (1990–91), ASEAN and other nations realized the geographical importance of India and the possibility of its being a major player in South Asia. But at the same time, there was disappointment in India with progress in SAARC. There was also the perception of India as mired in a permanent dispute with Pakistan. Other countries saw India in a straightjacket situation with very little to contribute towards regional cooperation. One of the important effects of September 11, 2001 was the realization that India's neighbourhood in its west could be an epicentre of terrorism in Asia. This event led to the realization of the inter-connectedness of security. Following the unilateral actions in Iraq by the US and the subsequent difficulties faced by it there, ASEAN nations realized that international relations could not be pursued along any single axis as in past years, and that ASEAN's security and stability required it to involve major countries and big powers.

India's Economic Performance The situation during the 'command economy' and the 'License Raj' era in India demonstrated the close inter-connectedness between domestic policies and their powerful influence on external relations. India was seen in a poor light when compared with the development of the Asian Tigers and China's economic growth. The 1991 foreign exchange crisis in India, when its reserves fell to a mere two weeks' worth of imports, then led to economic reforms and liberalization. The sequential rise of China followed by India today is the big story, and ASEAN seeks to leverage their growth and the improvement in their relations for its benefit.

Growth of Institutional Linkages with ASEAN India went through a long period of 'probation' before it was enabled to develop institutional links with ASEAN as a regional body. Singapore under Goh Chok Tong played a major role in promoting India's relations with ASEAN. Adopting a differentiated emphasis for each nation, India slowly built up its individual relationship with nations in the South-East during this period. The speaker highlighted the useful role played by the Confederation of Indian Industries followed by the Federation of Indian Chambers of Commerce and Industry in establishing good personal relations with the Singapore leadership. This led to major Indian firms being listed on the Singapore stock exchange and establishing tie-ups with Singapore firms. From 1992 India began to be included in the institutional processes of the ASEAN, when it was invited as sectoral dialogue partner of the ASEAN for trade, investments, science and technology and tourism, for which a joint coordination committee between

India and the ASEAN was formed.

Steady Progress in Partnership with ASEAN 1996 was a landmark year. At the Jakarta Summit, India became a full dialogue partner of ASEAN and a formal member of ASEAN Regional Forum (ARF), on par with the USA, EU, China, Japan, the Republic of Korea, and Australia, with consultation on regional security and other political issues. This was the second phase, marked by deepening institutional bonds set out in many formal agreements. In 2002, India participated at the Summit level at the Phnom Penh Summit. At the 2003 Bali Summit, three important documents were signed:

1) A Framework agreement on Comprehensive Economic Cooperation between India and ASEAN (signed by 10 heads of states and government, and Atal Bihari Vajpayee) in which India and ASEAN have formally agreed to set up FTA by 2011. This follows similar Agreements between ASEAN and China, Japan, and South Korea.
2) An Instrument of accession to the ASEAN Treaty of Amity and Cooperation in South-East Asia, which is a basic political foundational document, a necessary criterion to intensify dialogue in political, security, and other strategic issues.
3) A joint Indo–ASEAN declaration on combating terrorism that enables information and intelligence sharing as well as aspects of law enforcement.

Important Agreements Signed India and ASEAN signed two documents at the Vietnam Summit in 2004: the 'Partnership for Peace, Progress and Shared Prosperity' and the 'Plan of Action to Implement the India–ASEAN Partnership'. Both these provide a conceptual and executive framework for developments in diverse areas and are road maps for the future. With a signing of other notable bilateral Agreements such as the Indo-Singapore Comprehensive Economic Cooperation Agreement (CECA) in 2005 and the framework bilateral FTA agreement with Thailand, the progress made in the area of bilateral relations with the East could be considered positive.

'Arc of Prosperity' The East Asian Summit Process that was started in 2005 includes the ten ASEAN countries, and in addition Australia, China, India, Korea, Japan and New Zealand. The speaker described India's Prime Minister, Manmohan Singh's vision of this process as contributing to an 'Arc of Prosperity' where there would be the free flow of trade, investments, and ideas through greater connectivity between India, South-East Asia, and

East Asia. Further, the second EAS in 2007 decided to adopt an agenda for regional cooperation on energy security. It was posited that India's evolving relationship with ASEAN is a sum of its agreements with individual members and India enjoys differentiated relations with the group. With some, the emphasis is economic, with some it is defence, with some it is connectivity between India and South-East Asia and with some it is energy resources. With a few it is a combination of several of these.

Achievements of the Look East Policy The main achievements of India's Look East Policy are:

1) The systematic institutionalization of economic and trade interactions; this is substantiated by India's 2006 trade figures with East Asian countries, which shows impressive increases.
2) The broadening fields of cooperation, particularly in areas of defence as well as on political and security issues.
3) Prospects of greater connectivity through sub-regional institutions, such as in the field of energy, where Indian, Korean and Vietnamese companies are involved in Myanmar, and in sub-regional developments such as BIMSTEC. The speaker elaborated on this initiative, providing details about agreements such as the framework agreement on BIMSTEC Free Trade Area.

Urgency of Giving Importance to North-Eastern States Ranganathan emphasized that there was one aspect that needs to be addressed urgently if India's Look East Policy is to realize its full potential, namely, the importance given to India's North-Eastern regions. Some progress in this direction was the creation of road and transport links between the North-East areas and Eastern neighbours. Notable among these were several road links between Manipur and Myanmar, and the feasibility study of the Manipur–Myanmar rail link. The Asian car rally which traversed 8000 km from Guwahati across Myanmar, Thailand, Laos, Vietnam, Cambodia, Malaysia, Singapore, through to Indonesia 'broke the psychological barrier that India was a distant Western neighbour', in the words of Goh Chok Tong. India was not too far behind in its financial commitment to connectivity projects, as evidenced by its credit of US $57 million for upgrading the Yangon–Mandalay section of the railways and its investments and commitments to cooperation in education, human resources, tourism and communications. The ambitious India–Myanmar–Thailand road project needs to be realized at an early date. The importance of India's North and East connectivity to South-East Asia needs emphasis in the context of removing the feelings of alienation from mainstream India which is prevalent in those regions.

Important to Ensure Satisfactory Implementation of Policy In conclusion, Ranganathan said that India had to forge close links with its eastern neighbours in its own enlightened interest. To succeed, regional cooperation must be based on the principle of inclusivity, not exclusivity. India's links with ASEAN have bound it in a web of obligations and commitments in various fields with ASEAN nations; the implementation of these will have to be satisfactory if India's credibility and seriousness about its Look East Policy are not to be questioned. This is where China should not score over India, by default as it were.

ASEAN has made investments in India in the game of global realpolitik and it is up to India to fully reciprocate and optimize the goodwill for it in this vital region.

Presentation 2: Impediments to India's Look-East Policy—China's Reservations and Suggested Remedies

D.S. Rajan

Phases of Implementation Rajan began his presentation with a quotation from Manmohan Singh that India's Look East Policy is not merely an external economic policy; it also marks a strategic shift in India's vision of the world and its place in the evolving global economy. He highlighted the progress achieved so far in the implementation of India's Look East Policy since the early 1990s. In the first phase of its implementation, the main target had been to create links with the ASEAN, which had economic, political, and strategic importance in the Asia-Pacific region and a potential to become a major trade and investment partner for India. It was projected that in the second stage, the scope of the policy would be extended to include the Far Eastern and Pacific regions, facilitating India's enhanced links with a host of countries—China, Japan, Republic of Korea, Australia, New Zealand, Fiji, Papua New Guinea, and Pacific island states.

Benefits of Policy—Vision of Asian Economic Community The benefits of the Look East Policy in terms of both domestic economy and external economic relations were outlined. He added that the building blocks of India's Look East Policy, such as the Bay of Bengal Initiative for Multi-Sectoral Technical and Economic Cooperation (BIMSTEC) established in 1997 act as a bridge between South and South-East Asia. India's effort is to bring together such mutually beneficial partnerships in a web of Pan-Asian Free Trade Agreements (PAFTA) for building an Asian Economic Community (AEC) which would mark the formation of the third pole of the world economy, after the European Union (EU) and North American Free Trade Agreement (NAFTA).

China's Reaction to Indian Look East Policy

Points of Convergence and Divergence Beijing's emerging perceptions would have far reaching implications for the future course of the policy. Chinese and Indian policy statements show both convergence and divergence between them on the Look East Policy. Points of convergence were that both agree that a harmonious, peaceful and prosperous East Asia can be built with ASEAN as the driving force, and that non-South-East Asian countries could take part in the regional integration process.

Difference Regarding non-East Asian Countries On participation by non- East Asian countries, there was a subtle difference in China's stand. Prior to the Kuala Lumpur EAS gathering in 2005, China, according to reports, lobbied hard to stop India's membership. When the lobbying failed, thanks to the stand taken by most of the East Asian nations, Beijing chose the next best option, with an attempt to divide the EAS membership into two blocs: 'Core' states with China leading, and three peripheral states: India, Australia and New Zealand. China's approach was evidently based on its aim to dominate the EAS process.

Other Points of Divergence There are other points concerning Sino-Indian divergences on the matter of regional integration:

1) **ASEAN Structure** China's strong emphasis on the role of ASEAN + 3 with the PRC as the 'main channel' for East Asia cooperation contrasts with India's 10 + 6 (ASEAN plus 3 plus India, Australia, and New Zealand) approach.
2) **Regional Security Order** Secondly, on the issue of a regional security order, India's prescription for a 'polycentric' security concept for East Asia, in effect disallows domination of the regional security architecture by any country (China). Chinese strategic experts have indicated that Beijing is not worried about India's security intentions at the moment; their assessment is that despite India's Look East Policy, its power is limited to the Indian Ocean. At the same time, China's media alleges

that India's policy is designed to build a hedge around China by developing military relations with the PRC's surrounding neighbours. They especially mention India's strategy of monitoring China's missile systems from Mongolia, and the port calls by Indian warships including an aircraft carrier in the Asia–Pacific region.

3) **Efforts to Dilute Chinese Role—Beijing's Apprehension** Thirdly, China's apprehensions about efforts to weaken its role in East Asia's integration reflect its concerns regarding its territorial disputes in the South and East China Seas.
4) **Economic Cooperation** The speaker pointed out yet another point of divergence in China's silence over India's proposal regarding an Asian Economic Community, and also a Japanese proposal for a Pan-Asian trade bloc had been strongly attacked through the Chinese media. What comes out clearly, therefore, is that China will not accept any economic groupings which limits its leading role.

In sum, the conclusion was that Beijing viewed India's Look East Policy as a challenge to its central role in the Asia–Pacific region. The Chinese media have strongly criticised the US-India nuclear and defence cooperation, the recent Japanese proposal for a 'quadrilateral' initiative involving New Delhi, Canberra, Washington and Tokyo, and the five-nation (India, US, Japan, Australia, and Singapore) Naval Exercises in the Bay of Bengal in September 2007; all these are seen as directed against China. The speaker clarified that though these were media fears, they deserved due notice as anything printed in the Chinese media had the tacit approval of the authorities. He also observed that the PRC has chosen to move closer to Russia in order to use the ties with Moscow as a counter-weight to US presence in the region.

Competition and Cooperation Rajan observed that at the current stage, China perceived the need for a peaceful periphery in the interests of its modernization drives. It would therefore not obstruct India's Look East Policy, but accept it grudgingly, viewing India as a weak player in both trade and security spheres in East Asia. He predicted that Beijing's strategy for the present was likely to be one of competition or cooperation with India, depending on the circumstances. A competitive element may arise in the form of each side attempting to dominate East Asian markets.

Recommended Measures for India As a conclusion, Rajan suggested that India should address China's sensitivities and doubts on the implications of the Look East Policy and constructively take pro-active remedial steps aimed at reassuring it. We should work to strengthen bilateral economic relations and expedite the process of signing a Comprehensive Economic Cooperation agreement between the two sides. India's Look East Policy is already paying dividends; India should garner further support from the ASEAN, China's surrounding nations and Japan, and make its position stronger to neutralize China's apparent doubts. An India–ASEAN FTA agreement needs to be concluded at the earliest. The US–India civil nuclear cooperation and defence agreements have introduced a new element to India's Look East Policy, which should be exploited by India for entering the APEC as a member.

Long-term Scenario Uncertain Rajan's assessment was that the long-term scenario was fraught with uncertainties due to the regional power play already on between China and Japan. South Korean power too is on the rise and the entry of India would complicate the regional situation further, and pose tough challenges to the relationships between China, Japan, and India. The onus would be on the three nations, as major regional players, to act responsibly together for guaranteeing peace and stability in Asia.

Presentation 3: Maritime Aspects of our Look-East Policy

Vice-Admiral (Retd) P.J. Jacob

Admiral Jacob traced the genesis of India's Look East Policy which began after the collapse of the Soviet Union was traced. This policy was intended to be more than just a foreign policy alternative; it was meant to provide a development avenue as well, in synchronization with globalization and the resurgence of Asia as an economic powerhouse.

Recent Thrust on Policy Though there were attempts to keep India's presence active in the region through ASEAN, it was only in this century that India had given a big push to this policy by becoming a summit level partner of ASEAN in 2002, and getting involved in regional initiatives such as the BIMSTEC, the Ganga Mekong Cooperation, and the East Asia Summit (EAS) in December 2005.

Maritime Diplomacy an Important Component The speaker stressed that maritime diplomacy should now be an essential component of India's Look East Policy. India, he said, was in a position to contribute greatly to the safe movement and security of shipping along the SLOCs in the region by virtue of its location. With over 1,00,000 ships transiting the region carrying oil and other goods, it was important for India to ensure the safety and security of this seaborne trade.

Changing World Environment The changing world environment, the onset of globalization, rapid advances in communications, transportation and technology have together altered the social, economic and political environment. Though this change has increased legitimate trade and business, the same environment has also become conducive for organized crime due to the intensification of networks of interaction, and interdependence. This has led to nations in this region increasingly showing signs of interest in multilateral frameworks to build confidence and promote regional responses to economic, political, and security challenges.

Rationale for Cooperation About the rationale for cooperation amidst diversity, the speaker pointed out that the maritime region to India's East was home to vast geographical, historical, and economic diversity, and it was an area where many differing cultures, religions, ideologies, and political systems competed and struggled to survive or expand their own interests. In recent years, the Association of South-East Asian Nations (ASEAN) and the ASEAN Regional Forum (ARF) have developed multilateral and institutional regional security mechanisms at both the ministerial-official (First Track) and unofficial (Second Track) levels. He suggested that Track-1 initiatives were imperative to formalize regional cooperation agreements and Track-2 mechanisms could be useful for generating new ideas and fresh perspectives.

Growth of Maritime Crime Besides the relationships between nations, organized crime such as trafficking, gun-running, fish-poaching, and maritime piracy too has become a matter of growing concern, especially in the Bay of Bengal, and the Straits of Malacca. The speaker drew attention to various incidents of piracy and terrorism in the shipping lanes and also speculated on future crime scenarios unless there was a shift in the security environment in the region.

Joint Maritime Security Initiatives Other disasters such as oil spillage occurring due to possible terror attacks or a hijack of an offshore oil platform would result in crisis of serious proportions. Many multinational and bilateral naval exercises have been successful, including the exercises in the Sea of Japan with the US and Japan, as well as the recent Malabar 07. Bilateral arrangements with Thailand and Indonesia have been successfully negotiated for joint coordinated patrols by the three navies in the Bay of Bengal at the mouth of the Straits of Malacca . India's willingness to contribute to the capacity building of the littoral states in maritime security is demonstrated by the participation of Southeast Asian navies in the bi-annual MILAN exercises.

Development of Joint Capability in Disaster Relief India's maritime policy should make provision for the creation and sustenance of international cooperation in regional Humanitarian Assistance and Disaster Relief operations. The Tsunami of 2004 and the recent Yogyakarta earthquake in Indonesia have demonstrated the importance of multilateral interoperability. In the area of development projects, a maritime dimension has been included, such as the Kaladan Multi-Modal Transit Transport Facility which envisages connectivity between Indian ports on the eastern seaboard and Sittwe Port in Myanmar, thereby providing an alternative route for transport of goods to North-East India.

Current Indian Navy Regional Cooperation Activities The speaker described the various regional cooperative ventures of the Indian navy which were already underway. The launch of the Indian Ocean Naval Symposium in February 2008 would provide a platform in which maritime security agencies of the region discuss common issues bearing on international security. It was also mentioned that dialogue in the ASEAN Regional Forum, of which India has been a member since 1996, now includes regular discussions on maritime security issues.

Spectrum of Maritime Power Admiral Jacob clarified that maritime power is not singularly about the Navy; the pivotal role of maritime strategy in peacetime was also stressed. The traditional roles of the navy could be classified into four broad categories—policing, diplomatic, crisis, and military. The merits of the naval force which had the characteristics of reach and endurance, the ability to threaten and apply force in a finely graduated way, and use of warships as diplomatic instruments unlike any other kind of armed force were highlighted. These roles are naturally weighted to meet the nations prevailing maritime interests. In the current environment, it was felt that the policing and diplomatic roles were more predominant.

Indian Navy—A Potent Diplomatic Instrument The fact of India having a strong Navy and the anti-terrorist or piracy rationale for cooperation was highlighted. In view of the prevailing environment, it was felt that the littorals had no alternative but to pool their efforts and assets and cooperate in meeting common maritime objectives.

Measures to Intensify Maritime Cooperation The speaker outlined the various initiatives that could be taken by the countries both at the official (track-1) and the informal (track-2) levels. These included the following:

1) Increasing the frequency and broadening the ambit of joint exercises which help in identifying solutions to problems of interoperability.
2) Addition of more participants and venues to the biennial 'Milan' series of confluence meetings.
3) Versatility and impact provided by flag showing missions to be exploited to the fullest by allowing the navy to send ships to many more countries in the region.
4) Institutionalized approach to cooperation such as sharing of multi-locational relief supplies in the event of natural calamities and environmental disasters.
5) Sharing of information and access to relevant databases including revenue intelligence, poaching, SAR, meteorology and oceanology and the like and cooperation in terms of training and technology.
6) Strive towards common legislation for dealing with offenders and towards implementation of international and regional treaties and security codes.
7) Increase scope of participation in relevant conferences and seminars.

Perceptual Differences to be Overcome The point was made that despite best efforts for regional cooperation, actual implementation may prove to be challenging due to the difference in perceptions between major users of the trade routes and the littoral states that straddle these routes, as in the case of Indonesia, Malaysia, and Singapore vis-à-vis patrolling of the Straits of Malacca . It was further stated that the perceived infringement of sovereignty could also be a challenge, as in case of Malaysia, which had reacted strongly to the US deployment conceptualized under the Regional Maritime Security Initiative (RMSI), and had noted that the US should get permission from regional countries as it impinged on their national sovereignty.

The speaker hoped that the countries of the region would overcome individual reservations and put failsafe procedures in place for cooperative security. He stated that Indian Navy has transcended multifarious obstacles to ensure full cooperation in all regional initiatives concerning maritime security and international law and order at sea, as per the suggestions of The United Nations World Commission on Oceans.

Discussion

Content Analysis P.C. Nayak began the discussions with a brief background to his work on 'content analysis', based on mega trends in various newspapers on

India and its neighbours. He drew attention to the fact that relations between nations were changing because of international terrorism. India has been drawn closer to the USA because of this common threat. Similarly, ASEAN countries need India in their fight against this menace. He felt that even BIMSTEC was started as a regional grouping against Muslim fundamentalism. Next, the importance of the old 'Silk Route' to China has now been replaced by the 'Oil Route' through the Indian Ocean, and the one who controls the Indian Ocean and the Straits of Malacca will control the energy supplies to China. Similarly, he felt that the importance of oil would be replaced by gas in the future. In this context, Bangladesh will be compelled to sell its surplus gas to India in the near future. Finally, he felt that the first step in India's Look East Policy should be to Look East within India to the development of the North-Eastern states. The speaker concluded his remarks with a note of hope that the rice revolution, though later than the wheat revolution will encourage the development of eastern regions of India such as Bengal, Orissa, Assam, and the North-East.

On the issue of terrorism, the Chairman humorously remarked that even nation states that are very powerful, engage in terrorist activities that create fear in other countries. Ranganathan said that after social and moral erosion of US, the structure of international relations has changed from being axis-oriented to one of regional groupings. The example of ASEAN as a regional institution shows that various regions want to maximize their natural and common strengths. In this regard, he felt that India was trusted by many as a suitable economic ally. He differed with the earlier statement of Nayak that the BIMSTEC was created as an anti-Muslim grouping; he contended that it was a grouping of Bay of Bengal rim countries and already includes Islamic nations such as Bangladesh. Regarding the Indian Ocean and the Straits of Malacca, he said that these are common heritage of all mankind and it would be undesirable for India to attempt to 'control' them; but instead India should work to see that it is open to use by all. He fully agreed with the earlier speaker, on the disconnect between the North-East and the rest of the country, and the futility of looking Eastwards without paying attention to India's North-Eastern region. He suggested that development of the North-East should be given top priority. Gopal added that BIMSTEC had been created as an alternative to SAARC, which had been stymied by Pakistan.

Asian Economic Community not Feasible without China Jayaramu said that he agreed that India's national interest should be given importance in the formulation of its foreign policy. But he questioned the fears expressed regarding China's inclusion in the Asian economic community. He asked if it was feasible to actually have an Asian economic community without China. He also questioned the panel on whether the people from the Eastern region were given adequate representation in government services such as the Indian Foreign Service?

The Chairman and Ranganathan both emphatically confirmed that people from the North-Eastern region were serving with distinction in all the government services including IFS and their representation was more than proportional to their population. Rajan clarified that there was no question of keeping China out of Asian Economic Community. The only concern is to see that there is no over domination by any single power.

There was a lively discussion on the Sethu Samundram project. One of the members asked whether it was economically viable. The panel suggested that it was a technical issue and experts in the field have said that it is beneficial. As a part of the same discussion, the chairman remarked that the sentiments of the people matter a great deal and decision makers should give importance to it.

Piracy Different from Terrorism An opinion was expressed that maritime piracy and terrorism are two different things. The threat in the Indian Ocean is from piracy and should be treated as such. It is not for India to attempt to control either the Indian Ocean or the Straits of Malacca . This should be the responsibility of an international organization.

Vice-Admiral Jacob responded to these comments by clarifying that it was in India's interest to see that the shipping lanes in the Indian Ocean remain open. It is not only US ships that are escorted but all ships in the region are given protection in a multilateral framework. As regards patrolling of the Straits of Malacca , it is done jointly by India, Indonesia, and Singapore.

Not Necessary to Label as Friend or Foe Khaleeli said that on the Look East Policy, he would prefer to treat relations with China and Japan separately from other ASEAN countries, as they are in a different category as economic powers. He felt that from an Indian perspective, South-East Asia has progressed remarkably when compared to the progress made by West Asia, and India would do well to foster better economic ties with ASEAN countries. He suggested that it was not necessary to label China as a friend or enemy before progressing economic ties with ASEAN or with China itself. The position and potential of China are realities and India has to accept it.

Ranganathan agreed with Khaleeli that relations with ASEAN be carried out without the shadow of either Japan's or China's positions. Speaking about the Indian view of China, he said that it was not necessary to articulate it in terms of a friend or foe. Today, India needs China more than she needs us. We are increasingly dependent on trade with China. China benchmarks itself with the US, hence its standards are inspiring. However, as India's relations do improve with China and Japan, our acceptability to ASEAN countries will also improve significantly.

Need to Avoid Adversarial Approach with China On the issue of China, he agreed that its past actions do not inspire a positive outlook from India. While he may not be an ardent supporter of friendship with China, he is a strong supporter of avoiding a hostile or adversarial relationship with China. He said that one should make sure that the country with the second largest population builds a good working relationship with the country with the largest population. He also felt that it was not a crime for China, as the world's most populous state.

Conclusion

Focus of Seminar This seminar achieved the aim of focusing clearly on India's relations with the disparate littoral countries lying east of the Bay of Bengal. It is well understood in New Delhi that this region is growing in importance and potential, including as it does ASEAN as well as China, Korea (North and South), and Japan. The discussion at this seminar pointed to the need for addressing the problems of India's own North-Eastern states earnestly, for us to gain greater credence with ASEAN. The Asia Centre had earlier organized similar seminars on Myanmar and BIMSTEC. This has to be combined with sponsoring many more regional and country studies for the benefit of scholars, diplomats and businessmen, so that our diplomatic corps has a bigger and better base of human resources.

Potential for Cooperation The seminar brought out the abundant prospects of integrated regional cooperation in many fields, such as maritime, trade and economic, and political. Every country in this vast region has its own distinctive problems in its relations with India, which demands a high degree of sensitivity in our dealings with them. There is, however, an overall consciousness of solidarity in this region, which we can actively support, now that India enjoys greater acceptance as a benign power in South Asia, capable of exerting unselfish influence for the peaceful resolution of conflicting interests. While regional meetings and summits can set the tone for cooperation, they cannot substitute the country-specific approach India has to adopt in bilateral relations.

Necessity for Detailed Action Agendas The seminar rightly highlighted the need for India to avoid sending out a wrong signal of latent rivalry with China for preferential relations with ASEAN countries. The countries of the region are diverse and need carefully differentiated policies. 'Looking East' by itself is not enough without detailed action agendas which serve foreign policy in concrete particulars.

Chapter 13

India's Energy Security

ASIA CENTRE BANGALORE

'The Oil Crisis and India's Energy Security Outlook: Challenges and Options' Proceedings of the Seminar held on

March 24, 2012

Opening Remarks

The Chairman, Asia Centre, A.P. Venkateswaran, presided over the seminar. He welcomed the distinguished panel which would be speaking on this vital subject of energy. The oil shortage and rising oil prices were a major economic threat to a developing country like ours; the situation was worsened by the machinations of external powers whose strategy was at odds with our interests. We should not suffer from any sort of euphoria or joy at having got over the bipolar world because now the unipolar world poses a greater danger to us than the bipolar one ever did.

The Chairman then went on to welcome the distinguished panel which would be speaking on this vital concept of energy.

Senthil Kumar	Fellow, the Energy Research Institute (TERI), Bangalore
G.R. Srinivasan	Former Vice-Chairman of the Atomic Energy Regulatory Board
D.P. Sen Gupta	Visiting Professor at the National Institute of Advanced Studies, Bangalore
Sudha Mahalingam	Member, Petroleum and Natural Gas Regulatory Board

Introduction

Focus of the Seminar Setting out the background and focus of the seminar, the Director, Vice-Admiral (Retd) R.N. Ganesh, said that the country's long-term development plans were based on a high growth rate of 8 to 10 per cent. But India's rise, which was trumpeted so optimistically two or three years ago, is now threatened by the growing fiscal deficit, spiralling costs, and the widening trade imbalance; in all of these, oil plays a major part.

The energy scenario is a global problem and not an India-specific one. The 'Peak Oil' scare of a few years ago has receded somewhat, but the fact remains that oil is a finite resource with supply struggling to keep up with demand. The possession of oil or access to it has historically been a major driver of military strategies. The victims of the American invasion of Iraq and the NATO intervention in Libya were both countries that were rich in this resource. Storm clouds now gather over Iran, with the West possibly just waiting for an opportunity.

This uncertainty of the availability of oil and other fossil fuels to power its growth is a major vulnerability in India's economic strategy.

The distinguished panelists would make an overview of all energy sectors and assess their economic viability and production potential in the context of India's rising energy demands. And hopefully, options and policies would be identified for improving India's energy security outlook.

The Director then introduced the distinguished speakers.

Presentation 1: Conventional Energy Sources (Fossil Fuel & Hydro)

T. Senthil Kumar

Basic Energy Scenario in India

The total installed power production capacity in India is 1.85 lakh MW, of which coal-fired power plants contribute about 55 per cent and have been growing at a rapid annual rate of 7.2 per cent for the last five years. In the 11th five year plan, about 34,000 MW of coal-based power had been added; about 62,000 MW of coal-based power is proposed to be added in the 12th plan period.

Growth in Installed Power Generation Capacity Coal-based plants contribute about 55 per cent of our generation capacity, and gas-based plants about 10 per cent, with oil-based plants contributing less than 1 per cent. Thus, thermal power plants contribute about 66 per cent of our power generation capacity with nuclear power accounting for about 3 per cent, hydro-power plants about 20 per cent and renewable about 11 per cent. So coal-based power is the major contributor to the total power capacity and its share will continue to grow because of lower costs.

Electricity Production by Source—2010-11

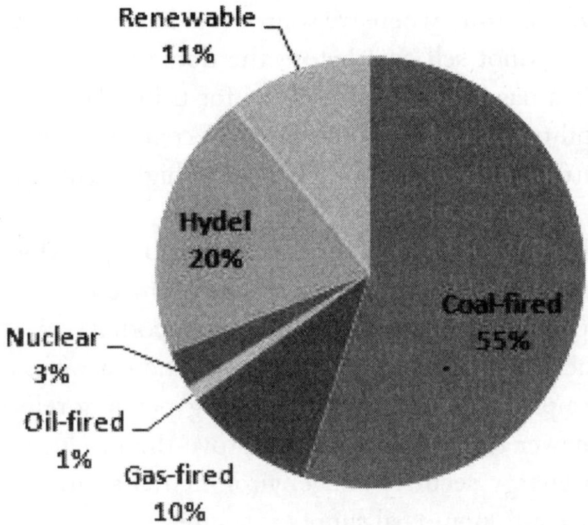

The speaker observed that we could meet our growth demands using coal for the next 20 years. The share of coal in power generation is expected to rise to 83 per cent at the end of the 12th Plan period (Apr 2012–Mar 2017). India has established reserves of about 106 billion tonnes (bnT) of surfaceable coal, but we currently mine only 0.5 bnT. India needs 1 bnT of coal for the next 25 years to meet the growth rate of 8 to 9 per cent.

In the 11th plan period (Apr 2006–Mar 2012), an addition of 78 giga-watts (GW) of power generation was planned, but only 66 per cent of the target was achieved. This has been the story for the last 25 years—there has been a continuous gap between planned and achieved figures. By 2012, we were planned to have added 210 GW, but what has been achieved is only 185 GW. The Plan calls for an increase of the power capacity to 835 GW, or an increase by 6 times by 2032, but we can see already in 2012 that we are not achieving it. Unless we achieve this 6-fold increase in power, we cannot achieve a growth rate of 8 per cent.

Demand-Supply Gap in Coal Coal demand in 2011–12 was 500 million tonnes (mnT), and is expected to increase to 850 mnT in 2017. As against this, the supply gap was 53 mnT in 2011–12, and expected to rise to 300 mnT by 2017. Coal imports are thus the only short term solution available to prevent the planned power projects from coming to a standstill. About 30 per cent of the coal for the power sector is currently imported, but this is not a long-term viable option, first because of the price (five times domestic coal), and also because the countries from where we source coal have restrictive resource policies. Indonesia does not sell coal before the domestic requirements are fulfilled, and Australia has imposed carbon tax for using coal. These factors decrease the availability and increase the price of coal in the international market. Since the utilities are unable to buy coal at higher costs, they resort to load shedding.

Most of the newly identified coal blocks are in the no-zone which requires environmental clearance. Environmental clearance procedures in the coal blocks need to be expedited to reduce the reliance on imported coal. Sustainable mining should be encouraged to augment coal production as well as to reduce the environmental impact. The introduction of long-pending reforms in the coal sector and of newer technologies will improve the production of coal. A balance between energy security and environmental security should be maintained so that a continuous coal supply is assured.

Ultra Mega Power Projects (UMPP) On the technology front, the latest development is the Ultra Mega Power Plant (UMPPs) of 4,000 MW and above, which are key thrust areas for the Indian power generation industry. Around 16 UMPPs are planned; the programme aims at improving the power situation by large doses of capacity addition based on super-critical technology. The major challenges faced by UMPPs are, again, environmental clearance and the price of imported coal. The efficiency of current power plants is about 30 per cent, but the UMPPs' have an efficiency of 40-42 per cent and super critical units about 45–47 per cent. In the 12th Plan, about 60 per cent of the plants will be of super-critical technology, and the National Mission for Clean Coal Technology plans to advance Super-critical technology along with carbon capture and storage technologies. Coal linkages will not be recommended in future for power projects that have less than 200 MW, unless they opt for super-critical technologies that result in reduced emission levels compared to the existing technology. Every 1 per cent increase in efficiency results in 2.5 per cent reduction in emissions.

Overview of the Oil Scenario The oil reserve in India is estimated at 750 mnT, and the production of indigenous crude is only 37 mnT. In the last fiscal year, we imported about 163 mnT. In India the use of oil for electricity generation is insignificant: oil is predominantly used in the transportation and residential sectors.

Gas-based Generation The share of gas-based power production is about 10–12 per cent. Gas-based plants offer significant advantages: they can meet fluctuating requirements, have lower emissions and shorter gestation periods. Their capital and maintenance costs are also much lower than coal-fired thermal plants. The efficiency of gas-based plants is about 30 per cent for open-cycle plants, and for a combined cycle plant where the waste-heat is cycled, it goes up to 60 per cent. The latest innovation is the micro-turbines where the capacity of the power plant is 1 KW and can be used with distributed generation centres, which cuts down the transmission and distribution losses. Gas plants can be modified to use methane gas (which is generated in landfills) and even bio-gas.

The production of gas in India in 2012–13 is estimated at 130 mmscmd (million metric standard cubic metres per day), which is expected to go up to 200 mmscmd by 2015–16. The proven gas reserve is about 1240 bnM^3 with the East Coast Basin (KG and Mahanadi Basin) having the largest reserve. Domestic production of NG in the year 2009–10 was 88.2 mmscmd and the demand was assessed at around 97.3 mmscmd. The petroleum ministry has projected that in the next five years gas consumption or gas demand will rapidly increase at growth rate of 6 per cent.

In the long run, gas-based plants will have a major role in our setup to meet the power requirement because of their great advantages in the areas of maintenance cost, emission levels, installation time, and environmental impact when compared to coal-based plants.

Liquefied Natural Gas Currently, India is importing 8 mtpa (metric tonnes per annum) of LNG which is set to increase to 30 mtpa by 2030. The demand for LNG has primarily been driven by petrochemical plants and refineries with gas-based power plants. The demand–supply gap will be reduced by setting up new terminals in the country. The issues and challenges in the gas-based plants are poor infrastructure of transporting the LNG available to different parts of the country. Differential pricing exists in the Indian gas market with APM (State-administered pricing) and non-APM pricing. The development of pipeline infrastructure is one of the key issues which are being addressed by the construction of the National Gas Grid of about 8,000 kilometres. Once the grid is completed it will ensure optimal use of the NG and LNG.

Hydro-Power The existing potential in hydro-power is around 38,000 MW. The 12th and 13th plans have targets of 12,000 MW and 30,000 MW of new hydro-power plants to be established in the country. The generation cost of hydro-power is Rs 1-2 per kWh for old plants and Rs 4-5 per kWh for new plants. Currently about 15,000 MW of hydro-power is under construction. Hydro-power has the potential to reduce the international commitment on carbon intensity by 15 per cent. Hurdles in the development of hydro-power are: (1) the stricter enforcement of environmental clearance for hydro projects results in longer gestation period for setting up new plants. Currently, clearance takes from 8–10 years, and (2) the supply chain for hydro projects is greatly extended because of inaccessible terrain.

Demand-Side Management India's energy intensity (energy consumption per unit of GDP) is 3 times that of energy-efficient economies like Japan or Germany. The Ministry of Power has taken a new initiative, called Perform, Achieve and Trade (PAT), to reduce energy demand in industries. This mechanism is likely to bring down energy consumption by 20,000 MW in the next 3 years. The other demand-side management methodologies which the government has employed are building codes for energy-efficient buildings, star rating of appliances, energy efficiency in public utilities like water pumping stations and street lights. Transmission and distribution (T&D) networks provide a very good opportunity for reduction of energy consumption. Restructured Accelerated Power Development and Reforms Program (RAPDRP) programmes are a major government initiative. Overall there is a scope for improving energy efficiency by 25 per cent at the transmission, industry and household levels.

Conclusion

1) Fossil fuels are a transitory fuel source until alternative fuels are established.
2) A careful mix of indigenous and imported fuel is a must for achieving a 9 per cent growth rate.
3) Reforms and technology adoption in exploration and generation need to be accelerated to meet planned targets.
4) Energy and environmental security requirements may conflict and have to be carefully balanced.

Presentation 2: Alternative Sources for Meeting India's Electricity Requirements

D.P. Sen Gupta

Importance of Quantification When discussing alternative sources for meeting electricity requirements, we have to consider our huge losses in electricity transmission and distribution. Our T&D losses are appalling—nearly a third of the electricity generated is lost in this process. Therefore, transmission, distribution, and utilization cannot be considered anything but a whole alternative means of energy generation.

Whenever people talk about alternative sources of energy, they tend to use adjectives: for example we have a 'huge' potential of solar energy, we have a 'massive' source of wind energy and so on; but very few people put numbers to them. Unless we put numbers to them, we do not know whether they are going to meet our demand. This is important because our focus is going to be on our future requirement. We are sadly placed as far as the Human Development Index is concerned. Even to try to get an HDI of 0.8, we still need roughly about 2000 units of electricity per annum per person. Keeping that in mind, the quantum of electrical energy we would need after 20 years with a population of about 1.5 billion, and a requirement of 2 Kwh each is 3.0 trillion Kwh of power. At present, coal, oil, natural gas, and hydroelectric power are usually clubbed with renewable energy. It is interesting to note that our wind power equals our nuclear power generation. However, we have no control over solar and wind energy, and as a result they have a very low plant load factor, as compared to thermal power plants which run 24 hours with a plant load factor of 79 per cent.

Energy Inefficiencies Of the 16.25 crore rural homes in India, only 45 per cent are electrified. Sen Gupta said that we had the dubious distinction of having 300 million Indians who do not have access to electricity and live like cave men just lighting a lamp in the evening. Even among urban homes, 6 per cent have no electricity. Electricity is a basic necessity; if we really believed in equity, we should provide it to our rural people who comprise 66.5 per cent of our total population—but we had decided to forget them. He doubted whether we could produce 2000 units per capita per annum by 2032.

The first priority was to save energy losses. Of every kilogram of coal, 40 per cent is lost in extraction, some is lost in the transportation, and in the plant (the laws of thermodynamics have to be obeyed), only about 0.171

kilogram is converted into electricity and put into the grid. The speaker said that though attempts had been made to improve this section, much depended on the quality of coal.

It was in transmission and distribution where the speaker said the losses were absolutely unforgivable. The losses are not so bad in the transmission lines—they have been planned and implemented by qualified people. But the distribution part comes under the state sector. And distribution lines have *grown*—they have not been *planned*. Totally wrong and irrational policies have been followed. A village *to be* electrified is connected to the nearest village that *has been* electrified. This causes random expansion of the grid, like Brownian motion. As a result, transmission and distribution losses in India amount to over 33 per cent of energy produced—and this should not exceed 15 per cent. In China, which is such a large country, the transmission loss is 10 per cent; the US has losses of 11 per cent. Losses mainly take place at 11kv and 440 volt level. For years we were told by the Electricity Boards that the losses were due to theft. But we have made measurements for five years in our Department of Electrical Engineering, and found that the losses are actual Ohmic losses due to the resistance in the transmission lines. There *is* a substantial amount of commercial loss, but technical losses should not exceed 15 per cent, at a liberal estimate. Sen Gupta estimated that if we reduced 10 per cent of our losses, it would amount to 30 gigawatts of installed capacity avoided. Thus, the best alternative energy source is to minimize energy losses.

Solar Thermal There are two types of solar power sources, solar thermal and solar photovoltaic. In India, we get about 250 days of reasonable solar radiation. It has been calculated that 3–4 hectares of open land would be required per MW of installed capacity. An installed capacity of 10,000 MW is planned by the year 2022. The acquisition of land is a difficult problem in this context.

Solar Photovoltaic Solar photovoltaic is fast catching up. It is a direct method of utilizing solar energy to produce electricity. For this too, 4–5 hectares of land is required per MW. About 10,00,000 hectares of open non-agricultural land is available in Rajasthan, Gujarat, MP, and parts of the Deccan plateau. The recent paper by Sukhatme assumes that 1 per cent of this land may be available for solar panels and calculates that 250 GW of solar thermal and solar PV with 7–8 hours each day for 250 days a year will have a Plant Load Factor of only 0.2. Rooftop photovoltaic cells need inverters and batteries for storage and are therefore costly, whereas solar thermal is being used widely for heating water and contributing towards reducing morning peak loads. Studies carried out in Thiruvananthapuram have demonstrated that solar energy by itself cannot meet the base load.

Wind Energy The total potential of wind energy is about 13 GW and expected energy on the basis of the analysis comes to about 91 trillion watt hours. The total installed capacity is 13,065 MW. We were getting a reasonable amount of energy, around 18,187 GWh in 2009–2010. We must explore and see how much solar and wind energy we may utilize. However, both solar and wind energy are expensive, costing about Rs 50,000 per kW. India has a total potential of 45 GW on land and this may be extended to 65 GW for off-shore.

Hydro-Electricity The sources of hydropower are locked up in the North-East and Eastern regions of the country. But there are technical and perhaps political problems because they are not the load centres; the energy is needed much more in the western and southern regions of the country where the economy is centered. Thus, there is a need to transport this power for thousands of miles, in some cases cutting through borders of neighbouring countries. This is technically feasible, but such transportation has its own set of problems. Problems of border crossings, rehabilitation and resettlement, issues of the environment and water-sharing agreements with neighbours will arise with large projects.

Biomass Sen Gupta strongly advocated the use of biomass gasifier plants for decentralized rural power and again emphasized the moral-ethical dimension of rural electrification, which was being neglected despite 300 million Indians living without electricity. Biomass exploitation will not only create local employment for people but distribution losses will come down drastically.

He would not however recommend bio-fuel as replacement for gasoline because it might have an adverse affect on our food production.

The electric power requirement of a typical Indian village is less than 100 kW. Almost 75 per cent is used in irrigation pumps. Presently, they get virtually free, un-metered grid supply of poor quality for few hours a day. The biomass available locally can sustain a plant of 25–100 kW.

Conclusion

1) Adding up potentially renewable sources we find that the total installed capacity comes to about 575 GW, and allowing for the plant load factors

we have about 1.23 trillion units as opposed to a need of 3.0 trillion units of electricity.

2) It is evident that minimizing energy wastage should be our first priority.
3) Installation of solar panels, wind generators and hydel projects, large and small, must all go in parallel.
4) The electrification of rural homes is of the utmost importance.
5) Alternative energy sources by themselves are unlikely to meet our needs; coal-based power generation has to be continued to provide a large section of the base load.
6) Nuclear power generation, though unlikely to provide more than 10–12 per cent of our installed capacity, is indispensable and is likely to grow in percentage as international pressure builds up for reducing coal-based power generation.
7) A proposal has been developed at NIAS that offers a very quick way to save energy: it is to advance IST by half an hour, that is, to UTC and six more hours instead of UTC and five and a half more hours. The NIAS analysis shows that we will save 2.3 billion units of electricity per annum and that at the crucial time of evening peaking energy. In this way we can save about 15 per cent of electricity. The NIAS paper has been published and it is with the government.

Sen Gupta ended his presentation with these emotive words from a Bengali song:

> *'Oh Mother Earth!*
> *I leave for you only two drops of tears*
> *I plundered you, and squandered what I plundered*
> *And when it was my turn to give back something*
> *All I could find in store were tears of repentance.'*

Presentation 3: The Oil Crisis and India's Energy Security—How Can Nuclear Energy Help?

G.R. Srinivasan

Why India is pursuing Nuclear Power India does not have the luxury of neglecting any energy source or neglecting energy conservation. We should think of our energy resources as complementary and not competitive; we cannot wait for one source to disappear before developing another one. As Senthil Kumar had told the audience, we are importing more than 70 per cent of hydrocarbons, and 30 per cent of coal. If China and India increased their coal imports by more than 40 per cent, it might give rise to a COPEC, a coal equivalent of the present OPEC.

Forecast for per capita consumption of 5000 kw/h	
Resource	**Projected Availability**
Coal	11 years
Uranium + Derivatives	40 years
Thorium	170 years

Table: Indigenous Resource Availability Forecast

Resource Availability Looking ahead to 2032, which Senthil Kumar mentioned, even with a modest per capita consumption of 5000 units which is lower than today's consumption in some countries, we will need 8 GW. With this rate of consumption our coal would last for 11 years. Uranium and its derivatives would last for 40 years, and Thorium in India would last 170 years. This was the situation regarding fuel availability.

Green Power Green power had already been discussed. The speaker felt that India had taken the right position by focusing on per capita emission for control of greenhouse gases. Those who were before us have polluted the whole world to improve their economy and wealth, and now they want us to reduce greenhouse gases. At the same time, greenhouse gases are not selective or preferential as far as victims are concerned. So one has to think about this and think about the pressure that will come 10 or 15 years down the line to reduce emissions.

Thorium Reserves We have vast Thorium reserves amounting to 25 per cent of world's reserves and correspond to 3,58,000 GWe-years. But Thorium is not a fuel; it has to be converted into Uranium-233 to use it, so it takes time. Due to progressive indigenization and future global players (like IT and Auto Industries), we will be a big global nuclear player 10 years from now; Srinivasan's estimate was that the nuclear industry would create around 10 million jobs. Dwelling on some of the advantages of nuclear energy, he said that nuclear energy fitted in well with sustainable development. There were advantages in transportation and it was less land-intensive. Also, it was not price-sensitive, as whatever the fluctuation in the price of Uranium, it comprised only 15 per cent of the overall cost. Thus, constant tariffs could be maintained. India follows the closed-cycle method as fuel taken out from NPPs is only partially used. Reprocessing increases the fuel capacity by 10 times and abundant Thorium by another 10 times. We have taken care to ensure that the NSG waiver gives us the right to reprocess fuel.

Brief History of Nuclear Activity Nuclear activity was started in India in 1954. The first nuclear power plant installed in India was a GE BWR Reactor at Tarapur (TAPS 1 and 2) in 1969. It is operating safely, reliably and viably even now. There are around 3000 manufacturers of components and structures for the nuclear industry and all the construction activity is carried out by private entities. Only the designing part is done by the Department of Atomic Energy. The Department of Atomic Energy has the unique feature of having control and experience on all phases of Nuclear Industry (front and back ends and Nuclear Power Plants as well as R&D) under one umbrella. Bhabha's three-stage programme is well on the way, and to his credit we have not needed to change it even after 50 years.

Thorium Technology Considerable work has been done in thorium technology. Contrary to some opinions, we have made good progress and are leaders in Thorium technology; we will be the pioneers 10 years from now and people will be coming to us for it. We have a reactor called Kamini that is running on Uranium-233 from Thorium. This is the only reactor of its type in the world. India follows the closed cycle system for obvious reasons as Uranium is scarce and because of fuel shortages. India is mastering reprocessing and enrichment technologies because these are also inputs for civil nuclear power plants.

Referring to the 3-stage process, Srinivasan said that in the first stage Uranium is used. Fortunately, from a nuclear power plant only 0.7 per cent of Uranium is used. The remaining 99.3 per cent is Uranium-238 which is converted into Plutonium. So there is plenty of retrievable energy left for the subsequent stages and the term 'spent fuel' should not be used—we should be calling it 'partially used fuel'. He said that as the audience may be aware, a 500 MW breeder reactor is being built in Kalpakkam and it may be operational in about two years.

Future of Indian Nuclear Industry India was earlier in the top 5 countries, but has slipped down as a result of slower progress. However, we have set ambitious targets for our nuclear power generation:

- 20,000 MWe by 2020
- 63,000 MWe by 2032 (40,000 MWe imported + 23,000 MWe Indigenous)
- 700 MWe PHWR and 500 MWe PFBR

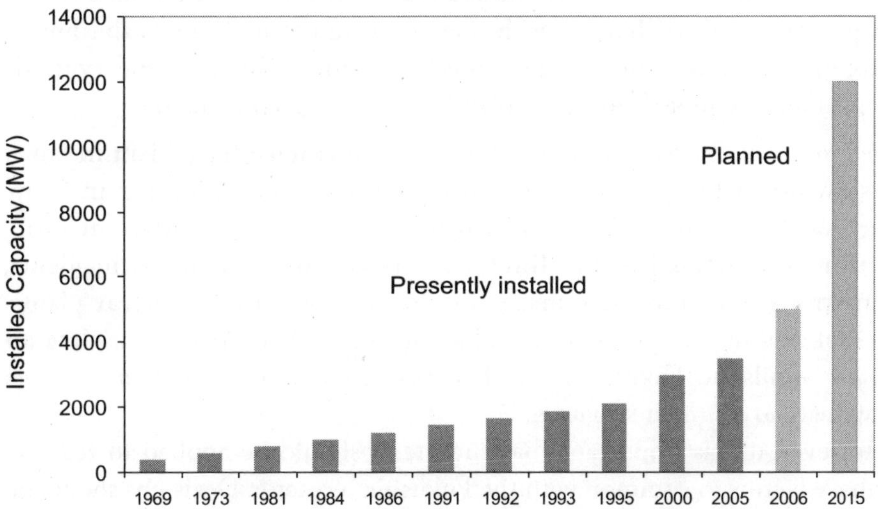

Table: Nuclear Power Generation Plan

The above targets will create huge business opportunities. At present there are four technologies—Westinghouse, GE, Areva, and Russian imported reactors, and offers from some other countries as well, but these are not at the expense of the Indian programme which will run in parallel, and in fact will be accelerated.

These targets can be achieved by supplementing indigenous and governmental efforts with imported nuclear power plants, foreign direct investment, and private sector participation (FDI is not permitted in owner or developer area yet, but could be started in the future.)

Energy Mix for India

The energy mix of India stands on four pillars which are:

1) Thermal power;
2) Renewable, including Hydro power;
3) Nuclear Energy;
4) Energy conservation, Smart Grid, lower T&D losses, improved energy intensity, and so on.

Extrapolation for a requirement of 8,00,000 MW installed capacity and a reasonable per capita consumption indicates a shortage of 70–80,000 MWe. This cannot be filled by anything other than nuclear power, and it can be filled by nuclear power only because of the abundant availability of Thorium in India. The speaker described Thorium as the fuel of the future, until the establishment of nuclear fusion as a bulk energy source. Thus, for fulfilling its energy needs India should use more Thorium which it has been given by nature.

Global Situation Post-Fukushima The Fukushima nuclear accident in Japan did slow down the progress of nuclear power capacity building in many countries. Public acceptance and world opinion are very different post-Fukushima, compared to the Three-Mile Island and Chernobyl incidents, when strong demands were made for closing down of all nuclear plants. Post-Fukushima, countries are conducting tests wherein they simulate an accident similar to Fukushima on their reactors to confirm if their reactors can withstand a similar situation.

However, it was important that such tests should be applied to reactors that have factors in common with the Fukushima reactor. Decisions should be based on scientific analysis and calculation, based on the vast global experience of over 14,000 reactor years of operation, and comparing the plants operating environment. Asking for all reactors to be shut down despite differences in type, location, geological environment and location, the speaker felt, was definitely over-reaction.

All countries have carried out a review of their nuclear programmes and of the 11 nations having more than 10 NPPs, Germany is the only one which is likely to phase out its nuclear plants. Others like the US and the UK are planning to build new NPPs.

Public Acceptance Issues Opposition to nuclear plants cannot and should not be disregarded. The challenge lies in convincing people who live near the nuclear reactor sites—the rural population. They have to be convinced that NPPs are not a threat to health and safety of population and environment.

Since the Chernobyl nuclear accident, that is, over the past 15 years, research has been carried out to ensure there is minimal or no damage to the public. Most reactors today are being modified based on the Fukushima accident.

Srinivasan covered several other public acceptance issues such as nuclear security and radioactive waste disposal. India works on a closed fuel cycle so the spent fuel or the used fuel is not a radioactive waste that has to be stored. He also stressed the need for an independent nuclear regulatory authority, which was in the process of being created by a Bill in Parliament.

Giving a few insights into the economics of nuclear plants, the speaker stated that the capital costs are much higher than for other energy sources. In all other respects there were advantages. At present, Indian NPPs generate power that costs Rs 2.83 per unit for all the twenty plants, which is comparable to thermal power plants. Tarapur generates power at 99 paisa per unit, which is comparable to many hydro-power plants.

Generation-3 reactors are more economical; more than 60 years of plant life and 90 per cent of PLF. These should be constructed at the earliest, otherwise the cost of production will increase. As far as contractual obligations are concerned, India has the best regime in the world to handle liability, totally addressing all the deficiencies which took place in the Bhopal gas tragedy.

Conclusion

1) India has built a strong foundation for its Nuclear Industry with many proven equipment manufacturers.
2) India has abundant Thorium. She must use it expeditiously and safely to combat the energy problem.
3) Nuclear power is the only alternative bulk source. However, all sources need to be exploited.
4) Public acceptance is important and must be constantly instilled.
5) Decisions regarding nuclear energy should be taken on a rational basis, with full regard to scientific facts.
6) Political consensus is important.

The nuclear industry requires clear, stable and long-term government policies. Nuclear energy is the only alternative bulk source of energy. When India's reaches its full potential, we would see that the IT wave was nothing compared to our nuclear industry. The costs would also be negligible when compared to the amount of jobs and revenue that nuclear power could generate.

Presentation 4: India's Energy Security in the Global Context

Sudha Mahalingam

Mahalingam explained to the audience that the Petroleum and Natural Gas Regulatory Authority of which she is a member is a regulatory authority outside the government, but mandated by Parliament with wide-range authority in the supervision, regulation, licensing and dispute resolution roles.

Global Scenario Coming to her subject, the speaker said that the main problem concerning oil is is the exploding global demand. Currently, the world is consuming about 87 million barrels per day (mbd), and this is growing primarily due to the demand from Asia with China accounting for over 50 per cent of incremental demand every year. This exploding demand comes against the backdrop of 'Peak Oil' fears, which was widespread in the recent past but which was, the speaker said, an overly pessimistic view.

Factors Affecting Availability Mahalingam then listed some factors that affect the availability of oil in the global scenario. Oil prices are crucially affected by what is called swing capacity. That is, for a daily consumption of 87 mbd, there needs to be a swing capacity of at least 5 to 6 million barrels to meet spikes in demand, without which we become very vulnerable. Another factor affecting availability was the instability in the MENA (Middle East and North Africa) region, which includes Iran. A third element is the race for gas. Shale gas is being touted as a game changer on the energy horizon. A fourth important aspect is that major oil companies like ONGC, Iranian National Oil Company, Rosneft (Russia), Aramco (Saudi Arabia), and Cantrell (Mexico) which are nationally owned, control about 70 per cent of global oil and gas and are generally not very transparent about their reserves. The last major issue is the piracy and vulnerability of the Sea Lines of Communication (SLoC) through which oil has to transit long distances.

Thirsty Asia According to the International Energy Agency estimate, the global demand for oil is growing at 1.6 per cent or 1.04 mbd in 2012. The major importers and producers are shown in the table below. Other major oil producers are Canada at 3.29 mbd, Mexico producing 3.0 mbd and UAE which produces 2.8 mbd. India produces only about 65,000 barrels as against its consumption of 3.3–3.5 mbd.

Big Importers	Big Producers
USA: Consumption 19.5 mbd. Imports about 50 per cent. USA's consumption is almost a quarter of the global consumption.	Russia: 10.25 mbd
China: Consumption 10 mbd Imports about 50 per cent of its requirements. Its oil consumption is growing at 7 per cent.	Saudi Arabia: 9.76 mbd
Japan: Consumption 5 mbd. Imports 85 per cent of its requirements. Post Fukushima, demand is likely to grow.	USA: 9.06 mbd
India: Consumption 3.3–3.5 mbd. Imports about 78 per cent of its oil requirements from the Persian Gulf. Consumption is growing at 8.4 per cent.	Iran: 4.17 mbd
South Korea: Consumption 2.5 mbd. Imports around 97 per cent of its consumption.	China: 3.99 mbd

Table: Major Oil Consumers, Importers, and Producers

Peak Oil Oil prices have risen drastically, but there hasn't been any major discovery of wells in the past 40 years. In a study of 140 major wells, it was found that most had dwindled drastically. This, in essence, means that the same old oil fields are being used even today. The Ghawar oil field in Saudi Arabia is currently being exploited with 40 per cent of water injection. When oil pressure drops in the field, water or gas has to be injected to maintain the pressure for the oil to come out. This has resulted in the depletion of fields like Cantrell in Mexico and Burgan in Kuwait. This was one of the reasons for the situation called Peak Oil.

Availability versus Price The availability of oil is a function of its price. If the price of oil is 30 dollars a barrel, probably no new discoveries would come on stream. But if oil is being sold at 120 dollars a barrel like today, people will invest to explore oil at a furious pace in all kinds of places. At present, the production cost of oil in Saudi Arabia or Kuwait is less than 1 dollar a barrel. In future if we have to mine oil in Siberia, North-East Asia, Sakhalin Islands, Arctic Circle, or in the deep sea like the Krishna Godavari basin, the cost of production may be about 15 dollars a barrel. Oil is neither peaking nor depleting; it is, however, going to be available in regions where it will be very difficult to mine, with a corresponding rise in the cost.

Effects of Unrest in the Middle East, North Africa Region The unrest in Libya drove out at least 1 million barrels of sweet Libyan crude from the global market. Every oil refinery has a particular configuration, and cannot switch sources or grades of oil. So when a million barrels of Libyan crude go out of the international market, it has a more significant impact on the global oil market than any other factor.

Iran's total oil production potential is about 6 billion. The Americans have been pressurizing us to reduce our imports from Iran by at least 15 per cent. Despite our public posturing, India may cut down on imports of Iranian oil; this will put our energy security at risk. This is because of the fact that Indian refineries are geared to refine Iranian heavy sulphur crudes, and it will be difficult to substitute it with crude from another source. This is a serious factor that could result in prices of oil going from $120 per barrel at present to $150–160 per barrel. Our oil import bill in 2010–2011 was more than US $100 billion; that was when the price of oil was $50–60 per barrel. In 2011–2012, it is going to be much higher.

This is a major worry for a country like India. Oil is going to account for more than one third of our import bill; this is made more acute by the fact that our exports are insufficient to pay for our oil imports.

The Race for Gas Nuclear energy need not be the only panacea for energy security. Gas is also an alternative route for safeguarding energy security. Currently, there is sufficient natural gas to meet the global energy requirement for the next 100 years. Gas is a wonderful fuel and is much cleaner than other resources like coal or oil. It is much more fungible than in earlier times, which means that it can be accessed anywhere, owing to the advent of Liquefied Natural Gas (LNG) which has enabled gas to be transported over long distances via ships and railways. Gas has a huge potential and is less whimsically distributed than oil. Iran and Qatar together have the world's largest reserves. The table below shows the rapid growth of the LNG trade.

Year	Exporters	Terminals	LNG Tankers	LNG Share of Gas Trade
1959	8	30	61	3 per cent
2010	20	90	300	30 per cent

Table: Growth of LNG Trade

Gas is a versatile fuel and can be used in transportation, power generation, industries, space heating, or cooking. In India, we have two LNG terminals at Dahej and Hazira with a third terminal being built at Kochi. Globally, gas is being transported via pipelines; developed countries have created grids of tens of thousands of kilometres. South Asia is only just beginning and the PNGRB is in the process of licensing and getting gas pipelines built in the country. The use of LNG in Asia is growing at the phenomenal rate of 30 per cent.

Shale—A Game Changer? The recent discovery of shale, which is essentially a form of rock in the pores of which gas is locked, has taken the US from being a net importer of gas to a position where they are thinking of exporting it. The US devised a process called hydraulic fracturing or 'fracking' for bringing the gas to the surface, and currently 18 per cent (likely to go up to 25 per cent) of US consumption is being met from shale gas.

Fracking Not Recommended for India Shale gas fracking is, however, not advisable in a densely populated and water-stressed country like India. It requires huge quantities of water and can result in poisoning of the ground water and damage to the earth's crust, raising the risk of earthquakes.

Security of Sea Lines of Communication Regardless of whether we are using LNG or crude, it will have to be transported long distances over the sea, as the sources of the resources are no longer near the markets for these commodities. Two-thirds of the world's oil trade of 87 million barrels per day moves over the sea. About 57 per cent of global oil and 45 per cent of gas comes from the Persian Gulf region; each day 17 million barrels of oil transit through the Straits of Hormuz. About two-thirds of India's crude imports originate from the Gulf, and the rest from Africa and Venezuela, which leaves us very limited scope for diversification. The security of the Straits of Hormuz is, thus, vital for India. China has an additional vulnerability as its oil imports have to travel through the Straits of Malacca. An additional matter of concern for India is that most of our oil installations and both LNG terminals are on the coast and are vulnerable to terrorist attacks. There is an urgent need to focus on security against this threat.

India's Energy Security India has a very energy-intensive growth paradigm. Not only the manufacturing industry but the IT and service industries too consume a lot of energy by way of high-rise buildings made of glass, chrome, and steel; these require artificial heating and cooling throughout the day and are thus extremely energy-intensive. The lifestyles and work requirements in these sectors, too, are hugely energy-intensive. However, India's energy consumption still trails GDP growth rate. The other point of importance is that the growth is not coming from coal or other sources but is largely hydrocarbon-led growth. Transportation is the biggest fuel guzzler.

As mentioned earlier, about 75 to 80 per cent of our energy requirement including LNG is imported. India's oil import bill was US $57 billion in 2010 and nearly US $100 billion last year. Our oil production has plateaued and we are excessively dependent on the Middle Eastern countries for oil and gas. The GCC supplies about 75 per cent of our oil and nearly 100 per cent of our gas imports. This means we need to have excellent political relations with these countries to keep our economic growth story going.

Energy Security Initiatives India is taking a number of steps to address energy vulnerability.

1) One of the important first steps is Enhanced Oil Recovery. India is investing a lot of money in ensuring that our oil fields produce any leftover oil by pumping in gas or water into the oil fields.
2) The oil sector which was earlier dominated by the government has been liberalized. Investment has been invited from the private sector, involving it in the entire value chain right from exploration to marketing. However, there has not been much interest shown by private players.
3) Strategic Petroleum Reserve is another area that needs action. India, which imports about 78 per cent of its oil, shockingly does not have a backup. India's inventory of crude in the refineries is enough for just 15 days operation. This is a huge vulnerability. All countries which are importers, including the entire OECD and the USA have their own strategic oil reserves. India is now thinking of how to develop such a reserve; a company has been set up for this purpose, and finances are being worked out. With the price of crude at about $120–150 per barrel, this is not the best time to buy oil to build up a reserve. Given the above, Mahalingam was of the opinion that a strategic petroleum reserve was still sometime away.
4) Other efforts to ensure our energy security are long term deals like the one with Australia to supply gas to the Kochi LNG terminal.
5) The setting up of independent regulators like the Petroleum and Natural Gas Regulatory Board which monitor the situation in the country and suggests remedial steps is a useful move.

6) Plans such as the setting up of neighbourhood pipelines like the TAPI (Turkmenistan–Afghanistan–Pakistan–India), the IPI (Iran–Pakistan–India), and the Bangladesh–India pipelines are yet to materialize and will take a long time to do so. The speaker therefore considered that LNG is the best way forward for India at present.

Tax Structure and Price Reforms Mahalingam brought out the need for price reforms in the PNG sector. She pointed out that kerosene and LPG are directly subsidized by the government while diesel is indirectly subsidized; however, the taxes on fuel are much higher than the subsidies. Of Rs 60, which is the price of a litre of petrol, the tax component is Rs 36. Our Ministry of Finance benefits from the price hike because when oil prices go up, the tax revenue also goes up without any additional effort on their part. There is a strong case for reviewing our tax structure.

Impact of Curtailment of Import of Iranian Oil Mahalingam stated that energy consumption in India is likely to go up and we could reach a situation where India would import as much as 90 per cent of its energy requirement. Saudi Arabia and Iran are the top two sources of Indian crude. Other sources include Iraq, Nigeria, and Venezuela. Whereas Reliance refineries in Jamnagar and Vadinar are versatile and can use the poor quality crude, the older public sector refineries would find it difficult to change sources. Any curtailment of Iranian supplies, therefore, would hit India badly.

Overseas Oil Equity Nine rounds of New Exploration Licensing Policy (NELP) have taken place and licenses awarded, but the big names are not interested in investing in India because it is not considered a prospective region, and the international players do not see it as having policy stability. Since India was not able to find oil within the country, it decided to go overseas and buy acreages. ONGC Videsh Ltd. (OVL) was set up as a 100 per cent subsidiary of ONGC to acquire assets in countries abroad. Total overseas investment until 2011 was US $11 billion in a total of 20 countries, out of which nine are producing assets.

Overseas Oil Investment Not an Energy Security Measure India's total overseas production in 2011 was 36 mmt (7,20,000 b/d) and 2 bcm gas. Physical deliveries are only coming from Sudan. However, in Mahalingam's view overseas oil equity does not improve India's energy security, for four reasons:

1) First, India is not the operator or major partner in any of the places where it has invested and therefore, it cannot re-route oil when it faces a domestic short supply.

2) Secondly, the articles of association do not seem to allow India to take its share in kind.
3) Third, even if this option is available from Sakhalin, for instance, the transportation of the oil would be difficult and exorbitantly expensive.
4) Fourthly, the major operators have entered into long term contracts for supply of the oil from these fields; thus, despite owning these assets, there is no guarantee that India will get access to this oil when it needs it.

Besides these, there are risks of regimes in the countries, where we invest, expropriating or even nationalizing our assets. India is not a powerful country and as a result, oilfields even in neighbouring Myanmar have been taken by Chinese companies.

India versus China Mahalingam made a stark comparison between India's and China's overseas investments and showed that:

1) China had invested US $65 billion plus a loan of US $77 billion, compared to the Indian investment US $11 billion.
2) China had built pipes and infrastructure, whereas India had not done so.
3) Indian assets were producing 7,00,000 b/d compared to China's 1.4 million b/d.
4) Chinese assets had strong autonomy while ours was restricted.

Cooperation, Competition, or Conflict Next, the speaker dwelt on the areas where India and China were in competition or conflict. The two countries were cooperating in Syria, Sudan, and Angola; in competition in Kazakhstan; and there was a potential for conflict in Arunachal Pradesh and the South China Sea, and also in the Indian Ocean and the Straits of Malacca region.

So there was a diverse set of relationships in different theatres which India had to manage with skill.

Natural Gas Natural gas forms about 10 per cent of India's energy basket, against the world average of 24 per cent. At current levels of reserves, we will have about 30 years' reserve/production ratio. The KG Basin discovery was touted to be a saviour for India. When gas was discovered in Bombay High, the government had formed a Committee and decided where the gas would be piped. Fertilizer plants were set up along the coast and it was done in a planned way for the development of the region. In contrast, when the KG basin gas was discovered, it was left entirely to private players who piped it all the way from

Kakinada to Gujarat to their own refineries. It is the role of the government to decide policy, and plan pipe grids to conform to regional development plans. Energy is too strategic a matter to be left completely to markets. If left to private players, they will only go to already developed areas. The speaker said that with signs that the KG gas was dwindling, it does not appear that our energy growth needs can be met by domestic gas. We are ringed by gas-rich neighbours—Turkmenistan, Iran, Myanmar, and Bangladesh—and we have to exert ourselves to gain access. We need to find answers to the security threats to these pipelines, and make it the responsibility of the supplier country to deliver to the border. The key to security was in the project structuring, and perhaps the involvement of international consortia. Both the TAPI and the IPI have problems.

Since we seem to be unable to solve the regional gas pipeline problems, the speaker concluded that the best option was to import gas. At present, we are importing LNG at three ports, but our trunk pipelines are a slender network; CGD (City Gas Distribution) licensing is also underway.

She wondered whether we could import power from Central Asia. There is enormous hydro-power potential there which is untapped. We could explore the possibility of joint development of Hydel projects with Tajikistan and Kyrgyzstan and power transmission through Xinjiang, across Ladakh. There was a Soviet era grid which could be restored. We have expertise in building transmission lines through difficult terrain in Ladakh and Himachal, so we could equally well build them across the Kunlun or Tienshan mountains. We must look at new solutions, and carry out feasibility studies before dismissing ideas.

Conclusion—India's Energy Future

1) **Overseas Investment** India's overseas investment is constrained by available choices as most of the preferred regions have already been taken. This means that India is left to invest only in areas like Sudan, Congo, or the Niger Delta where the political situation is bleak and there is no proper protection or rule of law.
2) **Dependence on Middle East** A vulnerability in India's energy security is its complete dependence on Middle East for its oil and gas supplies.
3) **Increasing Reliance on Domestic Coal** There is a need to use super critical technologies and other new Coal Technologies like CBM, Gasification, IGCC, GTL, and Pithead Plants.

4) **Gas Pipelines from Neighbourhood** Another strategy that should be followed is to procure gas from the neighbourhood via pipelines which ensures supply as it cannot be diverted.
5) **Use of LNG** LNG is the way forward and more LNG should be procured from global markets. The existing sources of supply in Oman, Qatar, Nigeria, and Vietnam should be tapped further. There are emerging sources of supply in Indonesia, Australia, and Malaysia which too should be given due diligence.
6) **Alternative Sources of Energy** There is a huge role for nuclear power, hydro-power, and renewable resources in ensuring India's energy security.
7) **Energy Purchase Agreements from Neighbourhood** Buying electricity from the extended neighbourhood like from Bhutan, Bangladesh, and so on, could also be another strategy.

Finally, Mahalingam said that there was no answer but to curb consumption. If every Indian and Chinese started consuming like Americans, this planet would not be able to bear the burden.

Discussion

Disruption of Oil Flow from Gulf Girish Dhume observed that it was quite possible for us to have a total disruption of petroleum supplies from the Gulf (75 per cent of our supplies) if the Straits of Hormuz close. What would be the impact of this worst-case situation?

Sudha Mahalingam replied that this would be a very grim scenario to even contemplate; the economy would come to a halt. Our only option would be to access some of Singapore's huge trading hub for oil. In the scenario described, only the military would get its supplies, other industries like automobiles would be grounded because they run on liquid fuels. But, she felt that there were too many big powers with vested interests that would not let the Straits of Hormuz close.

Dependence on External Sources for Fuel Addressing the question to Srinivasan, Hemachandra asked why we had to depend on some other country to supply Uranium.

Srinivasan replied that the paradox is that most Uranium-producing countries do not have nuclear power plants and vice versa. One need not be ashamed to import Uranium because the Uranium that is available in India can produce only 10,000 MW and is of poor quality. Say we import Uranium for imported reactors totalling 40,000 MW capacity. From the reprocessed fuel (which is our product, for which we have paid and have got international clearance), we could get 10 times the fuel or 400,000 MW worth. This means you have stored 10 times more energy. As mentioned in the case of oil, maybe it was better to acquire Uranium mines and do the mining abroad, as we have the expertise for it. Importing fuel is very expensive—we should do the value addition ourselves. Regarding Thorium, as mentioned it is a fertile material; to convert it into Uranium one has to have a large internal capacity—to convert 4,000 MW Thorium into Uranium one needs to have 40,000 MW of other plants where you can convert Thorium.

Waste Disposal Hemachandra further queried what would happen after 60 years when the reactor was decommissioned, and how the waste would be disposed of.

Srinivasan replied that there are three requirements for decommissioning nuclear plants—resources, a proper technical plan and procedure, and management commitment. All these three elements are there in India. At present, there is a cess being collected on the electricity from the nuclear power plant, which cannot be spent on anything except decommissioning. The operator remains in charge of the plant until the radiation is reduced to the background level. The operator remains in charge of the unit until the reactor is safely decommissioned. The AERB also ensures that the ability to safely decommission the reactor is part of the plant design at the approval stage itself.

Need to Import Uranium Mahalingam also responded that there are several levels of waste, high level and low level waste. The high level is vitrified and stored on site as of now. In the US they have been thinking of storing it in the Yucca Mountain in Nevada. But the public is not in favour of it. The 3 per cent cess on electric tariff from nuclear power plants which has been set aside is only for decommissioning purposes. It is an expensive proposition. Nobody in the world, including France and Belgium, which have high share of nuclear power have figured out what to do with the nuclear waste. The Bhabha vision is based on a three-stage nuclear power programme, in which the waste from the first stage which is a PHWR is going to be reprocessed and used in the second stage which is a fast-breeder reactor. We need to have a critical mass of the spent fuel from the PHWR to produce Plutonium for the second stage. Thorium cannot be used without Plutonium. To have Plutonium, we need to run fast breeder reactors. Therefore, one is dependent on the other. That is why we need to import Uranium.

Srinivasan added that till now there have been two plants that have been safely decommissioned—an American one where a fertilizer plant has been built on the site, and a French one which has been converted into a children's park.

The Potential of Nuclear Energy A member of the audience expressed the view that our power consumption is very low by international standards. Even taking the consumption in energy-efficient economies like Germany or Japan, the consumption is about 5,000 Kwh. Even if we come down to 2,000 Kwh which is still 4 times today's, there is not enough gas to allow that kind of consumption. We won't have 100 years of gas, but maybe 25 or 30 years. So he felt that nuclear energy was the only way ahead. Obviously we need to cut down consumption as well.

Srinivasan, while agreeing with the questioner, said that it would be wrong to think that nuclear energy is the answer to all power problems. As somebody has already pointed out, it cannot contribute more than 10 or 12 per cent. But 10 per cent of 8,00,000 MW is quite a lot.

Sen Gupta shared the questioner's view on consumption. We had to see how we could reduce our consumption and save wastage. We do not have to follow the American model of extravagance; we are short of energy and we have a large population to care for. Therefore, our objective must be to reduce losses and bring down urban consumption. If it is not possible to ensure 2,000 units per capita, let us reduce it to 1,000 units, but it should be properly used.

The Chairman remarked that although we were the first country in the world to undertake population growth control by the government, that campaign fizzled out. Our excessive population is a factor that we cannot overlook.

Utility of Rooftop Solar Water Heaters V. Vijay addressed a question to Sen Gupta: whether rooftop solar water heaters will have a meaningful impact?

Sen Gupta said one would be surprised to hear that the electricity boards sometimes have to produce 100 MW per minute during peak hours. If solar water heaters become a common feature, it would certainly bring down gas and electricity consumption.

Khaleeli observed that solar heaters were so effective that one could bring water to a boil in minutes after drawing it from the tap. This would be an efficient way to purify water for drinking in villages, which many people are unaware of.

Sen Gupta recalled that he had remarked that the heated water should be well insulated. Also, to store water and keep it hot did not involve a lot of cost. We have to study problems specific to us and find our engineering solutions and not merely follow other countries.

Feasibility of Hydropower Transmission Karanth asked when we have a small problem already from Arunachal Pradesh to get 80,000 MW hydro-power, how can we get power from even farther places like Kazakhstan? Is it feasible in terms from political and land area viewpoints?

Mahalingam replied that Pakistan had signed an agreement with Kyrgyzstan; we have to negotiate with neighbouring countries, supply some power locally, and transit the remaining. We need to improve our foreign relations with our neighbours.

Neglect of Distribution Infrastructure O.P. Goyal commented that we are talking about growth in energy and demand, and 1,84,000 MW demand for power after 30 years. From his experience, the area that does not get attention is the infrastructure in the distribution line. Very soon, probably in the next ten years, the transformers in Bangalore would phase out. So even if power were available we would not be able to use it. This is one area that requires attention.

Palk Bay Oil Exploration Vice-Admiral Jacob enquired about oil and gas in the Palk Bay area, and recalled that exploration had been put off because of the situation in the Sri Lankan area. He asked what the current status was, and whether the area was being looked at again for exploration.

Mahalingam replied that she was not sure whether this was one of the blocks in the nine rounds. Now that the situation had improved, there was no reason why it should not be included, except that this region is not considered very prospective. She would like to look at the data for this region before giving her answer.

Autonomy in Decision-Making Khaleeli, former ambassador to Iran, said that we were being criticized for not having good relations with some countries. However, the fault is not with those countries, but with our government, which doesn't exercise its own autonomy, and treats Iran like a terrorist state under pressure from the US.

He said that when the oil prices went up, in 1973, Indira Gandhi unveiled a policy which ensured our energy security from Iran and Iraq and the UAE; at that time we had a policy, we had autonomy and earned respect by the way in which we coped. Today, we are running after Saudi Arabia instead of Iran because the Americans say so.

Mahalingam said that she would reply with a small statistic. Originally, we were talking about a 150 mmscmd pipeline from Iran to India. Of this 150 mmscmd, 60 mmscmd were to go to Pakistan and 90 to India. The pipeline could have been laid in three years, and we could have simultaneously built a combined cycle gas turbine power plant. In three years this would have produced 24,000 MW of power. She wondered how long it would take to get the same power from nuclear sources, perhaps fifty years.

Closing Remarks

Concluding the proceedings, the Chairman, Venkateswaran, said that we had had a most interesting discussion thanks to this illustrious panel which had made such erudite and illuminating presentations.

He remarked that during the break some people had commented that in reading Madhavan's message he had been somewhat pessimistic. He had replied that the best definition of a pessimist is 'an informed optimist.' Khaleeli had spoken about Iran. Even if the pipeline had been built, the Americans may have bombed it or Israel would have threatened to do it themselves.

Venkateswaran thanked the panellists for travelling to Bangalore at the Asia Centre's invitation and taking the time to share their insights. He also thanked the audience for attending the seminar and participating in it to make it such a success.

The meeting ended with a vote of thanks to the Chair, the guest speakers, and to the audience for making the seminar a success.

Conclusion

Due to the relevance and timing of the topic, the seminar on 'The Oil Crisis and India's Energy Security' was enthusiastically attended. The speakers' presentations were all based on thorough research and were very well received.

The Phenomenon of Peak Oil Peak Oil was a scare some years ago when it was predicted that the world would run out of oil by the turn of the century. However, oil production or availability has not yet peaked. It is available, but in increasingly difficult terrain on land or greater depths in the ocean which currently makes it financially unviable to extract. With current price trends, more exploration can be done and the production of oil sustained. It is, however, a finite resource, and prices are extremely volatile. The situation is further complicated by cartelization and international power-politics.

Growth of Power Generation Capacity India needs to maintain a robust growth rate of 8 per cent or more in order to meet its developmental targets and raise the social and economic levels of its people, for which a corresponding growth in power generation capacity is a vital prerequisite. The growth rate of power generation capacity, however, is not encouraging, and the country is lagging by as much as 33 per cent in each five-year plan. The shortage of power will slow down the economy.

Demand-side Management A major point stressed by all speakers was the importance of demand-side management. There is a huge waste of power to the tune of one-third of the power generated. This is not a sustainable situation and urgent measures have to be put in place to at least halve this huge wastage. Generation, too, must be made more efficient, and power plants need to be modernized rapidly. Consumption target per capita can be reduced to 2,000 units per capita annually, instead of 5,000 units which is currently the norm in some European countries. We do not need to be profligate and adopt Western norms of per capita consumption.

Rural Electrification A country like India cannot ignore the requirement of power for the rural population. About 300 million are without basic electricity. This can be alleviated by solar power and the use of biomass, which also has the advantage of eliminating expensive and wasteful distribution lines.

Advancing Clocks An interesting option in this context was the proposal mooted by the National Institute of Advanced Studies to advance Indian Standard Time by 30 minutes. According to the authors Sen Gupta and Ahuja, this could reduce power consumption by as much as 15 per cent. Such a promising option needs to be evaluated quickly.

Development of all Energy Sources More than one speaker made the point that India does not have the luxury of developing only selected sources of energy. All sources need to be developed simultaneously, on a broad front. Nuclear power can be developed to contribute 10–12 per cent of the installed power generation capacity. This is essential to fill an otherwise unbridgeable gap in our energy resources. India has rich Thorium reserves, and it is imperative to exploit this. As leaders in Thorium technology, this sector gives India a huge commercial potential as well, and can be a resource-multiplier.

Sourcing Energy from Neighbourhood It is becoming apparent that the energy source of the future is going to be gas, both petro-based and more so, natural gas. To gain access to this resource we must move quickly to reach agreements with countries, like in our extended neighbourhood Kazakhstan, notwithstanding the well-known obstacles. We have already lost opportunities in Myanmar, whereas China has secured access to oil and gas at our doorstep. Some measures have been taken to import LNG on a long-term agreement.

Wealth of Hydel Potential in Neighbourhood Countries like Tajikistan and Kyrgyzstan have rich surplus potential for hydro-power, and imaginative solutions must be found to develop it under mutually beneficial arrangements.

India's Energy Security The conspicuous vulnerabilities that threaten India's energy security are:

1) The lack of a strategic petroleum reserve, which leaves us in a grave position if oil flows are interrupted for even two weeks.
2) Our over-dependence for oil and gas on the Gulf, which is a volatile region and has several political risk factors.
3) The lack of long-term power or resource sharing agreements with neighbouring countries, where others are moving in more actively.
4) The reliance on poor-quality coal which impedes the use of modern technology and creates environmental degradation.
5) International power pressures which disrupt our existing energy trade arrangements.

This seminar was a realistic appraisal of India's current energy situation, which gives no reason for sanguinity. In many cases the corrective measures are within our powers to implement, for example the elimination of transmission losses. Other factors are external, but India can and should move briskly to avoid being left out of the race for energy resources. Serious attention needs to be paid to the lack of a strategic reserve, based on which directives have to be issued to the appropriate government departments. Without energy security, India's plans to raise the social and economic levels of its people will be in serious jeopardy.

Chapter 14

India and Japan

ASIA CENTRE, BANGALORE

'India–Japan Relations:
From Near-stasis towards a Dynamic and Mutually Profitable Partnership'
Proceedings of the Seminar held on

September 29, 2012

Preface

The topic of the Seminar held by the Asia Centre in September 2012 was *'India-Japan Relations: From Near-stasis towards a Dynamic and Mutually Profitable Partnership.'*

The seminar was presided over by A.P. Venkateswaran, former Foreign Secretary and Chairman, Asia Centre, Bangalore. The following were the speakers:

D.S. Rajan	Director of the Chennai Centre for China Studies
N. Krishnaswamy	President, Indo–Japanese Chamber of Commerce and Industry, Chennai
Rajaram Panda	Senior Fellow, Institute of Defence Studies and Analysis, New Delhi

The presentations were followed by a question and answer session. The proceedings which appear on the following pages have been compiled by Vice Admiral (Retd) R.N. Ganesh.

Opening Remarks by the Chairman Asia, Centre

We have a subject which is very close to my heart. Because Japan was the first among all the countries to assert itself in what was called the Meiji Restoration and imitated Britain. If you have been to any of the Japanese museums, you would be struck by the portraits of Japanese emperors in British naval uniforms particularly in the 19th and the early 20th centuries. The Japanese were so good that they beat the West at their own game and flooded the international market with their manufactured goods, very much like the Chinese are doing today—cheaper and equally good.

The other quality of the Japanese is that they never gave up their basic culture. They stuck to it and this is something that comes across very clearly even today, if one visits Japan. The way they keep their temples and shrines is remarkable, often creating 'beauty out of nothing.' The Japanese do not have space—they create space through their art and it is amazing to see how out of normal, everyday things they create beautiful objects.

A quality of the Japanese which I admire is their stoic acceptance of whatever there is with a determination to improve it. We claim that we are very dharmic and karmic and so on but we buckle under the smallest challenge, but the Japanese do not. In the aftermath of the Fukushima accident the discipline that the people displayed cannot be seen in any other country in the world.

Coming to our own relationship with Japan, Rabindranath Tagore visited Japan, and so did a very remarkable gentleman called Radha Binod Pal, who was the member from India in the 'War Crimes Tribunal' which was established by the victorious Allied forces after Japan was defeated. To the surprise and chagrin of other judges he was the only member who gave a dissenting judgment; he wrote that war is such a thing that one cannot apportion blame to either side or label one side as the aggressor and another as the vanquished. He dissented on the death sentence awarded to Admiral Tojo. Today there is a separate room for him in the Yasoukini Shrine near Tokyo where all the Japanese War heroes are honored. And there is no politician worth his name in Japan who can afford not to go and pay respects to the departed souls at that shrine.

Japan was the only country against which atomic weapons were used not once but twice. When the decision to use nuclear weapons against Japan was taken, President Truman's own advisors advised him not to use an atomic bomb in a populated area given its enormous destructive power. These advisors requested Truman to drop the bomb on a beach or an open area where the power of the weapon will be known but lives will not be lost. Truman's reply was that he would like to use the weapon in a populated place as he would like the Russians to know that if necessary the US would use the weapon against them. So the Americans dropped it on populated areas not once, but twice, and about half a million were killed in each place.

I look forward to listening to our distinguished speakers, and to profit by their research and their knowledge of the area.

Introduction

India–Japan bilateral relations have never been the stuff of headlines. However, for the last 12 years or so, without it being much in the public eye, the Indian Navy and Coast Guard have conducted regular naval exercises with their Japanese counterparts. The exercises started in 1999 when the Indian Coast Guard rescued a Japanese ship that had been hijacked after a dramatic ocean chase.

The bedrock of Japanese policy is the US–Japan treaty that was signed after the Second World War. Japan has an export-oriented economy and understands that US buying power is not what it used to be. For India, Japanese technological prowess, their scientific knowledge, and their business practices are formidable strengths and we have a great deal to learn from them.

Today we are witnessing something which can be termed as 'normalisation' of Japanese policy. The Peace Constitution that was imposed on the Japanese by the Americans in 1959 forbids Japan to have any ship with war-making potential. But today Japan has a navy which is larger than ours; it has submarines, destroyers, shore-based maritime aircraft, and missiles with the range of 200 kms. Japan operates its ships to distances of about 1,000 kilometres on a regular basis and it has also deployed ships to the Arabian Sea. Where these changes will lead Japan would be something for our speakers to tell us.

Our seminar today will take a close look at the Japanese position in the Asia Pacific strategic structure. It will look at various strands of Indo–Japan relationship in the strategic, commercial, and security spheres.

Presentation 1: Japan–China Relations and the Asia–Pacific Strategic Equilibrium

D.S. Rajan

I am grateful to the Asia Centre for inviting me to speak to you on a subject that you are hearing and reading about almost every day, namely the China–

Japan dispute. The relations between China and Japan are of great importance in the context of strategic stability in the Asia–Pacific, and in my presentation I would like to dwell on this aspect.

The present China-Japan tension over a small island—the Senkakus—deserves to be noted in a broader context. It is not only the ownership of the islands which are involved: bigger and historical issues are involved in this dispute.

The Senkaku Islands (which the Chinese call the Diaoyu) are presently under the control of Japan and not the Chinese; this fact is important for understanding the character of the issue, because whenever China already occupies a territory there is no importance given to the issue. But because it is in the possession of the Japanese it is becoming a source of conflict. To go back in history, in the war of 1895, Japan wrested the island from China and after WWII the US took over the islands, and in 1960 as part of the US Japan Mutual Cooperation Treaty the US returned the Senkaku islands to Japan and this position still continues. Japan continues to argue (with the US agreeing) that the Island is governed by the 1960 US–Japan treaty to which China is raising lot of objections.

This being the historical context of the case, it is important to ask why this small Senkaku Island is attracting so much international attention with it becoming a flashpoint in the Far East. We know about the importance of the islands as a rich fishing base and they are also known for the natural resources. However, a broader historical and cultural context is necessary to understand the issue. Going back into history, Buddhism moved from China to Japan. In some sense, Japan owes its cultural strength to China.

However, in the contemporary context there is an important psychological factor also playing a role in the current row. China has become the second largest economy in the world, replacing Japan which had held this position for many years. This is a factor that has been affecting the Japanese and preying on their mind in their diplomatic relations and other fronts. Another lens through which to view the issue is that Japan is an oceanic country surrounded by the sea and China feels that Japan is making strategic adjustments is opposing China, which is a continental nation. Thus, China sees this overall conflict as a conflict between a continental and a maritime nation. So the issue has to be understood from a larger perspective. The Senkaku Island issue is not the only issue that is affecting the relations of the two countries—their historical past casts a dark shadow on relations between the two. Japan's role and actions in China in World War II has not been forgotten in China. Japan is not apologetic about it and China wants Japan to apologise for its role during that period. The textbook issue, the visit of the Japanese Prime Minister to the Yasoukuni shrine to pay respect to Japanese war dead—these, too, are issues that bother the Chinese and are creating tensions, and the Chinese feel that Japan is making strategic adjustments in its foreign policy. They see that their alliance with the United States, which is the cornerstone of Japan's foreign policy strengthening notwithstanding the so-called decline of the US. This is a factor that is taken very seriously by China, which has a dichotomous attitude towards the US—on one side it wants US technology and trade for its development, but on the other it is strategically very suspicious of the US and the Obama administration's 'Asia pivot' policy.

China itself has undertaken a foreign policy adjustment since the middle of 2009—to what may be termed a 'core-interest based' foreign policy. It is affecting China's foreign policy implementation: on the one hand it wants a 'win-win' relationship with the rest of the world, and on the other it is not willing to compromise on its territorial sovereignty including the Senkaku Island issue (the border issue with India also comes in this category.) China has not yet declared these to be core issues, but this stand is creating a tense situation. So both China and Japan are making policy readjustments. One can trace the relations in the context of their historical past and in contemporary developments which have led to both countries readjusting their foreign policies.

Recent Developments In September 2012, Japan nationalized the Senkaku Islands. It basically bought land in these islands paying about US $26 million and brought it under Japanese jurisdiction. This is a provocative factor that is complicating the relationship with China. However, one must look at the issue in its broader perspective. The reactions from China have been multi-directional—political, legal, and administrative.

China has so far been focusing on producing historical evidence to support its territorial claims. However, now the Chinese are taking certain legal and administrative steps. For example, in one of the islands in the South China Sea, China has established an administrative district to govern the Paracel Islands. Such administrative steps are very important—China has even issued a White Paper over the issue highlighting their claim over the Islands. This new form of assertiveness, both administratively and legally, is new for China and is something that India must take note of very seriously.

China has, however, not threatened to cut off trade links with Japan. They did this earlier in 2010 when the same issue had come up and had become a flashpoint, and China had suspended rare earth trade with Japan. This time, despite the rhetoric in Chinese media which states that the dispute will adversely affect Sino–Japanese trade linkages, no such step has been taken by the Chinese government.

This is also a result of the fact that both countries realize that they need each other. Sino–Japanese trade is about US $340 billion at the current point. The economic dependence between the two countries is particularly high even if we just look at Japanese investment in China. Trade and strategic factors are impinging on Chinese actions in the current dispute. China realizes that it is not going to gain in any manner by precipitating any long term conflict with Japan, which can affect the stability and prosperity of the Asia–Pacific region and its own economic interests. The Japanese, too, know that they cannot stretch it too far by becoming very assertive, especially in light of their liaison with the US.

Despite both countries playing the issue very carefully, there is a lot of rhetoric from the Chinese side. An influential retired PLA general is pushing for using the Senkaku islands and the surrounding areas as a practice grounds for the PLA Air Force and Navy. Despite such rhetoric there are steps on both sides to cool the tensions. The Japanese Vice-Foreign Minister has gone to China to discuss the issue. The basic drivers of this complicated Sino–Japanese relationship are going to remain strong for the foreseeable future and are going to influence the relationship.

Domestic developments also influence the situation. In November, China will undertake a power transition, a generational shift, and at this point, no Chinese leader would like to be seen as soft towards Japan and towards the Senkaku islands issue. This is another factor which needs to be kept in mind. I see one particular statement from the Chinese as being particularly important in which China says that it sees the Senkaku issue as an example of changes in the legal foundations of the international order in the Asia–Pacific region. This perception of the Chinese is very crucial. Beijing claims that Japan's ownership of the Senkaku Islands is changing the situation which had been established and concretized by the post-World War II Cairo and Potsdam Declarations, thus changing the international order in the Asia–Pacific.

Japan, for its part, suspects that China's military modernization and assertiveness in the region is changing the international order especially in North-East Asia. Both countries remain suspicious of each other's policy changes. China is perturbed by Japan's recent decision to lift the ban on arms exports, which they view as a negative development. While both sides are acting to cool tensions, the roots of the conflict are strong and there is no early permanent solution visible.

Japan's domestic situation is also not so stable as to enable it to take firm policy measures to change the situation. Asia–Pacific security is also affected by the changes that are happening in Korea and Taiwan. Rising nationalism, and disputes between Korea and Japan, the North-South Korea and South Korea–China hostility, and the China–Japan confrontation; all these create a threat to regional security. The situation is complicated by US policy and its naval build-up in the Pacific.

Implications for India The Japan–China conflict and the historically deep-rooted animosity between them are not conducive to a stable security environment in the Asia–Pacific region. India, which is keen to implement and extend its Look-East Policy to the Pacific nations, will find the situation very disadvantageous as it is in no position to take sides in the Senkaku issue. Even in the South China Sea dispute India is not taking any position. In the case of India's oil exploration project with Vietnam, when China expressed serious objections India was quick to explain that it was only a commercial enterprise, and expressed its unwillingness to take sides. So we are trying to be cautious in these strategic issues but the impact of the tensions in North-East Asia is going to be felt on India's policy-making.

Another way the Japan–China dispute will impact on India is in the economic sphere. Japan is wary of investments in China, and its business houses consider China unsafe with all the anti-Japanese rhetoric that is rife in the Chinese media. Will Japan divert their attention to India? To an extent this has already been happening since 2010 and during the visit of the Japanese Premier to India in December 2011. The Indo–Japan security relationship is unprecedented, as Japan has no such agreement with any country except Australia. This has China worried as it fears encirclement by Japan, Australia, and India. While there is no official statement on this subject in China, there are articles in their media which claim that these security links are moves to counter-balance China's influence.

Thus, there are fears in China about encirclement and fears in Japan about China's territorial intentions. India, too, has its apprehensions about China, as the strategic issues between the two countries have not disappeared, nor are they going to disappear in the foreseeable future. China's military modernisation and its growing power projection capability have generated fears in East and South-East Asia, including India.

The suspicion and fear between China, Japan, and India—the three pillars of Asia–Pacific stability and security—make the situation very complex and difficult, but it has to be addressed by these three nations. We have to wait for a few more years to see how it will be addressed and whether a stable situation will emerge in the region.

Presentation 2: Trade Relations between Japan and India: Present and Future Prospects

N. Krishnaswamy

Japan's history starts from the Meiji Restoration of 1868, before which it was a closed island without much linkage with the outside world, especially during the Tokugawa period, when the country was sealed from the outside world for over 300 years. But still, we can claim that India was the first country to export something to Japan long before written history. We exported the message of Buddha in 6th Century AD through China and Korea. Today, the morals, values, and practices of Buddhism are practiced in Japan in a sublime, silent way. It shapes their life and has, till date, a profound impact on Japanese polity, economy, and social life. The stoic nature of the Japanese, which the Chair mentioned, comes from their practice of the teachings of Buddha. The other major influence in Japanese society and culture is the teachings of the great philosopher Confucius.

Indo–Japanese relations were established following the visit of the first Indian Prime Minister Jawaharlal Nehru immediately after Indian independence; this year we are celebrating the 60th year of Indo–Japanese relations. Though there is not much warmth in the relationship, it is on an even keel and our bilateral relations are much stronger than, for instance, Sino–Japanese or Sino–Indian relations.

Following Jawaharlal Nehru's visit and the Indian promise to extend every possible help to the Japanese to rebuild economically, the first product we started exporting to Japan was iron ore, in a very big way. During this phase we also exported marine products, precious stones, and textiles to Japan. However, C.R. Rajagopalachari raised objections to the export of iron ore to Japan, saying that indiscriminate export of the ore would adversely affect the development of our own country.

In turn, once Japan became a little more developed it began exporting manufactured goods, steel products, and electronic goods to India. It must be pointed out here that from the very beginning Indo–Japan trade balance was always in Japan's favour as they were exporting high-value goods. This situation continues despite several plans and the liberalisation of our economy.

Despite the 1991 liberalisation, till 2002, the value of our trade (both export and import) did not exceed US $4 billion. Paul Krugman has said that the foreign policy of a country must be based on its economic policy. Unless we have a strong, self-reliant economic policy our political or diplomatic relations with Japan (or any other country) will always be erratic.

India was the first to begin trade with Japan, and exported huge quantities of iron ore; Japan was the world's second largest economy, its science and technology were at their height; despite all this, the economic relationship did not flourish as it should have. For a long time, Japan had its own misgivings vis-à-vis India. Nevertheless, liberalisation did improve the economic performance of India and step-by step, the Indo–Japanese bilateral trade reached US $13 billion by 2008–09.

More than any other country, Japan has studied, analysed, and recorded India's economic liberalisation meticulously. This was done by every Japanese delegation from 1991, whatever its level, sometimes excessively so. And every visiting Japanese delegation had a number of demands concerning the infrastructure and power situation in India, which they wanted to be fulfilled before investing in India. Indian leaders and government officials have always told the Japanese that India is committed to these steps and addressing these demands, but that they would take time; the Japanese, however, never had much faith in the stability of our economic reforms.

From our point of view the Japanese demands were being made without an understanding of the ground realities. The Government is fully aware of the need for power and infrastructure and so on. A recent incident involving the Japanese industrialists in the state of Tamil Nadu brings out this point. Japanese industrialists complained about the state of roads between Ennore and the Chennai port and asked that something be done about this as otherwise they would not be able to export their cars. Their Ambassador yielded to the pressure and came and met the Tamil Nadu Chief Minister, who assured him that the Government would take steps to address these demands and improve connectivity. But naturally, nothing changed dramatically. India, being a democratic country, there are numerous problems in the acquisition of privately owned land. The Japanese fail to understand the complexities of the issues involved and have been complaining time and again about the slow pace of land acquisition. This strengthens one's belief that the Japanese misgivings about our economic liberalisation and other steps that the government is taking to improve the situation are not based on pragmatism but are largely psychological.

However, after doing all this, the Japanese administration realized that this approach needed to be refined. Thus, in 2004, in consultation with the Ministry of External Affairs, they set up an Eminent Persons Group with representation from government, business, and academia, which possess deep knowledge about Japan. This group met four times between 2004 and 2006 and decided that India and Japan should enter into an economic agreement. This new wisdom, according to an article by a Japanese economist in the Asahi Shimbun, is partly a result of Japanese apprehensions about China and partly in the hope that India would be persuaded to sign a civil nuclear deal. With the unfavourable situation with China and the decline of the Western economies, the Japanese realized that India was a safe bet and the best option. The important outcome is that the Japanese now refer to India as a 'dependable friend', with a growing consumer market.

The level of discussion shifted from the Eminent Persons Group to the civil servants, and between 2006 and 2011, there were at least forty meetings. Both sides agreed in principle to a Free Trade Agreement (FTA) and signed a working protocol for the FTA in 2010. Despite a push by the Prime Ministers of both countries, it took another year for their Industry and Commerce Ministers to agree upon a Comprehensive Economic Partnership Agreement (CEPA), which was signed by India and Japan in October 2011.

The interesting point is that nobody in the industry or the exporters association knows how the CEPA is going to work or how it is beneficial to both countries. But it is important to note that the CEPA is an improvement over FTAs, which are restricted to specific purposes such as lowering of tariffs. In contrast the CEPA has a broader vision, and has targets like doubling of trade between 2011 and 2025 from US $13 billion to 25 billion. The CEPA is not focused on details like lowering of tariff or tinkering with custom duties, but has a broader vision and deals with larger activities and issues. As a result of the CEPA, tariffs will be reduced for about 90 per cent of goods on a regular basis; tariff will be reduced in stages to zero on almost all goods, in stages, within a decade.

Transfer of technology is a sensitive matter for the Japanese. They feel that they might lose their technological pre-eminence in the global market and therefore they never transfer their technology. India has signed almost 8,800 technology transfer agreements with various countries; of these, only 800 are with Japan. The CEPA, too, is silent about technology transfer. Despite CEPA, the Japanese are moving very slowly on two other issues. These are the movement of experts and trained professionals to Japan in varied disciplines like IT, nursing, and yoga. A second issue is that of not creating a monitoring body as this is not included in the CEPA framework.

A major aspect of Indo–Japanese relations is civil nuclear cooperation which is very important for taking the relationship to the next level. Prime Minister Noda of Japan has stated that he has faith in the Indian leadership and India's commitment to civil nuclear energy.

Thus, even though progress is slow, we have witnessed, in recent times, significant improvement on the past in various aspects; given that there are several factors driving the relationship in both countries, there is every prospect of continued improvement in the future.

Presentation 3: India–Japan Relations: Potential for Strategic and Defence Cooperation

Rajaram Panda

Introduction

After a long period of mutual neglect, the India–Japan relationship is evolving in a robust manner; it is evident that convergence of interests in the economic, strategic, and defence domains is going to be a defining feature of the 21st century in the Asia–Pacific region. After discovering economic complementarities, the two countries are engaged in strengthening defence cooperation to protect mutual economic interests and thereby contribute to a stable regional order. This is being done by way of mutual visits of defence ministers and senior officials of the governments, and a series of mutual agreements for cooperation in various areas.

The bilateral ties between India and Japan have also assumed a regional focus. This has been precipitated by the rise of China and the unpredictable nature of its postures on many bilateral and regional issues such as the South China Sea, energy and natural resources, maritime security, and territorial disputes. This factor of China's rise is impelling major powers in the region as well as the US to rebalance their mutual relationships. India and Japan are also driven to forge strategic partnerships, not only amongst themselves, but also with other friendly countries.

Another significant development that has taken place in the post-Cold War era is the growing bonhomie between India and the US. This too is being shaped to a great extent by a rising China and growing concern about China's power projection capabilities beyond its border.

Factors driving Indo–Japan Ties

Of all the factors that are driving India and Japan to forge a defence and strategic partnership, maritime issues and security of the sea lanes of communications (SLOCS) are the most prominent. The economies of both countries are heavily dependent on imports of oil and critical resources from the Persian Gulf, making maritime commerce vitally important. Japan's Constitutional limitation inhibits Maritime Self Defence Forces (MSDF) to deploy its Navy to international waters and, therefore, cooperation with Indian Navy becomes a strategic priority for Japan. As 90 per cent of Japan's oil requirements come from the Persian Gulf, maritime security is critical for Japan's economic future. Japan, therefore, considers India a strategic partner for closer naval cooperation, to tackle piracy attacks and terrorism at sea.

The Indian Navy has established its reputation in combating terrorism at sea and has successfully engaged in anti-piracy operations. The reputation of the Indian Navy and Coast Guard in Japanese eyes was enhanced when the Indian Navy and Coast Guard rescued the Japanese vessel MV Alondra Rainbow, hijacked by pirates from the South China Sea in November 1999. By doing so, India demonstrated that it can play an important stabilizing role in a volatile global security environment.

Significant High-Level Visits and Summit Meetings

A number of high-level visits have been exchanged between Japan and India in the recent past, which has given a fillip to bilateral relations. Prominent among these were:

- Prime Minister Mori's visit to India in August 2000, which saw the establishment of a 'Global Partnership between Japan and India in the 21st Century.' He also visited Bangalore, where the 'IT Cooperation between Japan and India in the 21st Century' was stressed and the Japanese PM emphasised the high potential for cooperation in this sphere.
- Against this backdrop, the Indian Prime Minister Vajpayee visited Japan in December 2001; during this visit it was agreed to continue the India–Japan Comprehensive Security Dialogue; the two countries further agreed to facilitate comprehensive dialogue and wider cooperation by way of expanding bilateral exchange in politics–military areas.

- During Koizumi's visit to India in April 2005, the two countries issued a joint statement entitled 'Japan-India Partnership in a New Asian Era: Strategic Orientation of Japan-India Global partnership' and announced an action plan called the Eight-fold Initiative for Strengthening Japan–India Global Partnership.
- In December 2006, during Indian Prime Minister Manmohan Singh's visit to Japan, the relationship was elevated by the signing of the 'Joint Statement towards Japan-India Strategic and Global Partnership.' Japan has funded many infrastructure projects in India, most notably the Delhi Metro subway system.
- Prime Minister Abe's visit in August 2007 provided an ideological basis for the relationship through his 'arc of freedom and prosperity' initiative, which he proposed in his address at the Japan Institute of International Affairs in November 2006. He emphasized that Japan should pursue 'value-oriented diplomacy' and justified Japan's closer cooperation with India, Australia, the US, and other NATO states, all of whom have 'shared values' of democracy, freedom, human rights, the rule of law, and the market economy. This 'Quadrilateral Initiative' was opposed by China and quickly faded.
- Prime Minister Manmohan Singh's second visit to Japan in October 2008 was notable for the 'Joint Declaration on Security Cooperation between Japan and India', signed in October 2008 under Prime Minister Taro Aso.
- Prime Minister Hatoyama's visit in December 2009 saw the signing of an 'Action Plan to Advance Security Cooperation based on the Joint Declaration on Security Cooperation between Japan and India.'
- In December 2011, Prime Minister Noda's visit to India further strengthened the existing agreements with the signing of the 'Vision for the Enhancement of Japan-India Strategic and Global Partnership upon entering the year of 60th Anniversary of the Establishment of Diplomatic Relations.'

Security Cooperation: Joint Naval Exercises

The decision of the Prime Ministers of Japan and India to start holding joint naval exercises in 2012 was a sign of the change in the relationship from an emphasis on shared values to active joint protection of shared interests. The move is seen as aimed to counter Beijing's strategic inroads into the Indian

Ocean region. So far, Japan had been engaged only in multilateral naval exercises wherein India too had been a part.

Combined anti-piracy and Search and Rescue exercises have been conducted since 2000 between the Indian and Japanese Coast Guards. The two Coast Guards exchanged a Memorandum of Cooperation on the occasion of Commandant Ishikawa's visit to India in November 2006. The heads of the Coast Guards of the two countries visit each other almost every year. They recently conducted joint exercises off Chennai in January 2012.

Although Japan withdrew from the trilateral Malabar Exercise in April 2011 due to the Fukushima nuclear crisis, India and Japan have increased mutual cooperation and interoperability based on NATO procedures: the joint drills will therefore be in the best interests of the two nations.

India and Japan already have significant security dialogue and cooperation aimed at tackling regional as well as global security challenges. There are the Comprehensive Security Dialogue, Defence Policy Dialogue, and Military-to-Military Talks. There have also been Service-to-Service exchanges between defence establishments of the two countries. The annual Indian Coast Guard–Japan Coast Guard Talks were held in 2009 and 2010 and the two countries have also carried out joint patrolling to counter piracy operations in the Straits of Malacca .

In June 2012, four Indian ships entered Tokyo after the first-ever Indo–Japan maritime exercises; their three-day stay there coincided with the commemoration of 60 years of diplomatic relations between India and Japan.

While India is wary of China's aggressive behaviour, it at the same time does not wish to take provocative actions. In this context, mutual port calls, such as the visit of the Indian Navy ships to Shanghai on their way back from the Tokyo exercises, could be a useful confidence-building measure.

Security Network

The recent territorial disputes between Japan and China, and Japan and South Korea coincide with China's military build-up and maritime expansion are complicating security issues and shaping those countries' approaches to the changing situation. In strengthening security networks, the US, Japan, Australia, and India are also expanding and strengthening their cooperation in addition to developing closer mutual security dialogues.

Japan and Australia have long developed bilateral alliances with the US. The fourth ministerial meeting of the Trilateral Strategic Dialogue between the three countries was held in September 2009. Japan and the US had the first high-ranking working level meeting on common issues including national security with India in Washington in December 2011 and the second meeting in Tokyo in April 2012. The third meeting is expected to be held in India.

Some analysts see the India–Japan–US trilateral dialogue as a move to contain the growing influence of China. Others see the buildup of new regional relationships as a contributory factor towards regional stability. Hardliners in Japan welcome the India–Japan–US trilateral dialogue on security cooperation, viewing it as India's endorsement of the strategy to cope with expanding Chinese naval activities. China has noted with apprehension that India and Japan have boosted regional cooperation in recent years in the economic and security realms. They have also broad-based their relations by including the US and Australia.

In an inter-dependent globalised world, where all countries are intensifying their mutual relations, China's concern appears to be to redefine the rules on its own terms, and any contrarian view is perceived in Beijing as anti-Chinese. China should understand that there has been a veritable renaissance in India–Japan relations with India embarking on market reforms, and Japan has found in India a large market. It is only during the past five years or so that both have started seeing each other as potential strategic partners and China's rise just coincided with this.

As Japan strives to struggle out from its long economic slump, the leadership is under pressure to look for new economic measures that might resuscitate the economy. With a view to this, Japan lifted the ban on arms exports, paving the way for Japan's air and marine forces to upgrade their hardware capability. China sees this as a threat and interprets Japan's decision as a re-shuffling of the international arms trade; Japan's competitiveness in military equipment might squeeze other countries' market share. As Japan now breaks into a politically restricted area, China perceives that Japan's move would create uncertainties in the Asia–Pacific region. China also fears that Japan sought and obtained Washington's approval to relax ban on arms exports as a part of their joint Asia–Pacific strategy to 'contain' China. That India would be a possible market for Japanese arms manufacturers also concerns China.

Conclusion

While the strengthening of the Japan–Indian strategic partnership is welcome, the ties must move to the next level for tangible results. This can be done by starting trade in defence technology as security cooperation without accruing economic benefits would not be sustainable for long. If Japan can relax its rules that facilitate transfer, sale, and joint production of defence technologies and military hardware, the strategic component of the bilateral ties would get teeth. Despite being a leading producer of advanced military equipment, Japan is constrained in engaging in arms trade with India. Japan's leading conglomerates such as Mitsubishi, Ishikawajima, Toshiba, and Kawasaki have advanced military technologies and have joined with leading US defence companies in various sectors for producing military hardware for American forces. India would expect similar defence relationships that would serve the twin objectives of strengthening defence ties and yielding economic dividends to both, thereby reinforcing the complementarities between the two countries.

Discussions

On conclusion of the presentations by the speakers the floor was opened to the house by the Chairman.

Insights into the Japanese Business Culture P.C. Nayak opened the discussions with some observations based on his experience as Industries Commissioner of Maharashtra. In that capacity, he had been responsible for bringing in one of the first Indo–Japanese joint venture into India in the form of the Yokogawa Company. The firm was called Yokogawa India. With this background he wished to address some practical aspects since the audience had already heard about strategy, tactics, background, and history from the guest speakers.

The first thing to remember, Nayak said, was that the Japanese do a lot of research, almost to the extent of 'analysis unto paralysis.' They would know more about us than we did about ourselves before they would even begin talking to us. This should always be remembered while engaging with the Japanese.

Secondly, like all businessmen, the Japanese also love money so it is important to point out the profit potential of the business venture to get them interested.

Thirdly, the Japanese do not understand or appreciate the concept of technology transfer. For them even a photograph of a factory is technology and they will not allow people to enter their factories with a camera. However, when he was Industries Commissioner in Maharashtra, he had taken a Japanese industrialist to witness how we export prawns, and that gentleman had taken hundreds of photographs there. It was important to go step by step with the Japanese; big ticket items like technology transfers put them off.

Fourthly, hierarchy was very important for the Japanese. There is always one man in the organization that makes the decisions. It is crucial to identify this person and establish a good rapport with him.

Fifthly, the Japanese have a great regard for government and hold the view that 'government is first and then industry.' Therefore it is prudent to involve the government in any collaboration with them. Nayak's enlightening remarks were followed by questions and remarks from members of the audience.

Prospects of Indo–Japanese Cooperation A question was raised about the nature of Indo–Japan cooperation and its prospects in the coming years. The panelists posited that there would be some adjustments which would need to be made in the mindsets of both companies and governments; though there will be some pull and push the general outlook would be positive.

Chinese Belligerence in Senkaku Dispute The Senkaku islands issue featured in the discussions with speakers as well as the audience raising concerns about the fact that the issue is a manifestation of the new Chinese aggressive nationalism. Several members expressed the view that China was becoming more and more assertive, as was also seen in recent developments in the South China Sea.

China–Japan–South Korea Triangular Relationship The management of the Japan, South Korea, and China relationship and the relationship of each of these countries with India were topics that were discussed at length. It was pointed out that on many aspects Japan was losing out to South Korea as the latter was willing to act faster and also engage in transfer of technology with India. While the Japanese company Toyota has been loath to transfer technology and is only now beginning to assemble units in the country, the South Koreans had shown no such reluctance.

There was a consensus that if India wishes to increase its role in the region it must decide the policy and posture it wants to adopt on various issues and then act decisively to back such a posture.

Conclusion

As the Chairman observed in his opening remarks, the Japanese have many admirable qualities that have imbued their art, society, and industry. P.C. Nayak made some penetrating observations about the Japanese attitude to the transfer of technology to other countries. He also underlined the Japanese respect for authority and in their belief that the Government took precedence over industry, and the effect that such a belief has in their business dealings.

The major part of the seminar dealt with Japan–India relations and the relations of China and Japan inasmuch as they impinged heavily on Asia–Pacific regional security. India's own security concerns are expanding and now include the East Pacific Ocean region. This is evidenced by the increasing use of the term 'Indo-Pacific' in the international security discourse. One speaker described China, India, and Japan as the 'three pillars' of Asia Pacific regional security. However, this term does not factor in the United States, which has a large stake in Asia–Pacific security, with security alliances with several countries in the North, West, and South Pacific Ocean. Aside from that, it is indisputable that Indian security horizons are growing eastwards, and in several aspects collide with the security boundaries somewhat pretentiously claimed by China.

It is in this specific aspect that Indo–Japanese relations assume an added significance. India does not seek to make military alliances in other regions, nor even in its own region. But there is a world of difference between military alliances and cooperation in security matters. The current scope of security cooperation between Japan and India is intended to sustain the hallowed concept of freedom of the seas and to rid the ocean waterways of the scourge of piracy, which is often viewed as the clandestine supporter of global terrorism. China would do well to encourage and even join such maritime security cooperation initiatives, as its energy flows through the same hazardous waters, rather than take the overly suspicious view that such cooperation is aimed against it. In this context, India has been prudent in resisting Japan's efforts to draw it into a quadrilateral strategic alliance with the US, Japan, and Australia, which was patently designed to contain China.

Insofar as the Senkaku dispute is concerned, although the popular view favours Japanese claims, in reality matters are not so clear-cut. The People's Republic and Taiwan both claim that the islands have been a part of Chinese territory since at least 1534. The Japanese annexed the islands in 1895, and thereafter the Americans took control of them after WW II. The Treaty of Potsdam had decreed in 1945 that all islands occupied by the Japanese were to be returned to China. In 1971, the US returned control of the islands to Japan along with Okinawa. So China may have a case when it expresses the apprehension that support for Japanese possession is tantamount to re-drawing post WW II treaties, which would upset the current international order.

But that is not to say that China is justified in its larger regional postures. It has time and again raked up centuries-old historical 'evidence' to claim territory. Its stance on its rights in the South China Sea is aggressive and disputable under UNCLOS. Its policy is to deal with the weaker states piecemeal, even using force on them one at a time, as it has done with Vietnam and the Philippines. The fear of China's military might is common to all states in the region, and many hope that India with its more benign power will provide a bulwark. India, however, is reluctant to assume this mantle, and rightly so, for it has urgent issues of development and economy on which it needs to focus. But India's caution need not become diffidence in the furtherance of its legitimate economic interests, as when it backed down hastily from an oil exploration agreement with Vietnam at the first hint of Chinese disapproval.

Indo–Japanese cooperation needs to be pursued more vigorously than it has; the fragmented approach in sectors such as security relations, trade, and cultural exchanges need to be unified in a coherent and integrated policy that addresses all these aspects to the mutual benefit of the two countries.

Chapter 15

India and China

ASIA CENTRE, BANGALORE

'Coping With a Rising China: Indian Perspectives'
Proceedings of the Seminar held on

December 22, 2012

Preface

A Seminar on the subject 'Coping With a Rising China: Indian Perspectives' was held by the Asia Centre in Bangalore on 22nd December 2012. The seminar examined various aspects of a rapidly rising China from an Indian perspective—the economy, the asymmetrical Indo-China strategic equation, and some implications of the proceedings of the recent 18th CPC Congress in Beijing.

The Seminar was chaired by A.P. Venkateswaran, Chairman, Asia Centre and India's former Foreign Secretary. The following were the guest speakers:

Mohan Guruswamy	Director, Centre for Policy Alternatives, New Delhi, former Advisor to the Finance Minister.
Vice Admiral (Retd) P.S. Das	Former C-in-C, Eastern Naval Command, and former member NSAB
C.V. Ranganathan	Former Indian Ambassador in China, Co-Chairman India-China Eminent Persons Group, former Convener National Security Advisory Group
Alka Acharya	Professor of Chinese Studies, Centre for East Asian Studies (JNU), Member India-China Eminent Persons Group, Member NSAB

The presentations were followed by a question and answer session. The proceedings which appear on the following pages have been compiled by Vice Admiral (Retd) R.N. Ganesh.

Chair's Opening Remarks

In his opening remarks, the Chairman pointed out the various qualities of the Chinese and their ability to stand up to Western domination. They are now making serious progress in attaining their long-denied status in the world, in the face of the aggressive pivot to the Pacific by the US. The Chairman recalled his experience in China and the subtlety and sophistication of the Chinese that sometimes made it difficult for the rest of the world to understand them.

Welcoming the audience and the guest speakers, Venkateswaran observed that there were many present in the audience who were both experienced and knowledgeable about China. He noted that the day's speakers comprised of an economist, a diplomat, a naval veteran and an academic, and was sure that their broad and varied experience would add great value to the proceedings of the seminar.

Introduction

The rise of China in all spheres has been the defining global development of the past decade. China has made impressive progress to claim the top rungs in global economic, industrial and military power.

Two main strands characterize the trajectory of the Sino-Indian relationship. The first is the security aspect, which has been dominant. After the heady days of *Panchsheel* and 'Indian-Chinese brotherhood', Sino-Indian relations plummeted with the 1962 conflict, which still looms large in the Indian psyche and has left its imprint on our attitude to China.

The second strand is that of bilateral trade, which is growing at a rapid pace and may have a moderating influence on the first. But here, too, there is the problem of an adverse trade balance.

This seminar is being held at a time when two landmark events have just taken place. One is the 50th anniversary of the 1962 conflict, and the second is the decennial change of the Chinese leadership. This is a timely juncture to take a fresh view of the India-China relationship in its totality and also to examine the internal and external implications of the recent changes in the Chinese leadership following the 18th CPC National Congress.

The Director then introduced the speakers, whose profiles are described briefly are at the end of this report.

Presentation 1: Sino-Indian Relations-Present and Future: An Economist's Perspective

Mohan Guruswamy

The Beginning of China's Economic Rise The story of China actually begins in the eighties, when I was a graduate student. Extrapolating India's and China's growth figures over various periods, I found some startling results. China was already growing at 10 per cent in 1980—the projections for 2050 and 2100 showed the world scene changing completely. I decided to make this the focus of my research and went to my faculty advisor who, however, put me off saying that India and China would never come to that situation, as there were other issues like backwardness and modernity involved. So that is where I probably missed my shot at fame and glory.

In 2003, I was prompted by a statement made by the Prime Minister at that time who said that we were now ahead of China and India was shining. I had a couple of research assistants and we examined it and found that far from doing better we were actually far behind China and were rapidly falling off the map. When I read my first paper in 2003 at an august gathering like this one in Delhi, many in the audience, refused to believe that the Chinese could do so well, and argued that my data was wrong. It took till about 2005 for the reality about China to sink in.

The US and the Chinese Economy

Delinking Dollar from Gold In 1974, Richard Nixon quietly delinked the US dollar from the gold standard, saying that the dollar was so strong that it didn't need to be linked with gold. Suddenly the dollar was floating in the air. It could print as many dollars as it wished. So, today of the world's monetary reserves 70 per cent are held in dollars, about 20 per cent in euros and a small amount in Pounds Sterling, Yen and so on. With the delinking of the dollar the US found a new way to prosperity. Earlier Japan, Korea and ASEAN grew on US consumption.

US Indebtedness and Chinese Growth With the printing of new notes becoming so easy, the US did not have to worry about budgetary and trade deficits. The Chinese growth story begins with this flood of dollars. And with dollars freely available, consumption increased, and so did borrowing. The US is the most indebted nation in the world; I am told the foreign debt of the US is 15 trillion dollars; its total collective debt from domestic debt, credit card debt, social service, security overhang is another 53 trillion dollars. So the average debt on every American will be something like 67,000 dollars, together with his credit card and unpaid mortgage. The Chinese hold all these notes and United States lives on credit. Selling to the United States is the basis of China's big growth.

The Wage Rise Another thing that happened was with the rise in wages in ASEAN, Korea and Japan these countries moved their manufacturing units to China to remain competitive. Today 70 per cent of Chinese exports come from enterprises that are owned by foreigners. A typical example is the Taiwanese company called Fox Conn, which is the Apple factory in Chengdu; Fox Conn employs 1 million people and the factory is a complete town with a population of two hundred thousand people; it has barracks, canteens, cinema theatres, entertainment, and even its own currency in the form of vouchers.

Chinese Trade Surplus The Chinese trade surplus with the United States is 200 billion dollars; but that surplus actually originates from Taiwanese, Hong Kong, Korean, ASEAN and Japanese companies. China has thus become a low-cost producer of goods and in this process became an industry-oriented economy. 52 per cent of the Chinese GDP today is accounted for by industry, about 30 per cent by services and 14–15 per cent by agriculture. This is the profile of an industrial state, where the bulk of the employment is in industry, and the bulk of the GDP usually comes from manufacturing.

India: The Post-Industrial Economy In India, on the other hand, services account for 52 per cent, industry 23 per cent and agriculture the rest. And when I say 'services', IT would spring to mind, since we are in Bangalore. But that is a very small part of services—the total employment in the IT sector in India is a mere 800,000. The biggest component of services is where you gentlemen and I have served, the Government. Public administration which for some strange reason is included in "services", accounts for 17 per cent and is growing merrily at 14 per cent a year. There are 23 million government employees, which is about the population of a well-sized European country. This is the situation in India, and I always say that India has the profile of a post-industrial state. We are aunique country—we area post-industrial society without having industrialized.

Current And Future Rankings China today is the world's second-largest economy with a GDP of 10 trillion dollars at purchasing power parity (PPP), USA's is 14 trillion dollars, and Japan used to be third. I say 'used to be' because in September Japan's GDP was at 4.6 trillion, and India's today is at 4.8 PPP. If you project these figures to 2050 the two big countries are China and India.

Citibank says that China's GDP (at PPP) will be 82 trillion dollars and India's GDP at PPP will surpass that at 83 trillion dollars. Goldman Sachs is more conservative and predicts that China's GDP will be 47 trillion dollars and India's will be 36 trillion dollars. After India, China and United States there is a steep drop in countries GDPs, with Brazil and Italy and seven other countries together not amounting to India. Even Japan would have gone to the bottom of the list. Both China and India are posting GDPs which are proportional to their population growth—the Chinese population has stabilized at 1.3 billion. China has an ageing profile, and the dependency ratio—the number of non-working to working people—is increasing. So, by 2050, 65 per cent of China will be dependent on 35 per cent of people. The majority will be old, and they do not have social security.

The older, non-working population does not consume, and China has hit that patch now. The Government of India has assured the United Nations in writing that we will stabilize the population at 1.3 billion. We have already crossed 1.3 billion. In 2050, we will be 1.6 billion and in 2097, 1.9 billion. That is the good news. The bad news is that the population in the South—Kerala, Andhra Pradesh, Tamil Nadu and Karnataka—is already tapering off. By 2030, the whole of South India will stop growing and start ageing. The states that are growing are Bihar, Eastern UP, Orissa, and Assam. The Bimaru states are growing and they will constitute 70–80 per cent of the country's population. Logically, money should be spent where the problems exist, but the per capita development expenditure figures in Bihar, Orissa and Assam are the lowest in the country. The highest per capita development expenditure in the country is in Jammu and Kashmir, Nagaland, Mizoram and Punjab and Haryana—all states that are either troubled areas or relatively prosperous. So the country's money is not going where it is needed, the federal system is not working well.

GDP and National Wealth Closer to our time, by 2020, China will surpass the United States in terms of GDP with its 24.6 trillion against the United States' 23.6 trillion. But while GDP makes a nation wealthy, it makes it collectively wealthy—it does not make the people wealthy. China's per capita GDP (at PPP) today puts it in the same level as Algeria and Albania at $4,300 a year. The United State's per capita GDP is $47,000. India's GDP is $4,000 in PPP terms. Even in 2050 when our GDPs are more than that ofthe US, America's GDP will be five times more than China's per capita GDP and six times more than India's per capita GDP. So, even when we think we will become wealthy, United States and Europe will continue to be wealthier—wealth is a relative thing.

GDP and National Power There is another notion that is widely prevalent in this country, that GDP means power: that the higher the GDP, the more powerful your country. People in India are excited thinking that we are going to be a super power—but things don't work like that. In 1870, Britain was at the height of its power and accounted for only 5 per cent of the world's GDP—the United States' GDP was bigger. In 1910, Japan's GDP was bigger than Britain's. When Vietnam and China defeated the United States and Korea, they did not even figure in the GDP rankings. When China defeated India, India's per capita GDP was twice that of China. This is a thing which we should never forget. Power has very little to do with GDP; the notion that GDP bestows power is false, and we would do well to discard it. India will surpass China and I am positive about that, I feel very optimistic about that. We will grow to be bigger than China, in terms of people and in terms of GDP. It might be messy, but India is like that.

GDP and Revenue It is very important for us to understand that the power of a country is determined by how much money its government has, and not how much money the society has. If the government has no money to spend, it cannot spend on development or improving the lives of its people, or providing for its Army or Navy or its Air Force. If the government does not collect revenue it has no power. India's current revenue-GDP ratio is 19.5. United States' Revenue-GDP ratio is 35, Britain's is 39 and France's 38. This ratio needs to be above 30 for the Government to have the money to spend. To use a simple analogy, your power is how much money you have in your pocket. If you wear nice clothes but you have no money in your pocket, you don't count.

So India has to increase its taxes to get the revenue-GDP ratio up, not let it go down by reducing taxes. But because CII and FICCI went to the Finance Minister and said taxes are too high, he is asking for reduction in taxes, instead of collecting more revenue. The business of the government is to collect taxes and to provide for people from taxes. China is increasing its collection of taxes; another thing that it has done is that it has decentralized. In 1950, 74 per cent of the Chinese wage bill used to be met by the Central Government and 26 per cent by provinces and local governments. Today, it has reversed that situation: 23 per cent of the wage bill is met by the Central Government and the rest is met by local and provincial governments. In India, 43 per cent of wages is accounted for by the Central Government, 45 per cent by the state governments and only 11 per cent is by local government. Local government is the level that directly affects the citizens, providing daily utilities and services. Instead of empowering local government, spending and power are concentrated in the central and state governments—local government hardly exists in India. So, that is the big difference again between India and China. China delivers more for every Yuan they spend, unlike us.

Now about India and China's relations: are we going to be friends? I don't think so; are we going to be enemies? I don't think so. Are we going to be rivals? Yes. We're going to be rivals. We can be competitors. This is something we have to live with. We will compete for resources, for attention, for space, markets, and we will compete everywhere. That does necessarily translate into enmity. Enmity exists between many countries which you would see if you went to a rugby match between France and Britain, or a soccer match between Argentina and Brazil. Knives fly there. The Chinese have a historical enmity with Japan, but Japan is also China's biggest trading partner and foreign investor. In the new world which has emerged, you do business with everybody. There is no reason why India and China cannot continue to do business with each other. India's problem is we have to nothing to sell to China. We sell commodities and iron ore in which there is no value addition; the profits go to a few, and the government gets a meagre revenue of 27 dollars per ton. But the economy gets no value addition. On the other hand, if you sell a car, which is nearly 800 kilos of steel, there is value addition at every stage of manufacture. A ton of steel costs about 560 dollars, and a car costs 10,000 dollars (Rs 5.5 lakhs). With value addition, the gains are spread among a larger number of people at different levels, and the government gets higher revenue.

Capital Outflow From the latest UN report which tracks such transactions, India has illicitly exported 123 billion dollars of capital since 2000. In addition, 97 billion dollars has been legitimately exported as capital. Tata has bought Corus and Jaguar and Mr Mittal bought steel plants. Indian companies buy shares and other companies because this is one way of moving money out. A total of 230 billion dollars left the country, and 170 billion came back as foreign investment. Interestingly, of this foreign investment, 47 per cent came from Mauritius. This is like a round trip with Indian business putting money which comes back to India; but unfortunately for India there is a net outflow indicating that there is loss of confidence in India. It is the thinking Indians who are losing confidence in India: the *aam admi* still has a lot of faith in India.

China's Currency Reserve I will come to one more aspect before I shut shop. There is much talk of China having piled up 2.8 trillion dollars as a foreign reserve. But these 2.8 trillion dollars don't earn any interest. Just as money in Swiss banks does not earn interest so also when a country invests abroad, it has to let the money lie idle in that country. So China has 2.8 trillion dollars in the USA and it can't take it back. If it takes it back, it would have to demonetize the dollars. It cannot just tear up the dollars—it would have to print the equivalent amount in Yuan, which would cause hyperinflation in China. If China tries to do anything else with that money, all kind of things could happen. If it doesn't do anything with it, the dollars appreciate at 4.3 per cent a year. So in twenty years, China's reserves will be dust. China is thus in a quandary. The Chinese give credit to the Americans, the Americans give credit to their own people to increase consumption, who then buy Chinese goods earning the Chinese more dollars. Economists describe this as a relationship between a dope peddler and a drug addict. At one stage of addiction, the peddler advances the addict money and keeps piling up the debt, because he has got to keep his business going. So, United States keeps the business going, and China keeps piling up the debt. It is all sitting there, in America. But recall that Richard Nixon delinked dollars; so the US keeps printing dollars without a qualm. This is why the world is in a very precarious situation. When is this system going to come to a grinding halt and topple over? People keep sounding warnings as they kept warning us till yesterday about the end of the world. Fortunately the Mayan calendar was wrong by 3 billion years. But the end of the financial system could happen anytime. Nobody thought that Lehman Brothers or AIG or General Motors would collapse. But these things happened. So China is sitting on this very fine thread of credit, and when you are in such a position everybody will have to be well-behaved. You cannot rock the boat, or be noisy. You have to go about quietly. But the problem with the Chinese is that they are noisy. They are always making claims on Diaoyu or the K6 power block or on Arunachal Pradesh and they upset everybody. And when people get upset, they do irrational things. The rational thing would be to let Chinese money remain there and get China to invest some more money in India. I keep telling my friends in the government to get China to invest in India. But the Chinese investment in India is decided by the Research and Analysis Wing, who fear that if the Chinese invest money in a port in Tuticorin it would compromise national security. The Chinese for instance want to build a high speed railway link in India. They need to invest their money somewhere, and India can absorb their capital. We can even give 4.8 per cent rate of interest, build freight corridors and build ports—they will agree because their money is becoming worthless. So we should let the

Chinese in. Last week, there was some good news when the National Security Advisor said that we were considering Chinese investments in Railways. The thing for India to do is to get them to invest and build a stake in India so that they have good relations with us. I think gatherings like these; people like you who are getting the message can tell our people in the decision-making apparatus that the Chinese are not stupid. They can invest their money, and they have plenty of it; they are in a desperate situation and they know that their reserve is dwindling in value. This is where we have to jump in and exploit the situation. There are people present here who are on the National Security Advisory Board, and have access to the decision makers. I am sure they will give these charts to Dr Manmohan Singh who, unfortunately, was educated in Cambridge University, and not in Harvard or Yale.

Thank you.

Presentation 2: Security Aspects of India-China Relations - Dealing with Asymmetry

Premvir Das

Ladies and Gentlemen, it is such a pleasure to be here and a privilege to share the podium with people of such immense expertise on the subject we are talking about. Ambassador Venkateswaran said in the beginning that despite his years in China he could not fathom the Chinese mind and I heard Ambassador Ranganathan saying from the left 'Amen!' So, what are ordinary mortals like me here going to talk about the Chinese? Mohan Guruswamy just said that power and economy are not related; I would change that slightly to say that they are not unrelated. Let me say that whatever I say here is my opinion and all of us know that in India there are as many opinions as there are people. So, here I am, to give you one man's opinion.

Need to Look Ahead Let us recall the media hype a month ago on the 50th Anniversary of the 1962 conflict. It is amazing that in this country we were almost celebrating 50 years of a military reverse. If Nehru had not asked us to push the Chinese back, if air power had been used, if the General concerned had not withdrawn from Sela Pass, if General Kaul had not been sent to Tezpur, the only place where you hear more 'ifs' is on the golf course. I think the world has moved on since then, and we have learnt from those reverses despite all the shortcomings. Let me give a few facts. If the Indian Army is one million strong today, it owes it to 1962. If the Indian Air Force is as strong today and is becoming stronger, it is because of the lessons learnt from 1962. The world has moved forward a lot today, the Chinese will travel to the Moon and I wish they do, the Indians are not far behind, admittedly in a stumbling, bumbling way. But the thing to do is not to look back but to look ahead and we can watch our stern, to use naval terminology, as long as we look ahead.

Asia-Pacific: The New Security Focus It is almost a cliché to say that the security focus has shifted to the Asia Pacific. But, there are reasons for that. After all, two of the four largest economies in the world are in the Asia Pacific. If in 15 years, they are joined by a third, namely India it will not be surprising. Four of the eight nuclear weapon states are in the Asia Pacific. If there are to be any additions, the chances are they will be in the Asia Pacific. Three of the four largest militaries are in the Asia Pacific, two-thirds of all terrorist movements worldwide are in the Asia Pacific, Al-Qaeda, Afghan Taliban, Pakistan Taliban and Lashkar E Taiba, Jaish Mohammad, Huji in Bangladesh Jamia Islamia in Indonesia, Abu Sayeb in Phillipines are all located here. The so-called rogue or problem states— Afghanistan, Pakistan, Iraq, Iran, and earlier Bahrain, Yemen, Syria—are all here. I have not spoken of energy centers, energy resources and more importantly the energy transportation routes, the Indian Ocean region. So, it is not surprising that the focus of global security concern is now on the Asia Pacific. And who are the players in the Asia Pacific? One can say America has got a fiscal cliff to climb. America is a hugely indebted nation, and is a diminishing power and so on. But, if one bases one's opinion on realities, the picture is a little different. The American economy in real terms is equal to the next three economies combined. In GDP terms, America will be well ahead of every other power for many years to come.

America in Asia The Chair said that America is now pivoting to the Asia Pacific. To that I would say yes and no. No, because America has always been in the Asia Pacific. Even in the Cold War, when it was not involved in Afghanistan, Iran, and Iraq or wherever, America's two largest bases were in the Asia Pacific—the naval base in Subic Bay and Clarke's Air Force Base in the Philippines. But their attention was focused on certain things for the last 20 years; that focus is now diminishing and one reason they are coming back to the Asia Pacific is the rise of China. America's disappearance as an Asia Pacific power in the near future is, I think, out of the question. It is true that their energy dependency is decreasing and will become zero in the next 10–12 years. But they are going to remain a major Asia Pacific power.

China This brings me to China and it cannot be gainsaid that China is a major Asian Power in every way. We all know about their economy, we just heard of its major military modernization programmes in aerospace and at sea, it is taking several actions to spread its influence worldwide, in Latin America and in Africa. It already is there in South-East Asia and South Asia. So there is no doubt that China is going to be a major player.

Japan One country that we tend to ignore is Japan. It is seen as a defensive and docile country which will not do much. But the fact of the matter is that last year Japan put out a defence doctrine which focused attention southwards, which means at sea and towards China. In the recent elections, the LDP has come back to power and the Prime Minister who is expected to be Shinzo Abe is known to be more nationalistic than his predecessor was. The Japanese navy is called the Japanese Maritime Self Defence Force, which makes it sound like some kind of a coast guard, but that is not true. The Japanese MSDF has the greatest naval capability in East Asia, in terms of maritime surveillance and anti-submarine aircraft; Japan has ninety two P3 type of aeroplanes. They are more than all similar aeroplanes held by India, China, Pakistan and the rest of Asia put together. So, we should not cast aside Japan as a non-entity in the Asia power equation.

Other Countries People generally tend to overlook Russia in the Asian context. Russia has not come to Camranh Bay for nothing—it is going to be an Asian player. Then of course there is India in its stumbling, bumbling way—India is like a runner in a steeple chase, jumping over one hurdle, then falling over another into the water, then getting out and running again. But India is continuing to run and there is no way that it cannot be a major Asian player. Then, there is South-East Asia, and Indonesia in particular. It is not just that they are a major economy; let us not forget that they sit astride the openings from the South China Sea into the Indian Ocean. There are also the energy centers of Southwest Asia and the Central Asian Republics.

Features of the Asia Pacific Security Region Many people say that the Asian equation is an India-Japan-China triangle. But I disagree. The Asian equation is more about a hexagon—India, Japan, China, Russia, South-East Asia, Central Asia, and South-West Asia—and I would suggest that a hexagon or polygon is more descriptive of India's security environment than any triangle. Another difference in the region is this: in Cold War Europe, the focus of confrontation was on land. The armies of the NATO and the Warsaw Pact countries were facing each other with tanks, guns, and tactical nuclear weapons all focused against each other on land. In the Asia Pacific the focus of concern is at and from the sea.

It is not surprising therefore that people have begun to term the Asia Pacific as the Indo-Pacific; most recently two days ago by a Prime Minister when speaking at the ASEAN Heads of States gathering and I agree with him. In the Indo part of the region there is the Indian Ocean where the concerns are essentially non-State. There is piracy, earlier in the Malacca States and now in the Gulf of Aden; there is maritime terrorism: an American destroyer was seriously damaged in Aden, a French tanker was attacked in the Gulf of Aden, the oil terminal in Basra was attacked by the Al-Qaeda group and we need not even talk about the attack on Bombay in November 2008. Yet there is little evidence of the possibility of nation-state confrontation. It is true that the Americans went into Afghanistan and Iraq, and they might go into Iran. But the possibility of intra-region nation-state conflict is not high.

In the Pacific part of the Indo-Pacific, all potential confrontation is between nation-states. There is no significant non-state actor threat, but there are problems between states: Japan and China over Senkaku, China and the Philippines over Scarborough Shoal, China and North Vietnam over Paracel and Spratly islands, China and Malaysia, China and Brunei, South Korea and Japan: the whole region is rife with potential or actual confrontation between nation-states, which is a different thing altogether. So, what we are seeing here are concerns of a non-state nature on one side of the Indo-Pacific and of a nation-state nature on the other. I think this is an important aspect to remember when we talk of security equations in the Indo-Pacific.

India's Concerns in the Region Now, let me examine what India's concerns are in this region because all discussion must stem from India's interests. First, whatever one might say, the fact of the matter is that India is, must be and will be a major Asian power. It may not be the predominant one, but it will be one of the major powers in Asia. Its interests therefore coincide geographically with the kind of power status it is seeking legitimately, and successive prime ministers have said that these interests stretch from the Suez on the one side to the South-East Asian Channels on the other and even beyond. This is an important aspect to remember in India's strategic security concerns. As a major regional littoral in the Indian Ocean region, India also has concerns including humanitarian assistance and relief in disaster situations such as tsunamis, in providing assistance for anti-piracy operations in the Western Arabian Sea, in maritime search and rescue and in ensuring safety of the sea lanes of commerce. India has also provided assistance to legitimate governments when asked to do so, for example in the Maldives in 1988 when the Kayoom Government was threatened by rebels and Maldives asked for Indian assistance; Indian troops landed in Maldives and INS Godavari was sent to apprehend the merchant ship African Queen on which the rebels were attempting their escape. They had taken with them some hostages to give them negotiating leverage. Godavari duly apprehended the African Queen, and the rebels were arrested and all hostages were rescued.

Thus, it has been part of India's responsibility as a major littoral to provide such assistance whenever needed. Closer home, of course territorial integrity stands at the very top of India's security concerns and interests. Equally, economic growth is also a security concern. Economic growth is a product of many factors, many of which Mohan has elaborated in terms of stability, good governance, and financial management. It is also dependent on energy and trade security which are vital for economic growth. This year, something like 70 per cent of all India's energy—oil and gas—will come through imports. This figure may increase to 80 per cent by the year 2020. So obviously that is a major concern. It is not just a question of locating the resources but also of the ability to transport it safely across the waters. The other factor is trade. This year, India's overseas trade may amount to approximately 750–800 billion dollars. Twenty years ago, the proportion of India's overseas trade to its overall economy was much less than what it is today, and fifteen years from now, it will be much more; especially in the category of exports, all of which is transported by sea. So we have to be very conscious of what these interests are and take measures to safeguard them. And finally, of course, we have to be on guard against not only maritime terrorism, but also terrorism of the type that we saw in November: terrorism on land is equally a concern. It is naïve to expect that there will be some arrangements with Pakistan that will result in the disappearance of the terrorism threat in this countryany time soon. Terrorism is too useful to the people across the border as an asymmetric tool. So we have to be prepared for that kind of environment.

India's Predominant Position in the Indian Ocean Let me end the 'India's interests' portion by saying that in its part of the world—the Indian Ocean region—India's ability to not control but to influence the geopolitical and the security scenario is very much greater than that of any other country. Look at its geography: open seas on both sides, far-flung island territories which give us capabilities which no other country has: Port Blair and Car Nicobar in the Andamans, both with air fields capable of operating the largest and the most capable aircraft in the inventory. In the southern part of India, Arakkonam,

Chennai, Thanjavur, Thiruvananthapuram, Kochi, Coimbatore, and Madurai all have airfields capable of operating the largest aeroplanes. So, the kind of capability that India has in this part of the world is not matched by any other state. The Americans on Diego Garcia have the capability, but we are not comparing ourselves with America; certainly with regard to any other state, our capabilities are much greater.

China's Interests I, now move on to China's interests in the region before we come to the India-China interface. Sitting in Bengaluru it would be very difficult to say what Chinese interests are. One has to be sitting in Beijing for that to discern the Chinese mind (which you have just heard is not possible to do). But I have found two things in my several visits to Chinaand discussions there. By and large, I see a general consensus in China that it is the major Asian power. It is consistent with its destiny to be that kind of power. Two, China will at some time be at par with the United States of America, whether that happens in 10, 20 or 30 years. As a goal to be achieved this aspiration exists, and it is consistent with China's view of itself as the Middle Kingdom. It is not a unanimous view because there are numerous rational Chinese who say that they must recognize the constraints under which they function. These people believe that it is better for China to be realistic; there was no sense in being too assertive, it was also necessary to present a soft face, and so on. In some things we are seeing a mismatch, but the sense which I get is of their being able to present a more co-operative face with India.

The India-China Interface What are the facets of the India-China interface? The negative facets are of course 1962, the nuclear and military help to Pakistan, the assistance of different kinds to our neighbors in South Asia, knowing full well that these affect India's sensibilities.

But now look at the positive facets. Bilateral trade, howsoever skewed, may approach $80 billion this year. Maybe we are exporting raw materials and importing manufactures, but things are changing and efforts to change it must continue. But $80 billion of trade is $80 billion of trade. Figures can't be discounted. That is one positive.

The second is China's involvement with India across the table in a number of multi-lateral forums—the ASEAN Regional Forum, the East Asia Summit, ASEAN Defence Ministers Plus, the Shanghai Cooperation Organization, India-US-China Trilateral and BRICS. In climate change and in some other matters we agree, on some other matters we may not agree. But there is engagement across the board.

And what I rate the third very important positive is the very muted Chinese response to the Agni 5 test, when they knew fully well what the purpose of Agni 5 is. It is not to reach Islamabad or anywhere else—it is to head towards their territory. But their response has been muted. So, there is bad news and there is good news.

China's Vulnerabilities Having said that, the Chinese also realize that they have serious vulnerabilities in the energy line running through the Indian Ocean region and no matter what they may do, they will not by themselves be able to ensure the security of this energy line. Their four-year presence in the Gulf means nothing. All any navy—whether from Norway, Italy, Thailand, or Singapore—needs to maintain a presence for this much time is fuel, water and provisions. But naval presence means the ability to operate under opposition if necessary, and to have the necessary maritime domain awareness and information, surveillance capability, and airpower. Right now, the PLA(Navy) has none of these three. A time may come when they may have all these three things, but that time has not come and the Chinese are the first to realize this constraint. One can see over the last four years a nuanced change in the way in which they are looking at things, in the way they understand India's capabilities here and their desire to engage. You could say that they are doing it because they are seeing India and US coming close together, or that they are seeing this pivot to Asia Pacific, and so they better have their own options in this area. But nevertheless that is the fact of the matter.

The India-China Military Equation What is the India-China military equation? I will make two caveats here. One, I am not going to touch the nuclear issue, because that is a different ball game, it requires a different seminar, and it is not a military question. My second caveat is that I am not going to talk numbers because, first, I don't know them, and second, there are people here who know much more about these numbers than I do. So, let me just state the overall facts and go in the order—Land, Air and Sea.

The Land Equation It is true that the Chinese borders' infrastructure has increased greatly in the last several years. It is true that they can mobilize quickly and deploy quickly around the border as they find it necessary. These two are given. Their ability to put in place on the border a military force, a land force—is much more than it was let us say 25 years ago. What about the Indian scene? We have been very slow on the border infrastructure. It is only now beginning to start, with some increase in our troop strength. So, yes, there is an asymmetry in the land equation on the border. Having said that, the ability of the Indian Army to impose unacceptable punishment on the Chinese is very much more than it was in 1962, at least militarily. What other penalties the Chinese might also get is another matter. But militarily, the ability of our army to impose unacceptable punishment on a military adventure is not to be discounted.

Airpower Equation Indian air power is in no way inferior to that of the Chinese. It is true that they have a larger number of aeroplanes, many of them quite old, but the operating conditions and environment, the places from which we take off, the places from where they take off at the higher altitudes create a situation where in air power terms, the IAF air power cannot be ignored by the Chinese when they make their calculations.

Equation at Sea There is no discounting or disputing the fact that the asymmetry at sea lies comprehensively in favour of India, unlike on land.

So, if you look at the totality: on land, the asymmetry is to our disadvantage, but our capability to impose punishment is quite high; in the air there is no asymmetry; at sea there is asymmetry to our advantage. I think the Chinese recognize this and to that is attributable in some measure the type of positions that they have been taking in recent times. Let me say that all this focuses on one caveat; that when we do our planning as security planners we do not at all worry about possible Chinese *intentions*—we plan on their *capabilities*. That is the *sine qua non* of military planning and I am sure that is being done in the Headquarters of the three Services.

China in the Indian Ocean Let me spend two minutes on a subject which everybody talks about, and examine China as a player in the Indian Ocean region. Let me begin with the constraints. How will it get out of its West Pacific clutch? One: they have the Japanese sitting on one side, they have the Americans sitting on another, and there is no access to open seas. Two: how does it access the Indian Ocean region without passing through the Straits of Malacca, the Sunda Straits, or the Lombok Straits; these channels are choke points against entry into the Indian Ocean region. Three: how does it operate credibly in the Indian Ocean? I have just mentioned some of the reasons why it cannot. Many people keep on referring to a thing called 'string of pearls'. What are 'strings of pearls'? China is busy developing some port facilities in Myanmar, in Sri Lanka and in Gwadar and the fear is that at some time to come, these facilities will be available to the Chinese. Seychelles has offered China port facilities and they have port facilities in Muscat. What are port facilities? The availability of port facilities enables a ship to replenish its food and water and gives an opportunity to its crew for some rest. They don't enable credible operations. Credible operations are enabled if these port facilities are converted into base facilities, which afford docking, repair, and air-supplied logistics, storage for equipment, spares and armament. When a country decides to provide others this kind of facility, they are making a major political decision. Let me tell you that at the height of our cooperation with the Soviet Union, when the Vishakhapatnam naval base had been developed based on a Soviet project report, with Soviet assistance, we never agreed to the Soviet request for their ships to enter Vishakhapatnam. One might say that India as a big country could resist such pressures. Will Sri Lanka be able to resist such pressures? Of course, they will be. China is 3,000 miles away. India is 26 miles away. There are 60 million Tamils sitting 26 miles away. So, to expect that anybody in Colombo would happily grant base facilities to China in Hambantota would be a little naïve. But, if it does happen it will be a serious failure of Indian diplomacy. It will show that we have not been able to give to our Indian Ocean interests the type of attention that we should have given.

Future Chinese Stance So, what do I expect in a Chinese approach to the security questions? I expect to see a continuing assertive posture in the East and South China Sea. Something or the other appears to be happening at Senkaku almost every day. We can expect to see a continuing assertive position on Taiwan and on Tibet, including Arunachal Pradesh which they call Lower Tibet—I cannot see any Chinese accommodation on Lower Tibet in the foreseeable future. Therefore, I do not expect a border conflict resolution any time soon. But the border is tranquil and that is the plus point in the scene. I expect to see a continuing Chinese effort towards establishing what they call a first Island chain capability at sea which means a line stretching from Japan, Taiwan and Philippines. Right now, they don't have credible operating capability in this part of the sea. So, I expect to see improvement and enhancement and I expect to see a greater Chinese effort to get what they call ability to carry out regional conflicts under informationalized conditions which means under high technology categories. I expect to see from them more efforts to developing flexibilities in the Indian Ocean region in whatever way; whether these will result in bases is something we will have to see.

India's Strategic Response So, what should be India's strategy in responding to this kind of scenario? Let me start off with the bottom-line which I have already mentioned, that we must understand their military capabilities and plan adequately dissuasive capabilities. We must recognize our advantages in the Indian Ocean region and enhance them to the extent that we can. We must advance our security cooperation agreements which we already have with a large number of countries in this region. Only two days ago, the ASEAN countries and India have agreed unanimously that they must promote maritime security cooperation. We must be more pro-active to ensure our interests in major IOR littorals—Bangladesh, Sri Lanka, Maldives, Seychelles, Mauritius, Gulf, Oman, and Muscat as we are already doing. But we must enhance our efforts.

Confrontation, Cooperation or Competition Let me end by answering the theme question that had been raised in the paper that Ravi Ganesh sent to us. What are we seeing? Are we seeing cooperation, competition, or confrontation? I think I will agree with Mohan completely that I am not even looking at confrontation between India and China. Both sides realize what it means, both sides understand the capabilities of the other side. There may be a very small skirmish, but they all know that the moment the skirmish last beyond two or three days, war possibilities loom around the horizon and neither of them are interested in that kind of scenario. We may see cooperation in a limited way—yes in some respects, as I have mentioned in multilaterals, and I am seeing signs of engagement. Six months ago, four Indian warships visited Shanghai and from all reports, the type of reception and treatment that the Chinese authorities gave them was more than that the Indian warships have ever received from many countries in visits in recent times. We have seen the recent visit of the Chinese Defence Minister to India, where he has said that they would like to do joint exercises at sea and I think that will come to pass. There is nothing wrong in India being proactive in engagement because it gives us more options, it broadens our strategic space, diplomatically and politically, and it only adds to the advantage. Do I see competition? Yes. One can see competition in location of markets, in location of energy sources, and in many other spheres. Some degree of competition and some degree of mismatch is bound to occur. But, by and large, I see a scene which is not hostile to India's security concerns in the foreseeable future. Thank you.

Presentation 3: Changes at the Top: Domestic Dynamics After the 18th CPC Congress

C.V. Ranganathan

Indo-Pessimism Hearing Mr Mohan Guruswamy, I must say my Indo-pessimism diminished a little because he gave a very refreshing perspective, looking far ahead in the future of the economic scenario. And hearing Admiral

Das, whatever lingering Indo-pessimism one would have had was completely wiped away. I think both speeches put a proper perspective on the enormous media hype that has built up the average Chinese man to somebody 10 ft. tall.

The 18th CPC Congress The speech of the outgoing General Secretary of the CPC extends to something like 46 pages of closely typed material which for my sins I had to go through rather carefully. The Chinese have had a 5-yearly Communist Party of China Congresses and at least from 1992, the transitions of power in the leadership of the Chinese Communist Party have been orderly and peaceful as far as the outer world could see. This has been largely because regardless of the fact that he himself had been the paramount leader for a long period, and Mao Zedong before him had been there almost forever, causing a lot of damage in his last year, that wise man Deng Xiaoping laid down that there should be a maximum tenure for Party leaders of ten years, and he also prescribed an age limit. So the conclaves which are attended in huge numbers by practically the entire top hierarchy of the Party and include advisors, Party school and leading provincial leaders sort out all intra-Party or factional differences within themselves. After the 1992 Congress the agendas for discussion are very well prepared, which is a huge transformation from the time of charismatic leaders such as Mao and Deng.

Hu Jintao—A Brief Portrait A brief portrait of the outgoing General Secretary of the Party Hu Jintao would be useful. He was the quintessential Party figure who joined the Communist Youth League as a student and was a witness to the Proletarian Cultural Revolution in Beijing. He then became a member of the Communist Party of China and was initially sent to somewhat backward provinces including Tibet and Gansu. It wasn't till the 1980s that he came back to the Centre. Unlike his successor Xi Jinping, he is not what the Chinese call a princeling. Hu Jintao had the patronage of both Deng Xiaoping as well as another very famous figure called Hu Yaobang, the General Secretary of the Party. In 1989, I happened to be present in China and I was a witness to the famous Tiananmen Square incident where the Chinese used force to disperse the demonstrators. The immediate occasion for people to congregate and show their dissatisfaction with the Party was the funeral of Hu Yaobang. The gathering then escalated into demands which met with rather autocratic handling by Deng Xiaoping, who after all was the father of nascent reforms and liberalism. But nonetheless military force was used to quell the perceived threat to the Party's supremacy, and the rest is history.

In 1993 soon after the demise of the Soviet Union, Hu Jintao became the head of the Central Party School, which is a think-tank of the Party. The collapse of the USSR had caused enormous investigation in China and the answer they came up with to avoid the Soviet Union's fate was to raise living standards, raise the GDP, emphasize economic growth and prove that the Communist Party was capable of delivery. As Head of the Party School, Hu Jintao is credited with having a coherent ideological approach to this crisis. As early as in 1997, Hu Jintao was inducted as Standing Committee member, though Jiang Zemin was still the General Secretary of the Party. He became General Secretary in 2002, President of the country in 2003, and Chairman of the Party Central Military Commission in 2004. So, looking at his tenure in high positions from 1992, he was a figure who had been in power for sixteen years; and as a strict observer of Party rules and discipline, it came as no surprise that he willingly handed over the offices of General Secretary of the Party and Chairman of the Party Central Commission when the time came. This was in sharp contrast to his predecessor Jiang Zemin who had held on to the Chairmanship for two years after he ceased being General Secretary. In 2013, Hu Jintao will also hand over the office of the President. His successor Xi Jinping paid him great tribute for following proper Party procedure which his predecessor had flouted.

Hu Jintao's Report at the Congress It is important to look at some aspects of this report because this is a legacy that Xi Jinping will inherit. Unlike earlier reports, this one does not spend innumerable pages about China's achievements. Achievements, undoubtedly, there were—after all Hu Jintao's era of ten years as General Secretary of the Party has coincided, as Guruswamy pointed out, with the Chinese economy becoming the second in the world, overtaking Japan and building up its exchange reserves. But, the emphasis is less on achievements and more on the defects and the deficiencies of the Chinese growth model. Obviously, the 2008 financial failure of the West had affected China deeply but more than that, the early emphasis of his predecessor as well as his own emphasis in his early days, on economic growth and stability at all cost, had resulted in enormous disparities in the domestic, economic and social situation of the people—the '*aam admi*' in China. Hu Jintao had the difficult job of justifying the Party's performance and restoring its credibility. He did this by tracing at great length the continuing lineage and the correctness of the Party, looking at the entire history of the Communist Party of China over 90 years.

The main theoretical guidance of the Party corresponds in Hu Jintao's definition to the four decades—one of Marxism or Mao Zedong Thought, followed by Deng Xiaoping Theory, followed by his predecessor Jiang Zemin's Three Represents, and Hu Jintao's own contribution to the mnemonics—the scientific outlook on development.

'The Three Represents' is Jiang Zemin's enunciation to open up the Party; not just confining it to workers and peasants which it was originally, but to all the 'productive work forces' which include entrepreneurs, businessmen, and intellectuals. Although people belonging to this category were bit slow to take advantage of this opening, today the Party stands at 82 plus million cadres which shows how vast the Party presence is in various aspects of China's national mosaic. One phrase which occurs again and again in the ideological part is 'Socialism with Chinese characteristics'. The Chair in his opening remarks spoke about the Chinese sense of exceptionalism. Here is a clear example of that exceptionalism: of the Chinese telling the world and their own people that socialism has to be with Chinese characteristics, which gives them the ideological freedom to evolve more liberal policies. This Chinese exceptionalism is also underlined in the clear disavowal of any imitation of the Western model. As I have said to the Chinese and this surprised them a lot, 'the only people I can compare you with are the Americans who also think they are exceptional.' Needless to say some may agree with me but there is never any real in-depth discussion.

Hu Jintao is extremely candid about recognizing China's deficiencies and two sentences in this I think are worth quoting in full: 'The issue of what path we take is of vital importance for the survival of the Party, the future of China, destiny of the Chinese nation and the well-being of the people.' The salience of this is that there is complete recognition of the Chinese model's lack of progress in political reform, social reform and even economic reform. It has been 'unsustainable, uncoordinated and unbalanced', in my view, these three words capture many aspects extending from social to the political scene where people are demanding more, and to the environmental scene. With this sort of frankness, Hu acknowledges what is wrong and brings in his creation of the scientific way of development.

Substance of Hu Jintao's Proposed Reforms Let me now turn to the substance of the reforms that he is suggesting. I mentioned earlier that they realized with the Soviet Union's collapse is that overall growth and well-being of the people form a compact where by the Party ensures its continuing survival; this obviously has to be done in a far better social milieu. The economic structural reforms that he is suggesting are: One, to ensure a balance between the role of the Government and that of the market; two, to follow more closely the rules of the market and ensure better administrative management capacity of the Government; and three, the recognition that a State cannot be lopsidedly only in favour of State-owned enterprises. The State should make it a level playing field with non State-owned enterprises. This has been talked about but it has been affirmed emphatically this time. The other thing is of course recognizing the great imbalance rural and urban development and ensuring a better balance between the two. Guruswamy earlier talked about taxes and how the Government of India can never hope to raise its revenue without increasing the taxes. In this case, there is a clear acknowledgement that if one has to ensure better distributive justice one needs to raise not only income tax but also indirect taxes. There are of course many other facets of economic reforms, but I have dealt with what is seen by the general public in China as well as the outer world about the monopolistic control of the economy through State-owned enterprises.

Turning to political reforms, the expression 'People's democracy' is used many times as being the soul of socialism with Chinese characteristics and the urging is to make 'People's democracy' more extensive. Now, what it actually seems to imply is greater supervision of the work of the Party cadres and the bureaucracy by the general public, close consultations with the people, particularly if big infrastructure projects are involved. There were recent reports in the papers about a chemical factory which was sought to be built was stopped because of people's protests that it would environmentally damage their surroundings. So, this is the point—that when projects are built, there should be greater consultation. Then, they talk of having greater consultation with the people before legislation and of extending the election system to non-Party members in local Congresses. Till now it has been dominated by Party members, but now the urge is to open it to more non-Party people and to duplicate the central structure of a National People's Congress where there is a change-over every five years. In 2013, there will be a new Prime Minister and a new President, and local Congresses should encourage debate and discussion and elected people should make a far greater contribution to local legislation. In other words, the thrust is on greater participation by the people under the overall supervision of the Party. In this manner it will become far more people-oriented, at least in theory.

The social field is one other in which there has been the biggest public protest because of the prevailing real and perceived inequities in access to education, health, and social security. There is therefore a great deal mentioned in the social reforms section about how the social security net has to now include all residents— urban and rural. One of the big reforms suggested is a change in the infamous registration system. In China, the average person is supposed to die where he is born and if he migrates in search of a job to a town from the countryside, he will have neither social security nor free health care, nor will his children have access to education. There are millions drifting around in towns with no entitlement, on the backs of whom China's infrastructure and roads, which are the envy of the world, are built.

The next important element is about the Party. I have already talked about not just the expansion of the Party but the envisaged role it will play in each of these segments of reforms. While it puts greater power in the hands of the Party cadre, it also imposes a greater responsibility, provided there is a corresponding awakening of the conscience of the people about their role in these proposals. So a great deal of the report is dedicated to a moral rearmament drive of the Party and this includes the rank and file as well as the Party leadership. Hu Jintao points to an impending crisis by posing the question 'Where is China heading?' and he goes on to say 'Combating corruption and promoting political integrity which is a major political issue and of great concern to the people is a clear cut and long term commitment to the Party. If we fail to handle this issue well, it could prove fatal to the Party and even cause the collapse of the Party and the fall of the State.' I have heard Chinese talking about the corruption and crisis. But, I don't recall anything put strongly as this at the highest Party level at the most august event that they have once in five years. He goes on to charge the Party to 'observe a code of conduct on clean governance, observe strict discipline, strengthen supervision over your families and staff, and never seek privilege.' Now I wonder whether this should be circulated in our country.

Bo Xilai Episode At this point it may be opportune to talk about a gentleman called Bo Xilai. Bo Xilai was a princeling, the son of one of the closest admirers of Mao, Bo Ipo, who lived right up to the Tiananmen Square incident. It was with him and a few other elders that Deng Xiaoping decided to send the army to disperse the demonstrators. Bo Xilai graduated out of Beijing University, joined the Party early, did a lot of field work in various provinces including in the Northeast in Liaoning and finally ended up in 2007 as member of the Politburo. In Chongqing, he was much applauded by the people for eliminating the mafia and in brief cleaning up the place. But all the time, Bo

Xilai harped back to the past. He recalled the slogans and the songs used in the Cultural Revolution period to infuse the public with a greater sense of public consciousness and serve society and it was rumored that he was aspiring to become a Standing Committee member of the Politburo to be elected in 2012. His wife, a prominent lawyer and business person, developed links to a Briton who was murdered, according to the Chinese by her, for which she has paid the price. Bo Xilai, too, had his own moral turpitude issues. So, the Party came down extremely heavily on him, withdrew his Politburo and National People's Congress membership so that he would not have immunity against prosecution. His prosecution is expected to take place soon.

Earlier I talked about Mao Zedong Thought being part of the hagiography or the pantheon of the mnemonics of Chinese theoretical guidance. The 1981 resolution of the Party came to the definite conclusion that the Cultural Revolution was a tremendous mistake by Mao done in his later years which has caused China enormous damage. So this case is a warning to all Party members, 'Do not draw Mao out of context for your own political ambitions.' But there were other charges against him. There is a procedure, a precedent and an expected maintenance of a low profile for leaders and Hu Jintao was the archetypical representation of such a Party figure. Bo Xilai had transgressed in violating this procedure and not living up to this expectation.

Acceptability of the State In any country, whether authoritarian or democratic, acceptance of the State depends on three things: contestation, participation and legitimation. Contestation in China never existed till 1992. What Mao or Deng said was everything. Participation is now being enlarged because of the tremendous amount of dissatisfaction with inequity, lack of access, the rich-poor divide, and the urban-rural divide Lastly, legitimation. There is absolutely no doubt in my mind that given rising prosperity, given a rising middle class, I think there was a clear cynicism about the Party. There was less and less commitment and this as I said within a hugely expanded Party membership also obviously applied to the Party cadre and Bo Xilai was of course the highest profile person caught. But, there is a very strong Disciplinary Inspection Commission Committee which makes an annual statement of the number of people proceeded against for corruption and I think this is something that we can look into.

On this subject of contestation, along with Alka Acharya, we are doing a study in Delhi of the 18th Party Congress and one of the rather brilliant papers produced was an examination of the Chinese use of the internet, particularly blogs, to be expressive. Now, one particular instance relates directly to the tremendous uses you can put the Chinese language to, because the language is so constructed that there are many homonyms and it is through the context and pronunciation that you derive the meaning. Thus advantage can be taken to express sarcasm or criticism. But there are red lines. You cannot under any circumstances criticize leaders of the Party. You cannot under any circumstances say 'Down with the Communist Party'. You cannot under any circumstances say that the Western model of democracy namely of separation of powers between legislature, executive and judiciary is what we want. But as the Nobel Prize winner Mo Yan said when he was criticized by dissidents outside why he was not being more forthright about the restraints on him, 'Great literature can be written in any way; it need not be noisy but in its own silent way it can prove certain points which the noise makers also want to make.'

China at a Crucial Turning Point I for one think that China is in a very crucial turning point and that unless at least some of the extensive reforms that Hu Jintao has suggested are rigorously implemented, what Hu Jintao wanted is not going to be achieved. But it is difficult to predict what will happen and all one can say is that China has become an even more interesting country to watch than it has been in the past thirty or odd years that I have seen it.

Thank you.

Presentation 4: Outcome of the 18th CPC Congress: Influence on China's External Policy

Alka Acharya

Myth of the Inscrutable Chinese I shall first dwell on the aspect on which I have been asked to speak: the foreign policy dimension that emanates from the 18th Party Congress—and then devote some time to implications for China-India relations. I will begin slightly tangentially by taking up this theme of this inscrutable Chinese that was mentioned by the Chairman at the very outset—the fact that it is very difficult to understand them. Over the years it seems to me that by harping on the theme of inscrutable Chinese, we have actually covered up the fact that we have actually used it as an excuse not to devote sufficient resources to understand the Chinese. In terms of the places where China is being studied, of resource people, of the number of people who know the language and who follow Chinese debates in their language closely, the situation is absolutely pathetic. We still do not have people who are monitoring China's varied developments and complexities on a regular basis. A few scholars gain some insights because of which they take contrarian positions; they are promptly dubbed as panda-huggers or China lovers. One's understanding, ironically, actually makes one a candidate for being labelled a panda-hugger. This kind of misconception abounds and it is high time we woke up to the fact that the need of the hour is to pump in several times the resources that are currently being devoted to building up our own reserves and strengths on studying China. We talk about how we completely accept Western views, and how important it is to develop an indigenous perspective on China: but we do not allocate the resources to develop that indigenous perspective. When doing my research as a PhD candidate, I was going through the Second World War issues of TIME magazine. I found one amazing article which was titled 'How to recognize our friends the Chinese from our enemies the Japanese', which went on to say that the Japanese was normally short and had a rather fierce expression, the Chinese was normally tall and had a benign expression! I feel we have been sliding into some kind of easy, broad, generalizations about what the Chinese are and it occurs to me as a student of international relations and of China and somebody who is asking 'What is it that makes the Chinese inscrutable? Why is it so very difficult to look at the Chinese as yet another large people who have emerged out of the colonial exploitative phase and are determined to rise and get rid of that past of humiliation, and to protect their interests?' Of course one can say that they have no right to impinge on our interests and all that—that is fine and valid—but one can at least begin with the notion that they are like any other society, and, like any other nationalistic people, they act in pursuit of their interests. So, let us then examine how and why it is that these objectives are becoming such a source of concern for a lot of people.

Significance of 18th CPC Congress Coming to the theme of the 18th Party Conference and its significance, I bow to Ambassador Ranganathan's insights. His long experience has enabled him to get his finger on their pulse. I am sure he does not subscribe to the inscrutability thesis so much. The significance of these Party Congresses is important to understand. The primary objective of the Congress is domestic; its implications are domestic, but the significance is enormous. The People's Republic of China today is the creation of the Communist Party of China, and the Party Congress is a most significant event because it has to do with a transition within the Communist Party organization. In short, we are now looking at the new leadership of China. We do not have sufficient material to assess what Xi Jinping's foreign policy agenda is going to be or how he is likely to shape Chinese foreign policy. We can only conjecture. If we look at the report, we will see that there are only three sections within that report which touch upon issues bearing on foreign policy concerns; even here we see that the treatment is more in terms of the effect on the domestic sector. Thus it is largely a domestic event; but given the fact that China's domestic and external concerns are now becoming increasingly intertwined, it is important to see what the significant issues that have been flagged out in this report are.

Run-Up to the 18th CPC Congress In the run-up to the Conference there were objective assessments about this major transition that was taking place within the Party. But it was amusing to see that the international coverage of the Congress was dominated by the Bo Xilai incident. In an informal discussion with Kevin Rudd who was passing through Delhi just before I came here, he explained to me that from his discussions with very senior officials it was clear that Xi Jinping's illness was not because of any sinister plotting, but that he had genuinely had a serious tonsillitis infection. There were different interpretations to the Bo Xilai episode in fact as well. I will just make a brief comment about this: It is a fact that Bo Xilai was projecting himself, that he was using Maoist revolutionary slogans to give voice to a sense of disquiet among a large range of people, and that he was touting a model which was specific to the place of which he was the Mayor. All these things were there and it was not as if he had not been doing it for some time. But his fall was related to the concern within the Party that somewhere, scholars have been talking about alternate models and criticizing the reforms. Implicit in Bo Xilai's Chongqing model was also criticism of the way the reforms were going on, but then he made the mistake of putting himself above the Party and as Ambassador Ranganathan just said, you cannot challenge the supremacy of the Party. It was being conveyed to lower-ranking people that this was a sin that would not be tolerated.

The New Leadership We have now information coming out about the kind of person Xi Jinping or Li Keqiang is, and there is a debate about the princelings and the Tuanpai who rise from the lower ranks. What we have to understand is that now the new leadership which is going to take China over the next 10 years is going to be one in which factionalism has come to be a part of normal Party functioning. When Deng Xiaoping started the reforms in 1978 with the backdrop of the Cultural Revolution, it was easy to forge a consensus on market reforms. Jiang Zemin and Hu Jintao built on that consensus; the new leadership in now to embark on the fourth generation reforms which in many ways will flow from what has happened, but they are going to be testing the limits of China's socialist character. Xi Jinping being known to be a votary of private enterprise, the question arises how he is going to weave that into China's socialism. Despite the existence of factions, it is not as if the Party is about to break up; and if we take this view the debates and discourses on reforms within the Party take on a much more manageable aspect. Xi Jinping is of course belongs to new generation of techno-savvy people, he is more experimental; this renewed moral drive that he will have to push has really shaken up China and there is a great deal of unhappiness and opposition to the imbalances that have appeared in Chinese society. These are also people who are experimenting with new ideas. It was reported that in 2010 as Vice-president, Xi Jinpingsent personalized text messages to one million cadres at the lower levels greeting them for the New Year. So there is a new dimension in terms of changes in the way the Party is going to be operating.

Sections Dealing with Foreign Policy Issues The 9th, 10th and 11th sections of the report address aspects which have bearings on external issues. One section focuses on national defence and armed forces. In this, the emphasis is on linking defence and development, and on the need to build a posture commensurate with China's international standing that is linked to its development interests. So, there are specific targets in the whole process of military modernization. But there is a very clear underlining of the fact that the Party controls the Government. That comes out very clearly in this section and there is emphasis on the Chinese-style path that integrates development of military and civilian sector.

In a section on 'One country, two systems' and the advancing of China's reunification there is a clear statement of the familiar precept that no concessions will be made on territorial sovereignty. But interestingly, they make the point that China has received international acceptance of its territorial sovereignty and approach to integration. They mention Taiwan, Hong Kong and Macau as instances of the international community's appreciation of the Chinese way of integration; they talk about the need to develop relations peacefully with the objective of further integration. The interesting aspect in this section which is aimed at a domestic audience is the claim of international approval of China's approach to integration; and this ties up with later statements on building a united country and an inclusive approach to minorities and groups which are somewhat disenchanted.

The last section describes how China views the world and here there are some aspects with interesting implications. Peace and development are identified as underlying trends of our times; yet the apprehension is expressed that this trend might not endure, resulting in turbulence. Similarly while the trend towards multi-polarity and economic globalization was deepening, some turbulence could arise because of non-acceptance of differing paths to development and different views on how societies should be structured. The report addresses the issues of the global financial crisis as well as signs of hegemony, interventionism, local turmoil, and the arbitrary use of force. This survey concludes with an expression of the belief that a peaceful global environment demands that countries recognize and respect each other's differences, allow all countries to evolve in their own way and cooperate to solve the problems of the world. This message has been at the core of China's White Paper on Peaceful Road to Development which came out in 2011.

Assessment of Foreign Policy Dimension The foreign policy dimension of Hu Jintao's speech can best be assessed by examining the main trends shaping Chinese foreign policy and its orientation in the contemporary period. An assessment of China's actions and the way in which these have been perceived, and then of the kind of concerns that confront Xi Jinping, will give an idea of the foreign policy implications.

Control of Foreign Policy in China There are two issues which have been part of the foreign policy discourse not just within China but outside, too. The first is the trend of multiple voices emanating from within China on foreign policy issues. There is a lack of clarity about who is in command; when there is the PLA that is increasingly pressing for hard-line positions on China's various global interests, or the Ministry of Foreign Affairs that now has now different interest groups, particularly that of state-owned enterprises driving the agenda of the foreign policy establishment. Questions have arisen about the role of the Supreme Leader over the last 2–3 years and the consensus has been that it is the PLA which is driving the agenda, particularly pertaining to the recent developments in the South China Sea. The Ministry of Foreign Affairs, under the State Council, is supposedly the principal actor, but it is clear that there is no supreme figure who wields the ultimate authority as it used to be in the days of Deng Xiaoping or Jiang Zemin. This is particularly so because the PLA is conspicuously absent in the Standing Committee of the Politburo.

The assessment is that the control of foreign affairs is undergoing a kind of evolution and an attempt is being seen to revive the authority of the Leading Small Group on foreign policy. This core group has the foreign minister, commerce minister, and representation from the PLA. The indications are that once again there will be a more cohesive and coordinated system of policy-making, ending the multiple voices that have created problems among China's neighbours and the world outside regarding the direction of China's foreign policy.

China's New Assertiveness The second issue over the last one year has been whether the understanding of China having suddenly adopted a more assertive stance is true, and if so, wise? The stronger proponents of assertiveness believe that China should now stand up and learn to say no; this is being seen in the media and it is having an impact on society as well. Serious scholars are, however, questioning the wisdom of revisiting or even discarding the Deng Xiaoping precept of keeping a low profile. Their argument is that Deng did not intend to use the low profile approach as a tactic, but as a long-term strategic maxim designed to allow China to build its resources and attain a better position to promote mutually beneficial cooperation from a position of strength. Stress therefore is on continuing on the path of peaceful development; since 2009 the pronouncements of the leadership are all about 'peaceful development' and 'peaceful rise'. About this time the evolution of this term—'development interests' has come about which is an interesting formulation that national interests must not be viewed from only a self-oriented perspective. Development interests would be inclusive of the interests of all cooperating parties.

Xi Jinping's first press conference after the 18th Party Congress did not talk much about foreign policy concerns; he merely spoke about the need to focus on strengthening China and on making it inclusive and harmonious with all minorities. His stress was on minorities, nationalities and different ethnic groups. In the end he just says that China has a lot to learn from the world, but the world also has a lot to learn from China. He makes the point regarding mutuality—that China's development is good for the world. This policy argument is something which has been in place for the last decade.

But nevertheless China's new assertiveness has become a concern. One source of this assertiveness is of course China's rise as an economic player, about which we heard from a previous speaker. This economic rise has enabled it to play a much more important role in global financial and commercial institutions. China has increased its contribution to the United Nations, it plays a greater role in foreign peace keeping institutions, it is talking about having a presence in the Arctic, and it is talking about the need to now formulate new regime in the cyber and space law. It is increasing its global presence and its involvement in global issues.

New Foreign Policy Priorities The question is whether this greater economic power and economic presence translate into a super power. That the Chinese firmly discard. They agree that they have the capabilities, so they would talk about issues which concern them and the world community at large. But they say they have no intention to become he gemonic or seek control. That is their line of argument and therefore this particular document talks about the priorities. It is clear that China's chief concerns are going to be the United States and how they emerge out of the global financial crisis. So China will give priority to the developed world.

Next come the other major powers; this implies countries like India and its neighbours, but specifically BRICS. From 2009 onwards there has been a debate with some holding that China should now focus on BRICS as its long-term strategic plank. These are people who actually negate the G2 concept saying that it is shortsighted to think in terms of a duopoly, that China's development interests would best be served by taking the BRICS as the plank for furthering its strategic interests.

Whereas earlier on, Chinese policy pronouncements spoke of the developed world, of the developing world and third world, now there is a need being increasingly articulated that the foreign policy must be much more specific and country-oriented. This view holds that there should now be far importance given to China's bilateral relationships keeping in mind various emerging trends. So we will definitely see a greater significance being accorded to BRICS, which would mean that India would be somewhere higher up in their concern. There is a lot of debate in this country about whether the Chinese take us seriously. In fact, the point inevitably arises every time the Chinese come, with them asseverating that India is very important to them. It is a fact that India is being studied with great interest and in great depth. My colleague Ambassador Vinod Khanna who has just been to the Chengdu conference came back and told us that Chinese students there are discussing their research on Kabir in flawless Bhojpuri; he said it was an eye-opener to him to see how much of work they are doing on India. They are trying to understand our history and our cultural dynamics in a way in which we are not. But, the developing world and the emerging economies are clearly the second rung.

The developing world is on the third rung. There were some reactions which mooted the possibility of the Chinese now neglecting the developing world. But what comes out clearly from the report is that the China would still continue to use its influence and power to give leadership to the developing world, because it is a strong arena for support, particularly at United Nations. It is clear that their priorities in the short-to-medium term are to focus on the developed world, and to get out the global financial crisis and all their concerns with the United States.

Achievements, A Source of Nationalism China's achievements have been a third set of sources of this nationalism, apart from the economic rise. From the time of the Olympics, the Chinese pride in the achievements of their nation became quite palpable. The nationalistic statements that are coming out from China cover a whole range. They are not from any specific community or interest group—they are from students and a range of scholars—and of course the pronouncements of the leadership of China's achievements are feeding this. It is definitely going to be a cause of concern. The Chinese spin on this is that it is not hegemonic, that this nationalism is an expression of pride in our achievements, and it is going to be peaceful. But that is an idealized representation.

The question for us in India will be how to interpret this nationalism. It is certainly going to be a constraint and I for one do not say that when they speak of public opinion as a constraint on their ability to take decisions it is just a kind of a blind. There is really a strong body of opinion which is emerging, and it is definitely going to be a restraint on the ability of the Chinese. When we talk about the Chinese suddenly taking a hard-line position on the boundary question, they do argue that people are beginning to question this. So we need to look into this more carefully, but I would say that it is going to be some kind of a limitation and is going to affect the way the Chinese project themselves. The emergence from the century of shame and humiliation, and their desire to proclaim that they have now arrived is part of that whole process.

China's Response to Regional Integration One more point about sources of the Chinese assertiveness has been the way in which it has ridden the waves of regional integration. When we look at South-East Asia on the one hand and Central Asia on the other, the Chinese have been successful in not only becoming central to the economic and political processes, but from being a participant in those processes, they are slowly coming to a position where they are determining the agenda. This may be done in a co-operative mode or they could use their economic clout to force their agenda. This is another area where we will have to keep our eyes open and analyse the trend. Of course, it is also important that we study these incidents carefully. In the case of the South China Sea which was given so much prominence, from 2009 onwards there has been a gradual escalation. But not much was heard about actions by the Philippines or Vietnam or Malaysia, nor was any importance to interactions between the US and China on the Law of the Seas convention. There are dynamics there which we need to study before we start taking positions.

Regional Role China's global role will continue in the dimensions that I have identified. Its regional role is undoubtedly going to be shaped by the recent talk about the US pivot. The Chinese view is that the US has never left the Pacific and they had always been there. Its concern is that an anti-China coalition is going to be created in the Pacific and in Southeast Asia. The question is whether the United States and the Chinese will be able to moderate their respective interests and work together. Judging from the time of Xi Jinping's Vice-presidential visit to the US in Jan-Feb 2011 to now, the statements reflect a sophisticated handling of the differences and there is an effort to accommodate each other. There are likely to be manifestations of both of these approaches.

The Choice before India India will therefore have to decide whether it wants to be seduced by the argument that our natural affinity as democratic countries necessitates cooperation with the US against the authoritarian country, or whether it looks closely at the reality and the arena of interaction between us and China.

Discussions

On completion of the last presentation the house was thrown open by the Chair for discussions.

China's Dollar Investments Akbar Khaleeli felt that since China had a surplus of dollars it would be more profitable for it to invest in mines and strategic resources in Africa and other places, rather than reinvest in America and get into the vicious circle that Mohan Guruswamy had described. This should be regarded as an important foreign policy factor.

Bimaru States Factor Moulik referred to Guruswamy's observations about the so-called Bimaru states with their abysmally low indices of social and economic progress, and asked how India could possibly overtake China, given that these very states were the ones with rapidly growing populations.

In his response Guruswamy said that as he had said earlier, total wealth had nothing to do with individual wealth. Huge income inequalities were piling up in India. Before the reforms started our income inequality was 0.3 per cent, and was now 0.6 per cent. But what he had talked about were overall growth figures, about overall growth figures, because size takes you up.

Border Dispute Resolved by ORF P.C. Nayak made the observation that the ORF seemed to have resolved the border dispute by giving Aksai Chin to China and Arunachal Pradesh to India—this could be seen on the internet.

Guruswamy responded that in the Constitution of India, the map of India does not include Aksai Chin. The present alignment was derived only in 1941. From 1890 we had the McCarthy-McDonald Line which is where we are today in actual ground terms. In 1941 some Russians were seen in Xinjiang so the British moved the border up again—they drew a new line and called it the border. The entire Great game was based on having buffers so that India was not contested and Russia was kept away. When the Constitution was written in 1950 there was no line—it was just dotted and left, saying that this was to be defined later. The McMahon line on the other hand, was clearly defined by a treaty with the Tibetans and the Chinese witnessed the treaty. The McMahon Line runs along the crest, or watershed; any cartographer would draw that line. What states do is create a strategic border. India cannot afford China any sub-Himalayan space—so there is no question of any negotiation there.

India China are Competitors, not Enemies Professor Jayaramu thanked the Asia Centre for putting together an excellent panel, two of them dealing with the domestic and 18th Party Congress and one dealing with economic issues and Vice Admiral Das speaking of the strategic. He said that he quite agrees with the common thread that the earlier first two speakers came up with; they said we are going to be competitors and rivals, but not enemies. That was fine, but we should keep our powder dry. Of course, military confrontation may not take place but skirmishes can.

Need to Work with the Chinese More Closely Professor Jayaramu also commented on the reference to the 'inscrutable Chinese'. If as Professor Acharya said we needed more funding, she was in the NSAB, which should take it up more seriously. He agreed with the speaker who had said that we should work with the Chinese more closely in multilateral forums. There was no point in us playing the American card and allowing the Americans to play the India card—those were outmoded ways of looking at it. Both India and China are important powers and need to come and work together. We talked about BRICS, but our political leadership doesn't do anything about it, and South Block cannot do it on its own unless the PMO supports it. We are going along with the Americans, whether in the G-10 or elsewhere, but not trying to explore possibilities for working with China. I quite agree that we should strengthen our linkages with the Chinese and work together at the multilateral forums.

Venkateswaran suggested that the Professor was slightly misled on this matter. We do cooperate with the Chinese in international and the Chinese themselves have expressed their appreciation of that. Sometimes we do not get a quid pro quo; that is a different matter. But we do cooperate with them. Ranganathan added that he agreed with that, and he had actually pointed that out.

Acharya, responding to the remark by Jayaramu that she should move more pro-actively about funding, said Ambassador Ranganathanwould bear her out that she had been making intense efforts for the past 10 years for increasing the funding: that was a sad tale, but it could be discussed later.

Referring to the Professor's comment that we should keep our powder dry, Admiral Das said that the theme of his military interface and equation was that no matter what the Chinese wanted or did not want to do, our military capabilities must be based on their military capabilities. So there is no question of this not being done. If confrontation was unlikely, it would be because of our having these capabilities.

Corruption in China R.A. Naik remarked that Guruswamy had made beautiful charts on different aspects of the economy; it would be interesting to see comparative chart of which country was more corrupt - India or China, and to estimate the effect of this on development.

The Chair interjected that in China, if one was caught for being corrupt, one was shot. In India, they let the corrupt out on bail to live on their ill-earned income.

Guruswamy responded that China is very corrupt, and one should not have any illusions about it. In June this year, Bloomberg news had a big story about how Xi Jinping's brother had amassed 1.8 billion dollars; Bloomberg was shut down in China in retaliation. But Chinese corruption is huge, but once in a while they make an example of someone like Bo Xilai. The illusion that it is only Indians who are corrupt is wrong—the Chinese are as bad.

Multiple Voices on Foreign Policy C.M. Reddy made the comment that Acharya had emphasized the fact that there was no single policy as far as many issues were concerned. He thought that was worth reiterating. The Finance Minister offered the excuse for our economic problems in India that it was because Hu Jintao could just wave a wand and everything would fall into place. That was not true and it is becoming much more obvious now that Hu Jintao did not have the kind of unilateral power to do things because his predecessor had packed the Standing Committee of the Politburo with his own people.

Need for Flexible Approach to Negotiation The second point Reddy made was about the relationship between India and China; we have to start with the premise that we have to negotiate with China, and balance the advantages. If we said that Aksai Chin for example is non-negotiable we would not be able to start at all. He was not saying that China had an inalienable right to Aksai Chin but negotiation was the need of the hour.

Acharya observed that Mohan Guruswamy had already taken a position which is more or less what Reddy was saying regarding Aksai Chin; the whole point was that unless we agreed that we would have to give something before we begin or at least recognized that it is open for discussion, we would not get anywhere.

Japanese Maritime Power and China's Acquisition of Naval Bases Venkatachalam felt that Admiral Das was very optimistic, which was good but we need to ensure that we do not become complacent. Admiral Das seemed to be quite forceful that a port facility in the South Asian region be it Gwadar or wherever else, would not necessarily become a base facility. He wondered what type of safeguards India ought to undertake so that it was not taken by surprise in case a port facility did become a base facility. That was his first question.

His second was how the Chinese view Japan as a maritime power and what the implications for China would be, in comparison to the American view, of an aggressive Japan in the region.

Admiral Das, answering the second question about Japan as a maritime power first, said that Japan has always been a maritime power. As far as China was concerned it was historically, like India, a continental power and would continue to be a continental power for some time to come. They did send Zheng He to the Indian Ocean twice, but they built the Great Wall, not a great navy. Our people sent the Cholas, the Satavahanas and the Pandyas all over South-East Asia but never built a navy. We are continental today and will continue to remain continental for some time because our concerns until now have been primarily continental. We are now understanding and recognizing our interests at sea and in the last several years, two decades specially, there has been a movement towards furthering our interests at sea and I think that is going to continue and it is not going to come down.

Regarding his optimism, Admiral Das said it was more a question of being pragmatic and realistic and being factual. He had traced the reasons why our asymmetries are to our advantage in certain areas, to our disadvantage in certain areas, and level in certain areas: in totality, the situation was that in any conflict we are not going to be easily defeated. Our ability to impose penalties on any adversary who wishes to enter into conflict is not negligible. That they may not defeat China is a different matter; but countries do calculate the balance between the gain and the penalty they can accept. Taking the totality of this he believed that the possibility of China entering into military conflict in the foreseeable future was not high provided we maintain our military dissuasive capability at the level with which we should.

Regarding port facilities, Admiral Das said that the so called client state has to take this decision for itself. It might get a trillion dollars or whatever, but it has to balance this against what it what it might lose. That is a calculation not easy to make for any country, and there is the factor of international opinion. As he had said, should any of these countries around us make their port facility into a base facility and give China military operating capabilities from that port then surely it would change the equation in the Indian Ocean region, where presently we are predominant.

India's Dependence on Defence Imports Muthu Kumar, addressing Admiral Das, said that he was happy that the Admiral had stated there would be no confrontation between India and China though there may be some skirmishes. He felt that we had been extremely fortunate: by the RM's admission, it seemed that the soldier's INSAS rifle was incapable of defending and we were going to import a standard weapon. Our Air Force weaponization is so poor that 99 per cent is imported. The aircraft are imported. The Navy is imported. He asked how we could sustain this kind of Armed Force and defend ourselves.

Admiral Das agreed that the INSAS rifle was at least 20 years old and required to be replaced; this was part of a normal ongoing process—things becoming out of date have to be replaced, and we have to find the best possible replacement. He did not want to comment on the INSAS rifle or on the weaponry of the Air Force—he thought enough efforts were being made. He would like them to be speedier, to ensure that our military capabilities were being enhanced; his own assessment was that by and large this was happening. He agreed there had been difficulties which could and should have been attended to. When the RM said that India is concerned about its military posture versus the Chinese he was absolutely right because this is what all of us are saying, because our military deterrence has to be sufficiently credible. Where there are gaps as in our border infrastructure, or in the Army troop presence in that area we have to make them good. He reiterated that when he said confrontation was not likely, he was not saying that it was not possible; he was simply saying the dimensions of the conflict are such that countries would have to do a serious calculation of what they would gain and what they would lose. Our interest mainly is that we should create the capability to be sufficiently dissuasive and credible. If we are doing that that's fine and the chances of a confrontation are not high—that's what I said.

Sino-Pakistan Nexus Acharya went on to make some observations regarding the Pakistan-China nexus. China's focus continues to be on economic development, but as it starts to look at its 'development interests', a term which as I mentioned is being increasingly brought into the discourse, the parameters of the Chinese modern economy will move beyond its national borders. In such a case, we would see a serious revaluation of many of its policies. With reference to Korea, the Korean peninsula and with reference to Pakistan, we have already seen a shift beginning. We need to monitor this carefully to identify options and opportunities that to break the China-Pakistan nexus. We keep talking about China's use of Pakistan for its own strategic interests and about Gwadar; can we visualize a scenario offering the Chinese the passage? It would cut the ground from many feet. That is out-of-the-box diplomacy and art of the possible. But we are seeing China shifting its positions, even on Korea, and we need to be alert to be able to take advantage of the opportunity it offers.

Guruswamy responded to Air Chief Marshal Major's remarks on the China-Pakistan nexus and agreed that it was very clear that one existed. The Chinese had given the Pakistan the Khushab 2 plant which is a plutonium line; they had given them all assistance in developing missiles—the new cruise missile which the Pakistanis have tested is a Chinese cruise missile which was originally got from Ukraine. This collaboration is an active programme which is on-going, and India should engage with the Chinese on that. They are now worried over India's relationship with Vietnam. The speaker had been in China the previous week and they had asked about our relationship with Vietnam. So he had told them that it was a relationship like theirs with Pakistan—higher than the highest mountain and deeper than the deepest ocean.

Indian Armed Forces Feel Let Down General Sampath Kumar said that he had no question, but as a soldier he wanted to make a small comment. In 1962, the Chinese attacked us brazenly and withdrew; that was our humiliation point. Then after the 1965 war, we gave away our gains. In 1971, we took 92,000 prisoners and freed them in a deal which did not settle anything. So today, the sentiment in the armed forces is that this country is letting them down. He asked why we were fighting at all. According to the General, this perception has percolated to the common man—the *aam admi*. Others may say that we must talk; but public sentiment and the sentiment of the armed forces are totally different. That is India's predicament.

The Chair thanked the questioner for his observations, and fully agreed with the General that we should not allow this easy-going approach with people who die defending our country; it was on television every day. People were waking up to this and he thought the Government should, too, rather than be indulgent with the Pakistanis or the Chinese or anybody else. He then thanked the General for his comments.

General Sampath raised a second point regarding our defence capabilities. But today, the actual fact was that there was very little left in the defence budget after pay and allowances, pensions and administrative expenditure. We had been in this situation for the last 25 years, and nobody had found a solution. The situation of the Armed forces as far as equipment was concerned was serious, and we have a long way to go to catch up.

Conclusion

In recent times China has pulled itself up by the bootstraps to claim the top rungs in all facets of comprehensive national power. A noticeable feature in China's advance has been clear indication of intent followed by a sustained and single-minded drive to attain its objectives. This characteristic has been manifested in several varied fields—in aerospace technology, in its rise from nowhere to become the world's leading shipbuilder, in the modernization of its military and in its economic surge.

But the rift of 1962 has never healed; for half a century, relations have stagnated in the 'cool to hostile' bandwidth. Chinese suspicions about India's intentions in Tibet and our protection of the Dalai Lama are matters never far below the surface. China's territorial claims on Arunachal Pradesh are kept alive by periodic diplomatic outbursts. China's covert and overt support to Pakistan in the military and strategic sphere is a major impediment to the betterment of relations.

The seminar covered various facets of the India-China relationship, and what a rising China portends for us. While well noting China's economic upsurge, the panel speaker struck a confident note for the long term because of several factors, a major one being the so-called demographic dividend India will enjoy with a young population.

The panel was unanimous that it was unlikely that China would adopt a confrontationist posture in its international dealings, particularly with India, although there would be rivalry and competition across the entire spectrum of Sino-Indian interactions.

The18th Congress and its impact on both in the internal and external dimension were analysed. There was agreement between the panel speakers that the changes in the leadership could bring changes also in China's style of functioning. Internally, it could be more inclusive with a greater representation of the people's concerns, and externally there was a possibility that China would become less dogmatic, show a softer international image, and focus on cooperative development.

An important facet of the seminar was the observation that India is not doing enough to study and understand China. If true, this is a puzzling phenomenon. While the current enthusiasm for intensifying the US-India relationship is well known, if not unanimously welcomed, India can ill afford to neglect the development of a deep understanding of our largest neighbour. There was a general consensus that there was question of India siding with any grouping in an anti-Chinese stance.

Sino-Indian relations could still go three ways from here—cooperative, competitive, or confrontational. The seminar has by and large leaned towards a mix of the first two scenarios. But as recent events have shown, China cannot be taken for granted, and their relationship with Pakistan strikes a jarring note in the context of their professed desire for warm and friendly relations with India.

Contributors

1. Dipanker Banerjee Dipanker Banerjee is a retired Major General who has studied strategic planning, disarmament, and regional and international security for over two decades. He has headed major think tanks and has participated in Track-2 dialogues with India's neighbours. He has been the head of the Institution of Peace and Conflict Studies (IPCS), at Delhi for the last seven years.
2. Alok Bansal Alok Bansal retired from the Navy as a Captain. He is a specialist in regional security with a focus on Pakistan. He contributes to journals and newspapers and has co-edited two books titled *Pakistan Occupied Kashmir: The Untold Story* and *Sri Lanka: Search for Peace*. His book *Pakistan at Crossroads: Balochistan in Line of Fire* is under publication.
3. M.K. Bhadrakumar M.K. Bhadrakumar was India's ambassador to Uzbekistan and Turkey. After retirement, he writes articles for journals and papers and is a columnist for two major national dailies. He has written extensively on Russia, China, Central Asia, and Pakistan and on the geopolitics of energy security.
4. Rajiv Bhatia Rajiv Bhatia has served in the External Affairs Ministry where he was responsible for India's relations with Bangladesh, Sri Lanka and Maldives. He was our High Commissioner in Kenya and Ambassador in Mexico, Myanmar and South Africa. He retired in 2010 and now lectures at the Foreign Service Institute, National Defence College and other institutions.
5. Rahul K. Bhonsle Brigadier Bhonsle is an Army veteran and a research scholar with the USI of India. His areas of interest include South Asia, future warfare and human security. He is a regular contributor to newspapers and journals and edits a monthly, *South Asia Security Trends*. His most recent work *Mumbai 26/11: Security Imperatives for the Future*, is an analysis of the Mumbai attack and its wider ramifications.
6. Sumant Chatterjee Brigadier Chatterjee is a graduate of the Defence Services Staff College, Wellington and the College of Defence Management, Secunderabad. He saw active service in the 1971 war with Pakistan and the

Kargil war of 1999. He has served as the Defence Adviser at the Indian High Commission at Dhaka.

7. Sreeradha Datta Datta is the Director of the Maulana Abdul Kalam Azad Institute of Asian Studies (MAKAIAS). While at the Institute for Defence Studies and Analyses (IDSA), she researched projects on the North-Eastern turmoil and Bangladesh . Her publications include *Bangladesh: A Fragile Democracy, The North-East: Complexities and Determinants* and *Caretaking Democracy: Political Process in Bangladesh 2006-08.*

8. Shanthie M. D'Souza Shanthie Mariet D'Souza is with the Institute for Defence Studies and Analyses (IDSA), and has a PhD in International Relations (American Studies) from the Jawaharlal Nehru University. Her area of research interest is Terrorism, Counter-terrorism, and insurgencies with special reference to Afghanistan. She has been a visiting Fulbright Scholar at Johns Hopkins University, Washington DC. She has conducted field studies in India and abroad, including Pakistan, Afghanistan, Jammu and Kashmir and India's North-East.

9. R.N. Ganesh Vice-Admiral Ganesh was the first Captain of India's first nuclear submarine. He retired from the Navy as the Flag Officer Commanding-in-Chief, Southern Naval Command. He has also been the Director General of the Indian Coast Guard. He was the Director General of the Indian nuclear submarine programme from 2000 to 2004. Currently he is adjunct faculty in the National Institute of Advanced Studies, Bangalore, and Director of the Asia Centre.

10. Eric Gonsalves Ambassador Eric Gonsalves joined the Indian Foreign Service in 1950. He served in Washington, London, Japan and in European Union. He has also been a Secretary in the Ministry of External Affairs. After retirement, he was Director of the India International Centre for several years. Currently, he is also the Convener of the Indian delegation of Bangladesh, China, India, and Myanmar (BCIM) Forum.

11. S. Gopal S. Gopal joined the Indian Police service in 1961 and spent most of his career in the Research and Analysis Wing (R&AW), from where he retired as Special Secretary. He has also headed the aviation research centre, an important wing of the intelligence apparatus. He contributes frequently to newspapers on strategic issues. He is presently a visiting professor at Manipal University and at the National Institute of Advanced Studies.

12. Mohan Guruswamy A post-graduate in Public Policy, International Affairs and Management, Mohan Guruswamy is an alumnus of the JFK School of Government, Harvard and the Graduate School of Business, Stanford. His career path has included teaching, senior management, journalism and government service as the Advisor to the Finance Minister. He now heads the Centre for Policy Alternatives, New Delhi. He is widely traveled in India and abroad, and

is the author of several books on policy issues, the latest being *Chasing the Dragon: Will India Catch-up with China?*

13. P.J. Jacob Vice-Admiral Jacob retired in 2001 as the Vice-Chief of the Naval Staff. An alumnus of the National Defence College, he has commanded the Eastern Fleet and also been the Director General of the Indian Coast Guard. He is a former member of the National Security Advisory Board and currently Chairman of the Global India Foundation

14. Prashant Jha Jha is a Kathmandu-based freelance journalist, a weekly columnist with *Nepali Times* and a writer for many papers and magazines in Nepal and India. He is also the correspondent for South Asia Intelligence Review and Janes Intelligence Review. His main focus is on the political situation in Nepal, the implications of the Terai issue, and Nepal-India relations. He is a regular speaker at think-tanks and international agencies.

15. Nirmala Joshi A PhD from the School of International Studies at the JNU, Professor Joshi is an expert on the Shanghai Cooperation Organization. She has been a visiting scholar at the Institute of Oriental Studies, Moscow. Professor Joshi retired as Professor in 2004 from the Centre for Soviet and East European Studies at the JNU. Since then, she has been the Director of the Central Asian Foundation, a New Delhi think tank.

16. Akbar Mirza Khaleeli Khaleeli has served as Ambassador to Iran and Italy, and High Commissioner to Australia. He has also served in Baghdad, Colombo and Amman. He is fluent in Persian, Urdu, French and Arabic. He is a student of comparative theology and cultures, with a deep interest in Persian poetry, vocal music and painting.

17. Srikanth Kondapalli Srikanth Kondapalli is Associate Professor in Chinese Studies at JNU. He is also an Honorary Fellow at Institute of Chinese Studies, Delhi, research Associate at the University of Stellenbosch, South Africa, and a Distinguished Fellow of the Institute of Peace and Conflict Studies, Delhi. He is educated in Chinese studies in India and China, and has been Visiting Fellow and Professor at Universities in Beijing and Taipei. He has published two books, co-edited a volume and contributed several articles in books and national and international journals and newspapers. He has presented several research papers at national and international conferences and is a guest faculty member at higher institutions of learning of the Armed Forces.

18. Natarajan Krishnan Krishnan is a veteran diplomat who has served as Ambassador and Permanent Representative of India to the United Nations in New York; on retirement he was assigned as Special Envoy of the Prime Minister of India in charge of the AFRICA Fund (1986-89). He set up the School of International Studies of Pondicherry University as its first Dean (1988-90), and was a Member of the Board of Trustees of the United Nations Institute

for Training and Research, and Member of the Executive Board of UNESCO in Paris.

19. SATINDER LAMBAH Satinder K. Lambah has held important positions both during service and after retirement. Currently he is Special Envoy in the Prime Minister's Office. Prior to this, he has served as the Convenor of the National Security Advisory Board (2004-05), Special Envoy of Government of India for Afghanistan (2001-02) and Chair of a Committee appointed by the Government of India on the reorganization of the Ministry of External Affairs and India's Diplomatic Missions abroad.

20. SUDHA MAHALINGAM Sudha Mahalingam is a Member of India's National Security Advisory Board and also of the Petroleum and Natural Gas Regulatory Board. She was awarded the first K. Subrahmanyam award for excellence in strategic studies. Mahalingam has published widely in academic journals, books and in newspapers. She speaks regularly in national and international conferences and lectures many audiences that include the armed forces, bureaucrats, police officers, and scientists.

21. FALI MAJOR Air Chief Marshal Major was commissioned into the Indian Air Force on December 31, 1967 as a helicopter pilot. He has served in important staff as well as operational appointments, including Deputy Chief of Integrated Defence Staff (Operations) and Air Officer Commanding-in-Chief, Eastern Air Command. Air Chief Marshal Major was the Chief of the Air Staff from 2007 to 2009. After retirement he was appointed by the government as Independent Director of the Board of Air India, the national carrier.

22. VED PRAKASH MALIK General V.P. Malik was the Chief of the Army Staff from 1997 to 2000, and planned and oversaw execution of the Kargil Operations in 1999. After retirement, he was a member of the National Security Advisory Board for two years. He writes frequently for newspapers and magazines, and has authored. *Kargil: From Surprise to Victory* as well as several papers on defence planning and security issues.

23. KESAVA MENON Menon is the Associate Editor of *The Hindu*, based in the Head Office at Chennai. He was its West Asia correspondent from 1994 to 2002 and reported and analysed events in West Asia and North Africa . He was the first correspondent to be posted by *The Hindu* in Islamabad, and covered the Mujahedeen take-over of Kabul in April 1992. He was the first and probably till date the only Indian correspondent to go behind Mujahedeen lines.

24. RAJA MENON Admiral Menon is a well-known naval strategist whose published works *Maritime Strategy and Continental Wars*, and *A Nuclear Strategy for India* are required reading at the Defence Services Staff College and other Armed Forces institutions. He was a member of government committees for higher Defence reorganization and creation of a National Defence University

and headed the team that wrote the Indian Navy's New Maritime Strategy. He is a visiting lecturer at all institutes of higher study of the Indian armed forces and the Foreign Office. Chairman, Task force on Net Assessment and Simulation, NSC.

25. DEB MUKHARJI Mukharji retired after serving as India's Ambassador in Nepal. He had earlier served as High Commissioner in Bangladesh and Nigeria. After retirement from the Foreign Service he was the convenor of the Indo-Bangladesh Track-2 dialogue and has anchored over a hundred TV discussions on Indo-Bangladesh relations. He is a regular contributor to newspapers and journals, and has published two books: *The Magic of Nepal* and *Kailash and Manasarovar: Visions of the Infinite* (2009). His interests include trekking, photography, reading and music.

26. B.R. MUTHU KUMAR Ambassador Muthu Kumar studied in Bangalore and completed his Masters (M.Phil) at JNU, in Delhi. He joined the Indian Foreign Service in July 1977. He has been the longest serving Indian Ambassador to Tajikistan till date, having served there for six years through a particularly difficult period in the nineties. Among his many tasks then was to supervise India's assistance to Afghanistan. He has travelled extensively in Central Asia. Before retirement he served as Ambassador in Belarus and then in Azerbaijan.

27. RAJARAM NAGAPPA Professor Rajaram Nagappa is a specialist in aerospace propulsion and has worked extensively in the design and development of solid propellant rockets. His interests are in missile technology and space weaponization. He has served in the Vikram Sarabhai Space Centre, ISRO as its Associate Director, and later was Pandalai Memorial Chair Professor at Anna University, Chennai. He has also taught at Technion-Israel Institute of Technology, Israel. He is a recipient of several national level awards for his scientific contributions. His recent work includes an assessment of the Pakistani cruise missiles and the Iranian satellite launch vehicle Safir. He has also participated in a study on China's Science and Technology capability.

28. SATISH NAMBIAR As Director General of Military Operations in 1991, General Nambiar led two defence delegations for talks with Pakistan. He was appointed the first Force Commander and Head of the United Nations forces in the former Yugoslavia. General Nambiar retired as the Deputy Chief of the Army Staff, and till recently was the Director of the United Service Institution of India. He served on a 16-member international panel appointed by the UN Secretary General on 'Threats, Challenges and Change'. In 2009 he was awarded the Padma Bhushan for outstanding national service.

29. RAVI NEELAKANTAN A career diplomat, Ravi has served in Bhutan, Japan and Moscow, and as Ambassador to Vietnam. He was Secretary (East) in the Ministry of External Affairs from October 2006 onwards. Earlier he was in charge of the West Asia and North Africa Division of the Ministry of Commerce,

where he also served as Member Secretary of the newly constituted Export Promotion Board. Ravi holds Masters' degrees in Chemistry and business management. Currently he is with the Centre for Public Policy at the Indian Institute of Management, Bangalore.

30. Madhavan Palat Professor Palat holds a Masters' and a Doctorate degree from Cambridge University. He has been professor at the Centre for Historical Studies, Jawaharlal Nehru University, and also a Senior Fellow, Nehru Memorial Museum and Library. He is a Visiting Professor of Imperial Russian History, University of Chicago and a National Fellow at the Institute of Advanced Study, Shimla. He is fluent in reading in English, French, German, and Russian, and has edited a number of publications including *Social Identities in Revolutionary Russia* and Volume 6 of *History of Civilizations of Central Asia*.

31. Sanjay Pulipaka Sanjay Pulipaka is currently a Fellow at the Maulana Abul Kalam Azad Institute of Asian Studies (MAKAIAS), Kolkata, India and is working on a project pertaining to developments in Myanmar. He was a Visiting Fellow at University of Cambridge (Lent Term 2012). Sanjay is also a former Fulbright Fellow and his areas of interest include political transitions, conflict transformation, Indian politics and international politics. Sanjay also has work experience in the realm of strengthening democracy at the grass-roots and in political and governance reforms.

32. D.S. Rajan Rajan has spent about 35 years as a Chinese and Japanese analyst, monitoring writings in the Chinese and Japanese language media. Of these 35 years, he had spent three years in Hong Kong when it was a British-administered territory, three years in China, and six years in Japan in two spells. Rajan has been the Director of the Chennai Institute for China Studies which also studies and analyses Japan and East Asia, for several years. He has published numerous articles in the print media.

33. B. Raman Raman served in the Cabinet Secretariat from 1968 as an external intelligence analyst. He retired from the Cabinet Secretariat in 1994 as Additional Secretary. After retirement, he started the 'Institute for Topical Studies' at Chennai of which he is the Director. He is Convener, Chennai Chapter of 'Observer Research Foundation' and was member of National Security Advisory Board from 2000 to 2002. He is a prolific writer with over 1400 published articles. He is a leading expert on security issues and regularly participates in TV panel discussions, seminars and lectures on National Security.

34. C.V. Ranganathan Ambassador C.V. Ranganathan served in a number of distinguished positions as a diplomat. He has been the First Secretary, Embassy of India, Beijing, China (1965–1968) and Commissioner of India, Hong Kong (1980–1983). He has been Ambassador of India to various countries including China and France. After retirement he continues to hold advisory and research

positions. He was the Co-Chairman of 'India-China Eminent Persons Group'. His writings have been published in books and periodicals in India and abroad. He co-authored a book *India and China – The Way Ahead* that has won critical acclaim. He was the Convener of the National Security Advisory Group (2002-2004), Emeritus Fellow and Founding member, CII, Institute of China Studies.

35. SHYAM SARAN A career diplomat, Saran has served in several capitals of the world including Beijing, Tokyo and Geneva and as Ambassador to Myanmar, Indonesia and Nepal. Saran was appointed India's Foreign Secretary in 2004 and held that position till his retirement from service in September 2006. After retirement he was appointed Prime Minister's Special Envoy for Indo-US civil nuclear issues and later as Special Envoy and Chief Negotiator on Climate Change. He has now concluded his assignment in government and returned to being a private citizen.

36. RAVI K. SAWHNEY Lt General Sawhney was Director General of Military Intelligence during the significant period from 1997 to 2000 when the Taliban were at their peak in Afghanistan. He therefore gained a close knowledge of developments in the region. Later he became the Deputy Chief of the Indian Army and in this capacity continued to deal with regional strategy till he retired from the Army in 2001. The government still utilizes his services in matters pertaining to Afghanistan. He is a member and distinguished Fellow of the Vivekananda International Foundation.

37. RONEN SEN A distinguished diplomat, Ronen Sen has had a unique range of experience. He was Secretary to the Atomic Energy Commission, and Joint Secretary to successive PMs from 1986 to 1991, providing policy inputs in foreign affairs, defence, atomic energy, and space. He has been Ambassador in Mexico, in Russia for six years during the tumultuous period after the break-up of the USSR, our first Ambassador in re-unified Germany and Ambassador in the United States as well as High Commissioner in the UK. He has held several assignments as Special or Personal Envoy of the Prime Minister from 1987 to 1994, and participated in around 180 multilateral and bilateral summits in six continents.

38. D.P. SEN GUPTA Professor Sen Gupta studied Physics and Electrical Engineering before he took his PhD from Liverpool University. He taught there for five years before he joined the Indian Institute of Science (IISc), Bangalore where he has taught and carried out research for about three decades. He has received awards for teaching excellence at both these institutions and also a special Chair for Energy Studies at the IISc. An Emeritus Fellow at the IISc, he is presently a Visiting Professor at NIAS, Bangalore. He has co-authored several books published abroad and recently by IISc Press and World Scientific. He has published a number of books for children.

39. Senthil Kumar Senthil Kumar is an Electrical and Electronics Engineer and an MBA in production management, with experience in consultancy in the fields of energy efficiency, renewable energy and power systems. Currently he works in TERI as a Fellow in the Industrial Energy Group. As a government-accredited energy auditor, Senthil has carried out around 100 energy audits for a wide range of industries including power distribution and water pumping systems. Senthil Kumar has published papers on diverse topics related to energy and edited a manual for practicing engineers on lighting called *Light Right*.

40. Kanwal Sibal Kanwal Sibal was Foreign Secretary from July 2002 to November 2003. He has been India's Ambassador to Turkey, Egypt, France and Russia, and is a member of India's National Security Advisory Board. Ambassador Sibal writes regularly for national journals and periodicals on international affairs. He has an MA degree in English Literature and a Bachelor's degree in Law. He speaks French fluently.

41. Veena Sikri Veena Sikri was India's High Commissioner to Bangladesh and Malaysia. She has also served in Indian Missions in Hong Kong, Paris, Moscow, New York and Kathmandu. She was Director General, Indian Council for Cultural Relations (ICCR), New Delhi. Since Retirement she has focused on academics and is a Professor, Ford Foundation Chair, Academy of Third World Studies, and Coordinator, Bangladesh Studies Programme at Jamia Millia Islamia University.

42. G.R. Srinivasan G.R. Srinivasan retired as the Vice-Chairman of the Atomic Energy Regulatory Board (AERB). He has over 50 years experience in the nuclear industry and is presently the Advisor, Nuclear Power business in GMR Ltd. Prior to this G.R. Srinivasan served in the Department of Atomic Energy for over 42 years. G.R. Srinivasan was Director Projects, Nuclear Power Corporation, where he was also responsible for Quality Assurance and Health, Safety and Public Acceptance.

43. P.K. Hormis Tharakan Tharakan served in the Indian Police Service and in the Cabinet Secretariat, Government of India. After retirement, he has served as Advisor to the Second Administrative Reforms Commission on Counter-terrorism and as Advisor to the Governor of Karnataka during President's Rule. Currently, he is a Member of the National Security Advisory Board, Member of the Advisory Committee of the Centre for Strategic Initiatives at the Indian Institute of Science, Chief Advisor (Strategic Studies), BrahMos Aerospace and Visiting Professor, Manipal University. He studies and writes on issues of strategic interest.

44. K. Yhome K. Yhome is a research Fellow at the Observer Research Foundation, New Delhi. Yhome took his PhD and M.Phil from Jawaharlal Nehru University. Before joining the ORF he worked for the portal on South Asia of the New

Delhi-based South Asia Foundation and as an editorial assistant for the *Indian Foreign Affairs Journal*. He also worked on projects covering energy, conflict, and terrorism for various organizations in South Asia. He has contributed chapters in edited books and articles in national and international publications. Presently, he is working on Myanmar's relations with its neighbours.

45. N. Krishnaswamy Krishnaswamy is the President of the Indo–Japanese Chamber of Commerce and Industry in Chennai. He has extensive and long experience of Indo–Japanese relations in business and industry, to which he has devoted a major part of his working years.

46. Rajaram Panda Panda is a Japan specialist who was till recently a Senior Fellow at IDSA, New Delhi. Prior to joining the IDSA, he was ICSSR Fellow and Research Associate at the Centre for East Asian Studies, JNU; Foreign Editor of *Newstime*, Hyderabad; and Chief Program Officer, The Japan Foundation, New Delhi. He has been Visiting Fellow at two Japanese Universities and the Australian National University, Canberra.

    Panda has presented a number of papers at national and international seminars and conferences on Japan's economic, political, and strategic issues. He is a frequent contributor to the print media on India–Japan relations. He is the author of 2 books and has contributed to several more, and published numerous research articles in professional journals in India and abroad.

47. Mohan Guruswamy A post-graduate in Public Policy, International Affairs and Management. He is an alumnus of the JFK School of Government, Harvard University and the Graduate School of Business, Stanford University. He lead an interesting career path that included teaching, senior management, journalism and in government as the Advisor to the Finance Minister with the rank of Secretary. He now heads the Centre for Policy Alternatives, New Delhi. He is widely traveled in India and abroad, and is the author of several books on policy issues, the latest being *Chasing the Dragon: Will India Catch-up with China?* He regularly lectures at institutions such as the Observer Research Foundation, Indian Institute of Public Administration, and at various Defence colleges.

48. Vice Admiral (Retd) P.S. Das Vice Admiral Das retired from the Indian Navy in 1998 as Commander-in-Chief of the Eastern Naval Command. Admiral Das has more than 170 published articles to his credit in newspapers and journals of repute and has been Co-Chair of the Maritime Working Group of the Council for Security Cooperation in Asia Pacific (CSCAP). He is a visiting speaker at all important Colleges of the Armed Forces and is a participant in several prestigious Track II India-Japan, India-USA and India-China strategic discussions in those countries and at home. He is a graduate of the Naval War College, USA, and holds a Master's degree in Business Administration. He has served as member of the National Security Advisory Board in the office of the Prime Minister.

49. C.V. Ranganathan C.V. Ranganathan joined the Indian Foreign Service (IFS) in 1959 and has served in a number of distinguished positions as a diplomat. He has been the First Secretary, China (1965–1968) and Commissioner Hong Kong (1980–1983). He has been Ambassador in China and France. Ranganathan is the Co-Chairman of 'India-China Eminent Persons Group' from 2006. He has published many articles and contributions to books, newspapers, journals, and magazines in India and abroad on international affairs. His book *India and China – The Way Ahead* that he co-authored with V.C. Khanna has won critical acclaim. Till recently he was the convener of the National Security Advisory Group. He is an Emeritus Fellow and former Co-Chairperson of the Institute of Chinese Studies, New Delhi

50. Alka Acharya Professor Alka Acharya is Professor of Chinese Studies in the Centre for East Asian Studies, School of International Studies, Jawaharlal Nehru University. She is also an Honorary Fellow of the Institute of Chinese Studies (New Delhi) and the Editor of China Report, a journal of East Asian Affairs.

She is the joint editor of the book *Crossing A Bridge of Dreams: 50 years of India-China*, published in 2002. She has contributed chapters to many books and regularly features in the *Economic and Political Weekly*. She has written widely on India-China Relations and other aspects of China's foreign policy. Her current research focuses on the settlement of the PRC's territorial disputes, India-China-Russia Trilateral Cooperation and the Chinese strategic response to the post-cold war globalizing politico-security architecture, with special reference to China's neighbourhood.

She is a member of the India-China Eminent Persons Group and also a member of the National Security Advisory Board of the Government of India.

Index